BRITISH ENVOYS IN JAPAN, 1859–1972

'Satsuma envoys paying the indemnity money at Yokohama for the Murder of Mr Richardson.' From *The Illustrated London News*, 1863

For

PETER LOWE

who has laboured hard for many years

on the history of

Anglo-Japanese diplomatic relations

The
Japan
Society
Founded 1891

British Envoys in Japan
1859–1972

COMPILED AND EDITED

by

HUGH CORTAZZI

with

IAN NISH, PETER LOWE and J. E. HOARE

GLOBAL
ORIENTAL

EMBASSIES OF ASIA SERIES
VOL. 1: BRITISH ENVOYS IN JAPAN, 1859–1972

Compiled and Edited by Hugh Cortazzi
with Ian Nish, Peter Lowe & J. E. Hoare

© Japan Society 2004

First published 2004 by
GLOBAL ORIENTAL
PO Box 219
Folkestone
Kent CT20 2WP

www.globaloriental.co.uk

ISBN 1-901903-51-6 [Case]

SPECIAL THANKS

The Publishers wish to express their thanks to the UK–Japan Joint
History Research Promotion Fund for their generous contribution
to the making of this book.

British Library Cataloguing in Publication Data
A CIP catalogue entry for this book is available
from the British Library

Typeset in Stone 9.5 on 10.5 by Mark Heslington, Scarborough, North Yorkshire
Printed and bound in England by Antony Rowe Ltd, Chippenham, Wilts

Contents

Preface

The aim of this book is to describe the personalities and activities of senior British diplomats in Tokyo and their role in the formulation and execution of policy towards Japan in the period from 1859–1972.

The first three parts consist of biographical portraits of the British heads of mission in Japan between 1859, when the first British representative Rutherford Alcock arrived in Edo as Minister Plenipotentiary, and 1972 when John Pilcher retired as Ambassador to Japan. We have deliberately ended this survey in 1972 as papers covering later heads of mission have yet to be released under the thirty-year rule enforced by the Public Record Office. The end of Pilcher's time as Ambassador also marks the end of an era. He was the last head of mission with pre-war experience of Japan and the last who had been a member of the pre-war Japan Consular Service. Moreover, while support for British commerce had been growing in importance in Japan since about 1960, by 1972 it had become one of the most important functions of the British mission to Japan and British relations with Japan had started a new phase.

The fourth part is devoted to some of the scholar diplomats who worked in Japan. One of these portraits is of George Sansom who played an influential role before the war in the British Embassy in Tokyo and during the war in the USA. Sansom should have become Ambassador if circumstances had been different. He was an outstanding scholar, but he belonged to the Japan Consular Service and the Foreign Office in those days mistakenly preserved heads of mission posts for generalists in the Diplomatic Service. Moreover Sansom's advice did not find favour with Robert Craigie who was the last British Ambassador to Japan before the war.

An appendix gives brief biographical details of some of the other British diplomats who are mentioned in the biographical portraits reproduced here or who may appear in other books about Anglo-Japanese relations in the hundred years or so covered by this collection.

This is not a diplomatic history of relations between Britain and Japan. It focuses on the British personalities involved at the diplomatic level rather than on the issues which dominated relations between the two countries. Naturally, however, themes such as treaty revision, the Anglo-Japanese Alliance, and frictions over China and Manchuria, which made up much of the work of British envoys, feature prominently in some of the profiles. Anglo-Japanese relations must be seen in the context of Japan's relations with the rest of the world, especially the United States, the European powers and

the leading countries in Asia. Inevitably, such international aspects can only
be covered peripherally in this study.

The British heads of mission in Tokyo and their staffs were not the only
people who contributed in this period to the development of Anglo-Japanese
relations. From the earliest days, businessmen, bankers, journalists, missionaries and those involved with cultural exchanges all had varying influence on
the Anglo-Japanese relationship.

Some of these portraits have appeared in various volumes published for the
Japan Society since 1991, but a good deal of new material has been included
to ensure that all heads of mission in the 113 years covered by this book are
portrayed.

□

In putting this book together I have been immensely helped by Ian Nish who
has written a number of the pieces included in this volume and has written
the introduction to part II covering the period 1900-1945. He has been most
generous with his help and advice on all parts of this book and I wish to put
on record my sincere thanks to him. Without his encouragement and support this volume could not have been produced.

I would like to thank all the contributors for allowing their essays to be
reproduced here. I am particularly grateful to Peter Lowe for introducing part
III and to Jim Hoare for introducing part IV. I also wish to express grateful
thanks to the British Embassy, Tokyo, for kindly supplying various portraits
of ambassadors featured in this book.

HUGH CORTAZZI
Autumn 2003

PART I

THE EARLY PIONEERS

1859–1900

'Landing' of Sir Rutherford Alcock, K.C.B., at Yokohama, Japan'. *The Illustrated London News*. 28 May 1864.

Introduction

SIR HUGH CORTAZZI

In the middle of the nineteenth century, with the significant growth in international trade and sea transport, which was then taking place, Japan's seclusion from the rest of the world was an anomaly which could not be sustained. Whalers and merchant ships increasingly wanted to put into Japanese ports for fresh water and supplies or to shelter from storms. European, especially British, as well as North American traders had begun to develop markets in China and consumers in Europe and North America sought tea, silk and other products from the Orient.

British interest[1] in Japan dates back to the decade of the trading post at Hirado in the period 1613–23, but after closing the post in 1623 Britain's East India Company showed only limited and desultory interest in trying to reopen trade with Japan. In 1673 a visit was made to Nagasaki by Simon Delboe in the *Return* and an attempt made to persuade the Japanese authorities to reopen trade relations with the company. However, the seclusion policy adopted by the *Bakufu* was being rigorously applied and the Dutch who had been allowed to maintain a small trading post on Dejima, an artificial island in Nagasaki harbour, were determined not to allow their competitors to trade with Japan. Delboe was forced to retreat.

In the eighteenth century some new interest was shown but no practical steps were taken to try to develop trade and the general consensus in the East India Company was that any resulting trade would not be worth the effort needed to force open the Japanese door. Captain Broughton[2] in HMS *Providence* visited the northern coast of Japan in 1796 and 1797 to undertake surveys. HMS *Phaeton* entered Nagasaki bay in 1808,[3] but the Japanese rebuffed these approaches. In 1813–14 Stamford Raffles, who had been appointed Lieutenant Governor of Java following the defeat of the Dutch in the island in 1811, seized the initiative. In 1813 he sent two ships to Nagasaki. The Dutch *Opperhoofd* (the chief of the trading post), however, refused to take orders from Raffles and stymied the British efforts.

In the 1820s British whaling vessels began to visit Japanese waters and there were clashes with local Japanese authorities. British interest, however, remained focused on China. In the 1830s there was some discussion of a

possible annexation of the Bonin islands to protect British settlers there, but
Captain Quin who visited the islands in HMS *Raleigh* in 1837 reported that
no formal occupation was needed. Meanwhile, the *Morrison* fitted out by
King, an American merchant, which was carrying Japanese castaways and
which had met the *Raleigh* in the Ryukyus, dropped anchor off Uraga to hand
over the castaways and some letters. The *Morrison* which was unarmed was
fired on by coastal batteries and had to withdraw. Henceforth it fell to the
Americans to take the initiative to open the Japanese door. The British were
preoccupied by the Opium Wars with China and Japan was peripheral to the
interests of the British government and its merchants in the East.
Accordingly, in the 1850s, they were content to follow the American lead.

Commodore Perry's expedition of 1852–54 opened the way for Admiral
Stirling's visits to Nagasaki in 1854 and 1855. The Anglo-Japanese
Convention of 14 October 1854[4] was regarded by everyone except the
Admiral as a most unsatisfactory agreement. The ports of Nagasaki and
Hakodate were to be opened to British ships for repairs and supplies while
other ports were only to be used by 'ships in distress'. Nothing was said in the
Convention about extraterritoriality, trade or consular representation. It also
contained Article VII which read: 'When this Convention shall be ratified, no
high officer (the Japanese words used mean 'ship's commander') coming to
Japan shall alter it.' This was at best ambiguous.

The most important steps to open Japan to foreign trade were taken by
Townsend Harris, the American Consul, appointed at Shimoda in the Izu
peninsula under the terms of Perry's convention of 1854, which had been ratified in 1855.

The Russians were also active and a 'Treaty of Peace and Friendship' was
signed between Russia and Japan at Shimoda.[5] This was followed by a supplementary treaty signed in 1857. The Dutch for their part fearing that they
might be left behind in the scramble for a share of Japan's trade concluded a
treaty with Japan in 1856 and a supplementary treaty in 1857 which had
implications for the development of trade with Japan.[6]

Harris's efforts culminated in the treaty between the United States and
Japan of 29 July 1858, which set the pattern for the other commercial treaties
between Japan and the Western Powers. The treaty between Britain and Japan
(the Treaty of Yedo with annexed trade regulations), concluded by the Elgin
Mission[7] on 26 August 1858, was based on the Treaty which Harris had negotiated although there were some differences.[8] In particular, the British treaty
included a most-favoured-nation clause which 'Harris had unaccountably
omitted' but it omitted the promise of mediation and friendly aid included
in Article II of the American treaty.

The first British official representative to reside in Japan was Rutherford
Alcock who was appointed as Consul General. He reached Japan in June 1859
and finding that this title did not give him sufficient rank among his diplomatic colleagues assumed the title of 'Plenipotentiary'. The Foreign Office
agreed and formally appointed him as 'Envoy Extraordinary and Minister
Plenipotentiary'. He quarrelled with Townsend Harris and had a real 'baptism
of fire'. But after Harris was replaced and Alcock returned from leave in 1864
the British Minister took the lead in relations with Japan. For the remainder
of the nineteenth century Britain became the leading foreign power in relation to Japan.

Alcock and, perhaps to a lesser extent, his successor Harry Parkes, faced some serious difficulties and dangers.

The British Legation had very limited information about Japan. The relationships between the Shogun, the daimyo and the court were not understood for some time and it was only in 1864 that the paramount importance of ensuring that the treaties were ratified by the court was recognized. Although some of the coast had been surveyed even relatively accurate maps were difficult to obtain.

The British Mission was a very small one and the head of mission had to carry a heavy burden of work. His deputy, if one was available, was the Secretary of Legation, a member of the diplomatic service who often had no previous experience of Japan or knowledge of the Japanese language. There might also be one or two junior secretaries, but they all depended on the support and expertise of the students who were trained in the Japanese language and who belonged to what became the Japan Consular Service. The leading expert became the Japanese Secretary to the Legation. All the staff, including the mission's doctor,[9] were often fully employed copying out in long hand the despatches, records, notes and reports which emanated from the mission.

Language was a major problem especially in the 1860s. At first as there were no competent interpreters between Japanese and English interpretation had to be through the medium of Dutch. This fact and the absence of equivalents in Japanese for terms and concepts in common use in English not only meant that conversations took a long time but there were frequent misunderstandings and nuances were missed.

Communications were slow not only within Japan but also across the seas to Europe and North America. There were no railways or telegraphs in Japan until the 1870s. Wheeled traffic could not use the main highways and major rivers had to be forded or ferry boats had to be used. At first there were no regular shipping lines and it could take four months or even longer for the British envoy to receive a reply from London. This meant that instructions, which might be based on out of date and inadequate information, were frequently either inappropriate or received too late. Inevitably, much had to be left to the man on the spot especially in the first two decades of resident British envoys.

Funds for the mission also presented difficulties. Initially, there were no banks in the settlements and the rate of exchange for the Mexican silver dollar in use in the settlements fluctuated. The British Government inevitably expected its representatives to be frugal and in the early years there was no understanding in London of the conditions in Japan.

But the greatest threat was to the security of the mission and its members. The treaties had been forced on a reluctant *Bakufu* and anti-foreign sentiments were strong with constant threats of violence against foreigners in the settlements and the few foreign diplomats in Edo.[10] These dangers were particularly acute in the first decade after the arrival of foreign representatives (the British Legation while housed at Edo in Tōzenji, a temple near Shinagawa, was twice attacked by anti-foreign samurai in 1861 and 1862), but anti-foreign behaviour was manifested at times until the last decade of the nineteenth century. The British envoy often felt unsafe.

Japan in the latter part of the nineteenth century was not a healthy place. Cholera and other infectious diseases were endemic. Water supplies were polluted and sanitary arrangements at best inadequate. Medical facilities were limited and there were, of course, no refrigerators or air conditioners. Hill stations such as Hakone and Karuizawa were developed, but it was not until the late 1890s that Satow established his house at Chuzenji to which he retired in the worst of the summer heat. Hugh Fraser, the British Minister from 1889–94, died at his post. His successor, Le Poer Trench, who was appointed to succeed Fraser, suffered a stroke in 1895 and had to be invalided home.

Fire was another danger as most structures were made of wood and easily combustible. In a major fire in Yokohama Ernest Satow[11] and A.B. Mitford[12] of the Legation lost almost all their belongings.

The British envoy had to deal with a merchant community, especially in Yokohama, which contained some very dubious characters who often behaved provocatively towards the Japanese with whom they came in contact. Relations between British diplomats and merchants were often fraught especially in the early years.

British policy towards Japan in the early years as demonstrated in the British bombardment of Kagoshima in 1863 and the allied bombardment of Shimonoseki in 1864 seems aggressive and Palmerstonian (although Lord Palmerston was only occasionally directly involved), but British Ministers and envoys, while determined to support the development of British trade with Japan and the rights of British subjects, sought peaceful solutions wherever this seemed possible. The late nineteenth century is often seen as the heyday of British imperialism, but British policies towards Japan, insensitive though they may seem to modern observers, were not racially motivated and there was never any suggestion of attempting to colonize or occupy any part of Japan.

The extraterritorial provisions of the treaties now seem unacceptable and highly discriminatory, but we have to bear in mind that at the time of the treaties of 1858 Japan had no modern civil or criminal code. Torture was common and justice in the normally accepted meaning of the term unobtainable in Japan. The Japanese understandably strongly resented the provisions and after the Meiji Restoration of 1868 treaty revision became a major preoccupation not only of Japanese politicians but also of foreign diplomats in Japan. The Japanese tried to do separate deals with one or more of the Treaty Powers, but they and the British finally recognized that a revised treaty between the two was a necessity if revised treaties were in general to be negotiated. In the Anglo-Japanese Treaty of 1894, which came into force in 1899, the British made significant concessions to the annoyance of some British residents in the treaty ports, although the Japanese for their part felt that they had been forced to make unfair concessions on tariff autonomy.

British trade with Japan in the nineteenth century was relatively limited but the settlements especially Yokohama and Kobe flourished. Gradually, travel in the 'interior' became easier and Japan began to attract the globe-trotters.

Britain played an important role in the development of the new Japan following the Meiji Restoration. While the Japanese understandably were determined not to be dependant on any one foreign country for help and expertise it is estimated that over forty per cent of the foreign experts[13] (o-yatoi gaikokujin) employed by the Japanese government were British. The British mission was inevitably closely involved with many of them. Parkes, in particular, pressed the Meiji government to employ British experts and use British machinery and technology.

British diplomats in Japan, beginning with Rutherford Alcock, became interested in Japanese art and culture. Alcock did his best to introduce Japanese art and crafts to Britain and was a serious student of Japanese art even if his tastes were limited. Parkes was among the founders of the Asiatic Society of Japan. Some of the young student interpreters in the Consular Service, especially Ernest Satow, W.G. Aston and J.H. Gubbins, went on to become leading scholars of Japanese history and culture.

□

The opening chapters of this first section covering 1859–64 may seem disproportionately long, but Rutherford Alcock was the pioneer and he and Neale, who was Chargé d'Affaires, while Alcock was on leave, saw not only the establishment of the settlements and the treaty system, but had to deal with significant threats to British interests, including two attacks on the British Legation in Edo, the murder of a British merchant near Yokohama (the Namamugi Incident) and interruption of shipping through the straits of Shimonoseki. These incidents led in 1863 to the British bombardment of Kagoshima and the allied bombardment of Shimonoseki in 1864 (described in Appendixes I and II). These were the two most significant incidents in Anglo-Japanese relations in second half of the nineteenth century.

Alcock, despite his verbosity and inability to explain clearly to the Foreign Office in London the complicated situation prevailing in Japan, was on the whole a sympathetic observer and deserves to be remembered just as much as Parkes, his domineering successor. Despite his limitations Neale, who was in charge while Alcock was on home leave from 1862–4, should not be dismissed as a weak and bone-headed ex-army officer. At the time of the Namamugi Incident in 1862 he showed cautious common sense. He followed up the incident with determination and persistence. The bombardment of Kagoshima could have ended in a British disaster if he and Admiral Kuper had not taken adequate precautions against Satsuma treachery.

Sir Harry Parkes was the longest-serving British envoy in Japan 1865–83. He was a brave but domineering envoy who must have been a very difficult man to work for and whose insensitive and rude behaviour was often deeply insulting to Japanese. But he steered British policy during the run-up to the Meiji Restoration so that Britain gained both prestige and influence with the new regime. He probably could not have achieved this without the able assistance and support of Ernest Satow[14] and A.B. Mitford[15] He and Satow did not get on but the latter's future success probably owed something at least to the favourable reports which Parkes must have sent about him. Parkes has been the subject of more studies than Alcock and my chapter on him is accordingly shorter than that on Alcock.

Little need be said here about the subsequent chapters on Francis Plunkett, Hugh Fraser and Le Poer Trench. They were all three competent career diplomats, well connected and with private means, who had joined the service as attachés without a formal university education. They do not stand out in the history of Britain's relations with Japan in the nineteenth century. Hugh Fraser, the only envoy to die in post, is overshadowed in popular memory by his wife Mary, whose memoirs[16] of Japan in the 1890s are still worth reading.

The outstanding figure in Britain's relations with Japan in the nineteenth century was undoubtedly the scholar diplomat Ernest Satow described in this book in two separate essays. The first in Part I covers his time as Minister at Tokyo from 1895–1900, the second in part IV deals with him as one of the leading scholar diplomats. His achievements both as a diplomat and a scholar were unique, but two other British scholar diplomats of the nineteenth century must be remembered and are covered in separate essays in part IV. The first of these was W.G.Aston whose writings about Japan, its history, literature and culture ensure his place in the list of outstanding Japanologists. The second was J.H. Gubbins without whose expertise envoys such as Plunkett, Fraser and Le Poer Trench would have floundered – especially in the complex negotiations for treaty revision. Gubbins following his retirement went on to write knowledgably about Japanese history. Neither Aston nor Gubbins ever became head of mission in Tokyo, but their contributions to British relations with Japan in the nineteenth century justify their inclusion in this survey of British envoys in Japan.

Select bibliography

Beasley. W.G.: *Great Britain and the Opening of Japan*, London, 1951. *Select Documents on Japanese Foreign Policy 1853–68*, London, 1955.
—— *The Meiji Restoration*, Stanford, 1972.
—— *Japan Encounters the Barbarians*, Yale, 1995.
Cortazzi, Hugh: *Dr Willis in Japan, British Medical Pioneer 1862–1877*, London, 1985.
—— *Mitford's Japan, Memoirs and Recollections 1866–1906*, 2nd edition, Japan Library, 2002.
—— *Victorians in Japan*, London, 1987.
Edited *Mrs Fraser, A Diplomat's Wife in Japan*, Tokyo and New York, 1982.
Daniels, Gordon: *Sir Harry Parkes, British Representative in Japan 1865–1883*, Japan Library, 1996.
Dickins, F.V. and Lane Poole, S: *The Life of Sir Harry Parkes*, 2 volumes, London, 1894.
Fox, Grace: *Britain and Japan, 1858–1883*, Oxford, 1969.
Hoare, J.E.: *Japan's Treaty Ports and Foreign Settlements: The Uninvited Guests 1858–1899*, Japan Library, 1994.
—— *Embassies in the East: The Story of the British and their Embassies in China, Japan and Korea from 1859 to the Present*, Curzon Press, 1999.
Jones, H.J.: *Live machines, Hired Foreigners and Meiji Japan*, Paul Norbury Publications, 1980.
Jones, F.C.: *Extra-Territoriality in Japan*, London, 1931.
Nish, Ian and Kibata, Yoichi: *History of Anglo-Japanese Relations, The Political and Diplomatic Dimension*, 2 volumes, London 2000.
Satow, Sir Ernest: *A Diplomat in Japan*, London, 1921.
Ian C. Ruxton (ed) *The Diaries and Letters of Sir Ernest Mason satow (1843–1929), A Scholar Diplomat in East Asia*, Lampeter, 1998.

1
Sir Rutherford Alcock
Minister at Edo, 1859–62

Rutherford Alcock

SIR HUGH CORTAZZI

Sir Rutherford Alcock was the first British Minister to Japan from 1859–1864. Born in 1809, he was the son of a London doctor and studied medicine fromthe age of 15. He developed an early interest in art, learnt Italian and French, studied for a year in Paris. At 21 he obtained his diploma in surgery. In the following year he joined an Anglo-Portuguese force supporting the Queen of Portugal. Alcock then joined the Spanish Legion. On his return to England in 1838 Alcock resumed his medical career. But he had contracted rheumatic fever at the siege of San Sebastian and, losing the use of his thumbs, had to give up his career as a surgeon.

In 1844 Alcock was chosen as a consul in China. He served in Amoy, Foochow, Shanghai and Canton. One of his young subordinates in China was Harry Parkes who later succeeded him as Minister in Japan. They got on well. Both believed in taking a firm line. Alcock declared that: 'a salutary dread of the immediate consequences of violence offered to British subjects . . . seems to be the best and only protection in this country for Englishmen',[1] but he did not believe in pushing things too far. His philosophy in relations with oriental peoples was one of firmness and determination combined with patience and persistence. He also had strong ethical principles and did not approve of the unruly and often unscrupulous behaviour of the British business adventurers in China. This was to be a source of trouble in Japan. One fault which he displayed in China and which was also to cause problems in Japan was his wordiness and the lack of clarity in his lengthy despatches.

ALCOCK'S ARRIVAL IN JAPAN

Alcock was appointed British Consul General in Japan in accordance with the
terms of the Treaty concluded between Great Britain and Japan by Lord Elgin
in 1858. In June 1859, he arrived in Japan by a Royal Naval ship (HMS
Sampson). He decided that, to be an effective representative, he needed a
higher rank and assumed the title of 'Plenipotentiary'. The Foreign Office
accepted this self-promotion and made him 'Minister Plenipotentiary'. After
a few days in Nagasaki Alcock went on to Edo bay where he arrived on 26
June 1859 in time for the opening of trade on 1 July, as specified in the Treaty
of 1858. Despite obstruction from the Tokugawa *Bakufu* authorities he
insisted on taking up residence in Edo and established his legation at Tōzenji,
a temple in the suburb of Shinagawa. One of his first acts was to arrange for
the exchange of ratifications of the 1858 treaty to be carried out with due
pomp.

The treaty specified that the ports of Nagasaki, Kanagawa and Hakodate
were to be opened for trade. The *Bakufu* authorities were reluctant to open
Kanagawa as it was on the Tōkaidō, and they feared trouble from anti-foreign
elements among the followers of the daimyo travelling on what was at that
time the most important of Japan's highways. They accordingly began to
develop facilities for traders at Yokohama, a fishing village across the bay
from Kanagawa. Yokohama was cut off by canals and foreigners there could
be largely isolated as the Dutch had been at Dejima in Nagasaki Bay during
the past two hundred years. Alcock fought hard against this deliberate
attempt to pervert the terms of the treaty, but British traders found the facilities at Yokohama acceptable. One of the first British merchants to establish
himself in Yokohama was William Keswick[2] of Jardine Matheson and
Company in premises which came to be known as Ei-Ichiban (i.e. England
Number One).

Alcock had to deal with other problems affecting the British merchants.
One of these was the currency to be used by the traders. Under the treaty all
foreign coins 'shall pass current in Japan' for one year after trade began and
the Japanese authorities were to provide Japanese coin weight for weight (silver and gold). Unfortunately, they had grossly underestimated the demand
for Japanese coins and in consequence of their scarcity Japanese silver coins
were at a premium. Another major difficulty was that the relative value of
gold and silver in Japan was five times whereas in the world outside it was
some fifteen times. The foreign business community, and in particular the
British, put in huge demands for Japanese coins whose supply had to be
rationed. This led to ever increasing demands, often on behalf of obviously
fictitious people including such imaginary individuals as Snooks, Doodledo,
Nonsense and Is-it-not. This infuriated Alcock who considered some of the
requisitions for coins were 'a positive disgrace to anyone bearing the name of
an Englishman'. Alcock's criticisms of the merchants were resented not least
because of the special privileges given to foreign officials who were able to
augment their salaries by up to 40% as a result of the favourable rate available for transfers of salary.

Another cause of friction was the restriction on visits from Yokohama to
Edo which was outside the limits set in the treaty. The ministers had very limited accommodation in Edo and there were no hotels where merchants could
stay. British subjects had to get special permits for visits to Edo as well as invi-

tations from their diplomatic representative whenever they wanted to go there.

One case which aroused a furore among the merchants was that of Michael Moss, a British merchant who was arrested by the Japanese in November 1860. Having been out shooting, he stayed the night in a farm-house outside the limits set in the treaty. While he and his servant who was carrying a wild goose were travelling back to Yokohama on the Tōkaidō his servant was arrested. Moss drew his gun and demanded the release of the servant. In the subsequent affray a Japanese official had half his arm blown off. This led to Moss being bound hand and foot and carted off. At first the authorities denied any knowledge of Moss's whereabouts but eventually delivered him up to the consul who under the extraterritorial provisions of the treaty arraigned Moss in the Consular Court. Moss was found guilty by the consul and two assessors and sentenced to be deported and fined $1000. Alcock, to whom the sentence had to be referred, thought that Moss was getting off too lightly and added a sentence of three months imprisonment to be served in Hong Kong. The business community considered Alcock's decision wrong and unfair. Moss, on arrival in Hong Kong, took out a writ of habeas corpus and an action for damages against Alcock for wrongful imprisonment. He won his case and was awarded $2000 in damages. Although British officials enjoyed shooting, Alcock had some justification in believing that Moss's behaviour (if repeated) could greatly exacerbate relations with the Japanese and that an exemplary sentence was called for, but he had exceeded his authority and did not take adequate account of the feelings of the merchant community.

It is clear from other evidence that members of the British merchant community in Yokohama in those days often behaved badly and arrogantly. Their sexual behaviour was also flagrantly different from those of the Victorian moralists. Alcock disapproved of the Gankiro, the foreigners' brothel in Yokohama, where syphilis and other sexual diseases were rife.

Dr William Willis, the legation doctor, who commented on the prevalence of sexual disease among the foreign community also condemned their general behaviour. In a letter dated 15 February 1863 he wrote:

> The English . . . are more hated than any other foreigners . . . We have all the air, if not insolence, of a dominant race; the facility with which we use our hands and feet in support of argument may elicit respect but not esteem . . . We may disguise it as we like, we are a set of tyrants from the moment we set foot on Eastern soil.[3]

A. B. Mitford, later Lord Redesdale, who was a member of Alcock's staff thought that his minister's criticisms of the British merchants, though bitter, were 'not more than the facts warranted'.[4]

Despite the bad blood between Alcock and the merchants in the early years, by the time he finally left Japan in 1864 the merchants paid a handsome tribute to his endeavours on their behalf. Certainly, it is clear from Alcock's despatches that he was never in doubt about the fact that the development of British trade was a, if not the, major objective of his mission.

When Alcock arrived in Japan all official communications had to be translated twice through the Dutch language. This left infinite possibilities of misunderstanding and caused vexatious delays. Alcock realized that he must have staff capable of communicating in Japanese and he ensured that high priority was given to the training of student interpreters in the consular service. Thus began the Japan Consular Service. He also made strenuous endeavours despite his age (he was 50 when he arrived in Japan) to learn Japanese. He and members of his staff collected each morning with 'our unfortunate teacher in the midst . . . bewildered and sore distraught, under a searching crossfire of questions for equivalents to English parts of speech'.[5] He found the written language particularly difficult. The almost total absence at that time of dictionaries, grammars and primers induced Alcock to produce two books devoted to the Japanese language. These were *Elements of Japanese Grammar for the Use of Beginners* which was published in Shanghai in 1861. The second was *Familiar Dialogues in Japanese with English and French Translations for the Use of Students* which was published in London and Paris in 1863. Neither book can be commended for use by the student today! But Alcock deserved high marks for effort, even if he only deserved a lesser one for achievement.

ALCOCK'S JOURNEYS IN JAPAN

Alcock visited Nagasaki on a number of occasions. In September 1859 he went to Hakodate to install Pemberton Hodgson as the first British consul there. His main problem was to secure accommodation, the Russians having got there first. Eventually, the Japanese agreed to allocate the British consul a temple which they had been preparing for the new governor.

In September 1860, after the climbing season had ended, Alcock managed, despite strenuous opposition from the authorities, to arrange for himself and a small British party to climb Mt Fuji. They were the first foreigners to make the ascent. On his way back to Edo Alcock stayed a few days at Atami. Alcock did not find Atami 'gay as a place of residence. Beyond the interests attaching to the study of village life in Japan, there is nothing whatever to amuse or give occupation'.

In May 1861, Alcock travelled with de Wit, his Dutch colleague, by land and sea to Edo.[6] He was not impressed by the miserable hamlets he saw in the Inland Sea. He noted at Osaka, in what today would be considered at the very least politically incorrect, that he had 'long given up looking at temples in Japan; for after seeing one or two, it is like looking at successive negroes – nothing but a similiarity of acquaintance, which you do not desire, can enable you to distinguish any difference between them'.

THE *BAKUFU* AND THE SAFETY OF FOREIGNERS AND FOREIGN MISSIONS

Alcock found dealing with the *Bakufu* authorities was at best frustrating; at worst they seemed to him to be deceitful and obstructive as well as insulting and threatening. As early as 9 August 1859 he sent a note to the Ministers of Foreign Affairs in which he complained that his officers could not walk outside their missions 'without risk of rudeness, offence and . . . violence of the most determined and wanton character . . . These outrages can only be considered as a reproach and scandal'. Alcock's protests had no effect. The first of many murders of foreigners occurred in Yokohama on 25 August of that year when a Russian officer was killed in the street. In November Alcock's servant was attacked before his eyes. In his note of 8 November to the Ministers of Foreign Affairs he gave a graphic account of the encounter with some drunken, armed samurai. Alcock became so frustrated that on 14 December he addressed a note to the authorities which contained a threat of armed retaliation. This earned a rebuke for Alcock from Lord John Russell, the Foreign Secretary: 'Time and patience may remove many of the difficulties of which you complain . . . You should endeavour rather to soothe differences than to make and insist on peremptory demands. Our intercourse is but duly begun; it should not be inaugurated by war.' Lord John's view from the safety of London inevitably differed from that of his minister enduring the threats and risks to life in Japan at that time.

On 14 January 1861 Heusken, the Dutch interpreter to Townsend Harris, the American minister, was waylaid and murdered on his way back from a visit to the Prussian legation in Edo. This led to an acrimonious quarrel between Alcock and Townsend Harris. The quarrel began after the funeral which the diplomatic corps against the advice of the *Bakufu* authorities had all attended. Alcock invited his colleagues to discuss what action they should jointly take. Alcock who took charge of the proceedings urged that, because of the failure of the authorities to provide for their security, they should all withdraw to the comparative safety of Yokohama. The other diplomats concurred but Harris demurred declaring that Heusken had exposed himself to attack by going out at night against the advice which had been given him. He failed to attend a second conference called by Alcock, telling him that, by withdrawing to Yokohama, the diplomats were playing into the hands of the Japanese authorities who would be thus relieved of 'anxiety, responsibility and expense' and they would never be able to return to Edo. The lengthy and bitter correspondence resulting from this quarrel was duly published in London and Washington. Both ministers appear to have behaved intemperately and neither was blameless, but Alcock who had been exposed to danger in many places and occasions cannot justifiably be accused of cowardice.

In fact, the ministers were able to return to Edo in March 1861 following discussions with *Bakufu* officials in Yokohama. However, their safety had by no means been assured. In July 1861, shortly after he returned to the legation following his journey overland from Nagasaki with de Wit, the legation was attacked in the middle of the night by *rōnin* (masterless samurai). Ten of their guards were wounded and two killed. The next morning the legation 'looked as if it had been sacked after a serious conflict'.[7] Alcock was provoked by the appearance after the incident of a Japanese official who called to congratulate him on his escape and prayed him 'to accept a basket of ducks and a jar of sugar in token of amity'. Alcock rejected this peace offering and demanded 'justice and redress, not ducks or sugar'.

Alcock's task in these days was complicated not only by the fact that it still took some four months to get a reply from London but also by the inability of the foreign secretary to understand the situation on the ground. This was partly Alcock's own fault because his meaning was often clouded by his emotions and verbosity. Alcock also could not easily call for assistance from HM ships in Far Eastern waters. These were limited and communications with them were subject to frustrating delays.

ALCOCK AS AN ADMINISTRATOR

Alcock, as Minister Plenipotentiary and Consul General, was, in charge of the total British official establishment in Japan and, because of the unavoidable delays in communication with London, had to take many decisions on his own authority which in posts closer to home would have been referred to the Foreign Office.

Policy towards Japan, the protection of British subjects and the promotion of British trade were no doubt the most important of his tasks. He also had to act in a semi-judicial capacity in view of the extra-territorial provisions of the treaty. As we saw in the Moss case, he did not always carry out this part of his responsibilities with due respect to the law. Beyond these important tasks he had to run an organization where the ordinary necessities such as stationery were unavailable locally and where there were as yet no banks and no telegraph.

The administrative problems which Alcock faced are set out in his despatch of 13 July 1860 in which he reported on 'the principal items of expenditure hitherto incurred upon my authority'. His total annual expenditure had amounted to £7,679. This seems a modest sum even by standards of the time.

His first concern was to ensure that the establishment of staff for the legation and the consulates was adequate to the tasks they faced. He requested the appointment of a Secretary of Legation to act as his deputy and take charge when he was away. Because of language problems he urged an increase in the complement of Dutch interpreters to at least five. He also called for the appointment of assistants to the consuls and for a medical officer for the legation.[8] Adding up all his recommendations he proposed an additional expenditure of £4,000 per annum. He concluded that 'the service cannot be efficiently and satisfactorily performed by a smaller establishment'.

Alcock's administrative problems were complicated by the fact that 'at present there is absolutely no exchange; and no funds can be obtained here or at any of the ports upon bills'. This despatch suggests that Alcock was a competent and reasonably economical administrator and coped well with the serious administrative difficulties he faced.

BRITISH TRADE WITH JAPAN

In his despatch of 11 July 1860, Alcock recorded that trade in the first year had amounted to nearly £1,000,000 sterling 'and with large profits'. He noted the beginnings of a trade in tea and silk. He understood that some 15,000 chests of tea and no less than 3,000 bales of silk had been exported. Merchants were, he said, counting on a supply of 15 to 18 thousand bales of silk being supplied while 'hundreds of tea-chests' were being manufactured in Edo. Other potential exports included vegetable wax and oils, mother-of-pearl shells, camphor and gall-nuts. He also referred to Japan's known mineral wealth although 'little progress has been made in conquering the repugnance of the Government to see any of the produce of their mines exported'. He had to add that: 'Of imports little can be said: the Japanese are only just beginning to show a disposition to buy any of our manufactured goods. This is a trade yet to be made, and wants must first be created in the natives.'

Before trade could develop the obstructionist attitudes of the Japanese authorities had to be overcome and security assured. Rightly he gave priority to these requirements, but throughout his service as minister he was conscious of the importance of developing trade with Japan.

ALCOCK AND THE RUSSIAN THREAT

On 18 November 1860, Sir John Crampton, HM Ambassador at St Petersburg, sent Lord John Russell at the Foreign Office a despatch in which he warned of a Russian push southwards towards Japan from their territories in the Far East. He declared: 'There is abundant evidence to show that the seizure of the Island of Matsmai[9] forms part of the Russian scheme of aggrandizement in the Pacific.' He added that 'the Japanese Government might be glad to know that both Sahalin [Sakhalin] and Matsmai are coveted in Russia'.

On 2 August 1861 Alcock addressed a despatch to Lord John Russell on Russian policy in the Far East. Having outlined the progress of the Russians in the area, he declared that Russia had gained 'a commanding position as regards the territories of China and Japan, and still more in reference to the great commerce of the Pacific'. He considered that one of the writers quoted by the embassy in St Petersburg had made 'a frank declaration of a policy of continuous aggression and conquest'. In Alcock's view, developments in the area called 'for the vigilant observation of the maritime powers of Europe, and of none so urgently, in view of the magnitude of the interests at stake, as Great Britain'.

Alcock was particularly concerned by the presence of Russians along the coast of Korea and in the Tsushima islands. A Russian corvette, the *Possadnick*, commanded by a Captain Barileff, was laid up in the Sound running between two of the Tsushima islands, 'apparently refitting, and quite dismantled, with workshops and quarters on shore'. Here Alcock's despatch becomes muddled and goes off into a sidetrack. According to information he had received the daimyo of Tsushima had written to the 'Taicoon' saying that he had been attacked by the Russians but did not need any assistance. There had followed the attack on the British Legation in Edo which 'was confidently affirmed, by the popular voice, to have been the act and deed of the Prince of Tsushima, in revenge for the violence and defeat he had suffered in his territories from the Russians'. Then, allowing his emotions to run away, Alcock went on: 'That all members of a Legation, with their Chief, should be thus indiscriminately immolated to the outraged pride of the Daimio, appeared to be considered in perfect accordance with Japanese traditions and habits.' He had to admit, however, that 'no legal or undoubted proofs have been attainable'. Indeed, the story about the involvement of the daimyo of Tsushima in the attack on the legation was a complete fabrication.

Reverting to the Russian threat he declared that he would not be surprised 'if at any hour the news arrived that, as a preliminary whet to this appetite for appropriation, Tsushima was in Russian hands'. This led him on to a discussion of what action should be taken to deal with the implied threat to British interests. One possibility would be for the British admiral in the Far East, Sir John Hope, if on close inspection he concluded that the Russians had 'any immediate intention of making a pretext for seizing Tsushima', 'to give their senior naval officer notice that this could not be permitted, on the grounds that it would prejudice our Treaty rights'. Another alternative would be for the British to take possession of the islands either by a convention with the Japanese in exchange for certain treaty rights they were anxious Britain should renounce 'or by force as a reparation or indemnity for injuries suffered at their hands in violation of the Treaties, for which no redress could otherwise be obtained'.

Sir John Hope, with whom Alcock discussed his proposals did not agree that the Tsushima islands 'could properly be considered as giving any command of the Straits, or being otherwise a desirable possession to Great Britain'. The admiral was, however, willing to take a look at the situation in the Tsushima islands and, if he concluded this was necessary, to give an appropriate warning to the Russians there. Hope, in a separate memorandum for the Admiralty, explained his views thus:

> I am disposed to consider even the temporary occupation of any portion of Japanese territory, as a measure of coercion, to be most inexpedient, in as much as it would not only strengthen, but justify, that jealousy of foreign intercourse which has given rise to by far the larger portion of the difficulties in which our Minister has been involved – an intercourse, in all equity let it be remembered, that we have forced upon Japan.

Alcock whose imperialist sentiments clearly exceeded those of the admiral concluded his despatch with an attempt in colourful terms to justify his attitude. He declared:

> And the day of grace seems nearly to have passed; with the beak and talons of the Russian eagle sharpened; and Japan not only without any alliance, offensive and defensive, to supply her with the strengths she wants to meet such a foe, but resolutely refusing to see her danger. The Japanese rulers are too much absorbed in measures for driving the other Powers from her shores, not seeing that they form their best security, and thus blindly would rush on to their fate.

Finally he declared:

> No doubt there are many people in England who would be quite ready to cry out, and condemn as flagitious the whole scheme sketched out. But to all such I would say, if the answer rested with me, there are necessities in self-defence, with national as with individual life; and that which is now threatened by Russia is vital to the interests without which our national life must perish. If no other or milder course be open whereby to avert it, the necessity would in this, as in a thousand other cases, prove its justification.[10]

Laurence Oliphant who was returning to Britain after having been wounded in the attack on the British legation accompanied Commander Craigie on a reconnaisance mission to Tsushima in HMS *Ringdove* and reported the results of these investigations to Hammond, the Permanent Under-Secretary in the Foreign Office, in a letter from Shanghai dated 2 September 1861. Craigie's mission was followed up in August 1861 by a visit by the admiral in HMS *Encounter*. In his report to the Admiralty Hope reported on the actions of the Russians and of the exchange of letters which he had had with Captain Barileff. In his letter of 28 August to Barileff, the admiral had pointed out that the treaty between Russia and Japan did not permit Barileff to create establishments ashore or to survey the coast without Japanese permission. He asked whether the Russian would leave in October as he had previously stated and whether he had any orders to create a permanent establishment. Barileff's reply in French took a tone of injured innocence, but affirmed that he had received no orders to occupy the island. The date of his departure was uncertain.[11] Partly as a result of British pressure and strenuous protests by the Japanese the Russians withdrew from Tsushima in the autumn of 1861.

ALCOCK AS A NEGOTIATOR WITH THE JAPANESE AUTHORITIES

Alcock's verbosity and his emotional reactions to events frequently detracted from his abilities as a negotiator and reporter. However, in the negotiations leading up to the British agreement to accept postponement of the opening of the additional treaty ports in 1862, Alcock showed both a readiness to make concessions where these seemed justified and an increased understanding of Japanese difficulties which he had failed to grasp earlier on. His firmness in negotiations at the time of the Shimonoseki affair (see Chapter 3), on the other hand, showed that he could remain firm in the face of recalcitrance.

Key meetings with the Japanese foreign ministers, leading up to Alcock's recommendation of a concession on the opening of additional ports took place in Edo on 14–15 August 1861. Alcock's lengthy and rambling despatch to Foreign Secretary Russell includes his account of these crucial meetings. We also have Oliphant's clearer record in his 'Compte-Rendu' submitted to the Foreign Office. Indeed, Alcock's despatches were so diffuse that Russell felt impelled to summarise briefly the position as he had gathered it from Alcock's correspondence. He noted that 'Alcock evidently does not wish to insist on the opening of the two ports which still remain to be opened according to Treaty. The question will be, whether we ought to waive the fulfilment of those articles, and if so, what conditions we shall ask in return for such concessions'.

Alcock in his despatch of 16 August said that: 'it is, indeed, impossible not to feel, here on the spot, that we have arrived at a turning point in the history of all foreign relations with Japan. He declared that a false step at this juncture 'might plunge the country into a civil war'. Excessive caution, on the other hand, might 'give such encouragement to the hostile agencies at work, that the position created by Treaties will be too far lost to be ever recovered by peacable means'. He thought that the Japanese anxiety to get agreement to the deferment of the opening of the ports and their embarrassment at the attack on the British Legation made this an opportune moment to try to develop a confidential dialogue with the Japanese ministers. The arrival of Admiral Sir John Hope and Sir Hercules Robinson, the Governor of Hong Kong, provided an excuse to seek a substantive meeting.

The Japanese Ministers eventually agreed to a confidential meeting. The *Ometsuke* (or 'Chief Spy' as Alcock called him) with all subordinates and attendants were excluded leaving the three 'Governors' of foreign affairs and Moriyama, their interpreter. Alcock kept with him only the admiral, Oliphant (Secretary of Legation) and Myburgh, his Dutch interpreter. With Moriyama on the floor between the tables and all the rest huddled close around, the discussions began in a tone so low that had anyone been behind the screens in the vicinity, the Ministers must have felt it would have been impossible to overhear'. The conversation involving double interpretation lasted for three hours and was adjourned to the following day. All in all, the conversation lasted some ten hours. It certainly helped Alcock to get a better understanding of the real position of the *Bakufu* in relation to the Mikado and of the problems which they faced.

Alcock felt that his persistence in remaining at the legation despite the armed attack on it 'while not without some risk' had gained him some advantages and that the position of the foreign representatives in the capital was now 'more firmly established'. He was encouraged by the willingness of the ministers of foreign affairs to explain their difficulties and considered that there were 'grounds for this improved feeling' with the Japanese. He had reached the conclusion after consulting his diplomatic colleagues that 'Of decided bad faith and unwillingness on the part of the Japanese Government to protect foreigners . . . there is not sufficient evidence. On the contrary I have come to the conclusion that they do really desire our protection.' But their inability to provide adequate protection compelled him to seek a British guard.

Alcock, however, a few paragraphs later reverted to form and declared that it would be long before Edo became 'either a pleasant or safe place of residence to the foreigner, exposed to the machinations of a race of political thugs, who take to assassination and massacre as a form of patriotism; for no criminals are so dangerous as those who can reconcile to their notions of virtue the pursuit of their objects'.

Alcock followed this with a lengthy review of the attitudes of his colleagues and of British business. He then turned to the proposal to delay the opening of the additional ports noting 'the grievous want . . . of more full and reliable information as to the actual Government of the country'. Behind the Tycoon and his councils 'in more or less vague and shadowy outline, though real in substance, only enveloped in a haze of mystery, are, first, the only acknowledged Sovereign of the country, the "Mikado" . . . But, although to the Mikado is due the profound respect and allegiance of every Japanese yet, as he is held not to meddle with the outer world and its vulgar interests, his demands upon them must be very small . . . Nevertheless, the Ministers told me the Mikado did, through his female Court, receive from time to time news of what was going on outside.' Alcock concluded that 'The Mikado is thus not altogether a myth.'

After a rambling discussion of history and the present position in Japan he noted that the Japanese 'know something . . . of our past history . . . in the East – how all began by a petition to trade, and ended by massacres and conquest . . . shall we wonder, or be impatient and indignant, that they distrust us.' He concluded that 'We must be patient, then, and either leave them to themselves – the only boon for which they would be really grateful – or consent to bear the natural penalty of a past it is out of our power now to change, unless we are prepared to justify their fears and hatred by making our trade a pretext for all the calamities of war and the conquest of the country.' He was sure that HM Government would reject the latter alternative. In that case Britain had no real alternative but to accept the Japanese proposal. Unfortunately, Alcock muddied this recommendation by suggesting that Britain should accept the offer of the opening of the port of Tsushima during the deferred period. (This idea fell by the wayside.)

He urged the conclusion of a protocol or convention recording that the deferment had only been accepted 'on the distinct assurance that the Tycoon hoped thereby to succeed in allaying the public discontent, from which all danger sprang, and that trade might go on without restriction or obstruction'. Lord Russell had great difficulties in making sense of Alcock's despatches.

Alcock, rather arrogantly, told the Japanese ministers that Britain 'was enabled to enforce her views . . . and if in the course of her future relations with Japan, she saw fit to waive any of her Treaty rights, it was not likely that any other Power would insist upon them'.

Alcock asked why he had not been able to call on any daimyo. The minister's reply was:

> In Japan it is not the custom for any blood relation to call upon each other. We are, for instance, both Daimios, but we have never visited each other. If you were to live here for ever you would never be able to call upon a Daimio.

At the second meeting the President of the *Gorōjū* 'and consequently the first Minister in the Empire' attended but 'under no circumstances does he ever take part in the conversation, and seldom manifests the slightest appearance of interest in what is going on. Upon the present occasion, however, he seemed occasionally to listen with great interest, though he never hazarded a remark.'

The ministers, commenting on the form of government in Japan, declared that this was very different from that of European countries.

> With us there is a spiritual Emperor, who really is the Emperor of Japan . . . Of course the Tycoon honours the Mikado, from whom he takes his investiture . . . The Mikado lives shut up in a house in Miako [Miyako i.e. Kyoto], and no one sees him; he is looked upon as a God, as sacred as if he was upon an altar; he has no communication with the outer world, and he does not know the actual circumstances in which the lower classes are placed; but he now and then receives rumours of discontent arising from foreign trade . . . It is our intention to inform him of the actual state of matters, but as he is invested with so much honour it will take some time . . . Osaka and Hiogo being in the neighbourhood of Miako, the Mikado is very much against their being opened; he has some very unruly subjects (this is a secret), and if they were opened there is no saying what collision might be brought about between the Mikado and the Tycoon . . . He is waited upon by women, and they get information and give it to him, and he occasionally writes to the Tycoon, and the latter occasionally writes and asks him about matters.

On being pressed by Alcock to say what assurance the ministers could give that, if the concessions requested were made, the discontent from which the dangers came would cease, the ministers could only assert that 'in the course of time the popular discontent will be abated'. They did, however, assure Alcock that they had no intention of seeking further concessions. (This, of course, they did during the mission to Europe.)

Alcock's recommendation that the British government should agree to the postponement of the opening of the additional ports was wise in the circumstances prevailing at that time in Japan, even if his arguments in support of his recommendation were rather muddled. The ministers' assurances were, however, of no practical value as they were in no position to influence opinion in Japan. The main interest of the meetings lies in what they reveal about Alcock who clearly enjoyed the conspiratorial nature of the discussions and about the ministers whose revelations should hardly have required such 'confidentiality'.

ALCOCK'S JUDGEMENTS ABOUT JAPAN

In *The Capital of The Tycoon* Alcock writes:

> Japan is essentially a country of paradoxes and anomalies, where all – even
> familiar things – put on new faces and are curiously reversed. Except that
> they do not walk on their head instead of their feet, there are few things in
> which they do not seem, by some occult law, to have been impelled in a per-
> fectly opposite direction and a reversed order

This comment has often been quoted, usually with approval, by writers about
Japan who put pen to paper after a limited stay. It is, of course, one of the
many myths about the Japanese.

In general, however, Alcock was a careful observer of Japanese life and
nature and, except in relation to the *Bakufu* authorities with whom he had to
deal, he was rarely anti-Japanese. His prejudices which were those of a
Victorian middle-class moralist inevitably coloured many of his comments
on Japan. He particularly regretted the lack of the Christian ethic.

Alcock could rarely resist the temptation of railing against the *Bakufu*. In
his despatch of 11 July 1860 he encapsulated one of his favourite themes,
namely the systematic policy of isolation and restriction on all foreigners
which together with 'insecurity of life, and denial of justice when either life
or property is sacrificed, are the greatest difficulties now to be encountered in
Japan'. He noted that relations with Japan were at all times 'at the mercy of
the Government of the day, and may be interrupted by a turn of the Tycoon's
fan'. Alcock's feelings on this score were understandable in view of the many
frustrations he suffered.

As we have seen, Alcock had no liking for Japanese temples and thought
nothing of Japanese architecture, but he was interested in Japanese art objects
and tried, for example, through the exhibits which he collected for the
International Exhibition in London in 1862 to promote the export of
Japanese works of art. He studied Japanese art with some care, if not always
with aesthetic discrimination. His book *Art and Art Industries in Japan* is a
competent survey of certain aspects of Japanese art which were available to
him. He wrote in this: 'Of high Art, such as has been cultivated in Europe
since the dark ages, the Japanese know nothing. But the range of true artistic
work in its application to industrial purposes in Japan is very wide, and more
varied than anywhere in Europe. There are a peculiar grace and delicacy, both
of design and execution, in all their work, even in utensils for the common
purposes of daily life . . .' In Alcock's view, 'all branches of Japanese Art, apart
from their popular picture-books, are decorative in their main purpose' but
he wanted to avoid 'any hasty inference that decorative Art should be
regarded as something inferior or ignoble'. His final conclusion which is a fair
one was that the lesson to be derived from the study of Japanese Art was one
of universal application – 'that only those who love their work, and find satisfaction in its excellence, can feel true pleasure in anything they undertake'.

HOME LEAVE 1862/3

In March 1862 Alcock, having arranged for a *Bakufu* mission to Europe to
travel in one of HM ships, departed on home leave. By this time he had come
to the conclusion that Britain should not insist on the opening on 1 January

1863 of additional ports as specified in the treaty but should accept the Japanese proposal to defer the opening of these ports until 1 January 1868. He accepted that a refusal to agree to postponement could provoke civil war and anarchy. Although Alcock recommended this concession, his own attitude subsequently hardened, as did that of Lord John Russell who was clearly irritated by the attempts of the Japanese envoys to extract further concessions from the British during their stay in London. By the time of his return to Japan in 1864 Alcock had determined that he would insist on the fulfilment by the Japanese of the terms of the treaties and that he would, if necessary, use force for this purpose. While Alcock was on home leave from 1862–64, Lt Colonel St John Neale, as Secretary of Legation became Chargé d'Affaires during his absence (see Chapter 2).

2
Lt Colonel Edward St John Neale
Chargé d'Affaires at Edo / Yokohama, 1862–64

SIR HUGH CORTAZZI

Lt Colonel Edward St John Neale

INTRODUCTION

Lt Colonel Neale (died 1866[1]) was in charge of the British Legation in Japan at a crucial period during the absence on leave of Sir Rutherford Alcock.[2] These were difficult and dangerous years for the British in relations with Japan. The British Legation in Edo was attacked for the second time in June 1862. The so-called Namamugi Incident occurred in September 1862. This led in due course to the bombardment of Kagoshima (the *Satsuei-sensō*) (see separate Appendix I) in the summer of 1863. The new British Legation at Gotenyama in Edo was burnt down in early 1863. The Straits of Shimonoseki were being obstructed to foreign shipping from 1863. Neale's staff at the Legation was small and inexperienced. The British merchants in Yokohama demanded tough measures.

In recognition of 'the patience, good temper, and firmness' which he displayed he was in November 1863 appointed a Companion of the Order of the Bath (CB),[3] a singular honour for a Chargé d'Affaires.

NEALE'S CAREER

Neale was a soldier before he became a consul and diplomat. His father Daniel Neale was a judge of the Supreme Court of Madras. His family stemmed from Hertfordshire where his grandfather had been a clergyman.[4] According to his entry in the Foreign Office List for 1867[5] he joined the 'Liberating Army' of Portugal on 20 September 1832 and was appointed to the Regiment of Scottish Fusiliers. He served throughout the protracted siege of Oporto and 'was present in command of a company in every action in which Brittish troops were engaged to the end of the war'. He was appointed to the staff of the British Auxiliary Legion of Spain in 1835, was Brigade

Major of the Light Brigade and took part in various engagements in Northern Spain. He was promoted Major in 1836 and Lt Colonel in 1837. He received the Spanish Royal Military Order of St Ferdinand (first class) for 'gallantry in the attack on the enemy's lines in front of St Sebastian, on 5 May 1836. In 1837 he retired from the Spanish Service to accompany Colonel Hodges, H.M.Consul General to Serbia. After two years at Belgrade he was appointed Vice-Consul at Alexandretta in 1841 and Consul at Varna in 1847. He later served in Bulgaria, Greece and Bosnia. He was appointed in 1860 Secretary of Legation in China where he accompanied the Minister (Sir Frederick Bruce) to Peking when the Legation was first established there in 1861. He was transferred as Secretary of Legation to Japan in 1862. After leaving Japan in 1864 he was not in good health and the Foreign Office decided against sending him back to Japan to act again as Chargé d'Affaires when they summoned Alcock home in late 1864. He was however appointed Secretary of Legation at Athens in April 1865 and in August that year was appointed Consul General at Guayaquil in Ecuador. He died at Quito in Ecuador on 11 December 1866. His posts were in those days almost all difficult and potentially dangerous assignments. No mention is made in Foreign Office records in the PRO (Public Records Office) about his wife and children, but his will,[6] which was signed in Varna in 1857 and for which probate was granted to his executor in April 1867, refers to his wife Adelaide, a daughter and two sons. When he died in Quito his son Henry St John Neale was with him.

BACKGROUND

Ii Naosuke (1815–60), the Chief Minister to the *Bakufu (tairō)*, who had been responsible for concluding the treaties of 1858 with the Foreign Powers was assassinated at Sakuradamon to Edo Castle on 24 March 1860 by *rōnin* from the Satsuma and Mito fiefs. The murder boosted the movement to 'revere the sovereign and expel the barbarians' (*Sonnō Jōi*). One of the leading members of the Shogun's Council of Elders (*rōju*) Andō Nobumasa (1819–71) tried to cement relations between the *Bakufu* and the Court in Kyoto which vehemently opposed the Treaties by arranging a marriage between an Imperial Princess Kazu-no-miya (1846–77) and the Shogun Tokugawa Iemochi (1846–66), but the marriage was strongly opposed by the anti-foreign faction and Andō was wounded outside the Sakashitamon to Edo Castle and forced to retire. This incident lay behind the decision of Shimazu Hisamitsu (1817–87), father of Shimazu Tadayoshi (1840–1897) the nominal daimyo of the Satsuma fief, to go to Edo to try to force the *Bakufu* to adopt policies which would stabilise the political situation and bridge the gap between the Court and the shogunate. It was on his way back to Kyoto that the Namamugi Incident (see below) took place. The reaction of the *Bakufu* to this incident demonstrated the government's weakness and the limits on its power to intervene in the affairs of the semi-independent fiefs.

The development of trade with foreign countries led to inflation causing hardship to the poorer samurai and ordinary Japanese. Some of the *tozama* daimyo who were not hereditary feudatories of the Tokugawa strongly resented the fact that the *Bakufu* had a monopoly control of the profits of this trade.

The attacks on Satsuma and Chōshū (see Appendix I on the British Bombardment of Kagoshima and Appendix II on the Bombardment of

Shimonoseki) led the two fiefs, which at first were strongly anti-foreign, to change direction and develop their military power. This was the foundation of the Satsuma-Chōshū alliance and the so-called Satchō oligarchy.

THE SECOND TŌZENJI INCIDENT

Alcock left on home leave in March 1862 before Neale had arrived from Peking. Charles Winchester[7] was left in charge until Neale arrived on 23 May 1862. Neale immediately decided that the Legation should return to Edo from Yokohama where it had been since the first Tōzenji incident[8] in June 1861. He was prevented by illness from moving to Edo until 12 June 1862.[9] One of his aims in bringing the Legation back to Edo was no doubt to demonstrate that he was in command and would not be intimidated, but he can have had little idea of the risks he was running, even though he was accompanied by a small British guard of 30 men from HMS *Renard*. In a despatch to Lord Russell dated 3 July 1862 Neale reported that 'a barbarous attack' had been made on the Legation by Japanese 'assassins'[10] shortly after midnight on 26 June resulting in the murder of two of the Legation's guards. The attack took place on the anniversary by the Japanese calendar of the first Tōzenji incident in 1861.

The Japanese authorities had appointed the daimyo Matsudaira, Tamba no Kami,[11] to provide protection for the Legation and some 535 men, partly from the daimyo's own bodyguard, were housed in detached wooden huts around the Legation. At about 12.30 a.m. the British sentry outside Neale's door challenged an intruder who attacked him. Neale emerging from his rooms found the sentry, Charles Sweet, dying from the sword cuts he had received. When the guard and members of the Legation assembled it was discovered that Corporal Crump was missing. His body, which was soon found, had received 'no less than sixteen desperate lance and sword wounds'. Some twenty minutes later detached parties of Japanese guards came to offer assistance. Some of these were 'intoxicated' and one, an officer, Neale 'caused to be expelled from the room'. They remained 'under arms' until daylight.[12]

At Neale's request Captain Bingham of HMS *Renard* returned to Edo with his ship and landed 'every available officer and man' augmenting the guard to 51. Neale immediately informed his diplomatic colleagues and Captain Vyse, the Consul in Yokohama, 'in order to avert over-exaggerated statements which would probably appear in local newspapers'. He also registered a strong protest with the Japanese authorities at their failure to prevent the assault. Neale was incensed by the fact that on the day before the night attack one of the Ministers of Foreign Affairs[13] had called to congratulate him that no 'disturbance or untoward event had occurred' on the anniversary of the previous attack.

The Japanese Ministers of Foreign Affairs told Neale that the attack 'filled not only us with great grief, but even His Majesty the Tycoon'. They 'were not a little astonished and pained to learn that two of the guards had met with a sad death.' They added that 'the culprit' had 'already committed suicide'. When Neale demanded to see the body he was eventually told that the body would be brought to the temple accompanied by many of the fellow retainers of the daimyo responsible for his protection. Not unnaturally Neale rejected this proposal. 'No assurances of any description' were given him about 'the future prospects of safety' of the Legation. To the Netherlands

Minister they said that they were 'ashamed' that they had not frustrated 'the evil design of the ill-disposed, and have thus caused anxiety to yourself and others; but as this originates from the disorderly state in which national feelings, owing to our nation clinging to ancient customs, we are in hopes of leading this inclination by degrees into the right course, and accustoming the national feeling to this change, to set the foreigners at ease.'

In writing to Rear Admiral Sir John Hope on 30 June about the need for the naval guard to be maintained Neale said that he was resolved to maintain his residence in Edo 'so long as reasonable degree of personal safety to members of the Legation prevails'.

When the Foreign Office in London received news of the attack a despatch dated 22 September 1862 was sent to Neale approving the action he had taken and his decision to remain at Edo. They found the Japanese response 'very unsatisfactory'. They expected Admiral Hope and the officer commanding the garrison at Hong Kong to take 'sufficient steps' for his protection, adding that it might 'be necessary to arm the Legation with three or four small cannon, to be mounted on a fit platform close to your residence'. Neale was instructed to demand compensation amounting to 10,000 pounds sterling in gold from the estate of the daimyo, in charge of the Legation at the time of the assault, for the families of the two murdered marines.

In the meantime, Neale had found it necessary to move back to Yokohama as a result of the 'harassment' of the marine guard and the difficulty of guarding the rambling buildings[14] used by the Legation at Tōzenji. This meant leasing once again the premises in Yokohama which had previously been given up. He proposed to visit Edo from time to time with members of the Legation until the new Legation being built on a hill at Gotenyama was ready.

Neale reported on 1 August 1862 from Yokohama that the Japanese authorities had not responded further to his protests about the attack on the Legation. He concluded that 'The policy of the Japanese Government consequent upon this outrage is now evident that of inaction and a stubborn resignment [sic] to whatever consequences may result.' On 27 August 1862 Neale reported that an infantry guard for the Legation consisting of an officer, two non-commissioned officers, and twenty-five privates from the 67th Regiment had reached Yokohama and quarters had been arranged for the garrison.[15]

THE NAMAMUGI INCIDENT

On 14 September 1862 Charles Lennox Richardson, a Shanghai merchant on a visit to Yokohama, accompanied by William Marshall and Woodthorpe Clarke, Yokohama residents, and Mrs Borrodaile, Marshall's sister-in-law, were riding on the Tōkaidō when at Namamugi near Kanagawa they encountered the train of the daimyo of Satsuma.[16] They were ordered off the road. After the leading members of the cortege had passed by, 'those who followed barbarously attacked'[17] the British party. Marshall and Clarke were seriously wounded. Richardson 'nearly cut to pieces, fell from his horse, and while lying in a dying state, one of the high officials of the cortege, borne in a chair, is stated to have told his followers to cut the throat of this unfortunate gentleman.' Mrs Borrodaile escaped unwounded, galloping to Yokohama, where she arrived 'exhausted and fainting'.

Neale, having discovered that the two wounded men were being looked after in the American consulate in Kanagawa, gave up his original idea of sending his escort of seven or eight men to search for the wounded on the high road and sent an armed cutter to Kanagawa to fetch the wounded men. However Captain Vyse, the British Consul in Yokohama, who had been absent, when news of the incident was first received, immediately on his return, without consulting Neale, took the escort with him on the road to Kanagawa.

According to Neale's despatch of 16 September 'The Settlement of Yokohama, as far as the Japanese are concerned, remained thoroughly tranquil and undisturbed.' But 'the British, and a few other members of the foreign community, thought it expedient to call a midnight meeting'. This meeting, under the chairmanship of Captain Vyse, passed a resolution calling for consultations with the 'commanders of the foreign forces' 'so that immediate steps may be taken so as to secure, if possible, the person of the Daimio whose retainers have committed the murder, or some of his high officers, in order to secure speedy reparation for this horrible outrage.'

A deputation from the British community, which called on Neale at 3.00am, informed him that they had already met Rear Admiral Kuper, who had just arrived from Hong Kong and who had agreed to attend a meeting at the French Legation at 6.00am. Neale, not yet having had the opportunity to meet Admiral Kuper, reluctantly agreed to attend the proposed meeting. He thought that the decision to meet at the French Legation showed 'bad taste' when the 'outrage' had been committed exclusively on British subjects. He also entirely dissented 'from the prudence or propriety of the impracticable and Quixotic coercive measures suggested'. This view he stated at the outset of the meeting at the French Legation, adding that if such steps, 'could with any chance of success, be carried into effect, I deem that to enter upon actual armed conflict with several hundred of armed Japanese, who are passing along the high road, and to seize the person of their Chief, would be tantamount to a sudden commencement of hostilities with the Government of Japan . . . Such a premature measure, I added, would be altogether unjustifiable, fraught with all the evils and consequences of actual war' including the stoppage of trade.' The French Minister concurred, but called for 'energetic measures for the defence of Yokohama and the Settlement by military patrols . . .' (It was eventually decided by the British French and Dutch naval commanders that 'the Settlement would be divided by nationalities and that guards from the ships of war of each nation would patrol in the neighbourhood of their own countrymen'.)

Neale commented:

A crisis has arisen on the present occasion arising out of the effervescence and irritation of the community, the disastrous tendency of which I have single-handed opposed myself to stem. I have not done so without obloquy. Much pressure was brought to bear on me, but I have been sustained by a strong sentiment of duty which dictated the urgency of resisting a precipitate and ill-advised course of action. . .which would. . .have instantly awakened into activity the civil strife which lies beneath the surface of events in this country.

Captain Vyse and the hot-heads in the British community were not satisfied and demanded that the record of their meeting and other relevant documents should be forwarded to the Foreign Office in London. Neale complied with this request drawing attention to the 'highly improper course which Her Majesty's Consul followed throughout the proceedings'. Captain Vyse had urged Admiral Kuper without consulting Neale to 'adopt immediate coercive measures'.

When Lord Russell was informed, he approved[18] the action which Neale had taken, commenting that 'his conduct seems to have been severely but unjustly attacked'.[19] The action proposed 'would have been an act of war, [the] Colonel is not authorized to make war.' He then set out the demands which were to be made for reparation. These were duly incorporated in somewhat modified form in Lord Russell's despatch[20] to Neale dated 24 December 1862. Neale was instructed to demand an ample and formal apology from the Japanese Government and the payment of 100,000 pounds. He was also to demand from the daimyo of Satsuma the immediate trial and capital punishment of the perpetrators of the murder[21] and the payment of 25,000 pounds to be distributed to Richardson's relations and to those who had escaped with their lives. If he was unable to obtain satisfaction he was to inform the Admiral on the station and 'call upon him to adopt such measures of reprisal or blockade, or both, as he may judge best calculated to attain the end proposed'.

Neale had continued to protest to the Japanese Ministers and to demand satisfactory arrangements for the defence of the Legation and the settlement. Although his instructions had not yet reached him demanding compensation for the attack on the Legation and the Namamugi incident, Neale visited Edo with Rear Admiral Kuper in his flagship *Euryalus* accompanied by three other ships which were then in Yokohama. They had an interview with the Japanese Ministers of Foreign Affairs (the *gorōjū*) on 23 September 1862. In his despatch of 1 October 1862 Neale reported that 'the general tone, spirit, and demeanour of the Japanese Ministers on this occasion were of a most satisfactory nature'. They were greatly relieved by Neale's resistance to 'a resort to immediate coercive measures'. Neale stressed to the Ministers their responsibility 'to afford efficient protection'. A temporizing communication from the Ministers to Neale dated 9 October led him to comment to them in writing on 12 October: '. . . your communication, under the plea of a necessary delay, after allowing the murderers to return to the Prince of Satsuma's domains, which you say are very distant, amounts to a denial of all redress'. He went on to demand that within ten days he should be furnished with 'such satisfactory, unreserved, and detailed information as to the real causes of this futile and dilatory action . . . as can be understood and accepted by me, as the Representative of a great nation which will not bear the outrages which have been committed on its subjects . . .'

This peremptory demand did not elicit a satisfactory response. Neale's position, especially without instructions, was a difficult one. In a despatch dated 18 November 1862 he recorded how a visit by the Legation to Edo was accomplished. Due notification having been given to the Japanese authorities, 'the boats containing the members of the Legation and guards are received by a hedge of yaconins [*yakunin* – officials], who restrain within certain bounds the crowd which assembles on these occasions'. They then walked to the Legation and the Japanese guards amounting to between 200 and 300 men, 'whose presence inspires little confidence, muster about their wooden huts on the rising ground around the Legation and along the avenue which leads to it'. Preparations for the night included the piling of firewood on the lawn and the trimming and hanging of numerous lanterns. Rounds were carried out hourly and the sentries, 'with the knowledge and concurrence of the Japanese authorities' were 'ordered to shoot all Japanese approaching their posts'. When visits were made to Japanese Ministers who resided about two hours ride away 'the British mounted escort, consisting of ten men, accompany the cortege' as did twenty to thirty Japanese horsemen. Neale added:

> notwithstanding these precautions . . . startling incidents are of not unfrequent occurrence . . . On one of the last occasions that I visited the Ministers . . . my horse plunged and reared amidst a general tumult, when two horsemen passed me, coming from behind at full speed, rushing through our ranks, striking the horses of our Japanese guards with heavy sticks, and pursued by the whole body of them.

Neale was now left alone with the few men of the British escort. When the Japanese retinue rejoined them he was told that 'they were adherents of the Prince of Satsuma'. When members of the Legation went out they were normally surrounded by Japanese guards, but when a daimyo procession was encountered they broke into single file 'thus exposing to isolated attack from passing retainers the foreigner they may be guarding'.

Neale reported on 12 December 1862[22] that he had called on the Japanese Ministers in Edo to carry out the instructions which he had by then received about the attack on the Legation. The response had been most unsatisfactory. The Ministers, while admitting that the attack had been made by one of the retainers of Matsudaira, Tamba no Kami, who had been given responsibility for the protection of the Legation, exculpated him on the grounds that the culprit acted on his own without the knowledge of others. They thought the demand for 10,000 pounds excessive but offered to pay in silver coin to the relatives of the murdered men 3,000 dollars (four dollars were roughly equal to one pound).[23] Neale later reported that Matsudaira, Tamba no Kami, was 'in very impoverished circumstances, and his estates mortgaged to merchants of Osaka'.

Neale's position was further complicated by the destruction by incendiaries of the new British Legation on Gotenyama[24] on 1 February 1863. This was fortunately not yet occupied; so no lives were lost, but it meant that the Legation had to continue to operate out of Yokohama with occasional visits to Edo. He then asked Admiral Kuper to return to Yokohama to confer with him. In February 1863[25] he reported that 'serious designs[26] are entertained by the Tycoon's Government to bring about a rupture in their relations with the Treaty Powers'. He suggested that 'A show of material force, coupled with conciliatory action on our part, would seem . . . as a general rule, the best calculated to consolidate our footing in this country.' He then compared the situation in Japan with that of other 'Asiatic' countries including Turkey in which he had served. He noted the Tycoon's rule was threatened by the attitude of the Mikado. He expressed the hope that Japan 'will pass unharmed through its present ordeal of political effervescence, for the Japanese are a shrewd and intelligent people, not subject to persevere in projects of impossible attainment'. He added that we should not lose sight of 'the main and sole object of our establishment in Japan, viz., the fresh field it has afforded for a prosperous trade, best secured to us by patience and forbearance'.

Over the next few months Neale had numerous exchanges with the Japanese authorities about a settlement of the British demands over both the second Tōzenji and the Namamugi incidents. In March 1863[27] he declared that in preliminary communications with the Japanese Government he would 'be impressed with the most conciliatory spirit so long as a reasonable probability exists of obtaining the reparations demanded'. He considered that 'the hardest blows we may be forced to strike should be directed against' the Prince of Satsuma. He trusted that a blockade of Japanese ports would not prove necessary, 'as in truth at the open ports the foreign residents would be the only sufferers'.

In his note to the Japanese Ministers dated 6 April 1863 Neale protested vigorously against the 'procrastination and evasion' they used in responding to British demands and demanded satisfactory replies within twenty days. If these were not forthcoming the British Admiral (Kuper) with the forces assembled in Yokohama, would 'proceed to enter upon such measures as may be necessary to secure the reparation demanded'. This amounted to an ultimatum backed up by force.

In fact it took until June 1863 before the issues were settled by the full payment of the compensation demanded. The Japanese authorities managed to delay and prevaricate up to the last moment. Neale was adamant that he would not be put off, but he was reluctant to use force to extract the compensation demanded, partly because the use of force could harm British interests and because he was doubtful whether it would be effective. He was also aware that the *Bakufu* were under pressure from the court in Kyoto[28] and were divided over what to do, although it is doubtful whether he understood at all fully what was happening within Japan at this time. To the *Bakufu* the British demands must have been a serious complication in their relations with the court, but the central issue for them was the court rejection of the treaties and the demand for the expulsion of the foreigners.

On 14 June 1863, after protracted negotiations, the *Bakufu* reached agreement with Neale to pay the full sum amounting to 440,000 Mexican dollars at the rate of five shillings to the dollar making 110,000 pounds in seven instalments with the first payment to be made on 18 June 1863 and the final payment on 30 July 1863. On 17 June, however, a few hours before the first payment was due, he received a message from the 'governor' of Kanagawa that orders had been received from Edo not to pay the money. Neale was understandably furious and on 29 June he asked Admiral Kuper 'to adopt such prompt coercive measures of reprisal, and such other measures as you may deem expedient, to punish in the first instance the Tycoon's Government for its flagrant breach of good faith, and calculated to bring them to a due sense of their engagements'. Before the Admiral could take any action the *Bakufu* had second thoughts and Neale, having made it clear that the agreement to pay in instalments had been abrogated, said that he would only accept payment in full. He was notified at 1.00am on 24 June 1863 that the money would be delivered that day. At 5.00am 'several carts arrived laden with dollars'[29] and coercive measures were called off.

However, a further complication immediately arose. One of the Japanese Ministers for Foreign Affairs[30] informed the foreign representatives, including Neale, that[31] 'he had been instructed by his Majesty the Tycoon, who is now at Miako [Miyako], and who received this order from the Mikado, to close the opened ports and to remove the subjects of Treaty Powers, as our nation does not wish to have any relations with them'. Neale immediately responded[32] expressing his amazement at the 'audacious nature' of the announcement which was 'unparalleled in the history of all nations, civilized or uncivilized'. It was 'in fact, a declaration of war by Japan itself against the whole of the Treaty Powers'. The other representatives also rejected the Japanese declaration. Lord Russell replying to Neale on 5 September 1863 said that the 'insolent intimation' had 'been properly answered' by Neale. He added: 'the mysteries of Japanese intrigue, and of the hostilities which are said to be pretended, and may turn out to be real, cannot be fathomed at this distance, and Her Majesty's Government will not trammel you with needless or unsuitable instructions.'[33]

It soon became clear that the *Bakufu* had no intention of taking effective action on the Mikado's instructions. A missive from the Ministers for Foreign Affairs dated 3 July 1863[34] expressed sorrow for the outrages and murders at the Legation and on the Tōkaidō and their hope that 'such events may not again occur to interrupt the friendly relations between the two Governments.' He and the other foreign representatives had been assured by the 'Tycoon's Envoys' that the Mikado's edict was 'a dead letter'.[35] This did not deter them from attempting in October 1863 to revert to this policy. On this occasion Neale[36] declined to go to Edo, having heard from his diplomatic colleagues that the purport of the Ministers' communication 'amounted to the total subversion of treaty rights'. The *Bakufu* in the event took no further action to implement the Mikado's instructions and informed the foreign representatives on 12 November 1863 that 'having changed her former policy' the Japanese Government asked for the return of the missive which the representatives had received and which had been signed by Ogasawara Jewsio no Kami [sic], when he was still in office.[37]

When the Foreign Office heard about this development Lord Russell in a despatch to Neale dated 11 January 1864 conveyed his 'entire approval of the conciliatory and judicious manner in which you have conducted yourself generally in these matters'. Russell added that it was Her Majesty's Government's 'earnest desire that nothing should occur to interfere with peaceful commerce, and they are prepared to make full allowance for the peculiar character of the Japanese Government. In short, the employment of measures of coercion and retaliation could only be warranted, in their opinion, by the necessity of prompt interference for the protection of the lives and properties of British subjects, or for the vindication of the honour of the British flag if assailed by wanton attacks on the part of the Government or influential nobles.'

The Japanese Government nevertheless once again reverted in January 1864[38] to the question of the closure of treaty ports and decided to send a mission to Europe to negotiate with the Treaty Powers for closing the port of Kanagawa-Yokohama. They cannot have expected a favourable response but under pressure from the Mikado felt obliged to try.

SATSUMA – RETRIBUTION

News which had been received in late July 1863 that US, Dutch and French vessels had been fired on[39] in the Straits of Shimonoseki led the US, Dutch, French and British representatives to meet and agree on 28 July 1863 on resolutions, which Neale transmitted to the Japanese ministers. The foreign representatives declared that 'the outrages and insults' to the vessels of for-eign powers would be resisted 'by a force the extent of which cannot at present be contemplated'. A settlement of this dispute was only reached in 1864 after Alcock's return from leave.

These developments did not deter Neale from proceeding 'to execute his instructions in respect to the Prince of Satsuma'. In Neale's view[40] the apol-ogy received from the *Bakufu* and the fact that the 'Tycoon's and Mikado's parties are fully occupied in their rival contentions' opened the way for action against Kagoshima. Admiral Kuper also presumably took the view that as yet British vessels were not involved in the Shimonoseki Straits and that the issues could at this stage be left to the Americans, the French and the Dutch. He accordingly decided that the British community would be safe if he left only HMS *Encounter* and two smaller vessels at Yokohama and departed for Kagoshima with the rest of his fleet.

The British bombardment of Kagoshima which was a major development in Britain's relations with Japan is covered in Appendix I. The 'negotiations' with the Satsuma representatives were conducted by Neale with his accus-tomed tenacity.

On his return to Yokohama Neale was able to report[41] on the astonishing degree of progress' made in trade with Japan despite all the political upheavals and insecurity. Imports into Japan from Britain in the first six months of 1863 had risen from some 331,000 in the first six months of 1862 to over 535,000 Mexican dollars, while Japanese exports[42] in British vessels had more than doubled over the same period from some 1.2million to 2.7 million dollars. However in October,[43] Neale was worried by the impression that 'the trade in staple product of silk was being gradually restricted to extinction' and he had felt obliged to take this up with the Japanese Ministers.

END OF HIS MISSION

Unfortunately, murders of foreigners continued to take place from time to time. A French officer Lt de Camus was assassinated on a country road on 14 October 1863. Nevertheless, shortly before Rutherford Alcock returned to Japan to resume his post as Minister Neale reported[44] on 1 March to Lord Russell that 'trade was steadily flourishing'. The main issue remaining was that of free navigation in the Inland Sea. He recommended an 'expectant and defensive policy' backed by 'a strong naval force' and a 'moderate military contingent available in China'. Alcock arrived the following day. He did not directly criticise in his despatches the role Neale had played during his long absence, but he also did not commend Neale. Was there perhaps an unfair hint of criticism of Neale in a despatch dated 31 March 1864 when he emphasized that the time had gone by 'irrevocably for concessions contrary to the spirit and intent of the existing Treaties'?

ASSESSMENT

Members of the British community in Yokohama thought Neale was insuffi-ciently robust in his response to Japanese threats and hostile behaviour. Satow[45] recorded in relation to the Namamugi incident that 'the idea had got abroad amongst the foreign community that Colonel Neale could not be trusted to take energetic measures which they considered necessary under the circumstance. In fact they found fault with him for preserving the cool bearing which might be expected from a man who had seen actual service in the field.' Satow commented in his account written many years later: 'Looking back now after the lapse of nearly a quarter of a century, I am strongly disposed to the belief that Colonel Neale took the best course . . .' Satow[46] recorded how in December 1862 he accompanied Neale to Edo from Yokohama. At Kawasaki they encountered 'an obstinate head ferryman' who did not recognize the British Chargé d'Affaires and refused to let them pass. Neale fumed 'with wrath'. At the meeting with the Ministers of Foreign Affairs, attended by Satow,[47] after the usual objections and difficulties raised by the Japanese, Neale 'at last lost all patience, which was no doubt what they were aiming at. He gave them a piece of his mind in pretty strong language.' The interview of about three hours ended without anything being settled. On this occasion Neale overheard Satow making a facetious remark. This elicited 'a terrible frown from the old gentleman'[48] and a rebuke for his indecorous behaviour. Satow was told that he would not in future be allowed to be present on one of 'these solemn occasions'.

Dr William Willis,[49] one of the Legation doctors, was at first inclined to share the views of the hot heads in Yokohama: 'Colonel Neale has little to recommend him. I doubt his courage, physical or moral . . . He is much despised here and looked upon as an old woman.' But Willis later accepted that Neale 'acted with great forbearance'.

In the absence of other comments and of any character sketch we can only try to draw a picture of Neale from his actions and his official letters. My impression is that he was a conscientious man who gave almost all his attention to his work. His courage, moral and physical, despite Dr Willis's comments quoted above, cannot be doubted. He was something of a martinet (understandable in view of his military background), had a short fuse, was often impatient and used language which was sometimes intemperate. His self-justificatory references in his despatches to his alone having prevented a war suggest that he felt rather lonely and isolated. This was not unjustified. He was probably not outstandingly intelligent, but he had common sense and his actions were usually restrained and cautious. He had no previous knowledge of Japan and did not know the language, thus often probably failing to realize all the complexities of translating from Japanese, with its tendency to use vague expressions, via Dutch into English. His subordinates had not yet had time either to master the language or the political situation.

His reports are not examples of the best diplomatic style, but at least they are more to the point, clearer and briefer than the effusions of Rutherford Alcock. In the circumstances his judgements were relatively sound. Lord Russell, the Foreign Secretary, at any rate approved of the actions taken by Neale and was relieved that Britain had not been intemperately forced into a damaging war with Japan. Russell's general stance was more pacific than that of Lord Palmerston, the British Prime Minister at the time, but Russell was just as determined as Palmerston to stand up for British rights and was prepared to allow a certain amount of 'gunboat diplomacy' in the Far East. His actions and those of Neale hardly comply with modern standards of international behaviour but they cannot fairly be judged other than by the standards of the time.

3
Alcock returns to Japan, 1864

SIR HUGH CORTAZZI

Rutherford Alcock

THE STRAITS OF SHIMONOSEKI

Alcock's main concern after his return to Japan in March 1864 was how to deal with the measures taken by the Chōshū authorities in 1863/4 to close the Straits of Shimonoseki to foreign shipping. Foreign ships had been fired on in 1863, but Lt Colonel Neale and Admiral Kuper had then decided that action must first be taken against Satsuma and its capital of Kagoshima not least because Satsuma was held responsible for the Namamugi incident in 1862 when the British merchant from Shanghai, Richardson, had been murdered. Satsuma having been dealt with attention turned to Chōshū. Satsuma and Chōshū were two of the strongest fiefs, among the so-called *tozama* daimyo, opposed to the Tokugawa *Bakufu* and were particularly critical of the concessions which the *Bakufu* had made to foreigners. Satsuma, following the attack on Kagoshima had come to recognize that an accommodation had to be made with the Western powers, but Chōshū had not in 1864 yet recognized that Japan was in no position to expel the foreigners.

The problem for Alcock and his colleagues in Yokohama in dealing with the problem of navigation in the Straits of Shimonoseki was complicated by the struggle between the *Bakufu* and the court, which was calling for the closure of the treaty ports and expulsion of the foreigners. Chōshū, which had its capital at Hagi, had a strong samurai and nationalist tradition and the daimyo family (the Mōri) like the Shimazu in Satsuma traced their enmity to the Tokugawa back to the battle of Sekigahara in 1603 when the Tokugawa had triumphed over their rivals. After the Meiji Restoration samurai from the two fiefs came to dominate the new government.

ALCOCK'S INSTRUCTIONS

Before he left London to return to Japan Lord Russell in a despatch dated 17 December 1863 told Alcock that he was to 'require from the Tycoon and the Daimios the execution of the engagements of the Treaty'. The instructions also contained the following explicit authorisation of limited naval action: 'The Admiral, with your concurrence, will be authorized, if he should think it advisable, to land marines and destroy the batteries, spiking the guns, which have been erected and armed for the evident purpose of interrupting the passage of our merchant ships, and which shall have evinced their hostile purposes by some hostile act.' The despatch repeated this last point in the subsequent paragraph which read: 'You will not, however, propose, neither will the Admiral be authorised to direct, the destruction of any such batteries, unless their hostile purpose has been clearly proved by acts of a hostile character.' Then, no doubt reflecting the reaction in parliament to the bombardment of Kagoshima (see Appendix 2), the despatch added: 'Her Majesty's Government rely on the Admiral for taking care that no unarmed and peaceable town should be bombarded.' However, presumably at the insistence of the Admiralty, the following qualifying sentence was appended: 'But when Her Majesty's ships of war are fired upon, that fire must be returned with vigour and rapidity.'

A subsequent despatch to Alcock dated 24 December 1863, perhaps reflecting a complaint from Admiral Kuper about Lt Colonel Neale's attempts to interfere during the Kagoshima bombardment Alcock was reminded that, although he had 'controlling authority' in matters of public policy, 'the manner in which such operations shall be executed must rest entirely with the naval and military Commanders. You have no authority to direct either of them [naval or military commanders] to undertake any operation, or to interfere with their directions as to the manner in which any operation should be conducted' On the other hand the commanders did not have 'any authority to undertake any military or naval operations of a special kind without previous communication with you and without your concurrence unless the honour of Her Majesty's arms, the safety of the lives and properties of British subjects, or some sudden and unforeseen emergency, should call for immediate action.'[1]

The government were also, as usual, frightened of the expense involved in maintaining a squadron in Japanese waters[2] and engaging in military or naval actions.

The instructions quoted above were regarded by Alcock as justifying the action which, together with the other foreign representatives in Edo, he authorized Kuper to take against the Shimonoseki batteries, which were obstructing shipping in the straits and harming British and other foreign trading interests.

However, on 26 July 1864 a despatch was sent to Alcock positively enjoining him 'not to undertake any military operations whatever in the interior of Japan; and they [HMG] would indeed regret the adoption of any measures of hostility against the Japanese Government or Princes, even though limited to naval operations, unless absolutely required by self-defence.' Nevertheless, the despatch added a caveat which could be seen as condoning action, which unbeknown to the Foreign Office Alcock had already authorized: 'The action of the naval and military forces of Her Majesty in Japan should be limited to the defence and protection of Her Majesty's subjects resident in Japan, and of their property, and to the maintenance of our Treaty rights.' Alcock was also reminded of an order in council giving him power to prohibit or restrict British-owned ships from entering 'straits or waters of Japan when such entrance or passage may lead to acts of disturbance or acts of violence, or may otherwise endanger the maintenance of peaceful relations or intercourse between her Majesty's subjects and the subjects of the Tycoon of Japan'.

These instructions, which did not reach Alcock until after the action in the Shimonoseki straits had been completed, were swiftly followed by a despatch[3] summoning Alcock home 'to explain the actual situation of affairs, and confer with Her Majesty's Government as to the measures to be taken.' Lord Russell was not well informed of the situation in Japan and it was very difficult for someone, brought up in a European environment and who had not travelled in the Far East, to grasp what was happening in Japan, a country, which at that time was remote and relatively unknown in Britain. The verbosity of Alcock's despatches also inevitably confused the Foreign Office.

The Foreign Office had to take account of the strongly held views of the Admiralty and the Treasury. It is not therefore surprising that Alcock's instructions were sometimes inconsistent. Moreover slowness in communications was a further complicating factor. In 1864 before the introduction of the telegraph a reply to a despatch could take up to four months to arrive.

Alcock, while taking the lead over measures to reopen the Straits of Shimonoseki, was careful to work in concert with his French, Dutch and American colleagues. He did not accompany the fleet as Neale had done to Kagoshima and did not therefore intervene directly in the operations. Alcock's task was far from easy. As he wrote to Russell in May 1864[4] 'the best-informed Representative of a foreign Power in Japan can only form his judgement on imperfect and contradictory data. The difficulties and embarrassments arising from the absence of all the ordinary channels of information open to the foreign Ministers in every other country, and the limited means of communication with the people, constitute serious evils.' He went on to deplore the 'lack of frankness and good faith' of the Tycoon's government.

Alcock had to deal with two main issues simultaneously. In addition to the action by the Chōshū authorities to close the Straits he had to ensure the defence of the settlement at Yokohama against the threats to close the port emanating from the Tycoon's government at the behest of the Mikado in Kyoto. Russell, who did not appreciate the way in which the two issues were interconnected, told Alcock[5] 'you should not require Admiral Kuper to act in a hostile manner against the Prince of Nagato [Chōshū], and . . . you should turn all your attention, and that of the Commander of Her Majesty's naval and military forces, to the defence of Yokohama.'

INSTRUCTIONS FROM ALCOCK TO ADMIRAL KUPER

The first action taken by Kuper[6] at the request of Alcock was in July 1864 to convey the two Chōshū samurai (Itō Hirobumi and Inoue Kaoru who had returned post haste from Europe) to the Chōshū domains to try to mediate between the powers and the Chōshū authorities. Kuper was determined on this occasion to have the most up-to-date intelligence and sent Major Wray of the Royal Engineers on HMS *Barossa* to ascertain as far as possible, 'without approaching too near the coast, the nature, extent, and position of the batteries forming the defences of the Straits'. Bearing in mind that the forthcoming operation was to be a joint one Kuper permitted a French and Dutch naval officer to travel on board the *Barrosa,* which was accompanied by HMS *Cormorant.* Captain Dowell of the *Barrosa* was told to 'be careful to economize the fuel of the vessels under your orders as much as possible, using sails wherever practicable'. Unfortunately Itō and Inoue's mission was abortive.

Rutherford Alcock[7] in late July summed up his assessment of the twin threats to British interests in Japan, the Tycoon's government having singularly failed to take effective action themselves against Chōshū. He told Kuper:

> It seems probable, therefore, that the best and least costly mode of providing for the security of Yokohama, and averting an attack which it might be difficult successfully to resist, with the means at command, would be to take the initiative ourselves, and attack the most forward and belligerent of the hostile Daimios in his stronghold.

The commencement of action, which had been agreed between the British, French, American and Netherlands representatives in Japan with Alcock as the senior representative in the lead, was delayed by the return of the Tycoon's envoys from Europe with a convention signed in Paris, by which the Tycoon undertook 'to open the Straits of Shimonoseki' within three months. The Japanese Ministers for Foreign Affairs decided to annul the Convention because if they had attempted to put it into force 'it is certain that civil war would immediately break out,' and 'friendly intercourse . . . would be destroyed'. Leon Roches, the French Minister, who had recently arrived and with whom Sir Harry Parkes was to have so much trouble later, does not seem to have been troubled by this volte-face.

A memorandum signed on 16 August 1864 by the British, French and American Ministers and the Netherlands Consul General gave the Admiral the go-ahead to take action against Chōshū. The main points made by the diplomatic representatives were as follows:

1. They absolved the commanding officers for responsibility for the defence and security of the settlement at Yokohama.
2. The Commanders were 'to proceed with all convenient speed to open the Straits of Shimonoseki, destroying and disarming the batteries of the Prince . . . and otherwise crippling his means of attack'.
3. If the Prince's batteries refrained from firing on the fleet they were nevertheless 'to destroy the batteries, and take such means as maybe deemed practicable, to secure a material guarantee against any future hostilities from the same quarter.'
4. They were to refrain from entering 'into any negotiations with the Prince, reserving the solution of all ulterior questions to the action of the Tycoon's Government, in connection with the foreign Representatives.'
5. There was not to be 'any demonstration of force in the vicinity of Osaka.'
6. Any part of the squadron not 'required for the maintenance of a free passage' was 'to be returned to Yokohama . . . as soon as the operations here contemplated shall have been completed.'

An account of the successful naval and military action at Shimonoseki and the way in which Admiral Kuper interpreted his instructions is given in Appendix II.

AFTERMATH

Alcock[8] reported on 26 September 1864 that the Tycoon's Government had offered to take on itself the whole of the claims of the Treaty Powers 'for the past acts of aggression on the part of the Prince of Choshiu, and either to liquidate such amount as shall finally be agreed upon, or open a port – Shimonoseki or some other eligible port in the vicinity of the Straits – at the option of the Treaty powers.' Alcock sought instructions, but suggested that if as a result of negotiations on the indemnity the powers could obtain 'ratification of the Treaties by the Mikado, and their acceptance by him and the Daimios' it 'would be worth more to Great Britain and all the Treaty Powers ... than many millions of dollars, or any sum that could be extorted from the Tycoon'. On 28 October 1864 Alcock[9] reported the conclusion of a convention under which the Tycoon's government undertook to pay an indemnity of 3 million dollars.

Alcock and his diplomatic colleagues took advantage of the presence of the squadron to visit Edo on 5 and 6 October 1864[10] 'accompanied by several ships of the squadrons' to press for early ratification of the Treaties by the Mikado. Alcock recorded that he had said to the *Gorōjū* that 'the root of all evil in respect of foreign relations was the want of accord between Mikado and Tycoon, and that the time had now arrived when ratification of existing treaties by the Mikado could no longer be deferred.'

Alcock[11] resented the element 'of censure and condemnation' in Russell's communications and defended his actions vigorously: 'What has been done was necessary to avert our expulsion from Yokohama and war as a certain consequence. My whole defence and justification is there, so far as the motive, the object and the means employed are concerned. The results speak for themselves. A catastrophe has been averted, the danger of war indefinitely deferred if not altogether prevented, and our position at Yokohama secured from all immediate risk.' Alcock added: 'the only way of proving ourselves strong and deterring Mikado and Tycoon from violating existing Treaties and expelling foreigners from Japan was to strike at the head of the anti-foreign faction, and discourage them from any designs on Yokohama, by demonstrating their hopeless inferiority in the field – by demonstrating, under circumstances which could not fail to carry conviction to the heart of every two-sworded Japanese, that the British naval and military forces were irresistibly superior.' Alcock's arguments carried the day and on his return to London for consultations he was praised rather than censured and promoted to be Minister at Peking. In those days China was regarded as more important to Britain than Japan.

CONCLUSION

Alcock did not, I think, act contrary to his instructions over the Shimonoseki bombardment although he interpreted, probably justifiably, instructions flexibly. He was the man on the spot and could not seek speedy clarification from London. If things had gone wrong he would have been the first to be blamed.

Russell's instructions were inconsistent and weak. He and the Foreign Office were ignorant of the real situation in Japan.

Judged by the standards of his time Alcock was generally successful as a pro-consular envoy although by today's standards he would be regarded as an imperialist with a limited outlook. His verbosity, the lack of clarity in his recommendations and his emotional judgements on people and events were also flaws, but as the first British envoy to Japan his achievements were considerable.

4
Sir Harry Parkes
Minister to Japan, 1865–83

Sir Harry Parkes

SIR HUGH CORTAZZI

Sir Harry Parkes (1828–85), who was the British Minister to Japan over a period of eighteen years from 1865 to 1883, was the longest serving British head of mission in Japan. His period of service coincided with the Meiji Restoration of 1868 and witnessed a time of unprecedented revolutionary change. What sort of a man was Sir Harry Parkes? How 'successful' was he as the chief British representative in Japan during his long term of office?

BACKGROUND

Sir Harry Smith Parkes, GCMG, KCB, was born in Staffordshire but was orphaned while still a boy. In 1841 he was sent to join relatives in Macao. He studied Chinese and in 1842 found employment in the office of the Chief Superintendent of Trade in Hong Kong which had been occupied by the British in 1841 and became a British colony in the following year. When the British plenipotentiary to the Chinese Court, Sir Henry Pottinger, left Hong Kong in June 1842 for the Yangtse Kiang and Nanking, Parkes was a member of his party. He worked as interpreter under Sir Rutherford Alcock who became Consul in Amoy in 1844. Parkes was in due course promoted to be Consul serving in Amoy, Canton and Shanghai. He travelled extensively in China. He was a member of Lord Elgin's mission to Peking in 1860. In the course of this expedition he was arrested by Chinese authorities and imprisoned for three weeks during which he was laden with chains for eleven days and threatened with execution. Lord Elgin wrote of him:[1] 'Parkes is one of the most remarkable men I have ever met; for energy, courage and ability combined, I do not know where I could find his match; and this, joined to his facility of speaking Chinese, . . . makes him at present the man of the situation.' Parkes was made a CB in 1860 and a KCB at the early age of 34 in 1862. In 1865, at the age of only 38, he was appointed Minister to Japan in succession to his old chief, Sir Rutherford Alcock.

CHARACTER AND BEHAVIOUR

Parkes was described[2] on his arrival in Japan by the Legation doctor, William Willis, as 'slim and rather below-the-middle size with auburn hair and red whiskers, a pleasant countenance with refined features, hands and feet much too large for gentility. The front part of the head is bald, the top very high. The features all express thought rapidly passing into action, the various appetites are not strong, I conclude.' Grace Fox[3] said that 'A large head, impressive brow, and alert blue eyes dominated his slight, short stature.' In 1878 Isabella Bird[4] thought that he was then still '. . . young-looking . . . scarcely in middle life, slight, active, fair, blue-eyed, a thorough Saxon, with sunny hair and a sunny smile, a sunshiny geniality in his manner, and bearing no trace in his appearance of his thirty years of service in the East, his sufferings in the prison at Peking, and the various attempts on his life in Japan.' (Willis commented[5] that, if you saw him smiling, you would think him such an amiable mortal quite deserving his sobriquet of 'Sir Smiles' but Willis had heard that Parkes was then (1874) said to be '. . . gouty and livery and not up to his old standard of making everyone miserable over whom he holds power.')

'Sunshiny geniality' was not the quality which struck members of his staff, nor probably his family. Willis asserted that Lady Parkes had '. . . a goodly amount of scolding and snubbing to put up with.'[6] He had written earlier:[7]

> Lady Parkes appears of a melancholy disposition and I fancy there is not much domestic happiness in Sir Harry's nature. He is a bustling pushing man and I believe has objects of desire dearer to him than home or family. He never eats a meal in time . . . Fancy on Christmas day [1866] Sir Harry dined in Edo and Lady Parkes in Yokohama. There is as little domestic bliss in the house as any I ever heard of. I believe he is one of those pushing elbowing men who [will do nothing] or anything except in so far as it advances himself. He would be, I am quite sure, unmoved if an earthquake swallowed up his wife and family, so absorbed is he in the game of self. Of all hateful husbands I can imagine it is a man who never eats, drinks or anything else at the same time other people do so.

Willis was being unfair. It is clear from other comments that Parkes was a reasonably social person. He enjoyed an occasional dance and he entertained frequently. F. V. Dickins who, with S. Lanee Poole, wrote the two-volume biography of Parkes which appeared in 1894[8] recorded that 'On Sunday evenings it was their custom to have some of the members of the Legation to dinner, and it was at these dinners I found it easiest to get him to talk on his life in China: he had the power of bringing the scenes described before his listener with wonderful clearness, till one almost felt the excitement of the moment he was talking about.' Basil Hall Chamberlain[9] noted how, after his arrival in Yokohama, '. . . having been prostrated by a fever, I was hospitably taken in by Sir Harry and Lady Parkes as soon as it was possible to move me from the uncomfortable Yokohama hotel of days to the British Legation on the Bluff.'

It is clear from Parkes's own letters that in fact he was very fond of his wife and children. When his wife died in England in November 1879, he was on his way home having obtained permission from the Foreign Office to come home on leave to see her. He wrote to F.V. Dickins[10] on 30 November:

I left Japan by the first opportunity after receiving the earliest warning that her illness was attended with danger. I lost not an hour in crossing America – but I arrived too late to hear her last wishes and injunctions, to smooth her pillow, and to close her eyes . . . I have now six children to take charge of, and feebly indeed shall I replace her in that charge, while the Legation will have lost the bright and good spirit to which it owed entirely whatever attraction it possessed.

Willis was also over-harsh in his judgement of Parkes' motives. Parkes was no doubt ambitious in the sense that he was gratified by the honours conferred on him and he doubtless welcomed the power which his position gave him. But, although by the standards of the time he was not badly paid (his salary on appointment to Japan was £3000 a year and he was granted a further £1000 for his outfit[11]), he was not motivated by pecuniary gain. In 1872 Parkes who was in London on leave and in attendance on the Iwakura Mission was questioned about diplomatic salaries by a House of Commons Committee. He considered[12] that all grades of the service in Japan were underpaid. In his case he had '. . . only just made both ends meet. I came away from Japan, after six years service there, poorer than I went.' When he was transferred to Peking[13] he accepted a reduction of £500 a year in the stipend attached to the Legation at Peking which had been demanded by a House of Commons Committee in a fit of economy. It has never been suggested that Parkes, unlike some of his diplomatic colleagues in Japan, ever profited from commercial transactions. Nor did even his detractors ever suggest that he was corrupt. His main motive was probably the old-fashioned one of carrying out his tasks as effectively and as conscientiously as possible.

Parkes was not demonstratively a religious man but in accordance with Victorian tradition he maintained a system of family prayers. Nor was he a profound man. But, as Dickins noted:[14] 'Men of action are not profound men, they are neither philosophers nor *erudits*. Their qualities are insight, decision, and courage moral and physical, and with these Sir Harry Parkes was abundantly endowed. If scantily "school'd he was yet learned" in the real knowledge of life, but he never lost a certain boyish ardour and simplicity. Although in his later time no student, he was always a great reader, a lover of poetry, and a devourer of as much modern literature as he could find time for. His wonderful industry extended to everything that bore upon his work.' He worked hard at his French. He was a '. . . most suggestive and stimulating President of the Asiatic Society.' A. B. Mitford, later Lord Redesdale who was a member of Parkes's staff in Japan, agreed:[15] 'Busy as his life was, he had read greedily, and he often took me by surprise in unexpected ways.' (Willis, however, disagreed:[16] 'Sir Harry never reads nor studies anything. He is shallow to a degree on every subject.') Parkes, despite the fact that he was an accomplished Chinese interpreter never seems to have worked at the Japanese language, but this is understandable. He was 38 when he came to Japan and was extremely busy. Moreover, he had able interpreters to work for him.

There can be no disputing his courage. Various attempts were made on his life while he was in Japan. The most dramatic of these was the attack by *rōnin* on the British Legation party on its way to the Imperial Palace in Kyoto for an audience with the young Emperor on 22 March 1868.[17] One man rushed at Parkes, '. . . cutting and slashing as he went, but fortunately missing the Minister. Satow had a narrow escape, for his horse was wounded close to his rider's knee, and part of the poor beast's nose was sliced off.' When Mitford ran forward to see what had happened, he found Parkes '. . . sitting on his horse, quite unmoved . . . As I came up with them I stumbled over something. It was a man's head.' As they wended their way back to the Chionin temple in Kyoto where the Legation was temporarily housed, Mitford was walking by Sir Harry's horse when Parkes turned to him and said 'Sensation diplomacy this, Mitford.' Satow[18] said of him: 'I do not think that his coolness and fortitude in the moment of peril have ever been surpassed by any man not bred to war.'

Parkes was courageous in other ways too. He was fearless in defending what he considered to be right irrespective of the position of the person he was speaking to. In those days travelling to the East, although much faster and easier than in the days of sailing ships, was still long and uncomfortable. In the treaty ports in the East disease was rife with smallpox, cholera and typhoid endemic. Indeed it was typhoid fever combined with overwork which caused Parkes's death in Peking in 1885. Parkes never hesitated in the face of these discomforts and threats to his life.

Nor did anyone doubt Parkes's application and willingness to work indefatigably. He had an insatiable curiosity and expected his staff to work as long hours as he did. He was thus a hard taskmaster. Mitford and Willis both found Parkes a maker of work. Mitford described him[19] as '. . . a very bustling man' '. . . full of whims, and seeming to seek out discomfort as he does danger for its own sake.' Willis[20] found Parkes '. . . a little pestilently active. He gets up at 5 in the morning and works all day plotting and scheming to get up a sensation. 'He is always muddling and meddling . . . He has the genius of misrule about him.'[21] 'Our chief is the most restless troublesome man you can imagine and seldom gives you leisure to do anything for one self.' Willis preferred a quieter life than he could obtain under Parkes!

Satow[22] commented that Parkes was '. . . entirely absorbed in the duties of his post, untiring in his endeavours to obtain a correct view of his surroundings, never sparing himself, and requiring from his subordinates the same zealous assiduity.'

Parkes was, as Satow also wrote,[23] '. . . of an active inquisitive temperament.' In Niigata in 1867 Satow writes:

> [Parkes] . . . signalized himself in the eyes of the natives by scrambling up to the top of a large shed under which a junk was in the course of construction, to get a view of the surrounding country, much to the horror of Mitford and myself, who were so orientalized by this time in our notions that we longed to see our chief conduct himself with the impassive dignity of a Japanese gentleman.

If Parkes cared little about dignity he was determined not to be set down by any of his diplomatic colleagues. Parkes's *bête noire* in the diplomatic corps in the days before the Meiji Restoration was Leon Roches, the French Minister. Mitford described Roches[24] as: '. . . a handsome swashbuckler, who had been an interpreter in the French army in Algeria. He was far more a picturesque Spahi than a diplomatist . . .'. He goes on to write:

It is not too much to say that Parkes and Roches hated one another and were as jealous as a couple of women . . . One day Parkes came into my room like a whirlwind, his fair, reddish hair almost standing on end, as was its way when he was excited. 'What is the matter, Sir Harry?' I asked 'Matter!' was the answer. 'What do you think that fellow Roches has just told me? He is going to have a *mission militaire* out from France to drill the Shogun's army! Never mind! I'll be even with him. I'll have a *mission navale!*' – and he did.'

Parkes's relations with some of his other colleagues were friendly enough. In particular he seems to have got on well with Von Brandt, the Prussian Minister. He did not, however, care for some of his American colleagues whom he suspected of double dealing.

Parkes was undoubtedly domineering in his manner. He was also very quick-tempered and his language was frequently most undiplomatic. In 1866 Willis[25] thought Parkes' manner with Japanese officials '. . . rather rough . . . he scolds them. Our last interview was the most rugged one I have yet seen.' Of a later interview with the *Gorōjū* Willis commented that this was 'A most stormy badgering style of interview. I can tell you Parkes is not overburdened with politeness to the Japanese. I almost fear he will goad them too far.' Satow who had to act as his interpreter in many of these interviews recorded how in Tokushima in 1867 '. . . Sir Harry [who had been kept waiting while Satow tried to procure three palanquins] lost his temper and swore he would not be kept waiting for all the d–d daimios in Japan.[26] In February 1868 Satow was pleased to be able to record[27] that Sir Harry was then '. . . in high spirits and in very good temper. We had no more of the interviews with Japanese officials at which he used strong language, and interpreting for him which used to be a painful duty, was changed into a labour of love.' Unfortunately, this situation did not last and Satow recorded[28] how in December 1868 Parkes '. . . lost his temper over the arguments used by Kido [over the treatment of Christians by the Meiji government] and made use of very violent language such as I do not care to repeat.'

Even Dickins noted[29] that Parkes's relations with Japanese representatives were often difficult and stormy:

With the ministers in the sixties, his manner was not always admirable but the conviction of those who knew him best is that he often lost sight of the Minister altogether, and thought only of some act or proposition that in his opinion – and his opinion was never hastily formed or unsupported by an ample basis of facts – militated against British interests or the welfare of Japan herself. As he grew older the irritability or whatever it was lessened and finally disappeared altogether.

Satow did not agree with this view.[30] Grace Fox[31] concluded: 'Granted that his outbursts of temper and arrogance often offended the sensitive, increasingly self-confident Japanese, the Meiji ministers sought and respected his advice from the beginning of their government.' Basil Hall Chamberlain[32] wrote of him: 'His outspoken threats and occasional fits of passion earned for him the dread and dislike of the Japanese during his sojourn in Japan. But no sooner had he quitted Tokyo than they began to acknowledge that his high-policy had been founded on reason . . . a high Japanese official . . . said to a friend of the present writer: "Sir Harry was the only foreigner in Japan whom we could not twist round our little finger."'

Parkes's actions were often not as rough as his language. After the Bizen incident in Kobe on 4 February 1868 when there had been trouble between men of the Bizen clan and the foreigners had moved from Osaka to Hyogo (Kobe) because of the disturbances in Osaka, the Japanese officer considered to be responsible for the incident, Taki Zenzaburō, was ordered to commit *seppuku*. Parkes had taken a very strong line after the incident but, when the heads of diplomatic missions considered the Japanese plea for clemency, it was Parkes[33] with the support of his Netherlands colleague who argued force- fully for clemency but they were overruled by the others who demanded that the punishment be carried out. After the attack on him in Kyoto in March that year Parkes very readily accepted the apologies of the Mikado's ministers. He could be and frequently was magnanimous despite extreme provocation.

His relations with members of his staff were also much better than his iras- cibility might suggest. He took care to commend good work in writing to the Foreign Office and did not claim for himself all the merit due to the Legation. Satow[34] who never cared for Parkes recorded:

> . . . he was strict and severe in service matters, but in his private relations gra- cious to all those who had occasion to seek his help, and a faithful friend to all who won his goodwill. Unfortunately, I was not one of these, and the result was that from the beginning we were never friends, down to the very last, though he never had reasons to complain of sloth or unreadiness to take my share of the work.

It is possible to surmise that Parkes disapproved of Satow's private life (he had a Japanese mistress and two children by her). Parkes may also have resented Satow's independent ideas.

Satow got across Parkes at a very early stage. In August 1866[35] Parkes, hav- ing given Satow and Siebold a quantity of official documents to translate, they addressed letters to him asking him to recommend that they should receive an extra £100 a year. 'This brought down his wrath upon our heads.' Satow wrote to his father that the service was not worth remaining in. He soon received a telegram telling him to come home. Satow then approached Parkes and asked for his resignation to be accepted. 'After a little humming and hawing, he finally produced from a drawer a despatch from Lord Clarendon [then Foreign Secretary], which had been lying there for several days, granting the applications of both Siebold and myself, and I conse- quently abandoned my intention of quitting the service.' In March 1868 Parkes, on the curious grounds that Satow had not been presented at the British court, decided that Satow could not accompany him on his call on the Emperor. He took only Mitford into this interview while Satow and others remained outside. This rule did not prevent Satow from being presented to the Emperor in May that year when Parkes handed over his credentials in Osaka. Was this snobbery or spite?

Willis[36] thought that 'Parkes killed a poor fellow called MacDonald by wor- rying his life out of him . . . McDonald died of softening of the brain brought on, I believe, by the acute general unhappiness of having to deal with Parkes every day.' John MacDonald, first assistant in the Legation office, died in May 1866 of apoplexy and softening of the brain.

Dickins[37] wrote: 'Out of his officers he got as much work as he could, but he never spared himself. With them his relations were most cordial (though he could both speak and act sharply at times) . . . His purse was always open to those in need of assistance after a frank and generous fashion that veiled the service . . . Though in official matters he went at once and straight to the point, and was apt to be somewhat brusque and exigent, especially with men of slow or confused minds, in all private relations he was one of the most long-suffering, friendly, and courteous of men. There was not an atom of factitious dignity about him, but one saw at a glance that the earnest and busy Minister was not a man to be trifled with – and no one ever attempted to trifle with him.'

All the above comments show that Parkes had outstanding qualities of courage, energy, drive and dedication. He was a difficult man to work for and his irascibility must have made him insufferable but he was obviously an outstanding head of mission. What did he achieve?

ACHIEVEMENTS 1865–9

Any fair assessment of Parkes must take into account his upbringing, the attitudes of Victorian England, the nature of British power in the second half of the nineteenth century as well as attitudes in Japan towards foreigners and their behaviour towards the first foreigners who came to work in Japan.

Parkes was largely self-educated. He had worked very hard to achieve his appointment to Japan at only 38 and was understandably contemptuous of those who were not ready to work as hard as he did or were not as quick in their perceptions. He certainly did not suffer fools gladly. He had had some bitter experiences in China and encountered many examples of official deceit. These all tended to make him highly suspicious of oriental officials.

Britain in the second half of the nineteenth century was at the height of its power. The Victorians believed that their achievements were the result of their own efforts and that Britain had much to teach developing countries of which Japan was one. British business needed markets and sources of supply and the Victorians were not in the mood to tolerate their business being frustrated by xenophobia or the seclusion policies of other countries.

Rutherford Alcock, Parkes' predecessor as Minister to Japan, had found the officials of the *Bakufu* with whom he had to deal deceitful, incompetent and frequently powerless. There were no proper criminal or civil codes in Japan. Torture was an accepted practice in dealing with criminals and executions were common. The xenophobia which the authorities did nothing to curb led to frequent attacks on foreigners and life in the treaty ports in the 1860s was distinctly insecure. The hierarchy of Japan which put the merchants at the bottom of the pile seemed topsy-turvy to the foreigners who found the merchants with whom they came in contact generally dishonest. It was thus hardly surprising that the merchants who came out from Britain included a number who were themselves dishonest. Life was nasty, brutish and short in the treaty ports in those early days and the chance to win a quick fortune tended to attract the rough and tough as well as the charlatans.

Parkes' instructions from Lord Russell, then Foreign Secretary, were modelled on those given to Alcock, his predecessor[38] and he was given freedom to act as the state of affairs in Japan seemed to warrant. He was to seek '. . . the abandonment of any pretence on the part of the Mikado or the Tycoon to violate treaties, and banish foreigners from Japan.' He was also to seek to ensure '. . . the faithful execution of these treaties [and] confirmation of the Treaties by the Mikado, or the formal admission that the Tycoon . . . required no sanction from the Mikado.' He was also to obtain '. . . the trial of all persons accused of murdering British subjects and their execution, if convicted.'

Parkes carried out these instructions faithfully. The American missionary and writer about Japan, W. E. Griffis,[39] declared:

> English scholarship first discovered the true source of power, exposed the counterfeit government in Yedo, read the riddle of ages and rent the veil that so long hid the truth. The English minister, Sir Harry Parkes, who risked his life to, find the truth, stripped the Shogun of his fictitious title of 'Majesty', . . . recognized the new National Government, and thus laid the foundation of the true diplomacy in Japan.

Ignoring the hyperbole, it is fair to say that it was largely due to Parkes that the Mikado's acceptance of the treaties was confirmed. This in its turn further undermined the Shogun's position and contributed to the fall of the shogunate.

In 1866, Clarendon, then Foreign Secretary,[40] instructed Parkes '. . . not to take sides or express an opinion for or against either party in the approaching contest. Britain's aim in Japan was not to seek political influence but to develop commerce.' In 1867 Clarendon's successor, Lord Stanley, reaffirmed the policy of neutrality, but[41] Parkes might '. . . promote as far as you can any system which, by securing to the Daimios a fair share in the commerce of Japan, will enlist their sympathies in behalf of foreign nations and so promote the development of trade.' Parkes[42] proclaimed British neutrality in the civil war of 1867/9 and called for 'a strict and impartial neutrality' by all British subjects. This proclamation did not endear him to some British merchants but Parkes did his best to ensure that the proclamation was observed. Grace Fox, however, noted that[43] 'His consent to the withdrawal of the allied neutrality proclamation in February 1869 hastened the government's defeat of the rebels in the north that June.'

Professor W. G. Beasley has concluded[44] that in his reports: 'Parkes shows himself as politically "neutral" in the sense that he was not greatly concerned about who won the struggle in Japan, provided foreign interests were defended . . . In fact, the one respect in which he can be said to have "interfered" was that he invariably gave his approval – often openly – to any plan that might result in greater stability.' Beasley stresses[45] that 'Parkes was more concerned to see law and order established in the country, that is, an environment in which foreign trade could flourish, than he was in the question of which of the rival groups should establish it.' 'In so far as Parkes went beyond his purely diplomatic brief, defined in terms of defending British interests, it was more in the service of "enlightenment" (*bummei kaika*) than of Satsuma-Chōshū power.'[46] Parkes defined his own objective in 1867 as being: '. . . to divert their [i.e. Japanese] attention from military glitter to industrial enterprise.'[47] He also constantly reminded the leaders of Japan of the need to make Japan '. . . into one firm and compact State, governed by uniform and just laws.'[48]

If Parkes himself was 'neutral', Satow and Mitford who were members of his staff were certainly not neutral. They cultivated the representatives of the *tozama* daimyo[49] with Parkes' approval. Parkes no doubt justified this in his own mind as an essential means of gathering information and intelligence. But he could not have condoned Satow's famous *Japan Times* articles of 1866[50] without compromising his neutrality. Satow asserted:[51] 'As far as I know it never came to the ears of my chief, but it may fairly be supposed to have been not without its influence upon the relations between the English Legation and the new government afterwards established in the beginning of 1868.' It is difficult to believe that Parkes who was very well informed did not get to know that Satow had written these articles. Perhaps he decided to turn a Nelsonian blind eye to them in the hope that they could be turned to British advantage. But Satow' s disobedience of the clear instructions from London may have been a factor in the coolness between the two men.[52]

Did Anglo-French rivalry and the jealousy between Parkes and his French colleague Roches who firmly supported the Shogunate make Parkes more inclined towards the supporters of the Restoration? This may have been a sub-conscious factor but there is no evidence to suggest that it was a material one.

The conclusion must be that in the first years of his mission Parkes's achievements were outstanding. He had certainly protected and furthered British interests and had for his part maintained a neutral position.

ACHIEVEMENTS 1869–83

During the second part of his long stay between 1869 and 1883 one important issue which took up much of Parkes's time was the problem of the formerly 'hidden' Christians who continued to be persecuted by the new Meiji government. This was wholly unacceptable to Western governments and public opinion. Parkes '. . . counselled that Western remonstrances should continue to be urged "with consideration and discretion". He understood the Japanese government's position. Roman Catholic proselytism at Urakami [in Kyushu] had assailed its dignity and authority. It was compelled to act if only to satisfy popular opinion which seemed to be vehemently directed against native converts . . . Events in time confirmed Parkes' faith in his personal influence with important Japanese ministers.' The persecutions were maintained but Parkes[54] '. . . continued to view the Japanese explanations tolerantly. He understood their intense national pride, their well-founded fear of Catholic proselytism, and the precarious position of the Emperor's government.' Britain and the United States opposed the view of the French Minister, M. D'Outrey,[55] that '. . . a strong and united demonstration of force by European powers would be the only effectual mode of preventing the recurrence of such acts and checking the intolerance of the Japanese government.'

Dr Gordon Daniels has asserted[56] that '. . . Parkes' approach to this problem was largely shaped by his hostility to Roman Catholicism, and particularly its Jesuit missionaries.' This is not supported by Grace Fox's account and it could be that Parkes was being politically sensitive and practical. Daniels goes on to note that, when on 9 February 1872 Parkes met representatives of the Evangelical Alliance, he rebutted their criticisms point by point:

> On this potentially emotive occasion Parkes exhibited qualities which are rarely associated with his East Asian diplomacy: finesse, sensitivity and extreme courteousness. He countered many criticisms with simple factual statements, and explained the complexities of Japan's religious difficulties. He concluded by urging patience in dealing with an enlightened, well-meaning government.

Parkes devoted much effort to helping and advising the Meiji government in its efforts to modernize the country. In doing so, he was doubtless motivated to a considerable extent by the desire to gain commercial benefits in the long run for Britain, but he also wanted to help the development of Japan. As Hazel Jones has pointed out,[57] Britain provided the largest number of foreign employees. Between 1868 and 1900 employees of British origin provided 4353 man-years of service. The next largest figure of 1578 man-years was France followed by Germany (1223) and the USA (1213). Parkes played an important part in this process. To give one example Parkes was primarily responsible for the appointment in 1868 of Richard Henry Brunton, the first of the *o-yatoi gaikokujin* of the Meiji government to construct lighthouses throughout Japan in accordance with the supplementary agreement of 1866. Brunton's appointment was as Chief Engineer to the Lighthouse Department of the Japanese government.

Throughout his service in Japan Brunton had the backing of Parkes.[58] He summarized his difficulties with other foreign employees and with his Japanese colleagues and assistants in these words: 'The conscientious and efficient conduct of work in Japan was a task which presented the most perplexing difficulties ... Resignation, insubordination, absence from duty, drunkenness, and other aberrations of conduct among Europeans employed in the Japanese government service, became frequent and distressing. On the other hand, the semi-ignorance of the native servants of the Emperor, and the self-esteem, craftiness and corruption of the Japanese underlings rendered cooperation by an honourable foreigner with them extremely irritating.' These latter problems frequently had to be taken up by Parkes and inevitably brought him into conflict with Japanese ministers. It is difficult not to sympathize with Parkes and the more honourable British employees in their difficulties. No doubt they would have done better to exercise greater restraint and tact but such reservations are readily made with the hindsight of history.

Among the many areas in which Parkes actively campaigned on behalf of British interests were telegraphs in which, after the Restoration, according to Grace Fox,[59] Parkes 'forestalled' a Shogunate concession to the Swiss and Austrian governments. Parkes was also an advocate of improved communications especially roads; but he also backed the Japanese desire to build railways. This involved his old crony and old China hand, H.N. Lay, but, as Grace Fox has pointed out,[60] 'There seems to be no evidence that Parkes or Her Majesty's Government tried to defend Lay when the Japanese government cancelled his commission . . .'

According to Hazel Jones,[61] Parkes sometimes overdid his interventions on behalf of British employees, for example, in the case of Alexander Pope Porter, harbour master at Hakodate, who was given a contract in 1874 as sailing master:

> The truculent Parkes took umbrage at the clause rejecting his mediation and charged Japanese officials with nefarious plotting. When he received no satisfaction, he carried his argument with Foreign Minister Terajima Munenori [with whom his relations were frequently strained] to irrational lengths.

But the most serious and contentious problem which Parkes had to face in these years was the question of treaty revision and the related issue of free trade versus protection. Dr Daniels has declared[62] that 'To Parkes treaty revision was a process that should proceed at a gradual, organic speed. This approach not only emanated from his basic philosophy, it coincided with the opinions of the British merchant community, which he sought to represent.' In fact, although Parkes's views were important, he remained the servant of the British government and the latter, no doubt primed by the arguments produced by Parkes, saw no need to hurry over treaty revision. Indeed, in London it was regarded as essential that, before extraterritoriality could be abolished, the Japanese should not only enact a 'civilized' criminal code and code of criminal procedure but should prove that they could operate it effectively and fairly. It was also felt to be essential for the sake of commerce that Japan should have adequate civil and commercial codes. At the Preliminary Conference on Treaty Revision held in Tokyo in 1882 Inoue Kaoru, its Japanese president, produced on 1 June[63] '. . . an altogether novel scheme of jurisdiction under which extra-territoriality wholly disappeared.' The American Minister nodded his approval, but Parkes submitted a memorandum in which he argued that, while the British government would sympathize with '. . . any efforts that might be made to bring the Japan into such a condition as to allow of the entire abolition of the consular jurisdictions, . . . the new Penal Code had only been one year in operation, and '. . . neither civil nor commercial codes were yet in existence. As late as the close of 1879 an able Japanese publicist declared that the laws did not duly protect the lives, liberties, and property of the Japanese themselves, and required very considerable reform before they could be generally approved by the Japanese people.'

At the conference which ended in July 1882 there were no fundamental differences of opinion[64] over the tariff question, although the President of the conference proposed a rise in the general *ad valorem* tariff from 7 to 10% in order to increase 'the stock of specie in the country'. But many leading Japanese preferred the protectionist system of the USA to the free-trade principles advocated by the British. They also resented the fact that Japanese tariffs remained fixed by the tariff convention of 1866 which Parkes had worked so hard to achieve at that time.

Revision of the so-called 'unequal' treaties had become a major Japanese national objective and aroused Japanese xenophobia and nationalism to such an emotional pitch that any Japanese who attempted to propose any compromise, such as Count Ōkuma Shigenobu, was subject to violent attacks. Parkes' objections to treaty revision, however well founded at the time, inevitably provided fuel for his enemies.

Parkes would not, however, allow British subjects to abuse the privileges of extraterritoriality. In 1876 J. R. Black published without Japanese permission (Japanese press censorship was severe) a vernacular newspaper called the *Bankoku Shimbun*. This was stopped by the Japanese authorities who fined Black and appealed to Parkes to prohibit the publication of Japanese newspapers by British subjects. 'Sir Harry[65] saw the absurdity of so interpreting the extraterritorial privilege as to enable the native press to evade the laws of the land by the simple expedient of placing itself under the protection of a foreign power.' He accordingly used the powers granted to him by Order in Council to prohibit such evasions. His action aroused the praise of Japanese leaders but the condemnation of some foreigners.

Parkes' efforts to influence Meiji government policies were often unsuccessful as Dr Daniels has pointed out.[66] In particular he failed in his efforts at

deterring the Japanese expedition to Formosa in 1874, although Sir Thomas
Wade, the British Minister in Peking, was able to help with the final settlement and was duly thanked by the Japanese for his efforts.

By the early 1880s Parkes who had lost his wife and was increasingly
unwell appears to have become still more arrogant and irritable in his official
dealings with the Japanese. In a letter to Dickins in 1881 Satow wrote:

> . . . you would not credit to what extent he is the bugbear of the Japanese
> public; in the popular estimation he occupies much the same position as
> 'Boney' with us fifty years ago. It has been going on for the past ten years . . .
> no one can deny his great qualities and his fitness to meet any dangerous cri-
> sis. His talents are however thrown away here. There is no analogy at all
> between the circumstances here and in China, where he learnt his diplomacy
> . . . here it is the square peg in the round hole.

Satow concluded that Parkes was not a 'diplomatist of the Talleyrand type'
able to respond to the nuances and subtleties of Japanese behaviour. Satow
was no friend of Parkes but his comments cannot be dismissed as simple prejudice if only because they match what we learn from other sources.

There can be no doubt that, if the Japanese had requested his recall, the
British government would have had to comply. But perhaps some Japanese
officials feared that such a step might jeopardize other Japanese interests or
there were influential people in the Japanese government who appreciated
Parkes' talents and help. His enemies instead used elaborate and indirect
means to. secure his removal.[68] The American journalist, E.H. House,[69] '. . .
was employed to write anti-British propaganda, and in a single year, 1875,
wrote two pamphlets which were designed to create consternation in the
British Legation. Between 1877 and 1880 House received further subsidies to
support the publication of the *Tokio Times*, a largely anti-British newspaper.
In this paper House[70] '. . . attacked British economic policy, criticised Parkes
bitterly, and argued violently for the abolition of extraterritoriality.'

Sir John Pope Hennessy, the Governor of Hong Kong,[71] caused a great deal
of trouble on a visit to Japan. Parkes in a letter of 1879[72] said that he had
invited him and his wife to dinner. He '. . . had to have an explanation with
him in consequence of the way in which he has been talking among the
Japanese and foreigners. I told him that, if I had visited Hongkong, I should
not have presumed to interfere with his business in the same way as he has
done with mine, and much other plain language, for I wished him to know
my mind. He defended himself but faintly, saying that he had been misrep-
resented, which, however, I know is not the case. I don't think he is
accustomed to get a good setting down from any one, and I think I gave him
one. We managed, notwithstanding, to part apparent friends, though he is a
man with whom I shall never be on good terms, as I utterly mistrust him.'

Another tiresome character for Parkes was Sir Edward J. Reed KCB, MP. In
January 1879 Parkes noted[73] that 'Reed, the late constructor of our navy –
who built the three new ships for the Japanese – is now here, the guest of the
Japanese Government who are making a great fuss about him. It remains to
be seen what each wants from the other, but I doubt whether Japanese
finances will permit of their giving Mr Reed [as he then was] orders for more
ships.' At the end of Reed's stay of three months Parkes recorded that he had
not seen much of Reed: 'He told me that the only expenditure needed by the
Japanese was *brains*.' Parkes[74] believed that Reed had influenced the Japanese

government to terminate the contracts of the remaining twenty-three members of the British naval mission in 1879 and had offered the Japanese men of his own selection.

Reed and Hennessy appear to have had contacts with House who[75] travelled to Britain at Japanese expense in 1881 to contact editors, politicians and men of influence and to undermine Parkes' position.

Parkes, despite his declining health, was still only 55 when he was transferred to Peking in July 1883. He clearly deserved another post and he was well qualified to return to China where he had spent his formative years. Peking was then regarded as a more important mission than Tokyo.

CONCLUSION

Whatever the frictions which had existed for many years between Parkes and Japanese leaders, he left with many expressions of thanks and goodwill. Were these just *tatemae* or did they represent Japanese *honne*? It is not possible to reach a final judgement so many years after the event but it is hard to believe that they were not at least to a considerable extent sincere. At a farewell luncheon given to him by the Emperor on 22 August 1883, to which all the members of the Japanese cabinet had been invited, the Emperor in a gracious speech[76] declared that, if British regulations had permitted, he would have conferred on Parkes the Grand Cordon of the Rising Sun but, because of the rules of the British court, he presented Parkes instead with a censer and flower vase '. . . which have been in my possession . . . as a token of my high regard for you.' On the evening of 27 August a farewell address was presented to Sir Harry on behalf of the British and foreign residents of Yokohama expressing their gratitude for all he had done to promote the well-being of the settlement. On Parkes' death Inoue Kaoru, then Japanese Foreign Minister,[77] sent a telegram saying 'His Imperial Majesty's Government cannot but feel great grief at the death of one who contributed so much to the improvement and progress of this country, and whose long residence has won so many friends among Japanese officials.'

Dr Daniels[78] has said that: 'Fundamental to Parkes' outlook was a critical view of Japan which failed to take account of its considerable achievements.' He went on to assert that such views were echoed by many people in Britain until the 1960s. It is hardly fair to make such a comment on Parkes who was in Japan at a time of revolutionary change and when Japanese xenophobia had been at its height. Japanese achievements were in those days largely confined to the cultural sphere and Parkes had little time to study Japanese culture. It is moreover the duty of a diplomat to take a critical view of the countries in which he serves. We may be sure that Japanese diplomats take a critical view of Britain. It is, however, essential that the critical view should be well based on observation and should be as fair as possible. Parkes was assiduous in collecting information and his judgements were, as Professor Beasley has pointed out, generally balanced although they were inevitably to some extent coloured by the age in which he lived and had been brought up.

Parkes' achievements cannot be dismissed lightly. They probably could have been greater if he had managed to exercise more restraint and tact. He was left in Tokyo for too long and British interests would have been better served if he had been transferred in the first half of the 1870s. But Parkes had received his appointment at the early age of 38 and the only obvious alternative post for him was that of Minister in Peking and this was not available at that time or Parkes was not then considered the top candidate. To have forced Parkes to retire early would have been unjust to a distinguished public servant and it is at least debatable whether in the long run his extended term of service in Japan was as harmful to British interests as Satow clearly thought it was.

Parkes cannot be faulted for lack of industry and application. Nor did he ever neglect British commercial interests. He rates a high place in the list of great British diplomats of the nineteenth century – a period when heads of mission, if only because of the slowness of communications, had much more discretion to act independently than they have today.

I would not have wanted to serve under Sir Harry Parkes (I have sadly been unable to find any evidence that he had much sense of humour and an ability to laugh at his own foibles). But I have to admire his fortitude and dedication.

5
Sir Francis Plunkett
Minister to Japan, 1884–87

SIR HUGH CORTAZZI

Sir Francis Plunkett

In the history of Anglo-Japanese relations in the latter part of the nineteenth century Francis Plunkett (1835–1907) has been overshadowed by the image of his forceful and abrasive predecessor Sir Harry Parkes. But Plunkett, who went on from Japan to more senior posts in Europe and who retired with a string of high honours, played a key role in the efforts, which were made while he was in Japan, to achieve agreement on revision of the 'unequal treaties' between the Western Powers and Japan. These efforts proved abortive but he was not responsible for the failure and his contribution to Anglo-Japanese relations deserves to be recorded.

Francis Richard Plunkett was the sixth son of the Earl of Fingall (an Irish peerage) and consequently had the courtesy title of 'honourable'. He was born on 3 February 1835 at Corbalton Hall in County Meath. He was educated at St Mary's Roman Catholic College, Oscott. He was appointed attaché at Munich in January 1855 when he was not yet twenty. From Munich he was transferred to Naples, then to The Hague and Madrid. In July 1859 he was appointed as a paid attaché at St Petersburg. In 1863 he was appointed Second Secretary at Copenhagen. After service at Vienna, Berlin, and Florence he was nominated in 1873 as Secretary of Legation in Tokyo under Sir Harry Parkes. He left Tokyo in 1876 and served as Diplomatic Secretary in St Petersburg, Constantinople and Paris before being appointed Minister at Tokyo in succession to Sir Harry Parkes on the latter's transfer to Peking. He was made a KCMG in 1886 while at Tokyo. (The notification of this award in a telegram from Lord Salisbury was timed to arrive on his birthday!) After Tokyo he served as head of mission to Sweden and Belgium where he was made a GCMG. In 1900 he was appointed Ambassador at Vienna and made a Privy Councillor. While he was in Vienna he was awarded a GCB and a GCVO. He retired in 1905. He died in Paris in 1907 and was buried at Boulogne. In 1870 he married May Tevis by whom he had two daughters.[1]

The Times of 2 March 1907, reporting the news of his death, recorded that in Vienna Plunkett had been liked in society and by his diplomatic colleagues. 'The Emperor constantly showed him marks of esteem, and gave him and Lady Plunkett upon their departure unusually flattering tokens of regard.' His 'kind and courteous bearing made him popular, while his keen interest in Austro-Hungarian affairs and solicitude for the welfare of the Dual Monarchy gained for him a place in the category of those diplomatists whom the Austrians cease to regard altogether as foreigners'.

On his first appointment to Tokyo as Secretary to the Legation under Sir Harry Parkes he came with his wife, two daughters and a governess. He was expected to live in the house built in the legation compound for the Legation Secretary. This was a single-storey house with a drawing room, dining room and three bedrooms (one quite small), a kitchen and various servants quarters, with a large open yard to the rear. Water came from a well in the garden. Plunkett refused to accept this house unless it was adapted to include an additional bedroom, a wine-cellar, storeroom and quarters for European servants. His wishes were apparently complied with.[2]

Plunkett seems to have been a competent diplomat and there is nothing to suggest in the Public Records that he was other than a satisfactory subordinate to his demanding boss. However, unlike A. B. Mitford who was also a diplomat and not a consular officer and had a similarly aristocratic background, there is no indication that he acquired any competence in the Japanese language. When in August 1875 he was sent on a mission to Korea and Tsushima he had to take with him a member of the Japan Consular Service, Vice-Consul Longford, to act as his interpreter.

Parkes had sent Plunkett to investigate the situation at Port Hamilton, an island harbour off the coast of Korea. As Gordon Daniels records,[3] Plunkett discovered 'that the thirty year-old description of Port Hamilton's sparse population was completely inaccurate for there were over three thousand Koreans living there'.[4] On their arrival at Port Hamilton the party seem to have been greeted rather like beings from outer space and had to undergo a 'ludicrous and unpleasant ordeal' during which the natives 'put their hands in our pockets, examined our clothes, tried on our hats, ran their hands up our sleeves and trousers'. They were served various fish dishes and expected to consume a 'horrid drink' of what seemed like sour saké [probably 'doburoku']. In Tsushima Plunkett had seen no signs of Russians, nor had he heard news of an advance of Russian troops or ships from Vladivostock. His expenses for the journey, as reported to the Foreign Office, came to 355.41 [Mexican] dollars.

Plunkett, who was not yet fifty, was appointed as Minister Plenipotentiary at Tokyo in 1883, but did not arrive until 15 March 1884. He and his family had travelled via Hong Kong on the P and O ship Kashgar which called first at Nagasaki where he was given a warm welcome. On arrival in Tokyo he paid a courtesy call on Count Inouye, the Foreign Minister. He was received in audience by the Emperor on 21 March when he presented his credentials. The letter from Queen Victoria was addressed to His Imperial and Royal Majesty, The Mikado of Japan. The audience seems to have followed the usual form. Subsequently he made courtesy calls on all Cabinet Ministers.

Plunkett seems[5] to have been an active diplomat. He travelled in Japan occasionally, but not extensively. One of his first trips was to Aomori, Hakodate and Sapporo in the late summer of 1884. He noted that in all the places in which he stopped there were Japanese Post Offices from which he was able to send telegrams in English or Japanese. He was treated with due honour and did not meet with any dangers.

Because of the continuance of extraterritoriality he had to supervise the consular courts. Among the routine matters which were dealt with by the Legation in these years were such issues as shipwrecks of which there were a number, changes in lightships and buoys, precautions against cholera and problems over applications for passports by British subjects wishing to travel outside the settlements, Japanese regulations on the sale of gunpowder etc. He was also responsible for concluding the perpetual lease on the Legation's premises (the present British Embassy).

The shipwreck in 1886 of the *Normanton* in which 23 Japanese passengers died caused much ill feeling in Japan as the crew managed to escape in the ship's boats and did not do all they could to save the passengers. Captain Drake, the Master, was eventually tried in the Consular Court in Kobe and being found guilty of manslaughter was sentenced to three months imprisonment.

Plunkett and his wife seem to have been hospitable. Plunkett would have liked to have had a ballroom built for the Legation residence but this was not approved.[6] Nevertheless, Lady Plunkett as she became was reported in the *Japan Weekly Mail* at one time as giving two receptions within a month. The Queen's birthday was celebrated (e.g. in 1886) with a grand dinner attended by Imperial princes and princesses and by cabinet ministers. The Queen's golden jubilee in 1887 was the occasion for major festivities in Yokohama. The jubilee committee in Yokohama decided to collect money for the establishment of a school in Yokohama to be called the Victoria school. Reporting on the festivities the *Japan Weekly Mail* for 25 July 1887 declared: 'The twenty-first was a day to be remembered with satisfaction by the British residents of Yokohama and Tokyo. If the celebration was preceded by some essentially British grumbling, it was carried out with a thoroughness not less essentially British.' A morning service at Christ Church in Yokohama was attended by the Minister and Lady Plunkett. In the afternoon the weather being surprisingly good for late June in Japan there were sports, including tugs-of-war and 'assaults of arms' on the cricket ground. Miss Plunkett presented the prizes. The British Consulate and other buildings were adorned with flags. 'All the British residents of Yokohama threw their houses open for the entertainment of their Japanese, American, and European friends from Tokyo'. 'Beef and bread were at a premium, and as for the less substantial accessories of feasting, they were practically unprocurable.' In the evening there were theatricals and dancing. All the ships of the British naval squadron in port were lit up and 'all around the port streamed the great beam of electric light from the *Leander*'. A supper for five hundred people began shortly after midnight in a huge tent that had been erected in the Naval depot. Plunkett, who sat at a table especially reserved for distinguished guests and the Corps Diplomatique, proposed the Queen's health in suitably pompous terms.

The Plunketts were present at the famous fancy dress ball given by Count Itō in April 1887. Miss Plunkett (presumably the elder daughter) is reported by the *Japan Weekly Mail* to have 'appeared in the gaily coloured dress of a

Russian Peasant Girl and one of the attachés as a Russian peasant, in black velvet and red silk sleeves. The Mail did not state what costumes were worn by the British Minister and his wife, but reported that there was 'a fine clerical figure of the later days of George II'. 'King John, in his royal crown and robes, moved about familiarly'. 'A portly Henry VIII was there'. Was Plunkett King John or King Henry VIII?

Plunkett seems to have had the usual interests of the British aristocracy. He and other members of the Legation applied for and were granted shooting licences. At one point the Legation were told that their request for the Imperial Fukiage Gardens to be kept open during daylights hours every day for skating had been accepted. The Plunketts attended the Yokohama race meetings and the Minister seems to have been instrumental in getting the Emperor to attend and to bring people down from Tokyo for the meetings. In 1886 Plunkett resigned after two years service as President of the Nippon Race Club, which was regarded as 'a thoroughly British institution' but he continued to belong to the Permanent Committee of the club.

Plunkett was also involved with a more serious institution, the Tokyo English Law School. The annual dinner in January 1887 was a very grand affair attended by Japanese judges, the Governor of Tokyo and the President of Tokyo Imperial University. After a ten-course dinner Plunkett proposed the health of the Emperor. All the Japanese who followed spoke in English.

A more important part of Plunkett's work was to keep in touch with the Japanese authorities over developments in the Far East, in particular over Korea where the Japanese were coming into conflict with the Chinese. This led to exchanges with Sir Harry Parkes in Peking. In a letter to Aston dated 17 January 1885[7] Parkes wrote:

> Plunkett has telegraphed me several times that the Cabinet anxiously desire to maintain peace, but that the party of action are crying out for war. But war for what and on what grounds? Plunkett also telegraphed yesterday that Japan was prepared to embark 50,000 men in thirty days. I replied that I doubted her ability to do anything of the kind, and that she had better be warned not to rashly engage in war with China, that France was fast making China a military nation.

No doubt this was sound advice from one of Parkes's experience.

The most important theme during Plunkett's stay was, as had been made clear in his instructions on leaving London, revision of the 'unequal treaties' of 1858. His efforts perhaps inevitably brought him into conflict with the resident British business community. He also clashed with them over his strictures on their attitudes towards doing business in Japan. For their part they criticised him severely for not doing enough to support British trade against German competition whereas in fact Plunkett took every opportunity to urge the Japanese not to show favouritism towards Germany.

TREATY REVISION

The voluminous files in the PRO about Treaty Revision during Plunkett's term of office in Japan show that Plunkett was willing to interpret his instructions flexibly and make appropriate concessions if these would secure a settlement, which would be acceptable in London. But Japanese opinion hardened more quickly than he or the Japanese officials with whom he was negotiating anticipated and the task of maintaining a united front among the representatives of the Western Powers was an impossible one.

Almost as soon as he had arrived Plunkett received representations from the British merchants in Yokohama and from British missionaries about Treaty revision. The merchants basically wanted to preserve their privileges especially in relation to consular jurisdiction, but also sought the opening of the whole country. The missionaries were more sympathetic to the Japanese point of view.

Plunkett was not inclined to take his line from the British merchants and displayed his willingness to be flexible from the beginning. On 10 April 1884 he reported to the Foreign Office that he had made alterations in the memoranda, which he had given to the Minister of Foreign Affairs, 'so as to bring them nearer to the spirit' of his instructions. 'I have softened considerably the stress laid in the original memorandum on the period of probation' during which Japanese would be expected to prove that their laws and administration of justice were acceptable. He rightly thought that this would be a sticking point for the Japanese and that concessions on this point would have to be made. In discussions with the Japanese Foreign Minister Count Inouye Plunkett said that he would take responsibility for waiving altogether the demand for a period of probation 'provided Japan would practically give me in another way the security to which I felt British subjects had a right'. This led to lengthy, arduous but unproductive discussions with Inouye and Yoshida, the Vice-Minister.

On 14 May 1884 Plunkett reported that: 'Neither Japanese nor foreigners care about Treaty Revision. What is wanted is a decent, practical "modus vivendi". Most people, and personally I entirely share this view, seem agreed that the time has come for admitting the first small end of the wedge, and the British merchant himself will, I am sure, be grateful to whoever has the courage to make the small beginning of gradual and prudent demolition, which will prevent the sudden collapse of the whole fabric of consular jurisdiction, which is what foreigners are so much afraid of.' Plunkett was still understandably cautious in view of opinion in both London and the settlements, but he saw that change had to be made fairly soon.

He was also conscious of the increase in trade, which could accrue if the whole of Japan was opened. On 22 July 1884 he reported that 'I have no hesitation in saying that the general interest of Great Britain is to create those fresh outlets for trade, and to help as far as she can, in the early opening of Japan to foreigners'. He noted that 'the home manufacturer and the General English Merchant have most to hope for from the opening of as many outlets for trade as possible. The shipping interest is most anxious for the opening of accessible ports.' But Japan had 'more real reason than anyone to desire the complete opening of the country'. In support of his thesis that concessions should be made he drew attention to 'the progress which Japan is daily making in Western civilization' and said that this was 'changing not only the relations between Japan and the Western Powers, but also is affecting the relations of these Powers amongst themselves as regards Japan'. The interests of the Powers were no longer identical and this caused a problem, as solidarity was needed in the negotiations.

Among the difficulties, which he faced was not only that of reaching agreement with the representatives of the other Western Powers but also the delays in receiving instructions. He reported on 22 June 1884, 'things are moving so rapidly in Japan that there is great disadvantage in constant references home, for by the time the answers are received from all the various governments, which appears to take from nine months to a year, the state of things here has altered and the instructions, when they arrive, are no longer applicable'. He stressed that 'the idea of a mere tariff treaty [which had been mooted] pleases no one'. He noted that 'Great Britain was the only Power which has made entirely adequate provision for the discharge of duties imposed on them'.[8] He was 'strongly of the opinion that it is prudent to make some concessions now, or at least at a very early date, in order to prevent serious complications in a not very distant future'.

Discussions continued throughout 1885. On 30 January 1886 Plunkett reported that he had spoken to Count Inouye and to Aoki Shūzō, the then Vice Minister, and pressed them to agree to a commercial treaty to last for 12 years and a jurisdictional convention which might be revised at the end of five years. He suggested that if Japan continued to make as much progress during this time the Foreign Powers would be prepared to make further jurisdictional concessions. Not surprisingly, the Japanese rejected this suggestion pointing out that they had no guarantee that the Powers would agree to changes in five years time.

On 21 March 1886 Plunkett warned that 'the importance of our Foreign Settlements is bound to decline'. He noted signs of decay in Yokohama and the foreign settlement at Tsukiji in Tokyo and pointed out that the 'Japanese seem to prefer, when possible, dealing direct with manufacturers in Europe'. They wanted to be free of foreign middlemen and avoid the commissions they had to pay when dealing through foreign merchants in the settlements. The Japanese saw the foreigners resident in the settlements 'as the main obstacle to the realization of their hopes for the recognition of the autonomy of Japan.'

Plunkett was appointed as the senior British delegate to the Treaty Revision Conference between Japan and the Western Powers held in Tokyo from mid-1886 to mid-1887. This was launched with the presentation of a joint Anglo–German note, prepared by Plunkett and his German colleague Baron von Holleben, which was based on the Japanese proposals of 1882 and provided for mixed courts including foreign judges. The Japanese seem to have thought this initiative a helpful one. They told the two Ministers that in recognition of their efforts to reach a settlement the Emperor wished to confer on each of them the Grand Cordon of the Rising Sun. Von Holleben accepted, but Plunkett, aware of the British rules about acceptance of foreign decorations, had to decline. However, the two Ministers were received in audience by the Emperor on 16 July 1886. Plunkett reported that the Emperor, after asking him to be seated, read out in Japanese a highly complimentary speech. The Emperor then told Plunkett that he wished to confer the Order of the Chrysanthemum on the Prince of Wales and proposed to send Prince Komatsu to England for this purpose.

The Treaty Revision negotiations dragged on for months with many disagreements, often over minor points, among the Western delegates. The first and second German delegates were frequently in open disagreement with one another. On 10 November 1886 the French delegate refused to admit that English should be the sole official language of the future courts. Eventually, a compromise suggested by the Russian delegate, whereby the official language of the courts was to be Japanese with English as the only for-

eign judicial language, seems to have been accepted. But all these time-con-
suming negotiations came to nothing as when the agreement was reported to
the Japanese cabinet it was turned down. Opinion in Japan was no longer
prepared to accept the derogation to foreign powers of their jurisdiction
within Japan.

The British merchant community who feared that Plunkett had given too
much away were critical, but *The Times* correspondent (possibly H. S. Palmer)
in an article which was dated 12 August and which appeared on 17 September
1887[9] noted that Plunkett was 'known to have been conspicuous throughout
for the display of a liberal and helpful spirit'. Praise was also lavished on the
'brilliant and indefatigable' Count Inouye who led for the Japanese.

PLUNKETT AND THE BRITISH MERCHANTS

In a despatch of 25 May 1885 to Earl Granville, then Secretary of State for
Foreign Affairs, which was published in *The Japan Daily Herald* on 20
September 1886, Plunkett wrote:

> I cannot help feeling that the days of 'foreign settlements' and 'enforced tar-
> iffs' are rapidly passing away, and that the small profits on which trade must
> now be carried on will make it every day more and more difficult for the
> English merchant to compete on the spot with the native, whom education
> and the telegraph are every day placing more on a par with him. If, there-
> fore, our home manufacturers hope to force the sale of our goods on these
> Eastern nations, they will have to look to native agents to do it, or they will
> find themselves beaten out of the field by the Germans and other foreigners
> who work at lower rates than we do.

On 26 July 1886 in a despatch from Nikko, where Plunkett was escaping
the summer heat, the Minister enclosed a memorandum by Vice-Consul
Longford on the import trade from Britain to Japan. Plunkett drew attention
to Longford's comments on the necessity for British merchants [to cultivate]:

> ... friendly and intimate relations with their Japanese customers. At present
> too many of them take little trouble to enquire what are the requirements of
> the local buyers, but methodically deal year after year, through the same
> channels, in almost the same articles.

When Japan was opened further the British merchants

> ... must awaken to the fact that Englishmen are not alone in the field, and
> that if they are not up and stirring, the new opportunities will be utilised by
> more active competitors from the Continent or from America.

These comments not surprisingly infuriated the merchants who protested
vigorously. In a letter to Plunkett they rejected his comments as 'unjust'.
They asserted that 'a Merchant is likely to consult his own interests better by
being on the spot to attend to the Japanese merchants, who receive orders
from all parts of the country, than by seeking business from the small country dealers themselves'. They also rejected his view that the English
merchants were losing their supremacy as premature. The bulk of the import
trade remained in their hands as in addition to imports from Britain they
were responsible for a large proportion of the imports from other countries.
Plunkett curtly acknowledged the merchants letter.

In May 1886 the British merchants found some encouragement in the instructions which Lord Rosebery, the new Secretary of State for Foreign Affairs, had issued to British missions in the Far East to support British commercial interests. There was in fact nothing new in such instructions and the controversy, which it aroused, was artificial. Plunkett took the view that the instructions did not require him to back one individual merchant but to support British trade interests generally. He believed justifiably that the Legation should remain neutral between British merchants.

The merchants separately accused Plunkett of not doing enough to stand up for their interests, which were being undermined by Germans who had the backing of the German Legation.

ANGLO-GERMAN RIVALRY IN JAPAN

In fact, Plunkett did all he could to counter what he saw as a mistaken Japanese penchant for things German. On 1 March 1886 he reported that he had taken the opportunity of 'a friendly conversation with Count Itō to speak at length of his marked preference for Germany and the harm that so mistaken a policy must necessarily entail on Japan.' 'I thought it wise to attack his Excellency thus abruptly, because Baron von Holleben, the new German Minister, has already passed Hong Kong. Itō was kind enough to say that I had given proofs of goodwill towards Japan during the two years of my residence here quite sufficient to ensure a friendly hearing, but he on his part must claim a similar freedom of rejoinder.' Plunkett said he knew von Holleben well and welcomed his arrival. The late German Minister Herr Doenhoff 'had steadily worked against British interests here'. Plunkett pointed out the danger for Japan of trying to play off Germany against England in the treaty revision negotiations. He complained in particular about pressure on the railway department to buy German products.

Itō said that there were two causes for the Japanese attitude. The first was 'the continuance for years after it ceased to be appropriate of the policy followed by Sir Harry Parkes ... Was it human nature that while being, as they considered harshly and unfairly treated by the British Minister, they should not to a certain extent, yield to the continued blandishments of the German Minister, who was steadily inviting them to come to him for support and consolation as the British Minister repelled them by his criticisms and advice.' Itō admitted that 'in this respect the policy of Her Majesty's Government had entirely changed for the last two years, but the seed previously sown had necessarily thrown out roots and they could not be eradicated at once'. The second cause was that 'after much careful thought and examination, it had been decided to form the new constitution and codes of Japan on the model of the constitution of Prussia and of the German codes'. 'The constitution of England was abandoned as a model because it was a growth of centuries, which could not be summarily transplanted to an Eastern soil, and it had no corporate shape in which it could be studied, or altered so as to be more suitable to the totally different state of things in Japan.' Plunkett pressed Itō to encourage the study of English arguing that English was the language of the East.[10]

Plunkett spoke to Itō again on the same subject a year later (his despatch of 8 March 1887) in forceful terms: 'I reminded Count Itō that nobody was more friendly than I to an independent Japan but that I should very strongly object to assist any further a Japan the wires of which were pulled at Berlin.' Von Holleben, the German Minister, who had heard of Plunkett's complaints protested to him. Von Holleben was particularly annoyed that the Japanese demanded that Germans whom they employed should speak English.

Plunkett, who had heard the complaints about German activities from British merchants, had also been approached by Inouye Masaru, head of the railway department, who had been a student in Britain in the early 1860s and who was bitter both about the pressure put on him by the Germans to buy German equipment and about Aoki Shūzō who as Vice-Minister for Foreign Affairs was likely to develop strongly pro-German policies. Plunkett seems to have taken a strong dislike to Aoki whom he regarded as pro-German and anti-British.

DEPARTURE

Despite Plunkett's quarrels with the British merchants they were seen off by many Yokohama residents as well as by many high officials and colleagues when they embarked on the Canadian Pacific *Parthia* in early August 1877 on his transfer to Stockholm. The *Japan Weekly Mail* commented that this 'was a demonstration worthy of the high esteem that the departing Minister has won in his official capacity and of the sincere regard entertained for Sir Francis and Lady Plunkett by all who have had the good fortune to make their acquaintance'. Perhaps the paper was just being polite but the paper also took issue with the *Hōchi Shimbun* which suggested that Sir Francis having become particularly popular among the Japanese 'by the liberality of his politics and the kindly courtesy of his ways, lost favour with his own nationals and was consequently obliged to leave Japan'. There was no truth in this suggestion. The government in London were most unlikely to take cognisance of the grumbles of British merchants in Yokohama and he was going on to another senior post. Lady Plunkett was not in good health and a change of climate was thought desirable for her. In any case he was due for home leave.

PLUNKETT AND SATOW

Ernest Satow who left Japan at the end of 1882 took his new post as Consul General in Bangkok in early 1884.[11] He visited Japan on leave in October and November 1884 and again to convalesce from June to August 1886. During this latter visit he and Plunkett visited in early August the Ashio copper mines together presumably from Nikko. The mining company did their best to make their distinguished visitors welcome. Tables, chairs and cooks were brought from the Seiyōken restaurant in Tokyo and the hill sides were illuminated with covered lanterns. A feature of the entertainment was 'a peculiar dance performed by the miners; a dance which is said to have been novel even to Mr Satow. Sir Francis went all over the works, inspecting even the shafts which were farthest underground.'[12]

Satow was on very friendly terms with the Plunketts. On 21 March 1884 in a letter to his friend W.G. Aston he wrote: 'I am very sorry not to be in at the Revision of the Treaties. And I like the Plunketts so much that it is a real grief to me not to be in Tokio during their reign.' In 1883 Satow had written a long memorandum to Plunkett about the need to abolish extraterritoriality,[13] which may well have influenced the latter's thinking in the negotiations. In 1895 he noted in his diary after taking up his appointment as Minister in Tokyo that Count Ōkuma had said to him: 'Since Sir Harry [Parkes] left H.M.G. had not sent any man of weight here. Neither [Sir F.R.] Plunkett, [Mr Hugh] Fraser nor [Hon P. H.Le Poer] Trench [the three British Ministers before Satow] understood Eastern problems. Very friendly but nothing more.'[14] Satow had hoped to be appointed to Tokyo in succession to Plunkett and might have gone there as early as 1885 but Plunkett who had been offered the post of Minister in Peking in succession to Parkes declined to move to China.[15] Satow's expertise and knowledge of the language could have been invaluable in the Treaty Revision negotiations which were concluded in 1894 before Satow was appointed to Tokyo. The Foreign Office was unwilling to grant equal status to members of the Diplomatic and Consular Service, which Satow had joined. And they had not yet come to recognize the importance of having in Tokyo a head of mission with a good knowledge of Japanese. Satow was in fact the only head of mission with an effective command of the Japanese language until the appointment of Sir Esler Dening in 1951. Plunkett and his successor Hugh Fraser had to rely greatly for advice from the Japanese Secretary of the Legation, J. H. Gubbins.[16]

ASSESSMENT

Bearing in mind Plunkett's ignorance of the language and culture of Japan the records show that he was a competent and generally agreeable head of mission. His judgements seem to have been fair and reasonable. He had served under Parkes, but does not appear to have used the same kind of hectoring style.[17] In negotiations he tried to be flexible and in his comments on the changes taking place in Japan he was generally sympathetic to Japanese aspirations. Plunkett may have been an old-fashioned aristocrat but his gentlemanly style no doubt pleased the Japanese with whom he came in contact.

6
Hugh Fraser
Minister to Japan, 1889–94

Hugh Fraser

SIR HUGH CORTAZZI

Hugh fraser (1837–94) headed the British Legation in Tokyo as 'Minister Plenipotentiary and Envoy Extraordinary' in the final stages of the negotiations, which led up to the signature on 16 July 1894 of the revised treaty between Great Britain and Japan. This replaced the so-called 'unequal treaty' signed by Lord Elgin in 1858 and led to the abolition of extraterritoriality in Japan. This was one of the most significant developments in Western relations with Japan in the nineteenth century and was one in which Britain took the leading role. His period of service in Japan was thus a crucial one concerning relations between the two countries. Hugh Fraser is much less well known than his wife Mary Crawford Fraser whose book *A Diplomatist's Wife in Japan: Letters from Home to Home*[1] was deservedly popular with its sensitive depiction of the Japanese scene.

FAMILY

Hugh Fraser came from the Balnain (Inverness) branch of the Fraser clan. His father, John Fraser, who seems in his youth to have been fond of duelling and something of a daredevil, had been an officer in the Light Dragoons in India. On selling his commission he had been appointed, through the good offices of his cousin Lord Glenelg, then Secretary of State for the Colonies, as Secretary to the Lord High Commissioner for the Ionian Islands which included Corfu. In this capacity he was appointed one of the first Knights of the order of St Michael and St George, an order founded expressly for services in the Ionian islands (later extended to cover overseas services generally).

CAREER

Hugh Fraser who was born on 22 February 1837 was sent to Eton at the age of eleven in January 1849 and remained at the school until December 1854.[2] He spent some of his holidays with his parents in the Ionian Islands where he met General Charles Gordon (the charismatic figure who became known because of his part in crushing the Taiping rebellion as 'Chinese Gordon' and who was killed in Khartoum in 1885) and fell under the spell of his personality. Almost immediately after leaving Eton Hugh Fraser was appointed as an unpaid attaché at The Hague in January 1855 (before his eighteenth birthday), but was sent to Dresden in the following month. Here, apparently for a wager, he swam down the Elbe from Dresden to Pirna. He moved to Copenhagen in November 1857 and passed an examination in August 1859 to become a paid attaché. He was appointed to the British Legation in Central America in September 1862.

Mary Fraser records[3] that Hugh whose headquarters were in Guatemala was on his own with 'a native clerk'. 'His only means of travel was a mule'. 'He used to tell me how he would journey from capital to capital through the forest, in uniform, cocked-hat and all, this latter for the benefit of any stray bandits that might have been driven there for shelter. They would not touch a foreign representative in a cocked-hat and gold lace, though they might have made a mistake and cut his throat in mufti. England [i.e. Great Britain] was a word to conjure with in those times.' When he visited Honduras and sent in his card as British Chargé d'Affaires to the President, 'that dignity looked it over and then burst out, "Who the devil are you? I never heard of any such person!" He never had and it took Hugh some time to explain himself.' Hugh Fraser wondered whether he had been forgotten by London who did not answer his requests for directions. 'He began to brood over his troubles, even going so far as to cuff the native clerk at times.' In the end he 'locked up the Legation, put the key under the door, and sailed away for England.' When he reported to the Foreign Office 'Authority [i.e. the official responsible for personnel] was infinitely amused. "Good Lord, my dear boy!" it said. "We expected you home ages ago – we had no idea that you would last it out as long as that."'

Hugh Fraser later served in Stockholm, Peking and Rome. In 1874 he met and married Mary Crawford[4] in Italy. After a brief engagement of six weeks they set out for Peking where Hugh Fraser had been appointed Secretary of the Legation and served for over two years as Chargé d'Affaires in the absence on leave of Wade, then British Minister to China. He was transferred to Vienna in 1879 and then in 1882 to Rome. In 1885 he was appointed Minister at Santiago, Chile, where his prime task was to be the settlement of claims resulting from the war between Chile, Peru and Bolivia. He had to serve on a three-man committee with Brazilian and Chilean colleagues. The Brazilian infuriated him and eventually Fraser determined to bring the proceedings to an end by imposing a compromise. His appointment to Tokyo was announced in April 1888 and he was glad to get away from Chile, but the Frasers did not arrive in Tokyo until 1 May 1889.

CHARACTER AND QUALITIES

Mary Fraser seems to have been devoted to Hugh Fraser, but her brief comments on his character[5] suggest that he was not an easy or sensitive husband.

His apparently dour Scottish character was in total contrast to Mary Fraser's Mediterranean and sensitive temperament.

There can be no doubt that Hugh Fraser was a brave man and cool when threatened. As a young man he might indeed have seemed foolhardy. Mary Fraser commenting on the anti-foreign bullyboys (sōshi) who threatened foreigners in Tokyo at this time said that Hugh Fraser refused to 'take the slightest notice of the agitation, and walks all over the town, quite alone, rather to my terror'.[6] On another occasion Gubbins, the Japanese Secretary to the Legation and Hugh Fraser's right-hand man, told her of an incident when 'quite close to our own gates they had suddenly been surrounded by a band of sōshi, armed with their favourite sword sticks. An attempt had been made to distract the Chief's attention by hustling him behind, and at the moment when he was intended to turn his head a sword was drawn to strike him in front. But he refused to look behind him, and kept his eyes fixed on the face of the man in front, who lowered his sword at once. H[ugh] laughed a little, and went on and finished his walk.'[7]

In addition to courage he had an austere sense of duty. This led Mary to say: 'I do not think Hugh would have been happy if he had been popular. He would have thought himself to have failed, in some respect, of duty.' He was never popular with the British community in Yokohama with whom indeed his contacts seem to have been very limited if not minimal.

His strong sense of duty ensured that he devoted his main energies to his work, which he appears to have tackled with both thoroughness and conscientiousness. Mary recorded that in Japan 'Poor Hugh is terribly busy, for all the hard work comes as a rule at the hottest time' and he often had to 'gasp over cipher telegrams'.

In his judgements of individual cases he appears to have been firm and unswayed by sentiment.

He was never accused of pomposity and although he did what was necessary in terms of protocol he did not allow it to dominate his attitude. Mary had to be presented to Queen Victoria before they went to Vienna, but Hugh refused to attend a levée although he did have a coat of arms registered.

Hugh Fraser seems to have had a jealous streak. At any rate Mary said that she had found it prudent to give up acting 'after three or four years of marriage. Violent love-scenes on the stage with good-looking men are not conducive to harmony at home.'

Mary was a devout Catholic. Hugh seems to have retained some anti-Catholic prejudices. 'Once Hugh got on to that subject, there was no arguing or pleading with him. His views were deeply rooted in the heavy soil of the "Early Walnut and Antimacassar" [presumably early Victorian] period, and, the soul of sweetness and reasonableness in every other relation of life, let that topic creep into any discussion and he was another person in an instant.'

He could be very inconsiderate in other ways. Mary suffered badly from rheumatism. Yet in Santiago when Mary urged him to go the police about a missing servant he insisted that they should walk half way across town and refused to call a cab.

Hugh Fraser could also be witty or, some might say, sarcastic. Mary records that for a reception at the Palace in Tokyo in 1894 she had 'found a brocade all over strawberries and in spite of Hugh's quotation, "Ce n'est pas la mode de s'asseoir sur son blazon" wore it bravely.'[8]

Mary Fraser described Hugh as having 'a philosophic temperament'. 'He never wasted time and effort in complaint when complaint was useless. Later in life he appeared not to notice ordinary discomforts and inconveniences at all . . . I remember once in Japan, when I had been away from the Legation for a couple of days, I asked the English butler what he had given him for dinner the evening before. "We gave His Excellency a very good dinner, madam." He replied assuringly; "a real old-fashioned English dinner – boiled bacon and cabbage, madam." And Hugh had never said a word!' Yet he had insisted on their appointment to Santiago in taking an English cook with them as he did not believe that native servants were reliable. 'He refused to be poisoned by the native messes, as he called them.' The Chilean habit of consuming large steaks at every meal did not appeal to either Hugh or Mary Fraser.

Mary does not comment on his attitude to money perhaps because this was not a suitable subject for a gentleman, but she does refer from time to time to the expense of running their establishments overseas and it is possible that Hugh Fraser, as a traditional Scot, was careful over money matters, but they cannot have been without private means. In the nineteenth century a British diplomat had to have a private income and Hugh had been an unpaid attaché for some four years. His mother and sister lived in apparent comfort in Bath even if to Mary there was an 'awful melancholy and dullness in all their surroundings'. As Minister in Tokyo he had an annual salary of £4,000, which was fair if not generous by the standards of the time.

Mary described her 'dear Hugh' as 'a splendid traveller' who entertained her on their difficult first journey to Peking with 'many queer accounts of his former sojourn in China'. The Frasers had two sons (Hugh and John). Mary was a devoted mother worrying greatly when her younger son was wounded in the stomach during the Boer war. There is nothing to suggest that he was not an adequate father, but travelling with children was clearly a trial. At one point she wrote: 'Hugh's nerves were always rather over-strung and just now in crying need of rest.'

In commenting on his rather complex character Mary wrote: 'Hugh was very patient, and his Highland ancestry had given him a sense of humour, that sword of the afflicted, grim and keen, against whose edge the storm burst in vain.' 'Hugh was rather a queer person in some ways. When he might be expected, and reasonably, to lose his temper, he would be quite likely to laugh, or to display a gentleness so utterly impersonal and yet so understanding, so sympathetic and so selfless that one looked up to him with a certain awe, as not being entirely of this world. At others, a trifle, unnoticed by anyone else, would stir that Scottish nature to its depths and for days he would brood over it, never speaking. One was left to conjecture what it might have been but one never, never found out – except by accident.' When the manager of an English store in Santiago wanted to marry the maid whom Mary had brought out to Chile at their expense Hugh treated the man concerned to an explosion of temper. Mary had to try to smooth him down. 'It was a long business, for Hugh had entangled himself in the depths of that Highland temper of his, where I could not follow him'.

Mary Fraser does not tell us much about her husband's hobbies and cultural interests. At one point she noted in China that he was knowledgeable about 'keramics' and at another that while in Central America he wrote a monograph arguing that the builders of the stone monuments at Copan in Guatemala 'were Mongolians who crossed over the straits from the north and wandered down'. It was in Central America that he got 'his guitar, which afterwards proved to be one of the great comforts of his life, a friend that never failed to soothe his soul when it descended into the pit of Celtic depression. And the marvellous airs! I cannot remember them . . . but I know that no music that I have ever heard was sweeter than that which he would whistle sometimes of an evening, strumming on the guitar.'

It is not clear how good a linguist he was. It is improbable that in those days he received much practical teaching in modern languages at Eton, but he presumably had to do some study of European languages, especially French, before he was granted a paid attaché appointment. His value to the Legations in Vienna and Rome would have been very limited if he had an inadequate knowledge of German and Italian. Mary writing of their stay in Chile said that he knew Spanish, 'perfectly', but was most reluctant to use it. During two postings to China where he worked for that great Chinese linguist Sir Thomas Wade and was a friend of Robert Hart, the head of the Chinese customs he must surely have learnt some Chinese, but it seems unlikely that he became at all fluent. In Japan he seemed to rely greatly on his Japanese Secretary, J. H. Gubbins and other members of the Japan Consular Service. All in all Hugh Fraser seems to have been rather taciturn even in English unless deeply roused.

IN JAPAN

The Japan Weekly Mail for the period when Hugh Fraser was Minister in Japan contains remarkably few references to him and his activities. It reported that the Frasers arrived in Yokohama from Hong Kong on 1 May 1889 by SS *Verona* and had an audience at the palace in Tokyo on 17 May. It noted that he was elected as a member of the Asiatic Society, but it does not seem from reports of the Transactions of the Society in *The Japan Weekly Mail* that he was an active member. In November 1890, the Frasers are reported to have attended the St Andrews Society Ball. They left Japan via the United States on leave at the end of June 1893. They returned to Yokohama on 24 February 1894 on SS *Ancona*. But the *Mail* had nothing of substance to say about Hugh Fraser until his death (see below).

TREATY REVISION

The most important theme for *The Japan Weekly Mail* in the Fraser's time was the subject of Treaty Revision.[9] This subject also dominates the papers covering the Tokyo Legation in the years 1889–1894 which have been preserved in the Public Record Office. It is clear from these papers and from Mary Fraser's account of her life in Japan that treaty revision was the dominant issue for Hugh Fraser during his service in Japan.

The substance of the Treaty Revision negotiations and the numerous communications between Hugh Fraser and the various Japanese Foreign Ministers during his time in Tokyo and with the Foreign Office in London cannot be covered in a brief portrait of him.[10] But there is one important question for which an answer should be given in any account of Hugh Fraser in Japan. Did his actions and comments have any significant influence on the outcome? It is not easy to give a definitive answer to this question, but it is clear from the papers in the PRO that Hugh Fraser, no doubt taking account of the advice of

J.H. Gubbins, his right-hand man and Japanese expert, took a realistic view of what could be achieved for British interests. He firmly rejected the emotional and reactionary views of the British community in Yokohama and urged on London a common sense approach.

At a meeting of Yokohama residents on 9 September 1890, as reported in *The Japan Weekly Mail*, three resolutions were passed which were critical of moves to revise the treaties. The most important of these declared that the time had not yet arrived 'when questions in regard to rights, whether of property or person, . . . can be safely subjected to the jurisdiction of Japanese tribunals . . .'. The resolution also said that it was not possible to estimate 'the period within which the unconditional relinquishment of extraterritorial jurisdiction in Japan can be safely promised'. A leading advocate of the resolutions was a resident named J. A. Fraser (not apparently any relation of the Minister).

Over a year before these resolutions were passed Hugh Fraser in his despatch[11] of 16 August 1889 had recorded to the Secretary of State in London a view from which he did not swerve: 'I do not think that there is any probability that Her Majesty's Government will be able to obtain additional guarantees [presumably about the administration of justice] on the part of Japan in relation to jurisdiction.' He noted 'the serious agitation' in Japan 'on the subject of the concessions they have already made'. Such agitation 'might take a more acute and dangerous form at any moment,' and 'such agitation in this country is apt to lead immediately to political assassination.' He thought that 'amongst the causes of our present weakness must be reckoned, I fear, a fault: that of requiring too much'. Bearing in mind that the Americans and the Germans had accepted Japanese terms, 'Alone, or with but weak support from the Powers I do not think Her Majesty's Government can obtain additional guarantees of Justice.' These were strong words, which would not make him popular with British residents.

On 25 June 1891 after he had called on Viscount Enomoto, then the Japanese Foreign Minister, he commented to London on the difficulties, which the Japanese Government faced over Treaty revision that it was difficult to know what was 'the dominant fear' of the Japanese Ministers – 'opposition at home or complications abroad'. He surmised that what the Japanese really wanted was 'the faculty of repudiating the Treaties altogether, on a plea that the revision clause had been rendered inoperative by faults on the part of the Treaty Powers. I do not think that any such faculty can be claimed in the actual circumstances . . . It is impossible now to assert that England stands in the way of Treaty revision.' Fraser commented that 'The foreign relations of the Empire are hardly satisfactory at this moment. The Japanese do not seem to have a friend anywhere, unless it is Russia, and their sympathy with Russia rests absolutely on fear, that is to say, principally on momentary panic.'

Separately Fraser rejected an approach by Mr Piggott (presumably Sir Francis Taylor Piggott (1852–1925)).[12] He told the Foreign Office that Piggott 'can have no knowledge at all of the recent history of the questions he writes on . . .', but demonstrated that he was critical of Japanese justice by declaring: 'Mr Piggott is wrong in his good opinion of Japanese jurists.'

OTHER ACTIVITIES IN JAPAN

In Hugh Fraser's time the other work of the Legation did not seem to include commercial work, which has become the primary task of so many of the British missions abroad today. Hugh Fraser's only involvement seems to have been to forward the returns of trade prepared by British consular posts in Japan.

Hugh Fraser had to cope with the unofficial visit in April 1890 of Their Royal Highnesses The Duke and Duchess of Connaught. I have given an account of this visit in my essay entitled 'Royal Visits to Japan in the Meiji Period'.[13] The Connaughts were clearly out to have a good time and cannot have been easy visitors. They did not endear themselves to the British Community in Yokohama by refusing the ball, which the community offered.

Hugh Fraser was not directly involved with the visit to Japan in 1891 of the Czarevitch who was attacked and injured on his way from Ōtsu to Kyoto, but the affair caused a major scare at the time.

Not least because British subjects in Japan were subject to the yet-to-be-revised treaties under British consular jurisdiction he was inevitably involved in consular issues. These included the tragic murder in Tsukiji in April 1890 of the Reverend T. A. Large, a British missionary. The incident, which was described at length in *The Japan Weekly Mail* dated 12 April 1890, appears to have been perpetrated by burglars and not to have had any anti-Christian motive. The *Mail* commented that 'The absolute immunity yet enjoyed by foreigners in Japan from all personal violence during the past twenty years, invests this sad event with peculiar interest.' After the violence and insecurity, which had prevailed in the years up to and immediately following the Meiji Restoration in 1868, the lives of foreigners in Japan had been relatively peaceful, but in view of the threats of violence against Hugh Fraser and others from *sōshi* at this time such a comment seems inappropriate.

The Times of 12 April 1890 drew attention to an incident, which did not enhance the British reputation for even handed justice. In July 1889 a Spanish subject fled to Japan from Manila to escape arrest. Arrested by the Spanish consular authorities he 'was thrown into the British gaol in Yokohama where he lay until 1 March 1890, without any form of trial'. When the Spanish authorities came to remove their prisoner from his cell to a steamer bound for Manila, 'they found the prison guarded by a strong posse of Japanese constables, who declined to let the man be taken from Japanese territory'. *The Times*, however, reported another case, which demonstrated Hugh Fraser's sense of justice. Campos, a Portuguese domiciled in Hong Kong escaped to Japan and was arrested by the British consular authorities in Kobe who held him for return to Hong Kong. This led to a protest by the Japanese Ministry of Foreign affairs to the British Legation. 'Mr Fraser took a singularly courageous and conscientious course. Disregarding the precedents set by his predecessors and the procedure prescribed by the Order in Council, he caused Campos to be liberated and then procured his arrest and extradition by the Japanese Government. This act, performed entirely, on the Minister's own responsibility, produced a most happy effect, and went far to teach the Japanese that they can always count on justice from Great Britain if only they succeed in getting her to listen to them.'

Hugh Fraser's contacts with Japanese Ministers were primarily connected with Treaty revision, although he no doubt drew on them for his political reporting. The reports kept in the PRO do not, however, suggest that Hugh Fraser had achieved any deep insights into the Japanese political scene. In his despatch of 30 October 1889[14] he wrote: 'It is feared that a real cabinet, one representing clear views and identical policy, can hardly be established without a serious conflict and the employment of material force; a measure to which no known leader would willingly have recourse.' In his despatch of 14 November 1889[15] he noted the continuance of the Satchō oligarchy commenting that 'The Satsuma men form a solid party and understand one another, but there is endless discussion, intrigue, and self-seeking in the Choshiu camp, and very little cohesion in the whole administration.'

Just before he went on home leave in June 1893 he commented on the confusion of thought in Japan, which was 'at all times remarkable for extremes of sentiment and violence of temper'.

Hugh Fraser relied greatly on J. H. Gubbins for whom he obtained the appointment of Japanese Secretary to the Legation, but it seems likely that Fraser's austere personality and uncertain temper may have made relations with his diplomatic secretaries difficult. There is a hint in one report in *The Japan Weekly Mail*, dated 27 December 1890, that there may have been problems with the Honourable W. G. Napier, his diplomatic first secretary. The *Mail* reported that M. W. G. de Bunsen another diplomat without any expertise in Japanese, had been appointed to succeed Napier whose departure was described as 'somewhat sudden', his term of service not having expired.

DEATH AND FUNERAL

Hugh Fraser who had only returned to Tokyo from home leave in March 1894 became ill early in May. He complained of pains in the stomach and was seen by Dr Baelz, the German Doctor who was the main medical practitioner for the foreign community at the time. According to the report by Dr Baelz, sent to the Foreign Office after Hugh Fraser's death by R. S. Paget who took over as Chargé on the death of his chief, a stoppage of the bowels was suspected. Castor oil and enemas having failed Dr Baelz called in a Japanese surgeon and they opened the small intestine, but the operation did not lead to a removal of the stoppage and a second operation was thought to be needed if the patient's condition allowed. Hugh Fraser however weakened and died on 4 June 1894. Dr Baelz commented that he was surprised by the absence of fever despite the existence of peritonitis. He did not think that there had been a malignant growth in the bowel. Hugh Fraser's illness must have been extremely painful at a time when abdominal surgery had advanced so little. Perhaps with modern surgery he would have survived.

Hugh Fraser's funeral took place on 6 June 1894. According to *The Japan Weekly Mail* of 9 June 'the body lay in state' throughout the afternoon, and 'was visited by a great concourse of mourning friends, among whom were the Japanese Ministers of the Crown and the Foreign Representatives. The floral tributes sent were numerous and beautiful.' The ceremony was apparently arranged by Josiah Conder, the British architect.[16] The coffin was carried out of the Legation at 3.00 and reached St Andrew's Church at 4.00. 'The steep approach and the narrow road presented serious difficulties for the great crowd of carriages that followed the hearse.' The tiny Church was packed. The full choral service was performed by Bishop Bickersteth. The interment took place immediately afterwards at Aoyama cemetery where a brick vault had been built during the previous night. 'Mrs Fraser was present from first to last, bearing with indomitable courage the terrible grief of this last parting.'

The Japan Weekly Mail in its obituary described him in these words:

> Mr Fraser was one of those rare men, who with abilities of the highest order and perfectly balanced judgement, live lives of perpetual self-effacement and find their highest reward in a conscientious sense of duty faithfully discharged. His abnormally retiring disposition narrowed the circle of his appreciators and impaired the public's estimate of his capacity ... If he lacked the power to dazzle, he possessed in the fullest degree that of inspiring confidence ... No British Representative ever acquired larger influence in this country or wielded his influence more conscientiously. The Japanese learned very quickly that Mr Fraser could be thoroughly relied on never to lend his support to any cause tainted by the least injustice ... Fate did not will that he should finally solve the complex problem of Treaty Revision, but that he materially facilitated a solution by the clearness of his insight and the dignified firmness of his methods, there can be no manner of doubt ...

Japanese newspapers seem to have echoed these sentiments. The *Nichi Nichi Shimbun* published the following statement:

> The singularly just and impartial views taken by him on all occasions were erroneously supposed by these narrow-minded persons to be unwarrantably friendly to Japan ... unswervingly true to the maintenance of the rights of his country, and in the discharge of his duties he was always heedless of what outsiders might say about him ... In private life, he was kind, modest, and reserved, winning the respect and love of everybody, both Japanese and foreign, that came into close contact with him. A man of firm resolution he was never moved from the path of duty by the clamours of his nationals in the settlements ...

Hugh Fraser, who was 57 at the time of his death, was the only British head of mission to Japan to die while still in post. He was also not honoured with a knighthood or an appointment to the Order of St Michael and St George. Surely as a conscientious and upright official, even if he lacked sparkle and flair, he would have been so honoured if he had survived.

7

Power Henry Le Poer Trench
Minister to Japan, 1894–95

SIR HUGH CORTAZZI

Power Henry Le Poer Trench

The Hon. Power Henry Le Poer Trench (1841–99), who was the fourth son of the third Earl of Clancarty, was born in 1841. His time as British Minister to Japan was the shortest of all British envoys in Tokyo, but he had served there as Secretary to the Legation from 1882 to 1889.

Trench was appointed as an attaché at Paris at the early age of 18. In January 1860 he was transferred to Constantinople, and in December 1861 to Munich. In July 1863 he 'passed second examination',[1] and in November 1863 he was appointed a Third Secretary. In August 1865 he was posted to Rio de Janeiro and in 1868 to Washington where he was private secretary to Sir Edward Thornton. In August 1870 he was promoted to second secretary and appointed to Florence, but he 'did not proceed' and stayed in Washington. From 1879 to 1881 he worked in the Foreign Office. In October of that year he was transferred to Rome. In May 1882 he was promoted to be Secretary of Legation and was posted to Tokyo. On his departure from Tokyo in 1889 he was promoted to Secretary to the Embassy in Berlin. While in Berlin until 1893 he acted on some eleven often brief occasions as Chargé d'Affaires. On 1 July 1893 he was appointed as Minister to Mexico. On 25 June 1894 he was nominated as the successor in Tokyo of Hugh Fraser who had died at his post and appointed 'Envoy Extraordinary and Minister Plenipotentiary to the Emperor of Japan and Consul General in the Empire of Japan'. According to his obituary in *The Times* of 2 May 1899 he had been 'specially selected' by Lord Rosebery, then Secretary of State for Foreign Affairs. 'in view of his previous services in Japan for a post which was acquiring more and more importance'.

During almost seven years in Japan as Secretary to the Legation Trench had become well versed in Japanese affairs. He had been Chargé d'Affaires in Tokyo from August 1883 after the departure for China of Sir Harry Parkes[2] until March 1884 when The Hon (later Sir) Francis Plunkett arrived. He was again in charge of the Legation from August 1887 after Plunkett was transferred until March 1889 when the new Secretary of Legation the Hon W.J.H. Napier assumed the post shortly before Hugh Fraser took up his post as Minister. *The Japan Weekly Mail* for 6 April 1889 carried an extensive tribute to Trench on his departure.[3] The paper noted that Trench had remained in Tokyo for such a long stint at his own deliberate choice, having turned down offers to transfer to Peking and Washington. One of his predecessors F. O. Adams[4] had produced an extensive report on sericulture while another R. G. Watson had written about education in Japan. Political economy, always having been a hobby of his, Trench had done a study of Japanese finance. 'His papers upon this subject were most valuable. Closely reasoned, accurate and concise . . . his report on Japanese Railways also received high praise.' Trench had made it his first duty to study the people and their institutions . . . It redounds to his lasting credit that without suggesting any violent contrasts [perhaps a hit at Sir Harry Parkes] or ruffling any prejudices, he succeeded in adapting himself throughout to the best canons of British diplomacy '. . . Mr Trench leaves this country as much esteemed by the Japanese as he is liked and trusted by his own countrymen.' After referring to 'his qualities that command trust and friendship' the article expressed the hope that he would one day return as British Representative [i.e. Minister to Japan].

Trench was much involved, especially while he was in charge of the Legation in the 1880s, in negotiations for Treaty revision. One important conversation about these negotiations took place on 28 December 1888 with Count Ōkuma Shigenobu, then Japanese Foreign Minister. This followed preliminary soundings about the new Japanese proposals for a revision of the Treaties which had been made with the US and German governments. Ōkuma explained to Trench that the Japanese Government were anxious to resume the negotiations which had been interrupted by the adjournment of the earlier conference in July 1887. The Japanese wanted '. . . to adhere as far as possible to the basis of the previous negotiations. That basis included two important points; the completion of Japan's Codes, and the arrangements to be made for the exercise of jurisdiction over foreigners.' Ōkuma thought that the 'Western Powers could not but admit that the progress, which Japan had made during the thirty years which had elapsed since the conclusion of the existing Treaties, was great.' Ōkuma said that 'The failure of the late conference had been caused by the strong pressure brought to bear upon the cabinet by the nation, which had condemned the scheme of treaty revision then put forward, on the ground that the concessions therein made to Western Powers were not consistent with the dignity of Japan.' Ōkuma explained that they did not think it 'desirable to assemble a fresh conference' but proposed to proceed 'by separate and independent negotiations with the Great Powers of Europe and the United States.' Ōkuma hoped the British Government would give a favourable reception to his proposals as he attached special importance to Great Britain's attitude. On being asked by Trench whether the new proposals had been communicated to any of the Treaty Powers Ōkuma admitted that they had been shown to the representatives of Germany and the United States and that the Americans 'had signified by telegraph their approval of the principles contained in them.' Ōkuma lamely added that 'ill-health and domestic bereavement had prevented him from communicating them to me [Trench] at the same time'.

Trench arrived in Tokyo as Minister to Japan on 20 August 1894 and took over the Legation where since Hugh Fraser's death Ralph Paget,[5] third secretary, had been Chargé. He had arrived in Yokohama on board the Canadian mail steamer *Empress of India*.[6] He came on shore in the steam- pinnace of HMS *Caroline*. On passing HMS *Redpole* her marines drawn up on deck presented arms. He was accompanied by Captain Norcock RN and by Judge Wilkinson [of the Consular Court]. On reaching the pier he was met by all the principal British residents then in Yokohama [many were away in the hills to escape the summer heat]. *The Japan Weekly Mail* noted that 'Mr Trench does not appear to be in quite such good health as when he left Japan nearly five and a half years' earlier'. This was put down to sickness in Mexico due to the climate there. At the British consulate a 'numerously signed address of welcome' was presented to him by Mr John Ricketts. This noted that on his departure in 1889 an address had been presented expressing their esteem and their regret at his departure. Trench made a short speech of thanks explaining his pleasure in taking up his new appointment and his gratitude for the support of the community.

On 23 August Trench was received in audience by the Emperor and presented his credentials. He was accompanied by Paget and J.H. Longford as well as by Marquis Kido of the Imperial Household Department. There was the usual exchange of friendly messages.

When Trench arrived as Minister the Sino-Japanese War (1894–5) was being fought and the war and its effect on British interests was his main concern during the months while he was in charge of the mission. The obituary of him in *The Times* of 2 May 1899 recorded that '. . . his health unfortunately gave way before long under severe strain of his duties during this critical period'.

On the day after his arrival in Tokyo (21 August 1894) Trench made his initial call on Viscount Mutsu Munemitsu, the Japanese Foreign Minister, who paid tribute to the way in which Paget had handled affairs in the absence of an accredited Minister. Trench clearly found Mutsu a difficult interlocutor. He noted, for instance, on 28 August that when he tried to ask about the way things were going with China Mutsu did not wish to talk about the war.

One of the first issues he faced was the Japanese response to British demands for Japanese recognition of the neutral status of Shanghai. Following an abortive meeting with Mutsu on 12 September 1894 Trench had called on Count Itō Hirobumi, the Prime Minister, and asked for his help over the problem. Trench in his report of this meeting noted that Itō was 'an old friend' from his previous service in Japan. Itō, he recorded, had been 'particularly impressed when I stated that any attempt to interfere with the trade and neutrality of that port might involve Japan in serious trouble'. Itō had then agreed to speak to Mutsu.

It would seem, however, from Trench's despatch of 28 September 1894 that Ito's intervention had not been successful. Trench commented:

> Viscount Mutsu appears to attach no importance to verbal communications and not to consider them official. Nor does he always take notice of paraphrases [presumably paraphrased to protect codes] of telegrams handed to him. Under these circumstances I thought it advisable to put in writing that Her Majesty's Government hold Japan to her undertaking not to undertake warlike operations against Shanghai or the approaches to that port.

On 18 October 1894 Trench recorded that 'Mutsu referred in rather bitter language to what he termed the unfairness of the Shanghai engagement'.

Much of Trench's reporting in the next few months was devoted to accounts of the progress of the war. He relayed both accounts in the Japanese press and reports from Captain du Boulay who with Taylor, an army medical officer, had arrived in October 1894 to act as military attaché and who had been immediately sent to join Japanese forces. He reported among other battles the capture of Pyong Yang and the fall of Port Arthur. On the latter he wrote in his despatch of 24 December 1894 that 'I fear there is no doubt that the inhuman butchery at Port Arthur lasted four days after the capture of that place by the Japanese.'

In his despatch of 14 November Trench reported:

> To all outward appearances China would seem to be at the mercy of Japan and to have been sufficiently humbled to gratify the feeling of hatred which existed before the war. But the feeling of hatred for China which was the original cause seems with every fresh success of Japan to prove herself equal to rank as one of the Great Powers, and this ambition seems in its turn to be making way to the conviction that Japan alone is well able to hold her own against any single European power.

Trench noted that the only two powers who were in a position to intervene [he used the word 'interfere'] were Russia and England [sic]. In his view the object of the Japanese Government was 'to set them off against each other. The rumours of a secret treaty between Russia and Japan 'originated with and [had] been circulated by the Japanese Government itself.' Trench added that the Russian Minister in Tokyo a Monsieur Hitrovo[7] [sic] was an Anglophobe with a 'capacity for intrigue'. At this stage Trench thought that any attempt by a single power to intervene would be 'fruitless.'

Count Mutsu Munemitsu in his memoir *Kenkenroku*[8] makes no mention of the issue of Shanghai and concentrates on British attempts at mediation which is not borne out by Trench's despatches preserved in the Public Record Office:

> When the Chinese Government sought the mediation of the great powers, the British showed their usual determination not to be left behind on Far Eastern matters. Despite the fact that Lord Rosebery's cabinet was on the verge of resignation and no longer had firm control in Parliament, Britain wished to be the first to mediate between Japan and China. As soon as the new British minister to Japan, Mr Trench, had arrived in Tokyo in mid-August, he called on me at the Foreign Ministry to serve semi-official notice that the British government would soon make some proposal regarding the termination of hostilities between Japan and China. On October 8, he informed me that he had been instructed by his government to inquire if the Japanese government would accept a suspension of hostilities on two conditions: a joint guarantee of Korea's independence by the great powers and the payment to the Japanese government by China of an indemnity for war related expenses. He added that his government had already discussed this matter with the other European powers and that the Russian minister in Tokyo would shortly be tendering us similar advice regarding a truce. Nevertheless, while I had frequent meetings at that time with the Russian, German, French and American ministers, none of them appeared to have any instructions from their governments on this question. Furthermore, in

as much as the Russian minister, Mr. Khitrovo, explicitly declared that the
Japanese government could not reasonably accede to any proposal so vague
as that forwarded by Britain, I found it difficult to believe that he would be
making a similar proposal anytime in the imminent future.

Was Mutsu's recollection at fault? Or was Mutsu referring to exchanges of
views in London between the Foreign Office and the Japanese Minister there?

As early as 7 September 1894 Trench had noted that the Japanese press
were 'daily becoming more excited' and referred to their enemy with contempt. On 24 December Trench recorded that Mutsu had assured him that
'Japan had no wish to dismember the Chinese Empire or upset the present
dynasty', but noted that 'the war party in the cabinet is at present omnipo-
tent'. By the time Sino-Japanese negotiations had begun in earnest Trench
was no longer active and Gerard Lowther, his Secretary of Legation, had to
deal with the issues which arose.[9]

One problem arising out of the Sino-Japanese War which involved Trench
in a good deal of work was the action of the Japanese authorities in boarding
and searching on 8 November 1894 the SS *Gaelic*,[10] a British vessel from San
Francisco. This was followed by the detention at Kobe of the French
steamship *Sydney* and the arrest of three passengers (two Americans 'travelling under aliases' and a Chinese) who were alleged to be engaged for service
in the Chinese navy.

A related issue with which Trench had to deal in the latter part of 1894 was
the issuing of instructions to British subjects about the maintenance of neutrality in the Sino-Japanese war.

Shortly after his arrival in August 1894 he received instructions to represent
Her Majesty's Government at the exchange of ratifications of the new Anglo-
Japanese Commercial Treaty. This duly took place on 25 August 1894 in
advance of publication of the text of the Treaty in the official Gazette in
Tokyo on 28 August 1894. In a despatch dated 31 August 1894 Trench after
summarising mixed reactions in the press, noted:

> People in Yokohama grumble at the prospect of coming under Japanese juris-
> diction and many of them are hostile to the Treaty, but the better classes and
> the leading merchants, knowing that Treaty revision was inevitable, are fairly
> satisfied with the Treaty. They are disappointed, however, at Osaka, Niigata
> and Ebisuminato having been struck off the list of open ports, especially as
> Osaka has a great future before it as a commercial port. They think that when
> England consented to the three above mentioned ports being closed to for-
> eign trade she ought to have insisted on Shimonoseki being made an open
> port. They also express great regret that Her Majesty's Government did not
> insist on British subjects being allowed to hold land in Japan, and as regards
> the Tariff attached to the Protocol, they consider the duties on several arti-
> cles of British manufacture as much too high, and instance cotton yarn, silk,
> satins, and silk and cotton mixtures.

The conclusion of the treaty led Trench to issue instructions to Consuls
about implementing the provisions of the Treaty including the issuance of
passports to British subjects for travel within Japan until the revised treaty
came into force in 1899.

Trench, of course, also had to report on Japanese internal politics. On 7
September 1894 he recorded that the general election which had been held
on 1 September had 'been unattended by those grave disturbances of the

public peace characterizing previous elections in this country'. 'The numerical balance of the various parties is not very much altered by the new election'. The government's position was strengthened by 'the unanimity which prevails that the Government must not be embarrassed by opposition during the war'.

In late February 1895 Trench suffered an 'attack of aphasia and paralysis' from which he never fully recovered. Gerard Lowther,[11] of the Legation, who had recently arrived in Japan, assumed Trench's responsibilities and signed despatches for Trench until he could be transferred home. Lowther then took charge of the Legation until the arrival of Ernest Satow in July 1895. After becoming ill Trench spent some time at Miyanoshita to recuperate. Soon after his return to Tokyo he moved to Yokohama before leaving for England via Canada on 10 May on *The Empress of India. The Japan Weekly Mail* for 11 May 1905 expressing the hope for his early and full recovery hoped to be able to 'welcome his return to a post where he has won universal respect and esteem'. The paper was surprised by a Reuters telegram reporting the appointment of Ernest Satow to Tokyo when Trench

> . . . had neither resigned, been transferred, nor placed en disponibilté. He has merely left Japan on sick leave . . . We can not sufficiently express the regret that will be felt by the community at losing Mr Trench. . .His countrymen . . . had ample opportunity to estimate his official abilities, to learn that their interests would always be safe in his keeping, and to appreciate his genial kindliness and profuse hospitality. Few British officials have ever been more sincerely liked and esteemed in the East.

Following his return to England Trench was not reemployed and in January 1896 he was retired on a pension. In London after his retirement he lived in Albion Street, London W2. He never married. On 30 April 1899 after a long illness he died and on 3 May 1899 he was buried at Highgate cemetery.

It is difficult, in the absence of private papers,[12] to give any convincing account of Trench's personality based on the available official papers and on local press reports. Even allowing for journalistic hyperbole it is clear, however, that Trench was well-liked in the British community and by Japanese with whom he came in contact. He was thus more than just a competent diplomat and 'a safe pair of hands'. As a bachelor his main interest may well have been his work. He obviously must have learnt a good deal about modern Japan during his period as Secretary of Legation in the 1880s, but he does not appear to have studied the Japanese language and had to rely, like his fellow members of the British Diplomatic Corps who served as Secretaries in the Legation, on the expertise of Gubbins and his colleagues in the Japanese secretariat.

8
Sir Ernest Satow
Minister in Japan, 1895–1900

IAN RUXTON

Sir Ernest Satow

Sir Ernest Satow (1843–1929) is generally regarded as the best qualified offi-cial and the most outstanding scholar of Japanese to have been appointed head of the British Mission in Japan. He would have liked to be the first British Ambassador to Japan but he was transferred in 1900 to Peking, then regarded as a more important post than Tokyo, in succession to Sir Claude MacDonald who needed a transfer following the Boxer rebellion. Sir Claude in the event became the first British Ambassador to Japan when the Legations were raised to the status of Embassies following the conclusion of the Anglo-Japanese Alliance in 1902. The mission in Peking remained a Legation throughout Satow's service there. He therefore sadly never became an 'Ambassador', although he became a GCMG and a Privy Councillor. The sta-tus of Ambassador was more important at that time than it is these days when every mission is called an 'Embassy' however unimportant the country involved. Brilliant but seemingly aloof, the best way to arrive at an under-standing of Satow is through his voluminous personal diaries and other papers kept in the Public Record Office. This brief essay introduces the man and his chief concerns during the above period, based mainly on his diaries.[1]

Satow arrived back in London from his brief posting as Minister in Morocco where he had been since September 1893 at the end of May 1895. He was almost 52. He had received a telegram from the Foreign Secretary Lord Kimberley (1826–1902) on 2 May offering him the Legation at Tokyo, and another confirming the appointment on 17 May.[2] This was the post for which Satow was the ideal candidate, having spent almost twenty years in Japan (September 1862 – December 1882 with two home leaves) successively as student interpreter, interpreter and Japanese Secretary to the Legation.

Since leaving Japan in 1882 he had been Consul-General in Bangkok where he had been promoted from the Consular to the Diplomatic Service early in 1885 and made Minister to Siam.[3] But he did not care for the climate or official corruption there.[4] Bouts of malarial fever rendered him ineffective, so that from June 1887 to October 1888 when he was offered his next post in Uruguay, he was on sick leave in England.[5] Uruguay was 'an earthly paradise in which he found nothing to do'.[6] Early in June 1893 he was transferred to Morocco where his task was to promote gradual internal reform through tact and patience. His success there led to his appointment as a KCMG.

NEW JAPAN: THE BACKGROUND

The Anglo-Japanese Treaty of Commerce and Navigation had been signed in London on 16 July 1894, providing for the abolition of extra-territoriality with regard to British subjects with effect from 17 July 1899, and the immediate introduction of an ad valorem tariff. This revision of the first of the 'unequal treaties' was an important turning point, both in Japanese history and in Britain's attitude towards Japan.[7] The First Sino-Japanese War had been won by Japan, leading to the Treaty of Shimonoseki, signed on 17 April 1895, but it had to be drastically modified after pressure in the form of 'friendly advice' from Russia, France and Germany (the so-called Triple Intervention). Japan was thereby forced to give up the newly ceded territory of the Liaotung peninsula in the southern tip of Manchuria, which included Port Arthur and Talienwan, in exchange for an increased indemnity from China.[8]

SATOW IN ENGLAND (MAY–JUNE 1895)

The Permanent Under-Secretary Sir Thomas Sanderson briefed Satow at the Foreign Office. They discussed the compensation that Japan would receive for withdrawing from Liaotung; the apparent rejection of Japanese reforms in Korea; and the Japanese annexation of Formosa, where the Chinese seemed to be supplying arms secretly to the anti-Japanese guerrillas, the 'semi-savage Hakkas'.[9] Sanderson told Satow that he should leave as soon as possible for Japan. The chargé d'affaires, Gerard A. Lowther, was doing well enough, but without Japanese language skills he was dependent on the legation interpreters, John H. Gubbins (who was then Japanese Secretary, and thus chief interpreter) and the second secretary Ralph S. Paget.

Satow also had meetings with Lord Kimberley who described Japan as 'our natural ally, as against Russia'[10] and stated that he regarded China as both 'unreliable and useless'. Britain should remain friendly to her, but not rely on her as a counterweight to Russia. Kimberley also remarked that he thought the English newspapers at Yokohama did a lot of harm to Anglo-Japanese relations. Japanese vanity should be humoured, and their goodwill cultivated. In an oblique reference to Sir Harry Parkes, British Minister in Japan 1865–83, he added: 'It was no longer possible to treat them as semi-civilised and to bully them; they must be treated on a footing of equality . . .'

Following the change of government from Liberal to a Conservative-Unionist coalition in June 1895, Lord Salisbury took over as both Prime Minister and Foreign Secretary. He was more sceptical about Japan's capability and reliability than Kimberley had been. When Satow wrote to him from Tokyo asking for instructions on 15 August, Salisbury in his reply of 3

October doubted whether the Japanese were capable of preventing Russia from obtaining an ice-free port on her eastern seaboard, which she could easily take by marching overland from Siberia. Satow was told instead to concentrate on the promotion of trade in the face of German commercial rivalry.[11]

Before his departure from England for Japan Satow was summoned to dinner at Windsor Castle on 25 June 1895 where Queen Victoria invested him with the accolade of a Knight Commander of the Order of St Michael and St George (KCMG), but apparently little was said. A more significant meeting took place on 11 August 1897 at Osborne House on the Isle of Wight during Satow's leave from Japan to attend the Queen's diamond jubilee. After dinner they privately discussed Siam and Japan:

> Then she said the Japanese prince [Arisugawa, in England for the Jubilee] was nice but not handsome, and I said Japanese thought him good-looking. Japanese women she thought were not so either. I said that travellers coming to Japan were shocked to find the men so ugly.
>
> She asked if Japan were not a very difficult post. I replied that fortunately the three powers [Russia, Germany, France] had made it very easy, and that being able to talk Japanese was a great help. She was much surprised at this, and asked if it were not a very difficult language. I said it was because one could not learn it by living in a Japanese family as one would do in Europe.

ARRIVAL IN TOKYO

Satow left Liverpool on 29 June 1895, and arrived in Japan on 28 July via New York and Vancouver. The business community and the Legation staff greeted him at Yokohama. The next day he called on Saionji Kinmochi, the acting Foreign Minister. On 1 August he met Itō Hirobumi of Chōshū, his old friend of Bakumatsu days, now Prime Minister. Satow congratulated him on Japan's beating China and discovered the conditions on which Japan would give up Liaotung. They also discussed Korea, Formosa and treaty revision.

On 9 August at 10 a.m. Satow had an audience with the Emperor and Empress, at which his credentials were presented. He was fetched in an Imperial horse-drawn carriage 20 minutes before. In the reception room Satow following the prescribed protocol, bowed three times and read his speech in English. The Emperor replied in Japanese, later translated thus: 'We are exceedingly gratified to think that a greater cordiality in the friendly relations existing between our respective countries will be facilitated by the fact of your many years residence in Our country and by your thorough knowledge of our national affairs.' Then Satow saw the Empress, who expressed pleasure at seeing him after so many years, echoed the Emperor's words on Anglo-Japanese friendship being enhanced and referred to Satow's being a 'great scholar in Japanese things'. Satow replied humbly before taking his leave.

THE MAIN POLITICAL ISSUES FOR SATOW IN TOKYO

China

The main problem with China from American, British and Japanese viewpoints was how to prevent her partition among the land-grabbing European powers and preserve the 'Open Door' to free trade. Satow wrote to Sir Nicholas O'Conor, then Minister in Peking, on 3 September 1895 that he supposed Salisbury's views would be the same as Kimberley's 'that China has shown she can never be of any use to us as an ally'[12] and agreed in a conversation with Admiral Buller later that month 'that China is hopeless in the matter of reform.' Her government system was 'thoroughly rotten'.[13]

When Satow saw Itō on 26 September he was told that Japan had tried desperately to come to an agreement with China over a sound system of government for Korea, but she had refused to cooperate, leading to the Sino-Japanese war. Satow himself told Count Inoue Kaoru of Chōshū (1836–1915), the former Foreign Minister (1879–87) and Minister to Korea (October 1894–September 1895) on 4 October that he thought Japan was a much better country than China to lead Korea's modernization. On the same day Foreign Minister Count Ōkuma Shigenobu denied that Japan had tried to pick a quarrel with China; the Japanese had been anxious about the Chinese navy with its powerful ships and foreign officers, but the Chinese army was poorly trained and led. Itō had told Satow that beating China had been easy.[14]

In 1899 two Chinese commissioners visited Japan. On 27 July Satow mentioned them in a private letter to Salisbury, commenting that they were unlikely to achieve anything significant:

> Japan does not wish to be tied to a corpse, nor to undertake the defence of China against Russia. Her chief care is for the maintenance of her position in Corea, and nothing but a Russian attempt to swallow up the Peninsula will in my opinion turn her aside from her present policy of lying low till her armaments are completed in 1903.[15]

After the commissioners left Satow reported again to Salisbury on 5 October that the Foreign Minister Aoki Shūzō[16] had talked to him 'in a very aggrieved tone' about their behaviour:

> By the way in which they went on they had made it impossible to have any serious negotiations with them. He added of course there had been no question of an alliance [between Japan and China], but only of a friendly understanding, which was frustrated by their conduct here.[17]

Korea

Korea had for centuries been a vassal of China within the Confucian hierarchy, and attempts by Japan to displace the latter were in general much resented in Korea and China. Korean hatred of the Japanese could also be traced back to the invasions by Toyotomi Hideyoshi in 1592 and 1597, and more recently to the unequal Treaty of Kanghwa forced on Korea by Japan in 1876.

When Satow saw Itō for the first time on 1 August he was asked if Britain had any interest in Korea. Discounting commercial considerations, Satow stated that like Japan, Britain wished to prevent Russian annexation. Satow asked Itō if Russia was planning to extend the trans-Siberian railway down to a port in Korea. Itō replied that they aimed at 'something much greater'. He read a memo from the Russian Minister stating that Russia expected Japan 'to conform her acts to her declarations as to the independence of Corea'. Itō and Satow agreed that neutralization of Korea guaranteed by several Powers would be better than independence, which would allow Russia to deal directly with Korea and 'obtain her aims more easily'.

On 25 August Satow reported to Salisbury that Viscount Miura Gorō had been appointed Japanese Minister in Korea. Satow believed he was a moderate in favour of gradual reform, but events soon proved him wrong. On 26 September Satow reported that Miura had refused a request by the Korean government for Japanese troops to subdue an armed rebellion. It was Satow's view that Korea was 'quite incapable of reform from within'. Itō himself believed that Korea could not survive as an independent state, but Japan could not prevent Russian annexation at this stage, because her navy, though increasing in size, was still too weak.

On 8 October 1895 a coup d'état occurred in Seoul. It was engineered by Miura Gorō, and the Korean Queen Min Bi was assassinated: as Satow discovered on 14 October, she had been beheaded. On the following day Satow observed in a letter to his friend F. V. Dickins that Korea would be 'another Morocco, a rotten fruit which no one may touch, and which will be carefully propped up lest it should fall into some one's hands of whom the others would be jealous to the point of fighting.'

On 13 February 1896 Satow received a visit from a Korean fugitive from Seoul, where the King had taken refuge in the Russian legation. He appealed strongly for British help for Korea, but Satow was unable to assist. In May he wrote to Salisbury that the Japanese viewed Korea as 'their Alsace-Lorraine'. On 4 June he told *Kokugaku* scholar Viscount Fukuba Bisei[18] that Inoue Kaoru had been 'in too great a hurry' in trying to reform Korea along European lines.

On 18 February 1897 the new Foreign Minister Ōkuma Shigenobu suggested to Satow that Britain might establish a legation in Korea, but Satow replied: 'It would probably excite umbrage in the minds of the Russians if we suddenly without any apparent reason converted our Consulate General into a Legation.'[19]

While on leave in England, Satow discussed Korea with Salisbury on 6 October. When Salisbury said the Russians wanted a port in Northeast Asia, Satow replied that a Korean port would be of no use, but that Port Lazareff (Wonsan on the east coast of Korea) in Russian hands would 'cause great popular commotion' in Japan.

Again on 2 March 1898 Satow received a noted Korean exile, Pak Yong Hyo, who asked if Britain would take a more active role in Korea. Satow said that Britain 'had no direct interests there. Only Russia and Japan had. But the latter neither spoke nor acted. Coreans must be patient for a few years.'

On 30 March 1899 Satow spoke with Aoki Shūzō, then Foreign Minister, who said:

> If Russia has Corea Japan cannot sleep in peace. Unfortunately the interests of England there are not sufficient to make it worth her while to support Japanese policy. But if Russia gets command of the peninsula she will have a great and damaging position as regards commercial nations. I observed that Japan would not be ready [for war] till 1903. He replied that she might be obliged to act before.[20]

Satow and Aoki talked again on 12 October about Russian moves on Masanpho as a coaling station and naval base for policing the Straits of Tsushima, which had been frustrated by Japanese land purchases.

Satow saw Itō for the last time on 2 May 1900 before returning to England. When Satow observed that all seemed quiet in the Far East, Itō replied that no one could tell how long it would last. Satow replied:

> As to war, I said no one could suppose it was to the advantage of Japan to fight Russia. Yet many people talked about it. Japan and Russia as to Corea like England and France as to Siam, a pretty woman with two suitors; no need however to come to blows. One thing however seemed clear, Russia regarded Japan as the only obstacle to her designs in the Far East.[21]

Formosa

Kimberley told Satow on 31 May 1895 that the government 'saw no reason for interfering about Formosa, though of course would rather they [Japan] had not taken it.' It was therefore not a political issue, but rather a commercial one for Satow, who had to preside over new consulates on the island as the Japan consular service was extended.[22] In particular he had to negotiate with the Japanese government over the camphor trade. Anglo-Chinese regulations of 1867 allowed foreigners to enter Formosa, buy and export camphor, but they were forbidden to manufacture it. In spite of this five or six British and German firms were in fact allowed to do so. When the Japanese took over in October 1895 they tried to enforce the regulations: several Chinese acting for the foreign firms were imprisoned. After protests by Satow and the German Minister Gutschmid, the camphor trade was conceded to foreign firms until the new treaties came into effect in 1899.

Opium was another matter. On 13 September 1895 Satow and Saionji discussed it. Saionji asked if it would be safe to take a permissive line, to which Satow replied that the British Opium Commission had said it was less harmful than alcohol, and that opium was frequently smoked outdoors by Chinese labourers, though he personally wished both 'could be done away with.'

Issues in Japan

With a new treaty only just negotiated and not yet in force, there were bound to be many issues which arose. The Yokohama branch of the China Association were against it as an 'undue sacrifice' of British (i.e. their) interests, as they told Satow in a memorandum.[23] They saw no benefit in further opening the country, unlike home-based British firms looking for new markets.

Leases caused problems, especially in Kobe. The Japanese tried to put a time limit on perpetual leases and effectively prevent foreign ownership of land altogether. Satow discussed the issue with Foreign Minister Nishi Tokujirō on 3 March 1898. Nishi thought there would be no objection. Satow replied that 'under the new Treaties foreigners would have the same rights as the law gave to Japanese and hence no need for fixing a limit. As to Kōbe I would wait till he got his information, but hoped he would eventually see that the Governor ought not to have fixed a limit on his own account when the agreement between the Japanese government and foreign ministers left everything to be arranged between the owner and the lessee.' He added that only Itō and he understood the situation in Kobe, as they had been present when the settlement was established.

Prison conditions and the access of Consuls to arrested foreigners were discussed on numerous occasions, as were certificates of origin for imported goods, taxes on land, and press laws. But the most sensational case was that of Mrs. Carew, accused of poisoning her husband with arsenic in October 1896. This was tried in the British consular court at Yokohama, under the old extraterritorial system. Satow found a way round having Edith Carew hanged and her sentence was commuted to life imprisonment.[24]

SATOW'S PERSONAL LIFE IN TOKYO

Satow would have been pleased to return to Tokyo, not only for professional but also personal reasons. It would give him the opportunity to spend time with his Japanese 'wife' Takeda Kane whom he could not marry as a diplomat and their two sons, Eitarō and Hisayoshi (also referred to as Hisakichi, and sometimes in the diaries as 'Cha-chan', an affectionate term used only in the Kantō region). Eitarō had been born in 1880, and Hisayoshi in 1883. They were therefore fifteen and twelve years old respectively when Satow returned in 1895. Lightly coded references to Satow's Japanese family are interspersed throughout his diaries, using other languages such as Latin, Italian and Spanish. For example on 26 March 1898 Satow wrote: 'Dined at Totsuka [Shinjuku ward, near the present JR Takatanobaba station] with tutti e tre.' The three here were Takeda Kane, Eitarō and Hisayoshi. Another frequent entry is 'Dined at Gembei [Totsuka] con los muchachos.'[25] Yet there are usually few details given. An exception is 30 December 1895:

> Started at 10 with the boys for Shidzuura near Numadzu, a brilliant day, on foot and to the top of the pass by 11.20 reaching Karuizawa at 12.15. Started again at 1.5 and walked to Hirai where we rested half an hour, and off again on foot at 2.55. Here Saburo [Satow's manservant] and Hisakichi took *kuruma*, while we continued on foot thro' Daiba and Yamashita, crossing a low pass just behind the village of Tōgo, and getting into the main road at Yamakiwa arr. at the Hōyōkan in Shidzuura at 5.15, standing betw. Saigō's villa and the Kai-hin-In a hospital. This is a new and elegant house. I gave a chadai [tip, pourboire] of 5 yen and we were well treated in consequence. There is a fine grove of pine-trees on the sandy shore, and the position is a beautiful one. Temperature much warmer than Atami.

There were also old friends, foreign as well as Japanese, with whom to renew acquaintance. Professor Basil Hall Chamberlain, in Japan since 1873, was still there. And among diplomatic colleagues Satow would have been pleased to find Albert d'Anethan, the Belgian minister, who had first been in Japan 1873–75 and his English wife E. Mary Haggard, sister of the novelist Sir Henry Rider Haggard, author of King Solomon's Mines, and of the diplomat Sir William Haggard. Other 'old Japan hands` included J.H. Gubbins who had taken over from Satow as English Secretary to the treaty revision conference in 1883. Henry W. Denison, an American, had acted for the Japanese foreign office as a legal adviser for many years, and the Englishman William H. Stone had advised on telegraphy since 1872.

Satow decided that he liked Lake Chūzenji near Nikkō better than Hakone as a retreat from Tokyo, especially in the hot summer months.[26] To F.V. Dickins on 21 August 1895 he wrote:

> Yesterday I came here, to a small house on the bank of the lake which I have taken till the end of September. I forget whether you know the place. It is

very small and quiet. The only other foreigners who have houses here are Gutschmid, the Lowthers, the Kirkwoods and a German savant name unknown.

And on 17 September he wrote in his diary that he 'rowed Gutschmid's boat in 12 min. over to Tozawa, where my house is to be built'. The villa which he had built is still used by the Ambassador. On 30 May 1896 Satow went with architect Josiah Conder to the building site and decided where the boathouse would be. Later he ordered a sculling boat for 70 dollars from A. Teck, probably to replace a leaky boat.[27]

Freiherr von Gutschmid did not remain long as German minister, being the author of several gaffes. The first was when he sent a telegram to Itō congratulating him on the Treaty of Shimonoseki, and then two days later joined in the protest about Liaotung.[28] The second was when he wrote a 'foolish note' to Saionji[29] and on 30 December 1896 he allegedly struck a student[30] with his whip. He was replaced by Graf von Leyden.

Asaina Kansui was employed as Satow's spy from 2 December 1895, in the days before MI6. He was from a *'hatamoto'* family, and his father had been Governor of Nagasaki. Asaina was also Governor from 1864–66 though he did not serve there. In March 1867 he was appointed Commissioner for Foreign Affairs, and in January 1868 Commissioner for Financial Affairs. Thereafter his career is unknown. Asaina appears in the official despatches as 'a confidential source' and gave Satow such materials as the shorthand notes of the financial committee of the Lower House. Sometimes Satow asked for specific information: on 12 March 1898 he 'told him to try and find out whether the Russians have informed his government of their desire to lease Port Arthur and Talienwan'. Asaina was paid regularly, usually in dollars or yen, but it is not clear how useful he was to Satow, and on 19 February 1896 Satow thought Asaina was trying to 'pump' him.[31]

On 11 December 1895 Satow was made President of The Asiatic Society of Japan, of which he had been a founder member in 1872, and to which he had frequently read papers in the 1870s. At one point on 30 November 1897 he discussed a proposal for winding it up with Chamberlain because there were too many 'twaddly papers', but it fortunately continues to this day. Satow lectured to the A.S.J. on "The Jesuit Mission Press in Japan" on 29 March 1899[32] and on 21 June at the Legation on "The Cultivation of Bamboos in Japan".[33]

Satow retained a scholarly interest in other languages, including Greek and Latin. He read Virgil with Mrs. Kirkwood, wife of the legal adviser to the Japanese government William M. Kirkwood (1850–1926).[34] He discussed Jesuit scholarship with a Catholic priest, Père Evrard. He frequently attended concerts and amateur dramatics, and was a keen member of a glee club, for which he persuaded Mrs. Blakiston (widow of Captain Blakiston[35]) to continue to play. He played whist regularly and was chairman of the Nippon Race Club in Yokohama, receiving the Emperor at the races on 29 October 1896. Other social engagements included dinners of Japanese Cambridge graduates on 24 January 1896 and 12 May 1898, and another of British and Japanese barristers at the Metropole Hotel, Tsukiji on 4 February 1899 to celebrate the founding of the Anglo-Japanese Inns of Court Association on that day.

FAREWELL TO JAPAN

On 29 March 1900 a telegram from Lord Salisbury indicated that he wanted to send Satow to Peking, and that MacDonald would 'not improbably take your place'. Satow replied that he was '[g]reatly pleased at this mark of Your Lordship's confidence" and accepted the transfer gladly, being better paid (£ 5000 rather than £ 4,000 p.a.) as well as more prestigious.[36] Several high-ranking Japanese regretted his departure, including Itō and Imperial Household Minister Tanaka Mitsuaki, to whom Satow said on 3 May that he 'was only the faithful representative of the friendly feeling of England, and whether I came back or not would make no difference'. His final audience with the Emperor and Empress was on 24 April and he sailed from Yokohama on 4 May.[37]

Note: For a full account of Satow in Tokyo see *The Diaries of Sir Ernest Satow, British Minister in Tokyo (1895–1900): A Diplomat Returns to Japan* edited by Ian Ruxton with an introduction by Nigel Brailey (Tokyo: Edition Synapse, 2003)). This is an annotated and indexed transcript of Satow's diaries for this period.

PART II

FROM THE ALLIANCE

TO ESTRANGEMENT

1900–1941

Postcard produced in Japan celebrating the Anglo-Japanese Alliance. *Courtesy Neil Pedlar*

Introduction

IAN NISH

Relations between Britain and Japan during the years 1900–41 fall into two periods: the period of the Alliance and its aftermath; and the period of estrangement. It is difficult to put dates to these periods since they merge into one another. The relations under the Anglo-Japanese Alliance (1902–23) were on the whole cordial, despite the existence of commercial rivalry between the allies. Good relations did not break down with the end of the Alliance. Partly this was because some of the goodwill of the alliance lingered on. Partly it was because the Alliance ended at the very time when United States-Japanese relations were at an all-time low because of American immigration legislation. Aware of her weakness, Japan decided that she could not keep on bad terms simultaneously with the new hegemonic power in the Pacific, the United States, and the British Empire. So Tokyo was a comparatively comfortable posting for a British envoy during the first three decades of the century. But the combination of the Manchurian Crisis of 1931 and the aftermath of the world depression made it a much less pleasant place until finally the embassy was closed with the outbreak of the Asia-Pacific War in 1941.

The Tokyo legation started the century with a senior staff of eight with outlying consuls numbering 13. It was converted to an embassy in 1906. Sir Claude MacDonald (1906–12) was the first ambassador appointed, though he had previously spent five years as minister (1900–5). In 1925 the profile of the staff was not substantially changed, with nine in Tokyo and 18 consular posts. Thereafter the embassy was enlarged, the Tokyo establishment growing to 12 in 1931 and 23 in 1941 with the consular numbers staying at 20.

The first three incumbents in the new century did not correspond to the stereotype of the career diplomat and had already had exceptional and exacting careers. Indeed the Foreign Office, whether deliberately or coincidentally, appears to have been looking for those whose past experience in Africa or elsewhere in Asia would be appropriate for the Japan scene. All three had had official experience in Africa: Claude MacDonald (Ch. 9) had several postings in east and west Africa; Conyngham Greene (as Peter Lowe's essay reminds us in Ch. 10) had been part of Milner's Kindergarten in South Africa; and Charles Eliot (Ch. 11) had had a remarkably diverse career, serving in Tangier, Samoa and Zanzibar. He was later recalled for the emergency in Siberia, before being re-admitted to the Diplomatic Service in 1919. In other words, all had previously had demanding postings and none came from an orthodox diplomatic stable.

But, despite the talk of reform and 'democratization' of the Diplomatic Service, the Foreign Office, after Eliot's retirement in 1926, chose to appoint the European style of career diplomat. A conventional type of representative was chosen for the Tokyo post which had of course been up-graded since the end of the war. John Tilley (Ch. 12) and Robert Craigie (Ch. 15) had little previous connection with Japan. As Chief Clerk, Tilley had presided over the reform of the Consular Service and was therefore aware of the problems of the Japan branch of that service. He was in any case highly regarded in Whitehall. And, as Antony Best shows, Craigie had had experience of negotiating with the Japanese because of his role in the two London Naval Conferences of 1930 and 1935 and acquired some contacts that way. By contrast, Francis Lindley (Ch. 13) and Robert Clive (Ch. 14) had both worked in Japan in the 1900s soon after joining the Diplomatic Service, though neither had become a linguist.

All seven representatives in the interwar period came from an educational background which was broadly similar, as Table I shows.

TABLE I

MacDonald (1852–1915) [Uppingham and Sandhurst] was appointed at age 48
Greene (1854–1934) [Harrow and Pembroke, Oxford] appointed at 58
Eliot (1862–1931) [Cheltenham and Balliol, Oxford] appointed at 57
Tilley (1869–1951) [Eton and Kings, Cambridge] appointed at 56
Lindley (1872–1950) [Winchester and Magdalen, Oxford] appointed at 59
Clive (1877–1948) [Haileybury and Magdalen, Oxford] appointed at 57
Craigie (1883–1959) [educated privately at Heidelberg] appointed at 54

The group had much in common; their educational background and their ages at the time of appointment were roughly comparable. The old private income requirement for admission to the Diplomatic Service had been removed; but they were comfortable rather than wealthy men. At the same time they were clearly different types. In an informal interview late in life, George Sansom said of Lindley for whom he had a high regard that '. . . he was a country gentleman, . . . the best example of the diplomat who, without great talents, had an enormous fund of common sense and experience. So, when a problem arose, he did what so few modern diplomats do, kept his temper. So he was able to cope with international crises.' By comparison, MacDonald was a soldier and fitted in well with the military-dominated governments of his day in Japan. Eliot had been a fellow of Trinity College, Oxford, and was a distinguished scholar in his own right, a scholar-diplomat in fact in the mould of the Meiji period - but more the former than the latter. He had in fact written about Japan in his *Letters from the Far East* (London, 1907).

Let us remember that Tokyo was recognized as a hardship post. For part of the uncomfortable summer months the envoy would go to the hill-station of Chūzenji near Nikko where he had the use of the villa which Sir Ernest Satow built beside the lake in the 1890s. French, Belgian and Italian representatives also had villas on the lakeside. Other embassy staff too, sought respite from torrid temperatures in Tokyo but had to rent houses in the resort. Ambassadors remained in charge while they were at Chuzenji but, while important papers were sent up to them, the bulk of the routine work was done in Tokyo by juniors. Occasionally, despatches were written to London from Chuzenji.

Nor was Tokyo accommodation always up to the standards of a European embassy and suited to the tastes of an envoy's wife. Dr Hoare makes clear that the Office of Works, the body responsible for buildings, did not always satisfy that harsh test. The earthquake of 1923 (*Kantō Daishinsai*) was certainly also a factor, since embassy buildings were badly destroyed and took almost a decade to rebuild. Life in the Tokyo embassy, especially in the 1920s, had the reputation of being harsh by diplomatic standards.[1]

So there were reasons for diplomats to be reluctant to accept a posting to Tokyo. We know most about the Lindleys who were in 1930 comfortably settled in Lisbon, a location they enjoyed. Francis Lindley accepted the ambassadorship, noting that it was 'promotion at last'. The prospect of moving to 'a big embassy' appealed to him personally. But then the family had second thoughts on the ground that it was so distant from Britain. Unlike European embassies, it was not possible to run home easily in order to discuss matters with officials or settle family issues. Still Lindley persisted. He set off from Southampton via Canada on 27 May and after stopovers en route reached the embassy on 2 July. It had taken him just over one month to travel to Tokyo. Yet, within two months of reaching his new post, Lindley was having second thoughts on his acceptance of the post.[2]

The special characteristic of the post at Tokyo was the existence of the Japan Consular service, which was both a weakness and a strength to any envoy. The officers of this service were trained as linguists, and tested within the embassy by the Japan Secretary, for a long period by J. H. Gubbins. They had often toiled for decades in Japan, e.g. as consuls at treaty ports and by extension in Korea, Taiwan and 'Manchuria'. They were experts in their fields. The task of the ambassador as a professional diplomat was to tap into the expertise of these consular officers. He was conscious of being a generalist, relying for local knowledge on his specialists. This was parallel to the wider debate in the British home civil service between generalists and specialists. For most ambassadors this was no problem. But some in the Diplomatic Service found it more difficult to adjust. Not all ambassadors were receptive of advice from the experts. This was to become one of the controversial points about the operation of the Tokyo embassy in the thirties.

In accordance with the prevailing thinking of the day, there was initially a concentration on the political side of embassy work. There was inevitably a political and strategic aspect to the Anglo-Japanese Alliance but, after it finished in 1923, there was a tendency for the relations between the two countries to become increasingly commercial. Hitherto the commercial side had been carried largely by the consuls at the ports. But it became necessary from the 1920s to create a commercial department within the embassy. Men were imported from the Department of Overseas Trade created in London in

1917 as a joint venture between the Board of Trade and the Foreign Office. These augmented the commercial experts on the ground in Japan. George Sansom, the most prominent of what came to be called Commercial Counsellors, said how glad he was to join the commercial section as it gave him 'great independence in running my own show, disposing of my own time and having to consult nobody.'[3] The diplomats, especially Eliot, did not care to interest themselves in the nitty-gritty of commerce, though commercial issues were increasingly becoming political ones.

That raises the question of communication at various levels. First with the Foreign Office. At the start of the century the method of Tokyo's communication with London was by despatch carried by boat, though sometimes by Russia's Trans-Siberian Railway, a route which often invited the attention of Russian intelligence, and by the trans-Pacific route. The telegram was an option; but its use was discouraged, except in an emergency, because of the parsimony of the Office. This put the diplomat until 1914 at a disadvantage compared to the local journalist who had greater discretion to pass his reports in a crisis by telegram, regardless of cost. Following the First World War, telegrams became the norm though detailed reports were still carried in despatches where there was a considerable time-lag.

British diplomats in Tokyo regularly complained about the one-sidedness of communication home. Many of the important insights in any overseas post came not from official despatches but from the personal letters sent from the ambassador to officials in the Office or to the Foreign Secretary himself. These would not ordinarily be printed or published and could therefore contain indiscreet material. While this practice worked well, it was rare for the outlying ambassador to get a response, except a rare missive from an official. It is hard to know whether to sympathize more with the ambassador who was in the dark but had the time to write or the Whitehall mandarin who was presumably in the light but claimed that he had not the time to pass on his insights. At all events, there were grounds for complaint that the staff in Tokyo were often in the dark about the global considerations or party political concerns, which were influencing policy-making in London.

An attempt was made to keep a balance between those who had experience of Japan and China in staffing the Far Eastern department in the Foreign Office. But, in spite of this balance, there was by the 1930s an underlying feeling, sympathetic towards China and hostile to Japan because of the latter's actions in China and entanglement with Germany. Advice from Tokyo was diverse; and Whitehall was sometimes inclined to accept the judgement of George Sansom on leave in 1934 and 1939 rather than that of the ambassador of the day. One would have to conclude that the Tokyo envoys rarely affected policy radically; and their views, however well reported, were often disregarded. We find this in Nish's article on MacDonald who recommends that the Anglo-Japanese alliance shall not be renewed in 1911, a view which was rejected. Smith's essay makes clear that Eliot is unhappy that his advocacy in favour of the alliance being continued has been overlooked. In Lindley's private letters to friends, he disagrees profoundly with what the Foreign Office and the League of Nations are doing in 1931-3 and admits that he cannot get his message across. Best shows, however, that his successor, Clive, was inclined to steer clear of controversies between the Tokyo embassy and London.

Communication within the growing British diplomatic establishment in Japan was also a problem. Inevitably there was an expansion in the size of staff to cope with the increasing tensions in the east Asian area. We have already written of the commercial staff who had to report direct to the Department of Overseas Trade. Then there were important commercial and financial missions like that of the Federation of British Industries delegation of 1934 and that of Sir Frederick Leith-Ross in the following year. There were also naval and military attachés and from the 1930s air and press attachés. It was almost an impossible task to coordinate the reports and reconcile the private viewpoints of these specialist members of the entourage. So, in the days before a unitary service came in with the Eden reforms of 1943, an ambassador's life was a complex one.

What influence did the British envoys have on the policy-making of the Japanese government? Until 1914 they had some degree of personal influence, though it should not be exaggerated. There was something special about the Alliance period when Japanese cabinet members would call round at the British embassy for a game of billiards and modify their policies to avoid giving offence to Britain. Thereafter it changed in two ways. Firstly, the ambassador lost some of the independence he had formerly enjoyed from his home government. He became a man under orders who had to convey London's wishes to the Tokyo government as Britain's spokesman. With the greater use of the telegram, he began to receive precise instructions and had relatively little discretion. It is doubtful whether British ambassadors had any overwhelming influence on Japan's policy in the interwar years. There had, of course, been many instances even in the Alliance period when Britain carried little weight. Secondly, Japan often preferred to deal with Britain through its London embassy rather than through Tokyo. Despite this, the Japanese Foreign Ministry in general, while recognizing that Britain's global power was waning from the 1920s onwards, continued to show respect for Britain until quite late in the 1930s. Indeed many Japanese diplomats who had been trained in Britain and some other Japanese leaders may have wanted the British alliance to be reinstated (though very few Britons did.) But this respect was not shared more broadly in government, especially in police and military circles. Thus Japan became an uncomfortable posting after 1938. Best's account of the last embassy before war broke out makes clear that Ambassador Craigie took an increasingly tough line towards Japan after the threats which British citizens faced at this time and the arrests which took place in 1940. (Ch. 15) The Burma Road crisis of 1940 shows that sentiment and nostalgia did not count for much.

9
Sir Claude MacDonald
Minister and first Ambassador to Japan, 1900–12

IAN NISH

Sir Claude MacDonald

$\mathbf{M}$acDonald's claim to fame rests with the long period of twelve years he spent as head of the British diplomatic mission in Japan. He went there first as minister from 1900 to 1905 and then became the first ambassador (when the two countries agreed to raise the status of their missions to embassies), and occupied that position till his retirement in 1912. The MacDonalds presided over the British Embassy in the halcyon days of the Anglo-Japanese Alliance, at a time when relations between the countries were closer than they have ever historically been.

Claude Maxwell MacDonald (1852–1915) was educated at Uppingham and Sandhurst and joined the army in 1872. As an officer in the Highland Light Infantry, he was posted as the War Office's representative at the British agency in Cairo during the Egyptian campaign of 1882. He was highly commended by Sir Evelyn Baring (Lord Cromer). He then occupied the position of consul-general, Zanzibar, in 1887–8 and went on to become consul-general of the Oil Rivers (later the Niger Coast) Protectorate, thought to be the most unhealthy and uncomfortable posting in the British Empire.[1] He was knighted by the Conservative government of Lord Salisbury in 1892, the year in which he married Ethel MacDonald (1857–1941). When Salisbury came back to power as prime minister and foreign secretary in 1895, he had to find a replacement for the minister at Peking. He chose MacDonald who had retired from the army and occupied the post from 1896 to 1900. It is often asked how MacDonald who had no experience of the East was chosen for this sensitive position. It appears that he had the strong recommendation of Cromer and had, by his activities in Africa, acquired the confidence of Salisbury. These years proved to be stormy ones for Britain, both from the Chinese and from the other powers: they were the years of high imperialism.

It may be that Salisbury reckoned that MacDonald, as soldier and avowed imperialist, was not ill-suited to the post. But, as contemporaries wrote, he was appointed '. . . to the indignation of the rest of the service.[2]

In spite of this, his years in Peking were agreeable and congenial for those immediately around him. He and his wife looked the part of Britain's representatives. MacDonald was tall, mustachioed and had the craggy good looks of a highlander. Lady MacDonald who was Anglo-Irish was also tall, good-looking, and tactful. They together established a tradition of hospitality at the legation which they were to continue in Tokyo. On the debit side, some have criticized his handling of his staff. The minister at Peking had the responsibility for the large number of members of Her Majesty's China Consular Service who were scattered around the treaty ports on China's coast and rivers. One author writes that MacDonald '. . . left China again without so much as clapping eyes on most of the consular officers whose careers and well-being lay in [his] hands.'[3] This criticism, if true, does seem to be an important one, even if it would hardly have been possible for him to have visited all the outlying consular posts. For those on the compound of legation or embassy, whether Peking or Tokyo, MacDonald was, however, the perfect family man, always solicitous about the 'bairns' of his juniors.

In the summer of 1900 the Legation Quarter in Peking was besieged by the Boxers. MacDonald and his wife were deemed lost. Obituaries were published and arrangements for the funeral were put in train. In fact, MacDonald survived. Because of his military background, he was asked to assume command of the community of the besieged, while Lady MacDonald was fully occupied, attending to the sick and arranging for food supplies. Shiba Gorō, an artillery major in the Japanese legation, was the chief staff officer and most effective collaborator of Claude MacDonald. He helped to establish a good relation between the two nations which he records in his account of the siege. The resistance of the defenders and the success of the allied expeditionary force, to which the Japanese contributed the second largest army, in pushing through to Peking and breaking the siege owed much to the cooperation of the Anglophile Shiba and MacDonald.[4]

MOVE TO JAPAN

The post of British minister to Tokyo was under consideration at the time. Sir Ernest Satow, the present incumbent, had completed five years in Japan and was then on leave in London. When the Peking siege began and MacDonald's life was in peril, Salisbury began to contemplate the despatch of Satow to Peking in order to supervise the peace settlement. There had earlier been a thought that MacDonald might move on to Tokyo. In succeeding telegrams of 16–17 September, Salisbury expressed his gratitude but invited MacDonald to return to England for recuperation. MacDonald, however, replied on 24 September:

> . . . the solicitude of Her Majesty and your Lordship with regard to my health calls for my deep gratitude. The anxieties and hardships of the siege do not, however, appear in any way to have caused my health to suffer. Under these circumstances, I feel that I should not be altogether justified in returning to England. I propose, therefore, that [sic] when my affairs are settled, say in three weeks from now, to leave for Tokio, and to arrange with Sir Ernest Satow to meet him en route, and confer with him.[5]

MacDonald described himself as a soldier-outsider in the diplomatic world. But there was something appropriate in a soldier being posted to Japan where in the Katsura government and among the *Genro* (elder statesmen) the power of the military was considerable. He may have lacked diplomatic finesse and been criticized for this by career diplomats but he was on the whole a sound and energetic British representative. Perhaps he was not unduly tested because the 1900s were a time of good Anglo-Japanese relations. But he had been tested in China and not found wanting. For the historian, too, he was interesting. He was a copious letter-writer. These were not intellectual letters, carefully balanced in judgement and cautious like those of Ernest Satow. They were chatty letters crammed with little bits of gossip, written in a firm hand and (if the historian may be permitted to fantasize) scribbled just in time to make the boat as it left from Yokohama pier. Unlike Satow, he did not think his private diplomatic letters needed to be copied so there are no 'MacDonald papers'. But his letters are scattered in the public record and in the private collections of his friends and contemporaries.[6]

ANGLO-JAPANESE ALLIANCE

MacDonald was very much the diplomat of the Anglo-Japanese Alliance. It is on that aspect that we shall concentrate here. By an odd coincidence he was in Tokyo for the negotiation of the first alliance, the second affiance in 1905 and the third alliance in 1911. In each case the prime negotiations took place in London; and, in Britain's case, it was global issues and imperial considerations which dictated the policy rather than the regional issues of East Asia. This meant that MacDonald and the staff of the Tokyo embassy had a reactive role. Their function was to maintain liaison with the Japanese government while most of the negotiations were channelled through the Japanese Legation in London.

Anglo-Japanese discussions of a fairly imprecise kind took place in London from the spring of 1901. Lord Lansdowne, the new foreign secretary, discussed possibilities with Hayashi Tadasu, the new Japanese minister. Before they embarked on more formal discussions, MacDonald was recalled for consultations and set off from Tokyo on 28 May. The degree of consultation was concealed since he was in any case overdue for leave. As we saw, he had gone directly to his new post in Japan the previous October without taking up the offer of convalescent leave in Britain after his ordeal at Peking. It was plausible, therefore, for Whitehall to state in public that he was visiting Britain to rest and recuperate and receive honours for his efforts in Peking without arousing suspicions about secret diplomacy. But there is evidence that he was fairly frequently consulted during the three months of his return.[7]

In his letters, MacDonald claims to have spoken to the king, to several members of the royal family and the Duke of Cambridge. Perhaps more significant, he travelled to Hatfield to discuss an Anglo-Japanese alliance with the prime minister, Lord Salisbury. MacDonald wrote: '(*En parenthèse* he was rather against the alliance)'.[8] Since Salisbury was later to be the member of the cabinet most resistant to a Japanese alliance, the visitor from Tokyo did not make a convert on this occasion. But it is nonetheless significant that MacDonald who owed his preferment in the diplomatic profession to Salisbury as foreign secretary, should have been assigned to talk things over at Hatfield after serving barely eight months in his new post. He also had several talks with Minister Hayashi who reported to Tokyo his distinct impression that MacDonald's object was to pave the way for serious negotiations. He was therefore seen in Japan as the mouthpiece of the British government and establishment and in the role, familiar to Japanese, of go-between. More formal negotiations began on 31 July. There was, however, something of a hiatus in August while the British ministers repaired to their summer retreats in the hills.

MacDonald himself had taken a holiday in the Scottish highlands and on the continent but his time for return to Japan was at hand. This delay worried Hayashi who was the pace-setter and begged an interview with MacDonald to which he was only too pleased to agree. In this farewell conversation on 30 August, Hayashi confessed that he sensed that Britain was reluctant to make the first move over 'the understanding'. He therefore beseeched MacDonald, when he returned to Tokyo to try to persuade the Japanese leaders, Itō and Komura, to take the initiative. His anxiety was in fact unnecessary because Komura Jutarō who had only taken over as foreign minister in September was not slow to study the papers and make the next move. He made this overture on 16 October which was a week before MacDonald returned to his post. But MacDonald was of course able to provide the Japanese leadership with some local colour about Britain's thinking at the time.

The alliance negotiations were carried through in spite of delays caused paradoxically by the senior statesmen on both sides. For Japan, Itō was reluctant to see a British alliance, though he finally agreed to come to London to put his seal of approval on it. For Britain, Prime Minister Salisbury was also reluctant to take on such a risky commitment as an entanglement with Japan, though he was a minority voice in his own cabinet. The alliance was signed on 30 January 1902 and published on 12 February. As MacDonald reported, the British treaty was enthusiastically welcomed by the Japanese people.

For the rest of MacDonald's stay in Japan the alliance dinners were to be an important anniversary in the diplomatic calendar. It was an important anniversary for the Japanese and an occasion which MacDonald with his gregarious personality relished. Whether in the British Embassy compound or at the villas at the mountain resort of Chūzenji, he and Lady MacDonald were generous hosts.

The alliance was soon followed by Russo-Japanese disputes which eventually led to war in February 1904. During the runup to the war MacDonald had a subtle role to play: he had to restrain Japan and, while avoiding any charge of interfering, advise her statesmen to consider carefully Japan's military strength. Probably this advice was not needed because the foreign minister and the elder statesmen had cool heads and delayed the final decision. Britain's selfish worry was to avoid being drawn into any war which arose. In the event the alliance never came into play. Britain remained neutral, though this did not preclude her from giving financial aid through the London money market after the war began and making coaling and repair hard for the Russian Baltic fleet as it made its way painfully to the East. The British Embassy in Tokyo reflected the feeling in Britain herself that Japan was a popular victor. Lady MacDonald was prominent in her work for the Japanese Red Cross and for charities for soldiers and sailors' families.[10]

THE ALLIANCE IS STRENGTHENED

In the negotiation of the second affiance which was concluded on 12 August 1905, it was again Hayashi, and not MacDonald, who bore the brunt of the negotiations. The foreign ministers, Lansdowne and Komura, were the same as before; but there was no suggestion that the talks would be carried on in Tokyo. The original alliance was due to continue until 1907; but there were reasons why both sides found advantages in carrying out the revisions – which were substantial – earlier. Unlike 1901 MacDonald was not recalled to London for consultation. The new alliance was made in London and took account of Britain's perceived imperial weakness. It was to stay in existence for ten years.

Following Japan's victory against Russia and the conclusion of the new alliance, the Conservative government decided to raise the status of its mission in Tokyo to that of an embassy. The Japanese were honoured and reciprocated. The result was that the existing incumbents, MacDonald and Hayashi, attained the rank of ambassador. There was, of course, the view that MacDonald had already served five years and was due for replacement. But, unlike Hayashi who was shortly instructed to return to Tokyo, MacDonald was allowed (by the new Liberal government) to stay in his post for another tour.

This desire to cement the alliance relationship symbolically led Britain to confer on the Emperor Meiji the Order of the Garter. Edward VII appointed Prince Arthur of Connaught to lead a Garter mission which conferred the decoration in Tokyo on 20 February 1906.[11] MacDonald was, needless to say, much involved. Personal decorations were also exchanged with great liberality. Ambassador Hayashi was given the KCVO, while MacDonald was presented with the GCVO and sworn as a member of the Privy Council in 1906 and also became Dean of the Diplomatic Corps in Tokyo.

MacDonald took a long-deferred leave in the spring of 1907. He was able to fit into the London scene without difficulty. Thus he reports on a dinner party where seated '. . . between John Morley and Jack Fisher last night I received much instruction'.[12] He was able to clear up some commercial matters, dealing with perpetual leases and possible British contracts in the South Manchurian Railway zone. He was able to take part in the early sessions of the army and navy talks in May to work out the strategic implications of the second alliance in the presence of Admiral Yamamoto Gombei for the navy and General Nishi Kanjirō for the army. Sir Claude probably made some contribution to the occasion with the benefit of his local knowledge. He returned to Tokyo by the weekly international train on the Trans-Siberian railway. Lady MacDonald lost all her baggage as was the hazard of that route.[13]

MacDonald enjoyed a period of leave in 1909 when the Chargé d'affaires was Horace Rumbold. While he was on good terms with his Chief, Rumbold records in his diary that 'Our Government did not trust their man here to be sufficiently energetic in his language and think he looks at things too much from the Japanese point of view'.[14] There were times when the minutes of the officials in Whitehall showed impatience, if not exasperation, with MacDonald who was very often suspected of not passing on their complaints with adequate forcefulness. He was a proud ambassador of long experience and felt that he had a feel for the ways of Tokyo. There is often a state of creative tension between Whitehall and a post abroad. That certainly came to exist with MacDonald. But George Sansom who was his private secretary writes of him with affection and understanding. It was an exceptional time for the British Embassy when Japanese cabinet members used to visit it frequently, admirals and generals called in to play billiards, and the Japanese social élite enjoyed embassy parties greatly. In view of the role of the military in Japanese political life after the Russo-Japanese war, MacDonald was an appropriate figure who was able to speak to the leaders on the same wavelength.[15]

Apart from Whitehall impatience there was also a growing dissatisfaction in commercial circles. Ambassador d'Anethan, a shrewd observer of the Tokyo scene, wrote that MacDonald '. . . has lately been very much attacked in financial circles . . . for not defending English interests with enough energy'.[16] Writers under commercial influence like Putnam Weale (B. Lennox Simpson) were hostile to him. It is doubtful what substance there was in these complaints. British interests had not made much progress as a result of the alliance and of the support given to Japan during the war; but that was scarcely the fault of MacDonald who, if he was Japanophile, was still intrepid in taking up with the Japanese matters of British national interest. Whitehall appears to have recognized this because it granted him an extension of his appointment in 1910 for two years.

PROBLEMS WITH WHITEHALL

In 1911 the underlying tensions between MacDonald and Whitehall came to a head. Japan, fearing that the alliance might not be renewed when it came to its completion date in 1915, asked for its renewal to be advanced. The British cabinet at its meeting on 29 March decided to propose that it be renewed straightaway till 1921, that is for ten years. On 3 April Japan and Britain entered into a new commercial treaty which finally gave Japan tariff autonomy on terms not unfavourable to Britain. In both cases, the decision had been taken in London with only limited consultation with the Tokyo embassy. MacDonald was clearly put out. Understandably MacDonald was indignant that he had not been asked for his views. On 5 April he sent off an urgent telegram:

> Next few years, particularly those during which the alliance has still to run, are of vital importance to Japan; and her policy in Corea, Manchuria and China generally during those years will be valuable indication to us whether we should renew alliance at its expiration or not . . . If we do not renew until alliance expires four years hence we can pretty well rely on tariff not being denounced before then and in other ways the uncertainty of renewal would be useful lever and also check to any unnecessarily forward policy.[17]

In reply MacDonald was told that the value of an American arbitration treaty must 'outweigh those urged by you on other side'. By implication he was being told that he was taking too narrow a view of the transaction. He did not give up the fight, however, arguing:

> . . . though a modification of the Agreement might with great advantage be made now, its definite extension at the present juncture should if possible be avoided.

Grey concluded that 'to modify without extending would create a most undesirable impression.'[18] The Tokyo embassy had been outpointed. Soon after MacDonald left by sea for Britain to attend the coronation of King George V. He was able to see the correspondence while he was in London and discussed the issue with Grey. But the consultations took place after the basic decision had been made.

On 13 July the third alliance treaty was signed in London in a more subdued atmosphere than greeted the earlier treaties.[19] It took account especially of Japan's annexation of Korea the previous year and omitted the clause dealing with Korean independence. This was the focal point of the treaty and of the ambassador's final tour. Not long after MacDonald returned to Japan in July, he launched himself on an energetic tour of northeast Asia. It was appropriate in the circumstances that he should visit Korea and the Kuantung Leased Territory where Britain had problems to resolve with Japan and examine the situation for himself Sidney and Beatrice Webb happened to meet the embassy party while they were on their way from Japan to China and recorded on 22 October:

> On [crossing] over the Yalu River into Manchuria, we ran across the British Ambassador, Sir Claude MacDonald who was journeying in state through Manchuria and Korea, as the guest of the South Manchurian Railway administration ... Although we had brought introductions, both official and personal, to the MacDonalds and to two of the attaches, they had not managed to see us. When we did meet at Antung, they were extremely desirous to be civil and they were, I think, [conscious] that they had not "played up" sufficiently.[20]

While this reveals much about the Webbs, it reveals something also about the MacDonalds. Although normally gregarious, they ran a mile from intellectuals, especially those suspected of having leanings towards international socialism.

1912 was a traumatic year for the Japanese. The Emperor Meiji died on 30 July and was buried in September in the presence of dignitaries from around the world, Britain being represented by Prince Arthur of Connaught. The ceremony was evidence that the new and modern Japan had been internationally recognized. General Nogi, one of the heroes of the Russo-Japanese war, and his wife took their own lives the same day as the burial. This showed that the ancient Shinto traditions and values of Japan were clearly still alive also. There was general recognition that it was the end of an era.

MacDonald had to address the question of whether the demise of the Meiji emperor would bring instability to the most stable and successful nation in Asia. He informed London what was known to inner circles in Japan:

> Intellectually [the Taishō emperor) is generally supposed to be somewhat wanting, and that is certainly the opinion the casual observer would arrive at after some moments' conversation.[21]

Sir Claude's view was that for stability to be achieved, he stood in need of a man of strength and knowledge of the ways of the world. He saw it as a role for Prince Katsura who had resigned as prime minister earlier in the year and was in St Petersburg when the Meiji emperor's illness became serious. He immediately returned, reaching Tokyo nine days after the emperor's death. He was then appointed to the post of Grand Chamberlain (*Nai Daijin*) and Lord Keeper of the Privy Seal.

Against this background of uncertainty MacDonald made his exit from Japan at the beginning of November. The Japanese press, never wholly predictable in its attitudes to the alliance, was united in expressing Japan's affection and appreciation of his efforts on behalf of Anglo-Japanese understanding.[22] His immediate successor, Chargé d'affaires Horace Rumbold, thought that he had served Britain's objects well, most notably by restraining Japan.[23] MacDonald, while he never became chairman of the Japan Society of London, did lecture to it in 1913 on the subject of his experiences – and those of Major Shiba – during the Seige of Peking Legations, a topic which he clearly regarded as one of the high-points of his adventure-laden life.[24] Sir Claude was not permitted to enjoy a long retirement and died in September 1915, much lamented.

Lady Ethel MacDonald had shared her husband's life in Tokyo and, like him, had enjoyed her long sojourn in Japan. Her role is described thus:

> Lady MacDonald was a model Ambassadress – very good-looking with a fine presence, clever and tactful: she entertained largely, and her kind nature and sympathy endeared her to all the English in Japan, especially the large colony in Yokohama.[25]

Lady MacDonald was renowned for her wit. When General Horatio Herbert Kitchener visited Japan in the summer of 1909, he acquired the reputation among the British community for meanness: for taking all he could get in the way of presents and giving nothing in return. 'Lady M.', (as she was widely known) commented, '. . . he would take a piece of sugar out of a bird's cage'[26] – a remark which, needless to say, travelled like greased lightning round the embassy compound. After her return to England, she lived for twenty-five years at Royal Cottage, Kew, which was allocated to her by King George V. For two decades she led an active life for charity, being especially active for the Overseas Nursing Association. In 1935 she was made a Dame of the British Empire in her own right. She died in 1941 at the age of 84, after seven years of illness.[27]

CONCLUSION

There can be no doubt that the MacDonalds presided over a special Anglo-Japanese relationship and may in the decade of their residence have contributed to that relationship. They were fortunate in having good access to Japanese ministers, bureaucrats, sailors and soldiers. One of the most baffling things for those in Whitehall was to understand the power structure in Japan, especially the role of the emperor and the elder statesmen. Unusually among diplomats, Claude MacDonald was able to throw some light on this, as when he attended a banquet on the occasion of the visit of the Royal Navy squadron to Tokyo in the autumn of 1905. In one of his private letters which did not betray many marks of Eton and Balliol, he wrote:

> His Majesty [the Meiji emperor] chatted most amicably with everybody around. The Imperial Princes, Arisugawa and Kanin, who sat on either side, treated him with marked deference but Marquis Ito and Count Inouye (the latter sat next to me) seemed to speak on absolute terms of equality and cracked jokes which made this direct descendant of the Sun roar with laughter. It was a great revelation to me and one which pleased me very much for though a Mikado he seems very human.[28]

The same inside knowledge of the Japanese scene suffuses MacDonald's Annual Reports which he wrote for the years 1907 to 1911. The Tokyo embassy was close to the Japanese bureaucracy which was inclined to disclose matters on which it might be secretive in other respects. Not least valuable in these reports are MacDonald's views on the personalities of the Japanese leaders which bear the stamp of his own authorship. He had been intimately involved with the Japanese scene for a decade, and earlier at Peking for another four. Although he had no knowledge of the Japanese language and did not try to acquire any, he was something of a Japanese expert by sheer length of service.[29]

MacDonald had been Britain's representative in Japan for twelve years and had therefore as minister and ambassador been the second longest-serving Chief in the British mission ever. He had presided over a decade of cordiality in relations (1900–11). At the time of his departure the relationships had entered into a decade of suspicion, though the alliance continued. Even Sir Claude, who was generally regarded as Japanophile, was aware of this deterioration. He had reservations about Japan's continental policy as we saw in 1911. In spite of this, he survived – partly, one feels, because the ministers in London liked his simple approach to foreign affairs; but partly also because MacDonald was the symbol of the alliance. To relieve him of his duties would have meant cutting the knot of Anglo-Japanese cordiality.

In the month before their departure, Sir Claude and Lady MacDonald made the gastronomic sacrifices which the British expect of their diplomats. They were entertained by the French embassy (16 October), the Russian embassy (17 October), Marquis Nabeshima (18 October), the Cambridge Club (18 October), the Swedish legation (23 October), the British Club (Eikoku kyōkai, 25 October), Prince Tokugawa (29 October) and the Tokyo Club (1 November). Such were the friends of the British ambassador in 1912. Long suffering and exhausted, the MacDonalds slumped in their seats on the 8.30 am train on 4 November from Shimbashi, bidding farewell to Tokyo for ever.[30]

10
Sir William Conyngham Greene
Ambassador to Japan, 1912–19

PETER LOWE

William Conyngham Greene (1854–1934) came from an Anglo-Irish background. Born on 29 October 1854, he was the elder son of R. J. Greene and the Hon. Louisa, daughter of the third Baron Plunkett and grandson of Richard Wilson Greene. He was educated at Harrow and Pembroke College, Oxford, where he was an open classical scholar in 1873. He gained first class moderations in 1874, a BA in 1877 and MA in 1880. Greene entered the Foreign Office with a Clerkship on 9 October 1877 when Disraeli was prime minister. He passed an examination in public law in March 1880 and served in Athens, Stuttgart and Darmstadt, The Hague, Brussels and Tehran. In 1884 Greene married Lady Lily Frances Stopford, daughter of the fifth Earl of Courtown; they had two sons and a daughter. The two principal diplomatic appointments held by Greene were in South Africa and Japan. In both cases he assumed post at times of accelerating tension and turbulence. Before turning to his service in Tokyo, it is necessary to consider briefly his experience in Pretoria.

After three years serving in Tehran (where he gained an allowance for knowledge of Persian), Greene was appointed Her Majesty's Agent in Pretoria, under the Colonial Office, with the personal rank as a Chargé d'Affaires in the Diplomatic Service. He assumed post on 25 August 1896. Greene arrived at a period of deep mutual suspicion between the British government, headed by the third Marquess of Salisbury, and the government of the South African Republic, headed by Paul Kruger. Boer hostility to the British was based on anxiety over the erratic extension of British imperialism and was driven by a tenacious resolve to defend Boer culture from British domination. The discovery of gold rendered the situation more combative because of the influx of Uitlanders keen to make money fast. Greene was faced with challenges that would have taxed the skills of the most hardened diplomat: he had to deal with the vacillating approaches of the government in London, an ambitious and ruthless British High Commissioner in Capetown (Sir Alfred Milner) and the obduracy of Kruger and his senior colleagues.[1] Greene succeeded Sir Jacobus de Wet as Agent in Pretoria. When he arrived the High Commissioner was Sir Hercules Robinson but the latter was soon replaced by Sir Alfred Milner.

The acrimony between Britain and the South African Republic need not have led to war. Younger members of Kruger's administration, notably the brilliant J. C. Smuts, were more conciliatory in approach: the passage of time, had caution prevailed, would have permitted a change in leadership in the South African Republic which could have led to the attainment of warmer relations with Britain.[2] This would have entailed the pursuance of moderate policies in London and Capetown. The heavy defeat of Lord Rosebery's Liberal government in the general election of 1895 led to the formation of a Unionist government, bringing together the Conservatives, headed by Lord Salisbury, and the Liberal Unionists of whom the most outstanding was Joseph Chamberlain. The most combustible element, however, came in consequence of the fateful appointment of Sir Alfred Milner as High Commissioner. Milner was deeply committed to the expansion of British control in South Africa and was reluctant to compromise. Chamberlain also favoured the growth of British power but he was, in part, constrained by the cabinet, notably by the Chancellor of the Exchequer, Sir Michael Hicks Beach. The latter eventually discerned the fundamental error in appointing Milner: he had 'outChamberlained Chamberlain' through his aggressive policy towards the South African Republic.[3]

Conyngham Greene arrived to achieve a diplomatic solution if possible. Left to his own devices, he might well have done so. On the eve of the outbreak of war in 1899, Greene engaged in important discussions with Kruger's State Attorney, J. C. Smuts. These occurred in July and August 1899: Greene encouraged Smuts to accept that the British government would respond positively to compromise proposals devised by Smuts. Milner disliked Greene's reaction to Smuts' initiative and criticized Greene for having gone 'much too far' in conciliation.[4] Both Greene and Smuts were handicapped by the prejudices of their superiors: Milner wanted to place the South African Republic under British control and Kruger wanted to rally the Boers against the British. F. W. Reitz, State Secretary in Pretoria, who was fond of *Treasure Island* by R. L. Stevenson, cynically remarked that Kruger's government was preparing to hand 'the black spot to Long John Conyngham Greene'.[5] And so Greene's endeavours to reach a diplomatic solution failed because of the intransigence of others. He departed from Pretoria on 11 October 1899 and was granted a temporary pension. He was knighted in 1900 and was appointed as Envoy Extraordinary to the Swiss Confederation. Subsequently he served in Bucharest and Copenhagen before receiving appointment as Ambassador Extraordinary and Plenipotentiary at Tokyo and Consul-General for the Empire of Japan on 1 December 1912. He was sworn a Privy Councillor in the same month. Greene served in Tokyo until April 1919.

Greene arrived in Japan during a time of fundamental transition in Anglo-Japanese relations. It differed from his experience in South Africa in that an alliance existed between Britain and Japan and there was no likelihood of armed conflict arising between the allies in the near future. But there were certain similarities with his service in Pretoria. The Anglo-Japanese Alliance was concluded in 1902; it was then revised and extended in 1905 and 1911.[6] The Alliance was important for both signatories and neither thought seriously of ending the agreement. However, storm clouds were beginning to gather. The interests of the two countries were gradually diverging. Britain wished to defend its global interests as best it could and had no interest in extending the empire before the outbreak of the First World War in 1914. Japan was a developing, expanding power and this factor was bound to produce friction. The catalyst was the Chinese revolution of 1911–12 which brought about the end of the ancient empire and the proclamation of a republic of China. Japanese civilian leaders and generals feared that instability in China could jeopardize Japanese interests. Some army officers and financiers began to increase support for the southern republicans, led by Dr Sun Yat-sen. Sun had lived in temporary exile in Japan in the first decade of the twentieth century and had cooperated with the nationalist adventurers (the *shishi*) of the Kokūryūkai (the 'River Amur Society' or 'Black Dragon Society').[7] The British foreign secretary, Sir Edward Grey, wished to discourage Japanese ambition in China while recognizing that some degree of Japanese expansion, as in Korea and Manchuria, was unavoidable. Clashing British and Japanese interests in China led to some of the most challenging problems faced by Greene during his six years as ambassador.

How well placed was Conyngham Greene for the demands of his new appointment? He was fifty-eight years of age in 1912 and had served in a wide variety of posts. He had been tested profoundly in Pretoria and, as we have seen, the situation there was beyond his ability – or the ability of any career diplomat – to surmount. Greene possessed a calm personality and he could bring a fresh perspective to bear on Anglo-Japanese relations, not encumbered by previous bias of having served in Eastern Asia. On the other hand, he lacked detailed knowledge of Japan and was compelled to learn fast. While conscientious and competent, he was not a man of deep perception or originality. He succeeded Sir Claude MacDonald, a soldier turned diplomat, who possessed much experience through having served in Peking and Tokyo.[8] It would have been preferable for Greene to have started in Tokyo in a placid period during which he could have established his bearings before concentrating on the more contentious issues. But the same could be said of his arrival in South Africa in 1896.

Greene was soon faced with the demands of the deteriorating situation in China and the associated criticisms of Japan advanced by the British Chargé d'Affaires in Peking, Beilby Alston. The latter had temporarily replaced Sir John Jordan who was on leave in Britain. A rebellion broke out in China in April 1913: the supporters of Sun Yat-sen took up arms against the autocratic president, Yuan Shih-k'ai. They were given financial support and arms by Japanese sympathizers including some army officers; Yuan proved successful in crushing the rebellion. A fierce debate resulted between critics and defenders of Japan within the Foreign Office in London. Suspicion of Japanese motives was growing and some officials entertained doubts as to the viability of the alliance in the longer term. Alston expressed his criticisms vehemently and Greene was compelled to respond. He sent a despatch to Sir Edward Grey on 12 September 1913 in which he pointed out that Alston could not prove that the Japanese government was undermining the alliance: 'I have endeavoured to make it clear that while there is little doubt that individual Japanese

were active in the recent events in China, there is no evidence that the
Imperial Government were a party to them.'[9] Greene argued that Japan
would consolidate its position in Manchuria and would not withdraw from
Manchuria in order to expand in central and southern China. He held that
the alliance remained a cornerstone in Japanese foreign policy. His South
African experience led Greene to remark that Lord Salisbury's government
had failed, during the 1890s, to prevent arms reaching South Africa and the
Japanese authorities were in a similar predicament over China.[10] Greene was
correct in stating that the Japanese government had no intention of ending
the alliance in 1913 but Alston was right to emphasize the emerging political
and economic differences between Britain and Japan as a consequence of
developments in China.

Britain had taken the lead in establishing occidental imperialism in China
during the nineteenth century. British firms dominated much of the trade in
the treaty ports. Grey and the Foreign Office were adamant in defending
British investments; they were determined to ensure that British influence in
the Yangtze valley was maintained. Curiously, Britain's relations with Japan,
France and Russia encountered increasing strain because of diverging interests in China between 1911 and 1914. Britain had an alliance with Japan and
ententes with France and Russia, dating from 1904 and 1907. Yet Britain's
partners in these agreements wished to foster their own economic ambitions
at Britain's expense in China. Railway concessions were particularly valuable
for combined political, economic and strategic reasons. Foreign avarice in
China was aptly compared by *The Economist* newspaper to an episode in a
famous Edwardian farce – 'It reminds us of a scene in *Charley's Aunt*'.[11]
Greene believed that the most sensible approach would be for Britain and
Japan to observe the continuance of each other's spheres of interest in the
Yangtze valley and Manchuria respectively.[12] The Gaimushō contemplated
developing the Anglo-Japanese Alliance into an economic, in addition to the
existing political-strategic, vehicle. Greene was not in favour of such a development, writing privately to the Foreign Office: 'If the Alliance is good
enough as it stands, why enlarge its scope? However that may be, it seems to
be beyond doubt that the Japanese are disliked and distrusted in our sphere
in China and that our co-operation with them would not be likely to be popular with our own commercial community.'[13] The permanent
under-secretary in the Foreign Office, Sir Arthur Nicolson, and Sir Edward
Grey concurred that Britain should not enter into a closer economic relationship with Japan.[14]

In March 1914 Greene delivered a note to the Gaimushō reiterating Grey's
determination to preserve the British sphere of interest in the Yangtze region:
'I have the honour to remind your Excellency that the Japanese interests
referred to cannot compare in magnitude or extent with the immense British
interests which have been so long established in the Yangtze region and
which are increasing every day; and I am to state that the policy of His
Majesty's Government aims simply at safeguarding these British interests by
maintaining control over the lines of communication . . .'[15] A change in
administration occurred in Tokyo in March 1914 when the government
headed by Admiral Yamamoto Gombei fell in consequence of serious bribery
allegations involving the navy. The new government was led by Count
Ōkuma Shigenobu, long an advocate of a more democratic system in Japan.
The foreign minister was Baron Katō Takaaki who had served successfully as

ambassador in London. Katō strongly supported the Anglo-Japanese Alliance but also favoured a more aggressive approach in advancing Japanese economic activity in China. Katō's marital links with Mitsubishi might well have stimulated his forward policy. Katō indicated, in June 1914, that Japanese interests in the Yangtze region would be advanced. In addition, he spoke privately to Greene to complain of the negative British policy.[16] Greene was broadly sympathetic to Japan but he entirely agreed with Grey's approach over China: 'I am glad we are all agreed about Japanese interference in the Yangtze Valley. Anxious as I am to help the Japanese, I cannot help feeling that while they will never let us into their spheres, they are trying to steal a march into ours, and this is not cricket between Allies'.[17]

Therefore, in the summer of 1914 Anglo-Japanese friction was growing and Greene was confronted with the problem of standing firm over British interests in China while not allowing this to rock the alliance too severely. At this point the grave crisis in Europe, resulting from the events in Sarajevo on 28 June 1914, led to swift descent into war in July-August 1914. Britain's relationship with Japan was important from several angles of approach. In fulfilment of the assumptions underlying British naval policy since 1907, the assistance of the Japanese navy was required in Far Eastern and Pacific waters. However, this in itself caused profound suspicion in the United States, Australia and New Zealand. They had regarded Japan with anxiety since Japan's defeat of Russia in the war of 1904–5. It was essential to maintain cohesion within the British Empire and Britain's relationship with the United States would be of crucial significance in the midst of a huge war. This contributes to explaining the way in which Sir Edward Grey dealt with issues concerning Japan's entry into the First World War. Grey was a skilful and perceptive foreign secretary but he erred in handling relations with Japan in August 1914. In his attempt to allay concern in the United States, Australia and New Zealand, Grey offended Japan by making obvious the lack of trust in future Japanese conduct. Grey's doubts possessed some validity but the maladroit way in which Japan was treated in August 1914 pushed the Ōkuma government towards a more assertive policy. Greene had to find the most appropriate diplomatic means, in 1914–15, of preventing a pronounced deterioration in Anglo-Japanese relations.

Katō Takaaki was the key personality in determining the response in Tokyo to the outbreak of war in Europe. Katō believed that Japan must participate and declare war on Germany. During the hectic activity in London following the British decision to go to war against Germany, Sir Edward Grey requested Japanese assistance on 6 August. Katō wished to act at once under the terms of the Anglo-Japanese Alliance. Japanese involvement would facilitate expansion in China. Grey feared that a Japanese formal declaration of war would alarm the United States, Australia and New Zealand. Accordingly, he endeavoured to dissuade Japan from formal entry and he tried to set limitations to Japanese actions. The Admiralty deemed Japanese naval assistance to be necessary in order to protect trade routes from a German squadron headed by von Spee and from German raiders. Greene was engaged in delicate exchanges with the Gaimushō. Katō emphasized that the Okuma government had decided to declare war on Germany, although he assured Greene that 'Japan's action will be strictly limited to measures which are absolutely indispensable ... British Government may rest assured that Japanese Government, in deciding her present attitude, had not been prompted by any desire for territorial aggrandisement or by any motives of prompting her selfish ends'.[18] Greene realized how necessary it was to establish a basis for Anglo-Japanese co-operation, the alternative being unilateral action by Japan. He implied some criticism of vacillation in London:

> It is, in my opinion, absolutely necessary that the intentions of His Majesty's Government should be made known as soon as possible . . . What we have to decide is whether it would be more advantageous for us to allow Japan to act alone, after having asked her aid, or to give in to her now, and by so doing so put her under an obligation which we can bring up when, after operations are ended, the process of cleaning up in China is begun.[19]

Grey was preoccupied in defining geographical restrictions to Japanese action. Operations should 'not extend beyond Asiatic waters westward of the China Seas or to any foreign territory except territory in German occupation on the continent in Eastern Asia'.[20] Katō informed Greene that his government could not accept the geographical constraints proposed by Grey. On 15 August Japan sent an ultimatum to Germany demanding withdrawal of German armed ships from Japanese and Chinese waters plus the surrender of the leased territory of Kiaochow in Shantung province of China, within one month. If Germany did not comply, by noon on 23 August, Japan would be in a state of war with Germany.[21] Therefore, on 23 August 1914, Japan entered formally into the First World War. Greene dealt with various diplomatic exchanges, involving Anglo-Japanese military operations against the German fortress at Tsingtao, and Japanese, Australian and New Zealand action against German-occupied islands in the Pacific. Considerable friction occurred, since the Japanese armed forces were determined to assert primacy and to make the most of this splendid opportunity to advance Japanese expansion in East Asia and the Pacific. The fortress of Tsingtao was duly captured in November 1914. By the end of 1914 the German-held islands north and south of the Equator had been captured, the Japanese occupying the more northerly islands and Australian and New Zealand forces assumed control of those below the Equator. The United States viewed matters with much concern but President Woodrow Wilson's Democratic administration had no shortage of problems to contend with in the Atlantic as well as in the Pacific.

The next stage saw Japan acting unilaterally, as Greene had feared in August. Predictably this comprised a resolute Japanese attempt to strengthen Japan's role in China. Within Japan different official and unofficial circles formulated specific and broad aims for political, economic and strategic exploitation of China. The Gaimushō wished to extend the leases of the territorial concessions inherited from Tsarist Russia in 1905. Financial interests (the *zaibatsu*) joined with the Gaimushō in wanting to develop Japanese activity in the Yangtze valley at the expense of Britain and France. The army was particularly interested in Manchuria. Unofficial groups included the nationalist societies, notably the Kokuryūkai, which advocated Pan-Asianism with Japan liberating Asian brethren from occidental domination: this would be assisted through persuading (or, more accurately, coercing) the Chinese government into appointing Japanese advisers, so as to consolidate Japanese influence. Thus the notorious 'Twenty-one Demands' materialized in December 1914 and this marked the start of another serious crisis for Greene to handle.

Katō met Greene on 24 January 1915 and gave him a summary of the demands but omitted the fifth group, as conveyed to President Yuan Shih-k'ai. Katō observed that the demands 'were not as far-reaching as some parties in Japan desired, but he was putting them forward with the hope that they would result in the establishment of good relations between Japan and China. They were made in pursuance of a scheme which had been elaborated long ago by him'.[22] The Foreign Office soon learned from a Russian source that Japan had put forward more extreme demands than those communicated to Greene. In an interview with a correspondent of The Times newspaper, on 10 February 1915, Katō admitted that he had forwarded 'wishes' in addition to 'demands': these included a preference for obtaining railway concessions in the Yangtze valley.[23] Greene visited Katō upon hearing the news from the correspondent (Katō had asked that it not be published) and the foreign minister replied truculently that Japan was prepared to act independently in advancing its interest, just as Britain had done in the past.[24] Katō modified his stance subsequently when faced with a robust response from Grey and a recommendation from the Japanese Embassy in London that he should adopt a more conciliatory approach.[25] Greene did all he could to achieve a more positive response from the Gaimushō. The Minister in Peking, Sir John Jordan, was critical of the 'British admirers' of Japan who had not revealed sufficient tenacity in protecting British interests.[26] Beilby Alston expressed blunt criticism of Greene in a personal letter to Jordan. He commented sardonically on:

> ... the faith which the Tokio [sic] Embassy appear to have placed in the Japanese all through that period in spite of all we did at Peking to enlighten them. The idea that they were not continuing to play straight never seems to have been shaken until the full text of the demands must have given Greene a rude awakening. They, the Japs., seem able to hypnotize our people over there – Greene wrote some time ago that he did not know what he would do if Katō was turned out of office . . .[27]

It was true that Greene had placed particular faith in Katō, bearing in mind the latter's close identification with the creation and maintenance of the Anglo-Japanese Alliance. But Britain could not afford a full-scale dispute with Japan in time of war, which could result in Japan deciding to change sides and support Germany. This was ultimately the answer to the criticisms expressed by Jordan and Alston. The Chinese president showed much skill in delaying concessions to Japan for as long as he could. Yuan's aim was to encourage foreign representations to Tokyo and to stimulate dissent within Japanese ruling circles over Katō's diplomacy. This proved a successful strategy up to a point. Britain, France, Russia and the United States protested at the scope of Japanese designs and at the want of frankness in Katō's conduct. Katō had already alienated the *genro* (elder statesmen) by refusing to consult them, as his predecessors had done. Katō's inability to compel Yuan Shih-k'ai to accept the Twenty-one Demands precipitated a domestic crisis from which Katō emerged the loser. The *genro* insisted on a full review of policy, the outcome being agreement between the Ōkuma government and the *genro* that an ultimatum would be sent, to Yuan, based on groups one to four of the demands while group five, which was of a generalized character, was withdrawn. China was in no position to fight Japan and Yuan had no choice other than to sign treaties in which he conceded an extension of Japanese rights in Manchuria and the Yangtze valley. It was an empty victory for Katō: his diplomatic reputation was under-

mined by the acrid international and domestic controversy and he resigned as
foreign minister later in August 1915.

Greene experienced disillusionment with Japan, as he revealed in a letter
to Sir Horace Rumbold:

> It has all been a very bitter experience for me after the close and personal
> relations in which I had been with these people during the critical stages of
> the war and up till the fall of Tsingtao. I need not tell you how disappointed
> I was, and so were my Allied Colleagues, when this was sprung upon us all,
> when our hands were full elsewhere. It is very typical of Japan, but it leaves
> an unpleasant impression behind.[28]

In a subsequent letter to Sir Walter Langley, Greene described the Japanese as
'opportunists to the backbone'. He added, accurately, that 'The fortunes of
war had placed the ball at Baron Katō's feet and he kicked it, that was all'.[29]
Diplomatic pressure from the Western powers led by Britain and the United
States, combined with the acrimonious domestic crisis in Tokyo, brought the
Twenty-one Demands crisis to an end in May 1915. It was a major watershed
in the evolution of the Anglo-Japanese Alliance. The Foreign Office, and
Conyngham Greene personally, were pushed towards the conclusion that the
long-term continuation of the alliance was not desirable.

Anglo-Japanese relations were still strained later in 1915 and into 1916.
Towards the end of 1916 changes in administrations occurred in London and
Tokyo. The coalition government led by H. H. Asquith was replaced by
another coalition headed by David Lloyd George. In Japan Ōkuma Shigenobu
was succeeded by Field Marshal Terauchi Masatake, a protégé of Prince
Yamagata Aritomo. Thus Japan reverted to a bureaucratic government of the
older type. At first sight this might have suggested that Britain would
encounter more difficulty but the Terauchi government presided over an
improvement in relations. The new foreign minister, Baron Motono Ichirō,
had served previously as ambassador to Russia and he wished to rectify the
damage caused by the adventurous China policy of his predecessor.[30] Motono
advocated a cautious policy of advancing Japanese interests in China more
gradually and of establishing cordiality in relations with the Occidental powers. Greene observed that 'we can hardly hope for a more friendly
Government than the present'.[31] Urged on by Yamagata, Terauchi worked to
achieve closer cooperation with political parties represented in the Diet. This
was in part accomplished with the establishment of the Advisory Council on
Foreign Relations which included representatives from the cabinet, privy
council and political parties.[32]

The exigencies of war in the form of the dire pressure faced by the Royal
Navy led the Lloyd George government to request Japanese naval assistance
in the Mediterranean and south Atlantic. Greene forwarded the proposal to
the Japanese government in January 1917. Motono made clear that Japan
would require assurances relating to Shantung and the Pacific islands occupied by Japan earlier in the war. Greene held that Japan was merely asking for
formal confirmation of the status quo and there was no point in arguing over
this. As a sign of good faith Japan swiftly agreed to provide the naval help
requested by Britain.[33] In return Britain acknowledged Japanese claims
regarding Shantung and the Pacific islands north of the Equator. Britain
requested reciprocal acknowledgement of the occupation, by forces from the
British Empire, of islands south of the Equator: this was forthcoming.

In April 1917 the United States entered into the First World War. Relations between the United States and Japan had encountered growing friction for the previous decade and the arrival of the United States as an ally compelled a reassessment of Anglo-Japanese relations. Greene produced an important analysis in a communication to Langley, sent in August 1917. Greene referred to the discrete sources of tension in relations, citing Japanese arrogance and opportunism; the long-term trend of Japanese expansion; the support for Indian dissidents expressed by some Japanese; economic aims advanced by Japanese companies with official endorsement; alleged Japanese aspirations regarding the Netherlands East Indies (Indonesia); Japanese ambitions in China; and racial strife, illustrated in problems concerning Japanese residence in the British dominions. Suspicion between the United States and Japan was deep and was unlikely to be reversed in the foreseeable future. Greene suggested that the Anglo-Japanese Alliance should be continued for the time being but that, in the longer term, the alliance might be merged 'in a triangular arrangement between Great Britain, the United States and Japan'.[34] Greene added that 'I cannot help thinking that the present hollow friendship cannot be continued and must in due course be resolved into some relation at once less intimate and more genuine; and that we might well try to bring in America on our side to redress the balance in the Far East'.[35] The Foreign Office was sympathetic but could discern only too clearly the difficulty of surmounting American isolationism which was likely to reappear after the First World War. However, the exchange between Greene and the Foreign Office pointed interestingly to the post-war debates in which Greene participated prior to the deliberations in the Washington Conference.

The Bolshevik Revolution in Russia in November 1917 led to renewed tension in Anglo-Japanese relations. Japanese leaders were alarmed at the instability in Siberia and the dangers this could pose for Japanese interests in East Asia. In addition, reports from Japanese representatives in Europe conveyed doubt as to the outcome of the war.[36] Some in the Japanese army believed that Germany would triumph and the Terauchi government revealed a less enthusiastic approach to cooperating closely with Britain in the latter part of 1917 and early in 1918. After lengthy debate on the merits of intervening in Siberia, ruling circles in Tokyo approved the dispatch of a military expedition in August 1918. Large-scale bribery was used in China to strengthen the warlord, Tuan Chi-jui. Domestic discontent in Japan over the price of rice caused serious riots which brought about the fall of the Terauchi administration in November 1918.[37] Speculation in Japan that German forces might break through decisively in March 1918 and lead to allied surrender evaporated in October 1918 as internal disaffection in Austria-Hungary and Germany contributed to the termination of the conflict. Greene reiterated opinions he had expressed in 1917 – 'the proposed League of Nations will ... create a new situation in regard to the whole question of alliances and enable Britain to merge the Anglo-Japanese Alliance – which I venture to think has lived its day and done its great work – in such a League'.[38] Greene thought that the alliance should be given 'a decent burial without hurting Japanese susceptibilities'.[39] It might be possible to achieve the former but it would be extremely difficult to fulfil the latter.

★ ★ ★

Conyngham Greene departed from Tokyo in April 1919. He retired with a pension in September 1919. Greene was succeeded eventually by Sir Charles Eliot who assumed post in April 1920.[40] Greene was invited to serve as a member of a small sub-committee established in order to assess the future of the alliance. His fellow members were Sir John Jordan, Sir William Tyrrell and Sir Victor Wellesley. They reported in January 1921 that 'A careful considera- tion of all the arguments both for and against the renewal of the Alliance has resulted in the unanimous conclusion that it should be dropped and that in its stead should, if possible, be substituted a Tripartite *Entente* between the United States, Japan and Great Britain, consisting in a declaration of general principles which can be subscribed to by all parties without the risk of embar- rassing commitments'.[41] If the United States proved reluctant to participate, the committee envisaged a new agreement with Japan so framed as to facili- tate American adhesion at a future date. The ambassador in Washington, Sir Auckland Geddes, recommended that the alliance should be continued, in a modified form, because of anticipated difficulties in inducing the new Republican administration of Warren G. Harding to cooperate. The new ambassador in Tokyo, Sir Charles Eliot, recommended extending the alliance.[42] The Foreign Secretary, Lord Curzon, was dismissive of the com- mittee's report. The Prime Minister, David Lloyd George, was quite sympathetic towards Japan. When the imperial conference met, in June-July 1921, he urged the extension of the alliance: he felt that while Japan looked after its own interests, Japan did not act more selfishly than any other power. Indeed, Lloyd George quoted part of Sir Edward Grey's address to the impe- rial conference in May 1911 in which Grey urged continuance of the alliance. Therefore, Greene's contribution to the debate did not influence the prime minister and the foreign secretary in the direction he desired. The Harding administration took the initiative in summoning a major conference in Washington in October 1921 and this led to the replacement of the alliance by a four-power agreement comprising the United States, Britain, France and Japan. Thus the United States helped to implement the kind of solution envisaged by Greene in 1917. The alliance ended finally in August 1923.

★ ★ ★

Conyngham Greene's diplomatic career was dominated by two major appointments in the course of which he contributed to deliberations of pro- found significance – in South Africa in the 1890s and in Japan between 1913 and 1919. Greene was a hardworking but rather colourless individual. He lacked the flamboyance of Sir Claude MacDonald or the erudition of Sir Charles Eliot. Greene was steady and realistic: he possessed the patient and conciliatory qualities required in a successful diplomat. He discerned the per- ils inherent in South Africa and worked to achieve a compromise. His efforts were thwarted by Paul Kruger and Sir Alfred Milner. In Japan Greene appre- ciated the value of the Anglo-Japanese Alliance at a time when Britain was encountering intensifying problems in Europe, culminating in the outbreak of war in July-August 1914. Greene lacked previous Far Eastern experience and when he arrived in Tokyo he was not fully aware of the diverse pressures that were pushing Japan in an expansionist direction. Thus he had to grap- ple with the arguments concerning the respective British and Japanese spheres of political and economic interest in China. Greene endeavoured to promote compromise but Grey and Katō were each resolute in defending their approaches. War in Europe temporarily averted further friction over the Yangtze valley and instead led to differences of opinion surrounding the circumstances of Japanese entry into the First World War. Grey's usual adroitness was missing in his clumsy attempts to define limits to Japanese activity in August 1914 and Greene had to point out to Grey that Japan must not be alienated. The Twenty-one Demands presented Greene with a formidable challenge: he understood that British disapproval of Japanese policy had to be conveyed but argument had to be contained amidst the greater demands of war. At the same time Greene's opinion of Japan changed fundamentally in 1915 and he regarded Japanese policy far more critically than before. This explains his advocacy of a new agreement to replace the alliance: Britain would move closer to the United States while obviating alienation of Japan. This was more difficult to accomplish than Greene appeared to believe. The significance of Conyngham Greene's service as ambassador is that it marked a decisive change in the climate of Anglo-Japanese relations, away, it might be said, from a certain warmth (if cooling gradually) to a bracing, chilling wind. The interests of the allies were diverging, as British decline became more obvious and as Japan's emergence as a major regional power became more striking. Greene was a loyal and competent facilitator of policy but he was not a commanding personality. Greene died on 30 June 1934, four months short of his eightieth birthday.

11
Sir Charles Eliot
Ambassador to Japan, 1919–25

Sir Charles Eliot

DENNIS SMITH

The name of Charles Eliot (1862–1931) has hitherto figured as little more than a footnote in the history of Anglo-Japanese relations, in part because he was directly involved with Japan as a diplomat and scholar for no more than the last decade of his life. However, he was one of a distinguished line of British diplomats in East Asia who made significant pioneering contributions to oriental scholarship; furthermore, his time as ambassador in Tokyo included the ending of the Anglo-Japanese Alliance. Eliot moved into a significant position in Britain's relations with Japan when he was appointed ambassador to Tokyo in August 1919. His first two years as ambassador coincided with the decline and final ending of the Alliance, which had been the keystone of Anglo-Japanese relations. There followed four years of readjustment to a new, less formal pattern of relationship. Eliot was a convinced advocate of close Anglo-Japanese friendship, and the abrogation of the Alliance was deeply painful to him. He had a deep and genuine regard for Japan and its culture and he despised the racial prejudice against the Japanese which was characteristic of his time and generation. Eliot's affection for Japan was vividly demonstrated by his decision to remain there after he retired from the diplomatic service, and he spent his final years researching and writing on Japanese Buddhism. Unfortunately, he was unable to translate his vision of Anglo-Japanese amity and co-operation into reality, but his genuine regard for Japan moved Major-General F. S. G. Piggott, himself no mean admirer of Japan, to write of Eliot that 'few, if any, men understood and loved their country's ally as much.'[1]

The tall, 58-year-old bachelor who stepped from a Royal Navy cruiser at Yokohama on 6 April 1920 to take up the position of ambassador brought with him an awesome reputation for intellectual brilliance. Indeed, even experienced Japan hands in the embassy experienced a frisson of apprehension. Eliot's appointment to Tokyo was the pinnacle of his career, and was the culmination of a varied, and indeed chequered, career which had shown spectacular promise in its early stages but had become extraordinarily becalmed during its middle phase.

Charles Edgcumbe Eliot was born on 8 January 1862, the son of an Anglican clergyman. He had a conventional upper-middle-class Victorian education, first at preparatory school, then at Cheltenham College and finally at Balliol, which he entered in 1880. By the time he arrived at Oxford, two of his principal personal characteristics had surfaced: sparkling intellectual brilliance combined with emotional and psychological fragility which had led to a nervous breakdown which had forced him to postpone going to university. At school, and then at Oxford, Eliot displayed striking linguistic aptitude. As an undergraduate he carried off a raft of prizes for both western and oriental classical languages, and during his life he acquired competence in close to twenty languages, including Arabic, Turkish and Chinese. Further, he became a substantial linguistic scholar, writing the first English-language grammar of Finnish and subsequently a Swahili instruction manual.

When Eliot left Oxford in 1886, he was undecided about his future, but a chance encounter with Lord Dufferin pointed him in the direction of the diplomatic service. Predictably, he passed the civil service examinations with ease and was posted to St Petersburg, where he could capitalize on his knowledge of Russian which he had incidentally acquired at Oxford. In 1892 Eliot was transferred to Tangier, and a year later he moved to Constantinople. Inevitably qualifying in Turkish, he stayed there for five years during which he developed himself into one of the leading authorities on the Ottoman Empire and what was then called the 'Eastern Question'. His expertise was revealed in 1900, when he published the highly regarded *Turkey in Europe*, writing under the pseudonym 'Odysseus'. By the time this work appeared, Eliot had served in Washington for a brief period, been knighted for service on the international commission set up to bring some order to the byzantine affairs of Samoa and been appointed consul-general at Zanzibar and commissioner of the British East African Protectorate.

Eliot would later tell one of his officials in Tokyo that his four years in East Africa were 'the happiest and most interesting' of his life'.[2] His appointment at the age of 38 put Eliot effectively in control of all British possessions in East Africa, and he seemed destined for the peak of the Foreign Office hierarchy. Instead, East Africa came close to prematurely but permanently ending his diplomatic career. Eliot became a passionate advocate of white settlement in what would become the White Highlands of Kenya, but the extension of white settlement could only take place at the expense of the Masai tribes who currently occupied the land. Eliot had taken a deep dislike to the Masai and was not averse to disturbing them. However, the Foreign Office was anxious to avoid confrontation with the Masai and Eliot was warned to take no action which might provoke it. Throughout his diplomatic career, Eliot showed a tendency to bend or even disregard his instructions from London if they contradicted his own deeply-held views. In 1904 this cavalier attitude to his political masters brought professional disaster when he continued to sponsor white settlement on Masai lands. Finally, London formally instructed him to reverse his policies, and Eliot responded by resigning from the diplomatic service.

Eliot had hoped that when he returned to Britain he could secure an official inquiry which would exonerate him and lead to his reinstatement, but no inquiry was held and his career as a diplomat appeared to be over. Eliot spent the next thirteen years as a senior university academic, first as vice-chancellor of the newly established University of Sheffield and then, from 1911 to 1918, as vice-chancellor of the University of Hong Kong. Eliot did not find life as a vice-chancellor particularly congenial, and he made sporadic but unsuccessful efforts to mobilize highly placed contacts to secure a return to official life. However, his university service did give him the opportunity to indulge his passion for marine biology and, more significantly, to collect material for and write a substantial part of his *magnum opus*, *Hinduism and Buddhism*, which appeared in three volumes in 1921. Eliot might well have remained an academic for the rest of his working life had it not been for the unusual circumstances which the First World War and the collapse of the Russian Empire created in East Asia in the summer of 1918.

On 2 August 1918 Eliot returned to the diplomatic community when he was appointed British high commissioner for Siberia. Eliot owed his appointment to the quite fortuitous fact that, being in Hong Kong, he could be at his post in Siberia shortly after the first substantial Allied forces landed at Vladivostok. The post of high commissioner was only temporary, but Eliot was so anxious to re-enter public life that he accepted it with alacrity, and was later to claim that it 'rejuvenated' him. Eliot was to have been the British representative on an Allied body responsible for co-ordinating the policies of the interventionist powers. However, Eliot would be the only commissioner appointed by a major interventionist state since both the United States and Japan did not make similar appointments and the co-ordinating body never functioned. In Siberia Eliot gained new renown as a linguist, and gained new fame as a provider of hospitality.[3] In general, he navigated the chaos of post-revolutionary Siberia skilfully. In early 1919 the Foreign Office found some difficulty in finding a successor to Sir Conyngham Greene as ambassador to Japan. On the strength of the accomplished manner in which he had acquitted himself in a very difficult situation, Eliot was offered the embassy in Tokyo.

Unquestionably, Eliot brought formidable qualities to his post. He was an acknowledged expert on 'the orient', having devoted much of his diplomatic and subsequent academic career to service in and study of the non-European world. When he arrived in Tokyo he had spent almost all the previous nine years in East Asia, first in Hong Kong and latterly in Siberia, and he had stayed for long periods in and immersed himself in the study of the most significant regions of the Far East, particularly China. He was reasonably competent in Chinese and he was putting the finishing touches to a major work on two of the great spiritual traditions of Asia. His previous diplomatic service had not involved dealing with Japan, and when he took up his post he did not speak Japanese, but he had visited the country several times, and his year in Siberia had naturally involved intense and sustained exposure to current Japanese policies in north-east Asia. On the debit side, Eliot had held no regular diplomatic appointment for sixteen years and the prolonged interruption of his career meant that he did not have the normal network of diplomatic and personal contacts within the Foreign Office, and this was a defect which three months' briefing in London in 1919–20 could only partially rectify.

Eliot took up his post at a decisive period in Anglo-Japanese relations, for the Alliance was beginning to come under serious scrutiny. Events during and after the First World War had brought attacks on the Alliance from numerous different directions. The Alliance was unpopular with the United States, where it was seen as an essential prop to Japanese expansionism on the Asian continent. Similarly, in China Japan's formal connection with Britain was viewed as a support for previous and current Japanese pressures on China. From a British perspective, the Alliance had been an essential plate in the armour defending Britain's interests in East Asia, first from Russian and then from German threats. The defeat of Germany and the disintegration of Russian power removed these dangers and consequently the Alliance appeared increasingly redundant. Also, Japanese activities in China and Siberia during and after the First World War often conflicted with perceived British interests, while the argument that the Alliance gave the British a restraining hand over Japanese policy seemed to be contradicted by events. Finally, the international environment which emerged out of the First World War was uncongenial to formal alliances. More specifically, the Anglo-Japanese Alliance and membership of the League of Nations might well prove incompatible. However, these threats to the Alliance took time to develop and converge. Eliot left for Japan on St Valentine's Day, 1920. The government's policy at that time, which was to retain the Alliance, albeit in a modified form, to take account of Britain's responsibilities as a member of the League of Nations, was almost identical with Eliot's own view. The ambassador-designate was convinced that the Alliance should be kept, and until its abrogation Eliot remained an unwavering supporter of it. After its demise he would be a regular mourner at its grave.

In the event, having Eliot, a staunch advocate of the Alliance, in Tokyo had no decisive impact upon the debate about its renewal since the final decision was taken entirely in London. Eliot's first substantial expression of opinion on the Alliance following his move to Tokyo was 'a masterly statement of the case for renewal', which impressed Curzon. Again in December 1920, Curzon found Eliot's stout defence of the Alliance more persuasive than the generally lukewarm report of the Foreign Office committee which had been specially constituted to consider the matter.[4] However, from February 1921 Canada began a concerted attack on renewal because of its adverse effect on Anglo-American relations, and by June 1921 the Alliance had become a main topic at the Imperial Conference. At that conference, Curzon still basically favoured renewing the Alliance, but its future was increasingly bound up with imperial and Anglo-American relations. By the summer it was clear that the Alliance's fate would be decided as part of the proposed international conference on Pacific and East Asian affairs, which was to be held in Washington. By this time Eliot had virtually no influence on decisions regarding the Alliance, and in fact he did not try to exert very much. As early as July 1921 Curzon was complaining that both information and views coming from Tokyo 'strike us as somewhat meagre'.[5] In Tokyo, Eliot was active in calming Japanese suspicions of Britain's policies, but he sensed that the Anglo-Japanese relationship based upon the Alliance was drawing to a close. After the abrogation of the Alliance had been arranged at the Washington Conference and it had been replaced by the Four Power Pact, Eliot wrote to Curzon that 'I confess that I regret the termination of the Anglo-Japanese Alliance, but it was really dead before its termination.'[6] Eliot may have been tempted to repeat the moral gesture he had made in East Africa nearly two decades before and resign over the issue, but he did not.[7] Instead, he remained in Tokyo with a brief to soothe Japanese feelings and work out a new framework for Anglo-Japanese relations.

After the Washington Conference Eliot was in a unique position as the only ambassador to serve in a country with which Britain had had a prolonged Alliance and which had been terminated by mutual agreement. It was a difficult, indeed potentially embarrassing, predicament. However, by June 1922 Eliot was able to put a brave face on the end of the Alliance: 'those who believe that real friendship between our two nations is possible cannot but feel some regret, be they British or Japanese, at seeing a close tie replaced by an advantageous understanding. But still a cause of chronic misunderstanding has been removed.'[8] In this second phase of his ambassadorship, Eliot fulfilled the normal tasks of assessing and keeping London informed of the nature and direction of Japanese foreign policy, of dealing with concrete issues between Britain and Japan and of sustaining and improving Britain 's image in Tokyo. All of these roles, were of course, complicated by the end of the Alliance, and because of the disappointments and sensitivities of the Japanese after the Washington Conference, it was vital that they be handled carefully. The Foreign Office was conscious of the delicacy of Japanese feelings, and soon after the Washington Conference Eliot had been specifically instructed to ensure that 'now that the Alliance has gone . . . [we] must do what we can not to make Japan feel we have abandoned her'.[9] These were instructions which Eliot obeyed to the full in both letter and spirit.

The least conspicuous, but none the less important, aspect of Eliot's work after the end of the Alliance was public relations. The state visit of the Prince of Wales to Japan in the spring of 1922 provided an early opportunity to improve Japanese attitudes towards Britain. The success of the visit was threatened by a series of thinly veiled anti-Japanese articles in *The Times* and the *Daily Mail* and by the Prince appearing to be uninterested in Japan during the early part of his visit. However, the Prince perked up as the visit progressed and Eliot believed that this brought a material improvement in Anglo-Japanese relations.[10] Eliot wasted no opportunity to bolster Britain's image in Japan. After the Kantō earthquake on 1 September 1923, Eliot pressed for urgent and substantial British assistance. He was only partially successful and was frankly disappointed by the British reaction, but he was instrumental in prodding the British government into donating £25,000 to Tokyo Imperial University to help restore its library. Eliot accompanied his subordinates on visits to numerous civil and military establishments throughout Japan, frequently impressing his hosts with the passable Japanese which he had acquired since his arrival in Tokyo. It is, of course, hard to assess Eliot's role in maintaining Britain's image after the end of the Alliance, but his contemporaries spoke highly of his efforts and it was, perhaps, in the words of *The Times* obituary for Eliot, 'a solid if not outwardly brilliant achievement'.[11]

When analysing Japanese foreign policy, Eliot, like most pre-war western observers, imagined the decision-making process to be a contest between 'the military party and the more peaceful elements in the State'.[12] Eliot believed that the latter group had established their dominance after the Washington Conference. Thus, in June 1922 he 'felt inclined to expatiate on the change in Japan's foreign policy, the apparent decrease in chauvinistic spirit of the nation and the abandonment of aggressive designs on China and Siberia'. He grudgingly gave the Washington Conference some credit for this, but he felt that the main cause was the failure of previous expansionist adventures to bear substantial fruit: 'all classes, and especially business people, cannot help feeling that half of the annual budget was devoted to naval and military expenditure with no adequate return, while many urgent needs were neglected'.[13] On a broader canvas, Eliot frequently referred to the weakening effect which Japan's post-war economic problems had upon its foreign policy. The range and depth of these difficulties discouraged foreign adventures and, in Eliot's final analysis, made Japan 'a weak rather than a strong power'.[14] One of the frequent refrains in Eliot's despatches was that Japan attached the highest priority to being recognized as one of the great powers and on being seen to co-operate with the others. He wrote that 'it is no exaggeration to say that they often put the manner before the matter, their national dignity before material advantage',[15] and he put great emphasis on the way in which Japan was treated and referred to by the British.

Eliot could point to specific examples of Japan's retreat from expansionism. The Japanese had retired gracefully from Tsingtao after the Washington Conference, and they had evacuated their forces from eastern Siberia exactly on time, despite attempts by the British, initiated by Eliot, to have them stay long enough to destroy large stockpiles of arms in Vladivostok.[16] In broader terms, Eliot opined that 'I do not think that any sane Japanese dreams of using force against Australia or Singapore, or of annexing the Philippines or Dutch Indies.'[17] Eliot was not completely starry-eyed about Japan's future policies, however. Writing in 1922, he warned that 'I do not, of course, mean to imply that an era of unbroken peace and guilelessness has commenced. The majority still believe in the mission of Japan, a vague phrase but not excluding ideas of conquest.'[18] Writing two years later, when the Japanese had been ruffled by the American immigration bill, Eliot cautioned London that 'in international relations the Japanese should [sic] take care to be correct and courteous but that if foreigners do not like Japanese methods they can go elsewhere'.[19]

Japan was most clearly interested in China, and there was very considerable interest in London in what would be the thrust of Japan's China policy under the new Nine Power Treaty, which had been one of the major achievements of the Washington Conference. Consequently, analysing Japan's ambitions and activities in China became a major part of Eliot's responsibilities between 1922 and 1926. When he tried to probe the roots of these policies, Eliot thought that he detected a certain ambivalence and even contradiction. On the one hand, he reported, Japan wished to be seen and clearly recognized as one of the great powers, and 'no international action must take place without the co-operation of Japan'. On the other hand, the Japanese obviously felt that they had a special position in China; during and after the First World War Japan had tried to expand its hold on China by political and military means, but after the Washington Conference they hoped to pursue their ends by economic means. However, the chaotic state of China was a grave disincentive to investment which might have been the spearhead of Japanese penetration of China. Consequently, Eliot wrote, Japan did not have 'a firm and consecutive policy' in China, but, generally, the Japanese were weak and indecisive in their dealings with Chinese affairs.[20] Eliot pressed on London his view that British and Japanese interests in China did not conflict and that Britain should pursue policies in tandem with Japan rather than with the United States, but such ideas found no favour and brought Eliot into conflict with the Foreign Office.

Eliot encountered almost no serious concrete difficulties in Anglo-Japanese relations after the Alliance ended. The one exception to this was the Singapore base project. Until the end of the First World War British interests in Asia had ultimately been protected by the Anglo-Japanese Alliance. However, a comprehensive review of imperial defence in 1919 had highlighted Britain's strategic weakness in Asia caused by the lack of any base capable of accommodating modern capital ships at precisely the time when the Royal Navy was coming to regard Japan as the hypothetical enemy. In June 1921 doubts about the future of the Alliance with Japan and steady pressure from the navy and the Australasian dominions persuaded the cabinet to approve the development of Singapore as a major base for the British battle-fleet. The British were careful to ensure that the Singapore base was excluded from the restrictions placed on new naval fortifications by the Washington naval treaty, and the project became the most important single element in British naval strategy in the 1920s. No amount of official evasion could conceal the fact that the Singapore scheme was aimed at Japan. It reflected the strident anti-Japanese tone adopted by the Royal Navy, which was in part a ploy to extract the maximum possible resources for the service from the Treasury, but it was also symptomatic of increasing forebodings of a threat from Japan which afflicted the Royal Navy.[21]

As ambassador in Tokyo, Eliot could not of course directly influence imperial defence policy, but he was troubled by the potential damage which building the Singapore base posed for Anglo-Japanese relations. Eliot never clearly opposed building the base, but he did warn of its impact upon Anglo-Japanese relations: 'Well-informed Japanese did not regard the proposal as a menace, but they were hurt that their old ally and professed friend should take an early opportunity after the Washington Conference of erecting fortifications as near to Japan as was convenient under the new regulations.'[22] Eliot wrote this appraisal shortly after the first Labour government had decided to suspend work on Singapore as part of its policy of stimulating further disarmament. Eliot had no influence on this decision on the Singapore base, but when the general election at the end of October 1924 produced a Conservative victory and a government likely to resume work on the project, Eliot wrote directly to Austen Chamberlain, the new foreign secretary, warning him that the Japanese-American immigration controversy had spawned an increase in anti-foreign feeling in Japan, and that the Japanese were unusually sensitive to foreign actions. At the very least, he pleaded for a conciliatory message to be sent to Japan, assuring them that Singapore was not aimed at curbing them, although 'I am bound to add that I don't think they will believe it'.[23] Eliot's hope that construction of the base would remain suspended was not fulfilled, although the project had to withstand a violent assault from Winston Churchill, then chancellor of the exchequer, before work on it was resumed. Eliot was left to try and mollify the Japanese and carry on his quiet public-relations exercises.

By the time the new Conservative government decided to resuscitate the Singapore scheme Eliot's influence on London had declined appreciably. Throughout his ambassadorial career, Eliot had irritated some of the most important Foreign Office officials with his opinions, his often convoluted method of argument and his occasional failure to follow instructions. The main London official whose patience Eliot tried was Victor Wellesley, who had been head of the Far Eastern department until his elevation to the post of assistant under-secretary of state in February 1924. Wellesley was a formidable influence upon Britain's policies in East Asia, and his increasingly exasperated comments upon Eliot's despatches reflect a belief that Eliot was too pro-Japanese and generally out of sympathy with the course which British policy was increasingly taking, especially in China. There was always an undertow of anti-Americanism in Eliot's opinions, and he disliked the gravitation of Britain's East Asian policy towards that of the United States at the expense of British relations with Japan. Shortly before he retired, Eliot made his views clear: 'So far as the East is concerned I personally feel that it is to our advantage to work with Japan rather than with the United States but I can imagine that considerations of world policy may dictate a contrary course.'[24] Victor Wellesley's view cut directly across that of Eliot:

> The fact is Japanese interests and British interests in the Far East do not harmonise while the American and ours are identical. It is this which makes cooperation with the Japanese so difficult and forces us more and more to cooperate with the Americans. Close contacts with America has become the only right policy for this country to pursue.[25]

In reality, the weight of the argument and of real influence lay with Wellesley, and although Eliot tried to initiate closer Anglo-Japanese consultation on Chinese affairs, Britain continued to incline towards the United States.

The estrangement between Eliot and senior officials in London contributed to the decision taken by Austen Chamberlain to retire him from the diplomatic service. While on leave in Britain in 1923 Eliot had received the impression that Curzon had assured him that, when his term in Japan expired, in early 1925, his appointment in Tokyo would be renewed or he would be offered another ambassadorship. Eliot passionately believed that he still had much to offer the foreign service, and correctly surmised that Chamberlain had decided to dispense with him because the foreign secretary's 'opinion of me has been mostly formed by information given by the Foreign Office. I may have enemies there.' Eliot lobbied for an embassy either in Cairo or Turkey; alternatively, he was prepared to accept the governorship of Singapore or Hong Kong. Chamberlain's claim that Eliot was being required to retire because of logjams in promotion within the diplomatic service provoked a riposte which reveals much of Eliot's self-confident character:

> I have a very exceptional knowledge of Asia, its inhabitants and their languages. How many people have you in the public service who know China, Japan and Russia as I do, or the near East. . . as I do? To throw away such knowledge and experience is simple waste and not . . . in the interests of the service as a whole.

Chamberlain would not relent and when, in October 1925, Eliot plaintively stated that 'I am helpless and you can treat me as unjustly and illogically as you like', Chamberlain coldly brought the correspondence to an end.[26]

After his forced retirement, Eliot did not return to Britain. He decided to stay in Japan and collect material for and complete his work on Buddhism in Japan. During his period as ambassador he had travelled widely in Japan searching for sources, and when he finally left the embassy in February 1926 he moved into the Nara Hotel and, with the assistance of a network of contacts in Buddhist institutions in Nara and Kyoto, he immersed himself in religious texts. In the years that remained to him, Eliot continued his lonely, solitary life in and around Nara. However, he did maintain contact with some of his closer associates from the embassy. Most notably, he became uncharacteristically close to George Sansom, then commercial counsellor; Sansom was in the final stages of completing his *Cultural History of Japan* and perhaps as an author Eliot felt close fellow-feeling with his erstwhile subordinate. By early 1929 Eliot had drafted much of his book on Japanese Buddhism, but his health was deteriorating rapidly and there is some suggestion that his vaunted intellectual powers were beginning to wane and progress on his book slowed drastically.[27] In December 1930 Eliot became seriously ill, and by February 1931 his condition was clearly terminal. He became determined to return to England, and he did set out for home but on 16 March 1931 he died as his ship passed through the Straits of Malacca. Japanese Buddhism was still unfinished and George Sansom undertook to complete it and prepare it for publication. The text was in some confusion and Eliot had been too ill to write anything on Nichiren. Sansom contributed a chapter on Nichiren and it took three years to shape the complete text into its final form. The complex and frankly imperfect work was only published four years after its author died.

It is not easy to assess Sir Charles Eliot's contribution to Anglo-Japanese understanding. Eliot himself was disappointed with the way in which the two nations drifted apart during his tenure of the Tokyo embassy. He was particularly distressed by the abrogation of the Alliance, but the important decisions concerning its renewal were taken in London, and it is difficult to see how the ambassador, geographically isolated in Tokyo, could have exerted more influence. Once the Alliance disappeared and it became necessary to build new frameworks for Anglo-Japanese relations, Eliot's instinctive empathy for Japanese sensibilities helped to project an image of a Britain which had not entirely abandoned its old ally. Eliot tried to reassure the Foreign Office that post-Washington Japan was not a threat to Britain's interests. As ambassador, he maintained a personal correspondence with four foreign secretaries, and the influence of his opinions emerges clearly in Austen Chamberlain's address to the Imperial Conference in October 1926 which, when discussing Japan's retreat into placidity, not only used the same arguments as Eliot, but also expressed them in virtually the same words as Eliot's personal letters.[28]

When Eliot tried to convince decision-makers in London that his conception of a close Anglo-Japanese relationship was desirable, he failed. The causes of that estrangement were fundamental, and the Foreign Office mandarins were too suspicious of Japan, and of Eliot's well-known pro-Japanese sentiments, for them to be able to accept his arguments. As one of Eliot's successors pointed out in 1931, Britain was now less important to Japan, which was concentrating its attention on relations with the United States, on the emergence of Soviet power in North-east Asia and on the the tide of change in China.[29] To the Japanese, relations with Britain were becoming little more than peripheral, while the British were increasingly inclining their East Asian policies towards those of the United States. The misfortune for a man of Eliot's convictions was that he was quite unable to reverse, or even slow, the estrangement of the former Allies.

12
Sir John Tilley
Ambassador to Japan, 1926–31

HARUMI GOTŌ-SHIBATA

Sir John Tilley

Sir John Tilley (1869–1951) was the British Ambassador to Japan from 1926 to 1931. His autobiography, *London to Tokyo*, was published in 1942, soon after the war broke out between Britain and Japan. His name does not appear in the *Dictionary of National Biography* and it seems that he has been largely forgotten. In contrast the achievements of Sir Miles Lampson (1880–1964) as British Ambassador to China from the end of 1926 to 1933 are still widely acknowledged. Lampson's association with East Asia dated back to 1906 when he went to Japan as secretary to the Mission of Prince Arthur of Connaught to invest the Meiji Emperor with the Order of the Garter. Tilley on the other hand had had limited contact with the region until he was appointed as Ambassador to Japan. Tilley was not a scholar-diplomat such as his predecessor Sir Charles Eliot (1862–1931) or Sir George Sansom (1883–1965), who was the commercial counsellor under Tilley.

Tilley was born on 21 January 1869. Educated at Eton and King's College, Cambridge, he entered the Foreign Office in March 1893. He was first assigned to the Eastern Department, where Sir William Conyngham Greene, who was to be Eliot's predecessor as ambassador to Japan, was also working. Tilley's next assignment was to the Far Eastern Department at the time of the first Sino-Japanese War and Tilley described the experience as his 'first, though distant, acquaintance with Japan as a world power'.[1] In his late thirties, he worked in Constantinople for several years as a first secretary. As the Foreign Office and the Diplomatic Service were still in theory separate, he had to effect a temporary exchange with a member of the Diplomatic Service. The two services were amalgamated in 1916 by the work of a committee appointed to consider reforms. Tilley participated in the committee as the Chief Clerk of the Foreign Office.[2] Apart from his experience in

Constantinople, he worked mainly in London, but towards the end of 1920 he was asked to go to Brazil as the ambassador. Tilley described this as a 'thunderbolt', although 'of a pleasant nature'.[3] He remained in Brazil until 1925 when he learnt that he was to be appointed to Tokyo. Tilley, who was 56, does not seem to have been consulted before the Foreign Office sought Japanese *agrément* to his appointment. In June and July 1925 before he had been informed of the Foreign Office's decision, he was surprised to find friends congratulating him on his appointment to Tokyo.[4] Tilley accepted the appointment and sailed for Japan on 7 January 1926.

TILLEY IN JAPAN, 1926–31

The five years Tilley spent in Japan can be divided into two periods. The first was from the time he first arrived in Japan until he was granted home leave in January 1928: the second started in October of the same year when he resumed his job. In the first half, Tilley did not enjoy his life in Japan at all. It seems that he took an instant dislike to the country, although this feeling might be exaggerated in *London to Tokyo*, which was published in 1942 after the outbreak of war. The first reason why Tilley felt his life so difficult was that when he arrived only two years had passed since the Great Kantō Earthquake and Tokyo was still in the early stages of rebuilding. 'The old Embassy house, . . . everything in fact, had been destroyed in [September] 1923.'[5] The new embassy building was completed in 1932, but Tilley had no chance of living there. The physical discomfort in a 'bungalow' infested with rats was almost unbearable.[6]

Secondly, the Taishō Emperor died in December 1926, and national mourning continued for a full year. The emperor had been weak since childhood, and he was a 'lunatic'[7] when Tilley arrived in Japan. His eldest son was acting as Regent, whom Tilley initially did not rate highly.[8]

Thirdly, although Britain needed Japanese cooperation during this particular period, Tilley failed to secure it.[9]

Since the Anglo-Japanese Alliance was abrogated at the Washington Conference of 1921–22, the 'decline of British popularity' and the 'downward trend' persisted. According to F. S. G. Piggott, the military attaché under Eliot, 'outward relations with Japanese of all classes seemed as good as ever', but 'the very fact that we were always on the look-out for opportunities to maintain good relations meant that their maintenance was to some extent artificial; fundamentally they were not the same as in old days, when no special efforts were required'. As Eliot made 'unremitting efforts' to stop the fading of British popularity, Piggott thought Eliot's departure together with the death of Katō Takaaki (1860–1926) was a heavy blow to Anglo-Japanese relations.[10] This seems to imply that Piggott did not think highly of Tilley as ambassador. He later wrote that he was pleased when a change of ambassadors took place in 1931:

> . . . I had known Sir Francis [Lindley] slightly twenty-five years before when he was a junior secretary, and I now had the pleasure – a pleasure shared by several others at the War Office – of reading his pungent dispatches from Tokyo; a spade was invariably called a spade, much to our satisfaction.[11]

In the meantime Britain was facing serious problems in China. The Chinese were rapidly becoming aware of their inferior status in international society and began to make efforts to recover their rights. As Britain was the country, which from the middle of the nineteenth century had the largest interests in China, she was the first to be singled out as the target of attack. British trade in south China had been paralyzed because of a boycott against Hong Kong. Britain tried to cope with the situation in cooperation with other powers and wanted in particular Japanese assistance.

The Japanese Foreign Minister then was Shidehara Kijūrō, who had been a career diplomat. His diplomacy has been praised in Japan, and he wrote in his autobiography published in 1951 that he rated British diplomacy highly and tried to adopt the same general guidelines.[12] However, in the mid-1920s, the British government were displeased with Shidehara's policies towards China, because he did not seem to be willing to cooperate with Britain. He had the reputation of being 'anti-English' and instead, in favour of conciliating China and the United States.[13] Shidehara was unpopular among the British, because the interests of Britain and Japan often conflicted. The two governments, for instance, differed over whether tariff autonomy should be granted to China or not. Before the Peking Tariff Conference opened in October 1925, Britain believed that agreement had been reached to grant tariff autonomy step by step in return for effective guarantees for the gradual abolition of *likin*, a kind of internal customs. Nevertheless, when the conference met, the governments of Japan and the United States decided to grant to the government in Peking tariff autonomy in full and at an early date. In addition, Shidehara tried to secure low customs duties for Japan. As a result the conference was prolonged without the prospect of any early settlement. Another example was Japan's lack of military cooperation when Britain dispatched an expeditionary force to 'defend' the Shanghai International Settlement from the advancing Kuomintang in 1927. Shidehara considered that military intervention in China was counter-productive. Tilley's role as ambassador was to protect British interests; so he was displeased with Shidehara whom many British thought was only interested in enhancing Japan's economic interests.[14]

When the change of government took place in Japan in April 1927, however, Tilley learned 'with horror' that the new Prime Minister cum Foreign Minister, Tanaka Giichi, spoke neither English nor French, and intended always to have an interpreter at his side. Tilley disliked using interpreters and knew several European languages as well as a little Turkish, but had given up 'the attempt to learn any Japanese beyond a few ordinary expressions'. Tilley and all his colleagues greatly lamented the departure of Shidehara, 'who had a perfect command of English and an equally perfect command of his temper, and who was, moreover, very reliable in what he said'. Shidehara was a man similar to themselves. His retirement led Tilley to wonder whether he had done the former justice. Tilley wrote a farewell letter to Shidehara regretting his resignation as Foreign Minister; Shidehara wrote a charming letter back.[15]

Ex-army general Tanaka, however, was much more interested in closer communication and cooperation between the two countries than Shidehara. The change he brought to Japan's China policy was welcomed by Britain, and Tilley found him 'pleasant to deal with', although he did not rate highly Tanaka's talent as a politician. In December 1927, Tilley came to think that Tanaka had 'very little to say':[16]

... The Prime Minister at first gave me the impression of being a man of some determination who knew his own mind. Unfortunately, although these qualities do in a way belong to him, they are not backed by much power of thought. Consequently he dashes off without very well knowing where he's going. This has several times become evident in his dealings with China: ...[17]

The Tanaka government sent expeditionary forces to China in 1927 and 1928. The Sino-Japanese military clash at Jinan in May 1928 led to a serious deterioration in relations between the two countries. As Japan became the sole target of the Chinese boycott, she started to seek cooperation with Britain. Uchida Yasuya, former Foreign Minister, was sent to Europe in the summer 1928 partly to promote such cooperation. In the meantime, China started to show goodwill to Britain and the trade situation improved for the latter. Britain no longer needed Japan's support. On the contrary, close relations with Japan might have destroyed the favourable position which Britain secured in China.

Tilley was on home leave while the relations among the three countries thus changed drastically. When he came back to Japan in October 1928, his job turned out to be much easier and life more enjoyable. The Japanese started to make tremendous efforts to entertain Tilley and improve the prospect of Anglo-Japanese cooperation. Although the efforts were fruitless at the international level, Tilley himself at least was much happier.

ENTHRONEMENT OF THE SHŌWA EMPEROR

The latter half of Tilley's ambassadorship started with celebrations. On 28 September 1928, Prince Chichibu, the second son of the late emperor, married Matsudaira Setsuko. The couple received greetings from ambassadors and ministers on 4 October. This was followed by a banquet a week after and a luncheon on 12 October. Princess Chichibu was the elder daughter of Matsudaira Tsuneo, an able diplomat and the fifth son of the former daimyo of the Aizu domain. The princess was born in Walton on Thames, Surrey, while her father was serving as a secretary at the Japanese Embassy in London. Although the Matsudairas left England when she was only eight months old, the princess was quite Westernized as she attended a high school in the United States where her father was Shidehara's successor as Japanese ambassador.[18] After the wedding, her father Matsudaira Tsuneo was due to leave for Britain where he had been appointed Japanese ambassador. Prince Chichibu had also stayed in England and studied at Magdalen College, Oxford, although after a term he had left because of the illness of his father, the Taishō emperor. Tilley liked both the Chichibus and the Matsudairas.

The Shōwa emperor was enthroned in November 1928. All the foreign representatives including Tilley went to Kyoto where the ceremony was held. They were the guests of the Japanese government and expected to witness the emperor ascending the throne. They were among the immediate onlookers during one of the ceremonies. Together with them were only the imperial family and the highest officials.[19]

Although the ceremony was 'extraordinarily picturesque',[20] Tilley was aware that it was an 'invented tradition'.[21] He compared it with another invented tradition, namely the British coronation ceremony, but noted three points of difference. First, he noticed that the Japanese crowds were kept at a considerable distance from any route along which the Emperor was to pass and there was no cheering. Secondly, he observed the extreme remoteness of the emperor and empress even from their guests including himself. Although they shook hands with foreign representatives, they never spoke. Thirdly, he thought it strange that the emperor ascends the throne by the grace and favour of his own ancestress, although after all it was claimed that she was a goddess.[22]

Tilley could not believe that there was any popular enthusiasm for the emperors. He had already noticed that a considerable proportion of the crowds who prayed for the Taisho Emperor during his illness were organized schoolchildren and boy scouts.[23] Although the press reported that enormous crowds of people flocked into Kyoto for the enthronement, he could not believe it, because he did not see any sign of them. He felt that the feeling of awe to the throne was maintained with difficulty and imperial ceremonies were rather a triumph of organization than anything else. While there was no spontaneous cheering along the route when the emperor passed, Tilley was impressed with the tremendous shout of three banzais conducted by Prime Minister Tanaka in front of a palace during the ceremony:[24]

> . . . to the European mind the general idea suggested by the treatment of the Emperor . . . is rather that of a Being who must be propitiated than a Father of his country who must be surrounded with affection. To the Japanese mind this outward display of veneration of the Emperor may have seemed . . . a natural respect for symbolized authority. At the same time it is really of quite modern invention dating only from the time of the Emperor Meiji, and is strictly inculcated by the authorities rather than spontaneous. In earlier days and for centuries many of the Emperors, although the object of some theoretical veneration, lived lives of miserable poverty and neglect and were merely made use of by the Shoguns for such purposes as the latter thought convenient. It seems to me doubtful whether this compulsory veneration of the Sovereign, in its modern developments, will conduce to the stability of the Throne better than attempts to win the genuine affection of the people; indeed, given the great development of education in this country, I imagine that the present system may have the opposite effect to that intended.[25]

However, Tilley was not absolutely sure whether his observation was correct. The experts at the embassy told him that there was still a very strong feeling towards the emperors among the peasantry away from Tokyo.[26] He also noticed that almost 'no Japanese would say what he thought to a foreigner on such a matter, nor, indeed, would he say what he thought to anyone at all but an intimate friend, for fear of trouble with the police'.[27]

The enthronement ceremony was followed by a lot of entertainment for foreign representatives: a garden party, a performance of Miyako-odori [Dance of the Capital], a trip on Lake Biwa, an excursion to Nara, banquets both in Japanese and Western style. Tilley seems to have enjoyed most of them. After spending about ten days in Kyoto, the representatives returned to Tokyo on 19 November.[28]

In May 1929, a Mission led by the Duke of Gloucester, younger son of King George V, arrived in Japan to bestow the new emperor with the Order of the Garter. On arrival at Tokyo station the duke was met by a group of British schoolchildren outside the station who had been told not to cheer, 'in deference to Japanese custom'.[29] Among many events during the duke's visit to Japan was a 'mammoth' garden party at the British Embassy: 'Sir John having been determined to invite all available British to meet the Duke . . . British from Yokohama of every degree; Indian women in their saris – wives of merchants – a Scout Parade, Salvation Army lasses who busily tackled the middies from HMS Suffolk in their traditional style, whilst teachers from all over the country, including elderly persons from distant outposts, poured forth exuberant and impassioned loyalty to anyone handy.' The party was a tremendous success.[30]

Tilley's evaluation of Japan in this period rose to a certain extent. He wrote:

> The people are mainly . . . peaceable and frugal in their own lives; they are neither adventurers nor warlike, nor fond of display. I should not even describe them as hardy although they may be accustomed to hardship and are certainly ready to endure hardship if necessary. There seem to me excellent reasons why they should wish their Government to refrain from dangerous or extravagant enterprises, and why, happily, we need not expect that Japan will kindle war on this side of the world if she can possibly help it.[31]

He also wrote in the annual report for the year 1929 that the Shōwa Emperor had 'since the enthronement, developed unexpectedly', and his bearing, manner and voice showed greatly increased self-confidence. Shidehara, who returned to office after the Tanaka cabinet fell in the autumn of 1929, was described as being ready to work with Britain. In other dispatches written at the beginning of 1930, Tilley stated that 'in the main, Japanese policy [was] wise and farseeing, and by no means always selfish'; that 'Japan's constant schemes and intrigues in China [were] exaggerated'; and that she would not be so foolish as to annex Manchuria with a population of twenty millions of another race, which was constantly growing by immigration, and thus to annoy both China and the United States.[32]

OBSERVATIONS OF JAPAN AND THE JAPANESE

As Tilley had given up the attempt to learn any Japanese beyond a few ordinary expressions, all Japanese with whom he made friends spoke good English. Apart from Prince and Princess Chichibu and Matsudaira Tsuneo, he liked and respected Tokugawa Iyesato, Makino Nobuaki (Shinken) and Chinda Sutemi.[33] All of them spent one of the happiest periods in their lives in Britain. Tilley preferred Japanese naval officers to soldiers, because the latter usually spoke no English and were 'less inclined to be friendly'.[34] On the whole, Tilley's autobiography makes one aware of the class difference in Japan in the 1920s.[35] People whom Tilley mentioned were mainly peers or the highest officials. For example, Tokugawa Iyesato, 'unusually fine example of the old territorial nobility',[36] was heir to the last shogun. On the other hand, the names of ordinary people including servants at the ambassador's residence were hardly mentioned.

Tilley seems to have had few friends in Tokyo not only among the Japanese but also among the diplomatic corps. He had known the Belgian ambassador for many years and talked with the American and German ambassadors, but he wrote that he never knew well Paul Claudel, the French Ambassador from 1921–27 and a poet.[37] This situation was very different from the social life of

Lampson in Peking, who enjoyed good communication with fellow minis-
ters. Lampson formed a friendship with Yoshizawa Kenkichi, the Japanese
Minister to China, and was invited to Yoshizawa's residence several times.[38]
On the other hand, Tilley described the life of diplomats as follows:

> It is quite obvious that the relations between an Ambassador and his staff
> must be something quite different from those between the various members
> of an office in London, more especially at distant posts. It must be remem-
> bered that the idea that diplomats are constantly entertained by the people
> of the country where they live is generally speaking, entirely fictitious. For
> one thing, apart from official entertainment, it is only in the English-speak-
> ing capitals that people habitually entertain, even each other, in their own
> houses, and since the War this has become more true than ever. Diplomats,
> therefore, depend chiefly on each other for society.[39]

In his autobiography, Tilley complained about not being invited to
Japanese houses, and even when he was invited, he sometimes had to spend
tiresome hours because the hosts hardly spoke English.[40]

His communication with the Foreign Secretaries back home was also insufficient. He wrote that he talked with Sir Austen Chamberlain twice and with
Arthur Henderson once. 'I did not therefore feel that I had any sort of personal relation with my chiefs. I cannot recollect anything in the nature of a
personal letter, and very few private letters of any sort.'[41] His attitude was
completely different from that of Eliot and Lampson. Eliot believed that it
was his duty to explain the situation in Japan and things Japanese to the
Foreign Secretaries, and without expecting answers, continued to write private letters. Lampson worked directly under Chamberlain when the latter
was enthusiastically working towards the Locarno Treaty and came to be
deeply trusted by him. There were naturally a certain number of private letters exchanged between the two. Lampson was a good writer; both his
dispatches and diary are long, detailed and thus useful for historians.

Tilley was fortunate to have many competent staff at the embassy including Sansom. He delegated various tasks to them. For example, when he wrote
the general summary of the annual report for the year 1929, he acknowledged that the remaining sections had been written by his staff.[42] Thanks to
their capable support, observations sent from Tokyo seem mostly accurate
and some are valid even today: The situation of the Diet in those days for
example, was described as 'pathetic'. Although manhood universal suffrage
was introduced in 1925 and the first general election was held in 1928, a parliament sat only for two months per year, and the impression Tilley gained
was that its members were intellectually incapable of discussing any subject
of importance intelligently.[43] The education of the public by the press was
also considered to be extremely poor, because its criticisms on current events
were generally of the feeblest kind. The general public had no other choice
but to believe what they read in the papers, because their own knowledge and
intellectual powers were limited especially in relation to foreign affairs. They
seemed to have taken interest only in matters of local interest.[44]

Slowness of apprehension and decision-making were also noted. Tilley considered this was partly due to a definite fear of being trapped by the
Europeans, but he also mentioned other reasons – the temperament, education and the necessity to refer every point to a multiplicity of advisers.
Even when the matter had been fully considered, those who should make

decisions were inclined to wait further to see how things were going to turn out. No one wanted to take responsibility and turn into a scapegoat. Tilley wrote, 'political and civic courage [the Japanese] have not'.[45]

Another problem Tilley noticed was the low status of women. Women tended to be completely excluded from social gatherings and even when they were allowed to attend some, 'only those who had had a diplomatic training talked at all'. The exception was only when Tilley visited Taiwan in January 1929. A dinner was given for him by the Governor-General and guests included a large number of Japanese, both men and women. He wrote: 'The excitement was that this was the first time that ladies had been included in such a banquet. It was a very friendly gathering.'[46] However, the general situation was not improving. In March 1930, the Ministry of the Imperial Household announced that invitations to the imperial garden parties would, except in the case of diplomats, no longer be sent to unmarried daughters, because the presence of girls on such occasions was a Western custom.[47]

Tilley felt that Westernization and the spread of English culture in Japan was insufficient, but that efforts to assimilate Western civilization were on the decline. On the contrary, he noticed the inclination of reverting to Japanese tradition. In 1927, he wrote that 'hostility to Great Britain' did not arise from the abandonment of the alliance, nor from fear of the British base at Singapore, but from some deeper 'nationalist feeling, not only in favour of Japan for the Japanese, but of Asia for the Asiatics'; and it was as 'the enemy of Asia generally' that the British were looked upon.[48]

He also observed that the system of teaching English to Japanese students was very unsatisfactory, and expressed concern that the Ministry of Education might reduce the hours for the study of foreign languages.[49] In fact he took a keen interest in education and made a number of contributions in this field. It was through his efforts that the Shakespeare medal and a library of beautifully printed books were presented to the Imperial University of Tokyo. He attended oratorical exercises at various schools and universities. His interest encouraged and inspired all those engaged in teaching and learning English. The very successful visit and lecture tour by art-historian and poet Laurence Binyon of the British Museum, who gave a series of lectures, was also largely inspired by Tilley. An exhibition of English water-colours was opened under the supervision of Binyon.[50] However, Tilley later wrote of British visitors to Japan:

> Unfortunately, the Japanese with whom our visitors made friends were the cultivated class, men with wide views of human affairs, whose influence in their own country was diminishing in favour of the ultra-nationalists, who cared nothing for cooperation, intellectual or otherwise with Europeans, unless it could contribute to the aggrandizement of Japan.[51]

Perhaps Tilley was aware that the same could actually be said of himself.

During his stay in Japan, Tilley visited various parts of the country including Kyūshū and Wakayama where he was entertained by former daimyos of those regions. In November 1929, he went to Korea, Mukden, Dairen and Peking. In Peking, the Tilleys spent a week with the Lampsons. Tilley also enjoyed his visits to Nikko and Chūzenji, where he revived the use of the Ambassador's summer villa, a two-storied Japanese-style house first used on a regular basis by Sir Ernest Satow when he was Minister to Tokyo in the late 1890s. He claimed to be the one who first started using a car in the region

to avoid friction with the Nanking government and were vacillating over Manchuria. He predicted: 'I shall not have a great deal to do here.'[4] I quote this to illustrate how the actions of the Imperial Japanese Army which were about to take place on 18 September came to the British Embassy as a surprise. It is arguable that the army had been skilful in keeping its intentions secret and taking the various embassies and even the Japanese government by surprise. Within two months of reaching Japan, Lindley was faced by a serious regional crisis between China and Japan over the latter's treaty rights in north-east China, generally known as Manchuria, and this escalated into an international crisis which involved not only the Powers individually but also the League of Nations as a peace-making organization. Sir Francis, so far from being idle, suddenly became the most active of British diplomats overseas and had to try to interpret the delicate balance of forces struggling for the upper hand in Japan and forecast the outcome of the power struggle.

Lindley has been summed up in an affectionate assessment: 'He was a rather tough old character in some respects and very outspoken in his likes and dislikes.'[5] Undoubtedly he brought to his post considerable experience as a diplomat and had had tough postings, mainly in Europe. Most notably he had been in Riga at the time of the bolshevik take-over and was left in charge of the embassy after the withdrawal of Sir George Buchanan. This experience had given him a deep suspicion of Soviet Russia (as it later became). He saw it as expansionist and as Britain's main global problem. He then served successively as minister to Austria (1919–20), Greece (1922–3) and Norway (1923–9) and ambassador to Portugal (1929–31).

He had had no experience of the Americas and was sceptical about American ambitions in the East. The United States had during the 1920s taken over from Britain the role of the major outside player in the Japanese economy and society. Lindley deplored the fact that cricket, 'our national game', was 'in a less satisfactory condition in Japan' and had symbolically been displaced by the loathsome baseball.[6] Though he remained on good terms with W. Cameron Forbes and Joseph C. Grew, successive American ambassadors in Tokyo, he seems to have been convinced that it was the inclination of administrations in Washington to strike poses in East Asia without any intention of seeing things through and to rely on Britain 'to carry the baby'.

His likes and dislikes were vocally expressed. He was not favourable to the Foreign Office as an institution and was courageous in defending his views against the mandarins in Whitehall. He had never had a desk in the Office and so was not overawed by officials there. He thought that ministers and top officials in Whitehall were distinctly lacking in experience of East Asia and in the understanding of a foreign postings. Lindley belonged to that group in the foreign service who were profoundly sceptical of the League of Nations, of collective security as a means of preventing war and of the use of sanctions against an aggressor. He had disliked it long before he set foot in Japan and was to distrust it more when he saw the way in which the League's councils and committees handled the Manchurian Crisis which was developing. In private correspondence he railed against Whitehall for its unquestioning acceptance of impracticable League principles. Moreover Lindley was critical of Sir Miles Lampson, his colleague at Peking, for encouraging China to rely on the League and building up her expectations.

PERSONAL AGONIES OVER MANCHURIA

The Manchurian Crisis matured quickly. Soon after the initial railway 'explosion' on 18 September, the Japanese Kwantung army pushed out from
Mukden, the focus of Japan's rail network, occupying Chinese cities in all
directions without encountering long-lasting resistance. The Chinese
responded by appealing to the League of Nations in Geneva, thereby con-
verting a regional issue into an international one in a way that greatly
embarrassed the Japanese government. Just as China's Nationalist government did not really control affairs in Manchuria, Tokyo was not able to
control its own military there. Moreover Japan was not specially adept at
operating within the procedures of the League where Britain had a leadership
role. The Foreign Ministry was embarrassed and conveyed that frustration to
Lindley.

His embarrassment increased when the League passed a resolution on 24
October calling on the armies of both Japan and China to pull back from
occupied territory within a prescribed time limit. Evacuation was unacceptable to the Japanese who opposed the resolution through their ambassador
to the League, Yoshizawa Kenkichi. Moreover there were rumours circulating
around Geneva that Japan's action warranted the application of economic
sanctions against her. Lindley's problem was that he was not privy to the attitude of the British Government on this resolution which had been prepared
and sponsored by the French. He had to assume that it had the backing of
London and was promoted also by the substitute British representative on
the League, Lord Robert Cecil, who became one of Lindley's particular bêtes-
noires. He leaves this private account of this 'most harassing time':

'The proceedings at Geneva have really been a first-class scandal. All the
members of the Council dying to get away and yet attempting to settle the
vital interests of a country like Japan . . . Sheafs of telegrams in cypher to deal
with and answer or act on before a sitting fixed perhaps a few hours ahead.
And the Japanese Government expected to reach decisions and give fresh
instructions in a few hours or less. Naturally they just dug their toes in and
refused to budge. We have come in for all the blame and are abused like pick-
pockets in any paper. This is mainly due to the forensic zeal of Lord Cecil
who seems to have treated the wretched Yoshizawa as if he was in the dock
at the Old Bailey instead of a delegate conscientiously carrying out instructions his government has been given no time to modify. The result of all this
is that Japan is in ugly mood and will accept dictation from no-one – certainly not from the League. My only object is to prevent the latter turning
this absurd Manchurian rumpus into a world war.[7]

Lindley was especially alarmed at the hostility of the Japanese press and the
political power of the military party which was determined to resist sanctions. The more extreme among them were already talking of leaving the
League. The Japanese, both in government and the media, took a hostile view
of Britain's attitude. Lindley himself felt exposed to personal criticism on two
grounds: firstly, that the British government was openly anti-Japanese while
France and the United States had dressed up their criticisms of Japanese
actions more tactfully than London; and secondly, that he personally must
have been misinforming and misadvising London. These criticisms were of
course unfair because he did not agree with the supposed 'British line' which
Japan was condemning. He was to be placed in an awkward position for the

eighteen months the crisis lasted, satisfying neither his home government nor the government to which he was accredited.

In fact, the views of the Foreign Office mandarins were not too far removed from Lindley's position. In reality, Whitehall officials thought that there was not a remote possibility of sanctions being applied. When the National government was reformed in November with Sir John Simon as foreign secretary, Lindley was courageous enough to write of 'the naive follies of Reading and Cecil' – the previous ministers. But for the rest of the crisis he continued in his private correspondence to the court and ministers to fulminate against a government which still seemed to follow Cecil's views rather than his own.[8] Lindley was also disappointed about US Secretary of State Henry L. Stimson's statement of 7 January 1932 declaring Japan's actions to be unacceptable to Washington but making clear that he was unwilling to do anything positive about it.

The next problem was Shanghai which was occupied (apart from the International Settlement) by Japanese armies in February 1932. Lindley feared that the world powers might take offensive naval action and get into conflict with Japan on Chinese soil in a way that naval powers could never win. He again took a serious view of the danger: '. . . a false step might precipitate catastrophe'. External criticism of Japan's actions would only harden opinion in favour of the army and navy; a tough international stance would play into the hands of the Japanese. Lindley reassured London that Japan had probably stumbled into a situation at Shanghai where her prestige was at stake and was not seeking territory in central China. On what grounds he made that claim is not clear. But his exasperation is evident in the following letter:

> I have had the hell of a time trying to prevent Cecil and our Pacifists bringing on a world war of which we should bear the brunt. Nor is the danger really over yet because they so mishandled the Manchurian business last October that it is impossible to get it on an even keel again. At that time they did every single thing which I told them would be fatal. A blunder of that magnitude can't be put right. Some-times I have felt quite worn out with anxiety and have often thought of asking the FO to send out some one else. Fortunately the Conservative element in the Cabinet predominates; and Sir J. Simon is different from that senile rat-catcher Reading.[9]

The Shanghai incident was fortunately brought to a negotiated settlement in May by the skilful use of international diplomacy under the auspices of the League. Interestingly Lindley felt that the Shanghai crisis was a sideshow compared to Manchuria. But it was good luck for him that his deduction that the Japanese would be restrained in their actions there turned out to be correct.

Lindley's advice led to accusations in Britain that he was becoming pro-Japanese in his judgements. His Tokyo colleagues and acquaintances did not accept this. Nor did his old friend, the American ambassador, Joseph Grew, who had known him in pre–1914 days during postings in Cairo. Grew always spoke of 'good old Lindley' whom he regarded as robust and realistic in his judgements.[10] While the Foreign Office on one occasion administered a stern rebuke, it by and large took a tolerant view of Lindley's effusions, concluding that he was over-wrought and was affected by his anti-League bias and his anxieties about Soviet Russia. Lindley saw a lot of the League's commission

of enquiry into the Manchurian emergency under Lord Lytton during their
two stays in the Japanese capital. He probably had foreknowledge of the con-
tents of its report which was signed on 4 September and published on 1
October. He wrote:

> I expect a stormy autumn after the Report of the League Commission on
> Manchuria is out. And I foresee a very disagreeable struggle with my own
> Government who are bent on complete subservience to America in the hope
> of favours in debt settlement. To my mind a fatuous idea. So I shall have to
> do my best to defend British interests in the Far East from being sacrificed for
> nothing. As it is, I am in bad odour with our Geneva enthusiasts whom I
> frightened with prudence much against their will.[11]

While there was resentment in Japan against the Lytton report, it did not
become a major issue as the Manchurian question passed back to the corri-
dors of the League for discussion. That process was interrupted by the
campaign undertaken in the new year by the Japanese forces in Manchuria in
the Chinese province of Jehol to the north of Beijing which created a bad
impression in Geneva. But the British representatives on the spot in Tokyo
and Peking appear to have been fairly confident that the aim of the Japanese
General Staff at the end of their campaign in Jehol was to round off its position in Manchuria (now renamed Manchukuo) rather than to embark on an
invasion of northern China. This minimalist view of Japanese ambitions
suited Britain and the British empire. If Japan confined herself to the north
of the Great Wall, she was likely to present less of a threat to Britain's global
interests.

Nonetheless, London felt that Japan should be taught a lesson. Under the
severe pressure of public opinion, the British cabinet decided on 27 February
1933 to discontinue the supply of munitions to Japan and also even-hand-
edly to China. This limited arms embargo did not attract the support of any
other Power and was eventually withdrawn a fortnight later on 13 March.
Lindley commented that, as seen from Tokyo, the embargo policy held nothing but disadvantages for Britain; the situation he faced would be easier were
it known by the public that sanctions were out of the question. Another proposal which followed soon after was that the Powers should withdraw their
ambassadors from Tokyo. Asked to comment, Lindley wrote: 'I cannot sufficiently deplore the proposal which will do nothing but harm. Anything in
[the] form of a rebuke would be deeply resented by Japan.'[12] He was so convinced of Japan's strength and willingness to challenge world Powers that he
was opposed to any international attempts to discipline her.

MANCHURIAN AFTERMATH

In the resolution finally adopted by the League in February 1933, Japan was
mildly censured but some criticisms were directed at China. This was merely
a tap on the wrist for Japan. But she did not like to be criticized internationally and retaliated by giving notice of leaving the League of Nations. Her
relations, therefore, became frosty with all the powers: hostile to the League
and to Britain by extension. Lindley was embarrassed. In a letter unprecedented for an ambassador to write, he regretted that he had failed to bring
home to London 'the peculiarities of the case which political prudence,
common sense and above all a regard for British interests demanded . . .:

I blame myself grievously for my failure to convince HM Government of the risks they were running by allowing matters to take their course according to the fixed and immutable principles of the League. I now find myself faced with the imminent danger, if not the actual probability, of the supreme failure of not having prevented a disastrous and avoidable conflict with the country to which I am accredited.[13]

Once a ceasefire had been declared in the area, the Foreign Office privately examined the criticism that Lindley's embassy in Tokyo had been pro-Japanese throughout the crisis as many were saying. This seeped through to Tokyo. George Sansom, the commercial counsellor, defended the Tokyo embassy's views resolutely.[14] This was supported by W. R. Connor Green, an official who had previously served in Tokyo but had returned to the Japan desk in London. He reversed the criticism, writing that, when he had been in Lindley's embassy, 'we were never given any indications as to what if any was HMG's policy . . . The Embassy tried to point out exactly what was going to happen. We were right every time.'This was a bold defence even if one that the historian can scarcely accept today. Over Japan's intentions at Shanghai and Jehol the embassy was fortunate to get it right.[15]

From mid-April 1933 Lindley who had not taken leave between Lisbon and Tokyo spent six months in Britain. En route via Canada he was interviewed by a journalist from the *Winnipeg Free Press*. He reported that Lindley said that Japan had much provocation from the Chinese for their actions in Manchukuo and that Japan's friendship means more to Britain than China's. Lindley denied these statements and claimed that he had merely reiterated the arguments contained in the Lytton report. But the allegation created a stir in Canada, in the press in Britain and in the House of Lords where Cecil once again drew attention to the pronouncedly pro-Japanese stance of the ambassador.[16]

In London Lindley had the expected consultations with the Office and the Japanese ambassador over the difficult commercial situation affecting various members of the British Commonwealth. The MacDonald government was under pressure to take action against Japanese cotton goods in British Empire markets. The situation with India, Australia and West Africa was difficult.[17] It seems likely that the decision to send George Sansom to Simla in June in order to take part in the conference arising from the decision to terminate the commercial convention between Japan and India owed much to Lindley's recommendation. Sansom was to advise both the British and Indian governments but also to explain Japan's position over the cotton goods trade.[18] Lindley also drew up an important memorandum for the cabinet on the Far Eastern situation on 20 May. He also met Neville Chamberlain, the chancellor of the Exchequer and strongest member of the cabinet, and seems to have told him that, if Japan had not an outlet for her population explosion in China, there was the possibility of immigration trouble in British colonies. This idea which was not unique to Lindley impressed some leaders; and his views are quoted at meetings of the Committee of Imperial Defence.[19]

The impression that Lindley was on an evangelizing mission found its way to Tokyo. Lady Sansom wrote that he had been doing some mighty spade-work and she was amused at '. . . the picture of the delightful man [Lindley] with his understanding of Japan's sheer necessities and forceful trading habits, stumping up and down the Office'. The impression he made in Whitehall is buried in the archives. The fact that he returned to his post for a mere three months prior to his retirement is also something of a mystery. He reached Tokyo around Christmas 1933 and presented a message of British goodwill from the foreign secretary to the newly-appointed foreign minister of Japan, Hirota Kōki. This was, of course, reciprocated. It was with some relief that Lindley was able to report that Britain had reverted to the '. . . well-tried policy of making friendly relations with Japan the cornerstone of our Far Eastern policy'.[20]

Lindley suffered a bout of ill-health which delayed his departure from Japan. He must have regretted the delay because a major crisis blew up in his final weeks. The so-called Amau (Amō) Declaration was reported in the press on 17 April 1934. It was a detailed and provocative statement made unofficially to journalists by the press spokesman (jōhōbuchō) of the Foreign Ministry. It was tantamount to an assertion of Japan's independent responsibility (tandoku sekinin) in China and her opposition to military help and political loans being given by other Powers there. It threw down the gauntlet to the Powers and particularly to the United States which had for a decade and more been trying to build up a new and stable China. In the light of the global protests which resulted, it was left to Lindley and to Ambassador Grew to seek clarification of Japan's true position and to secure the toning down of the Amau declaration by discussion with Foreign Minister Hirota. This they broadly achieved.[21]

Lindley left Tokyo for good on 28 April. He had his final audience as ambassador with King George V on 2 June. Though he had earlier entertained hopes of being offered a final post in 'a good European embassy',[22] he gladly went into retirement one week later. He felt, he wrote, liberated from the stultifying atmosphere of 'The Office':

> I can't describe my joy at being quit of the Foreign Office and all its works for good. Bureaucrats are top dog and it is impossible to get anything done.[23]

We may presume that it was at this time when he had cast off the burdens of office that he penned this light-hearted verse:

> Thou who seest all things below
> Grant that Thy Servants may go slow
> That they may study to comply
> With regulations till they die.
>
> Teach us Lord to reverence
> Committees more than common sense.
> Impress our minds to make no plan
> But pass the baby when we can.
>
> And when the tempter seems to give
> Us feelings of initiative,
> Or when alone we go too far
> Chastise us with a circular.
>
> Mid war and tumult, fire and storms
> Strengthen us we pray with forms.
> Thus will Thy Servants ever be
> A flock of perfect sheep for Thee.[24]

This 'hymn for use in government departments', as he called it, may reflect a hurt done to Lindley by the Foreign Office during the Manchurian Incident, especially the portion in italics. At all events, it hints in a jocular vein at his view of an institution that was ripe for reform.

Many thought his retirement was a waste of human resources. Sir Samuel Hoare, formerly secretary of state for India and currently foreign secretary, publicly expressed his regret at Lindley's departure from the public service: '. . . he retired from public life far too soon! He has decided to retire to Hampshire; instead of which, he could still be devoting his valuable services to the Empire'. This confirms Lindley's undoubted dedication to the long-term interests of the British Empire and his reputation for conservatism.[25]

After the close of Lindley's professional career in Japan, he had many admirers there, among the strongest being the Sansoms. George Sansom who as Commercial Counsellor was a highly regarded member of Lindley's embassy, was interviewed by Professor Allan Nevins at Palo Alto on 11 June 1957. He said that Lindley's good point as ambassador was that he 'used his experience and kept his temper'. Interviewed on this subject following the Suez Crisis of 1956, Sansom drew a contemporary parallel. He said that Lindley's approach was in marked contrast to that of the protagonists of the 1956 crisis, namely Anthony Eden, John Foster Dulles and even President Dwight Eisenhower. He kept his cool and held his tongue. Lady Sansom also spelt out Lindley's virtues in even greater detail:

> . . . what a superb public servant he was. And particularly valuable here in these last years when it was advisable to keep a wary eye on America whose policy as a rule has been neither good nor bad but simply all over the place in partial enthusiasms. That we the British should not be left carrying the baby may not sound a noble aim, but by Jove! it was practical enough. And in such matters Sir Francis was throughout able and shrewd and coura-geous.[26]

Retirement was alien to Lindley's vigorous nature. He was still active at the age of 62 and mapped out a new life for himself.

On the one hand, he settled in the rural paradise of the Weir House, Old Alresford, Hampshire. There he indulged his passion for fishing and became the chairman of the Test and Itchen fishing association, and an official verderer of the New Forest.

On the other, he became chairman of the council of the Japan Society of London in 1935. Since Lindley's tenure in Tokyo was relatively short, his con-tribution to Anglo-Japanese relations comes equally from these Japan Society years. This was likely to be a difficult assignment because the society had been riven apart by the Manchurian Crisis.[27] He was to continue in office until 1949 when he found it necessary to retire owing to advancing age. Sir Francis died at Alresford on 17 August 1950, one year after his wife.

14

Sir Robert Clive
Ambassador to Japan, 1934–37

Sir Robert Clive

ANTHONY BEST

S ir Robert Clive (1877–1948) holds a curious position in the history of Anglo-Japanese relations, for although the period in which he was ambassador to Japan has been the object of much study, the man himself remains a mystery.[1] This is particularly so when he is compared to those who preceded and followed him as ambassador to Japan, Sir Francis Lindley and Sir Robert Craigie. The reason for his relative anonymity is not difficult to explain. Unlike Lindley and Craigie, he did not spend much of his time in Tokyo arguing with the Foreign Office or with his British counterpart in China.[2] These may have been years of diplomatic fluidity but they were not ones of controversy between the British Embassy and London.

Sir Robert Clive was born in 1877 and entered the Foreign Office in 1903. He first went to Japan from 1905 to 1909 as Third Secretary at the Tokyo Embassy and then had further East Asian experience as the Counsellor at the Peking Legation from 1920 to 1923. Prior to his term as ambassador to Japan he had served for a long period as the Minister to Tehran, where he had successfully negotiated an end to the British extraterritorial regime in Persia.

Clive arrived in Tokyo in July 1934 at a difficult time in Anglo-Japanese relations. Since the final act of the Manchurian Crisis when Britain had initiated a month-long arms embargo against both Japan and China relations between London and Tokyo had become tense. The central issue was the inability of Britain and Japan to agree about the future of China, notably because Japan was seeking to implement its own Monroe Doctrine in East Asia, which would allow it a veto over Western dealings with the Chinese. Another pressing problem was the rise of antagonism between the two countries over trade issues. A huge surge of Japanese exports into the British colonies in Asia, including India, had led to an outcry from textile producers and the protectionist lobby in Britain and accordingly quotas had been introduced to curb Japan's incursion. This in turn provided ammunition for those in Japan who sought to whip up anti-Western sentiment and a raison d'être for the desire to create an economic sphere of influence in East Asia. As if these were not enough another contentious issue was rapidly coming to the fore, the future of the naval limitation process that the United States, Britain and Japan had initiated at the Washington Conference in 1921/22.

At the same time, however, there were countervailing forces in operation that sought to dampen down the burgeoning ill feeling. In London the development of the threat from Nazi Germany had led some politicians and officials, particularly the Chancellor of the Exchequer, Neville Chamberlain, and his civil servants in the Treasury, to conclude that Britain could ill-afford tensions with Japan and they were thus interested in cultivating a rapprochement. Similar thoughts were entertained in some quarters in Tokyo where there was an interest in finding common ground over China and a mechanism that would allow Japan naval equality in principle with Britain and the United States. However, not all were sanguine about the prospects of renewed friendship; most notably the Foreign Office in London felt that Britain had to proceed cautiously in its dealings with Japan lest it offend China and the United States. This then was the complex environment within which Clive had to work.

Before he could even become acclimatized the fluid nature of Anglo-Japanese relations plunged Clive into the middle of a controversy. In his first meeting with the Japanese Foreign Minister, Hirota Kōki, on 5 July 1934 the latter raised the possibility of Japan signing non-aggression pacts with Britain and the United States in order to pave the way for an agreement over naval limitation. This overture provoked much debate in London about whether Britain should use this opportunity to orchestrate a rapprochement, an episode that has been extensively analysed by historians such as Ann Trotter, Hosoya Chihiro, and Gill Bennett.[3] Clive's role in these events was largely to act as a messenger and to try under orders from the Cabinet to get Hirota to elaborate on his proposals. His efforts were in vain, and the whole affair seems to have heightened his innate caution.

His suspicion of the Japanese was further reinforced by the welcome provided by the Japanese to the mission sent by the Federation of British Industry (FBI) in September and October 1934 to investigate the potential for British trade and investment in Manchukuo. The FBI mission was unofficial and supposed to deal solely with commercial issues, but the Japanese government and media treated it as if had a political purpose much to the embarrassment of the British Embassy. The most problematic aspect of the mission was that on its arrival in Japan Clive discovered to his horror that an audience had been arranged for its members with the emperor. Clive's initial reaction was to prevent the audience from going ahead but once it was clear that this would mortally offend the Japanese he demurred.[4] However, this episode, added to the artificially cordial atmosphere cultivated by the Japanese, aroused his distrust. At first glance it might appear that he was allowing an adherence to traditional diplomatic formality to cloud his judgement, and that he should have welcomed this outpouring of Japanese affection which was surely just what Britain needed at this juncture. However, what Clive surmised, perhaps under the prompting of his astute Commercial Counsellor, George Sansom [later Sir George], was that there was no real substance to Japan's words of friendship beyond a desire to persuade Britain to accept a subordinate position in East Asia.[5]

After this baptism of fire and with his wariness duly reinforced, Clive settled down to a more normal routine. Over the next two and a half years he became a careful observer of the political scene in Japan, although by his own admission he found Japanese thinking difficult to understand. In November 1935 he noted in exasperation to King George V's private secretary, Sir Clive Wigram:

> The inner workings of the Japanese are often beyond our comprehension and one learns with time never to judge these people by our own standards or to expect them to react as we should.[6]

In regard to British policy towards Japan Clive did his best to make sure that Britain steered a middle course neither engaging in outright appeasement nor leaning towards the construction of an anti-Japanese bloc with the United States. In January 1935 following Japan's abrogation of the Washington and London naval limitation treaties he produced a lengthy and strongly worded despatch in which he opposed the view recently propounded by Lord Lothian that Britain should draw closer to the United States. Instead he argued that Britain should seek to use its long-standing ties to Japan, such as memory of the alliance, to act as a 'moderating influence' and to see whether Hirota's vague overtures could be made into something more substantial.[7] This analysis was well received in the Foreign Office. Indeed the Permanent Under-Secretary at the Foreign Office, Sir Robert Vansittart, who resented the intrusion of amateurs such as Lothian, praised Clive's professionalism and ordered that the ambassador's views should be circulated to the Cabinet.[8]

However, it was not easy to follow such a balanced policy, as ironically the enthusiasts for rapprochement in both countries tended to make progress more rather than less difficult. The problem with the Treasury was that its enthusiasm for a deal with Japan clouded its judgement. Notably in the autumn of 1935 Chamberlain sent out the government's chief economic adviser, Sir Frederick Leith-Ross, to assist the Chinese with currency reform and attempted to link this endeavour to a political settlement of the region's political problems by proposing that Britain and Japan should offer a loan to China in exchange for Chinese recognition of Manchukuo. In September 1935 Leith-Ross arrived in Tokyo and attempted to sell this idea to the Japanese, but neither the Foreign Ministry nor the Finance Ministry were interested. In a state of disappointment he then proceeded to China where he again flew the recognition kite, only for it to be shot down by a firm Chinese rebuff. This sort of amateur diplomacy did not impress Clive and during a visit to Shanghai in November to meet the British Ambassador to China, Sir Alexander Cadogan, he informed the latter of his fury about the whole business.[9]

On the Japanese side there were also elements that strove for better Anglo-Japanese relations but here, too, the approach, as far as Clive was concerned, was fundamentally flawed. The leading Japanese figure in 1936/37 pressing for a rapprochement was the new Ambassador to Britain, Yoshida Shigeru. From the first Clive was not enthralled by the prospect of Yoshida in such a key position. In March 1936 on learning of the latter's appointment Clive noted in a letter to Wigram, now the private secretary to Edward VIII, that

Yoshida was 'a very agreeable smiling little man' but that he was not of the calibre of his esteemed predecessor, Matsudaira Tsuneo.[10] Clive's fears about Yoshida's judgement were confirmed in the autumn of 1936 when he learnt that the latter was, without explicit approval from Tokyo, attempting to interest Britain in an over-arching settlement of all problems in Anglo-Japanese relations. Afraid that Britain might take Yoshida seriously Clive sent a number of warnings to the Foreign Office, stating that the new ambassador was not so influential in Tokyo and that he had only been sent to London to save his face after the Imperial Japanese Army (IJA) had vetoed his appointment as Foreign Minister in March 1936.[11]

Clive may therefore have had some hopes that a settlement of Anglo-Japanese difficulties was possible but he was not prepared to support rushed and ill-conceived diplomacy to support such a goal. Moreover, from late 1935 to 1937 his belief in the need for caution was reinforced by a revival of Japanese bellicosity both by its rhetoric about its foreign relations generally and by its policy towards China. In particular the IJA's support for the autonomy of north China and for the smuggling of Japanese goods into this region, thus evading paying duty to the Chinese Maritime Customs, suggested that there was little point in expecting Japan to negotiate reasonably. In addition, Clive was outraged in October 1936 when a number of Royal Navy ratings visiting the port of Keelung in Formosa were arrested and then beaten by Japanese police. Clive believed that this incident was symptomatic of Japanese arrogance and its lack of respect for British interests and was therefore convinced that Britain should push hard to achieve a satisfactory settlement of this incident, which he hoped would bring the Japanese to their senses. Indeed, in this episode he took a harsher line than the Foreign Office and feared that his forthright refusal to compromise might have annoyed the latter.[12]

Clive's increasingly tough stance towards Japan had both its admirers and detractors. Among the former was the Commander-in-Chief China station, Admiral Sir Charles Little, who noted approvingly to the First Sea Lord, Admiral Sir Ernle Chatfield, in July 1936 that Clive recognized that the only language that the Japanese understood was force.[13] The Foreign Office also generally approved of Clive's actions and assessments, which were much in line with its own thinking. However those in Britain who longed for a return to Anglo-Japanese friendship saw Clive as failing to take advantage of some crucial feelers from the Japanese and therefore acting as an obstacle to their goal. In his diary entry for 3 March 1936 the Japanophile former army language officer and Reuters journalist in Japan, Malcolm Kennedy, noted that during a lunch he had with two prominent supporters of close Anglo-Japanese relations, H. A. Gwynne, the editor of the Morning Post, and Arthur Edwardes, the financial adviser to the Manchukuo government, Clive had been heavily criticized. All three men had lamented the fact that Clive had recently turned down an offer from the IJA to provide a 1,000 man guard of honour at the ceremony to commemorate the recent death of George V, and noted that he had also blundered over the FBI mission's audience with the Japanese Emperor in September 1934.[14]

Divisions also existed within the embassy in Tokyo. In 1935 the War Office decided that in the interests of better Anglo-Japanese relations it would appoint the stridently Japanophile Major-General F. S. G. Piggott as its military attaché. Clive was not impressed with this choice on the grounds that 'It might be embarrassing to have on my staff an officer on whose judgement I could not rely and with whom I might differ on broad questions of policy.'[15] Unfortunately, the War Office was adamant and Piggott duly took up his post in the summer of 1936. Almost immediately his views began to clash with those of Clive, for Piggott was convinced that the general mood within the IJA favoured a rapprochement with Britain. Clive was prepared to acknowledge that the IJA's mood might have recently improved but, drawing on the opinion of the vastly more experienced Sansom, he argued that this did not by any means suggest that an agreement was practicable, for any terms acceptable to Japan would necessarily offend China and the United States.[16] Clearly, Clive felt that of his Japanese experts, Sansom and Piggott, the former was by far the more reliable and after his return to London in the summer of 1937 he lobbied for Sansom to be promoted as a means of ensuring that he stayed in Tokyo.[17]

Towards the end of his tour of duty Clive again became more optimistic about the prospects for Anglo-Japanese relations. This had nothing do with the machinations of the Treasury, Yoshida or Piggott, but was rather linked to the appearance of Satō Naotake as the Japanese Foreign Minister in March 1937. Clive had a high opinion of Satō and believed that he was a genuine Anglophile who would work for real reconciliation. He felt, however, that Satō had to be allowed to bring around the IJA in his own time and that Britain could not and should not try to force the pace of events by making any ill-timed overtures.[18] Given time and latitude Clive believed that Sato could achieve a great deal; he noted to the head of the Far Eastern Department, Charles Orde, in March 1937 that 'my own view about the immediate future is that the Japanese are likely to be less aggressive and more amenable to reason than they have been in the last few years'.[19]

Clive's time as ambassador came to an end in May 1937 immediately after the coronation of George VI. On his departure Japan appeared to be clawing its way back from international isolation and seemed ready to engage in talks with Britain on a basis of equality. Such hopes were, however, soon to be dashed, for the government of which Satō was a member collapsed at the end of the month and in July 1937 fighting broke out in north China. Clive's optimism thus proved to be woefully misplaced. The Sino-Japanese War would lead to new, even more serious problems in Anglo-Japanese relations, but Clive had now bequeathed these to his successor, Sir Robert Craigie. Clive did not, however, throw off the Japanese yoke entirely, for he soon found in November 1937 that his new posting, Brussels, was to be home to an abortive conference to end the Sino-Japanese hostilities.

Sir Robert Clive thus took the helm in Anglo-Japanese relations in a particularly difficult period. The overall impression that Clive gives is of a diplomat who was very much in tune with the thinking of the Foreign Office. He was a cautious man who wanted diplomacy handled in the traditional channels or not at all. He did not dismiss the chance that Anglo-Japanese rapprochement was possible but at the same time felt that it could not be forced or hurried. As such he appears as the quintessential careful diplomat and as a man deserving of the description given him in the Dictionary of National Biography, namely that he was 'a superb public servant'.[20] Whether Britain needed a more dynamic figure who was less likely to toe the Foreign Office line remains however a matter of debate.

15
Sir Robert Craigie
Ambassador to Japan, 1937–41

Sir Robert Craigie

ANTONY BEST

The reputation of Sir Robert Craigie (1883–1959) as ambassador to Japan in the years 1937–41 is one of more controversial subjects in the history of inter-war Anglo-Japanese relations. Two schools of thought have appeared in an effort to assess his impact; one has portrayed Craigie as a man inexperienced in Japanese affairs and thus too easily given to unwarranted acts of appeasement in an attempt to win over the nebulous Japanese moderates'.[1] The other school has in contrast drawn a picture of a realist all too aware of Britain's weakness in East Asia and determined to use his substantial skills as a negotiator to prevent the outbreak of a potentially disastrous war for Britain.[2] In attempting to present a portrait of Craigie, both schools have focused primarily on the various crises with which he had to contend, such as Tientsin in 1939, the *Asama Maru* and Burma Road incidents in 1940, and the final path to war in 1941. In addition, there has been much debate over his contentious Final Report in 1943, in which he criticized the Churchill government for not having done enough to try to prevent war from breaking out. There is, however, a danger in concentrating simply on these crises because, although they are important, they do not necessarily lead one to see the broader motives behind his thinking: to get a real understanding of Craigie's attitude towards his role as ambassador one first has to look at his career in the years immediately preceding his appointment.

One of the most important things to note is that before he reached Yokohama on 3 September 1937 Craigie had never held a position within the Far Eastern Department at the Foreign Office or been posted to East Asia, and does not even appear to have had any substantial links with the Japanophile lobby in Britain. He instead emerged as a figure of some prominence in the field of Anglo-Japanese relations due to his role as Britain's chief negotiator in the naval limitation talks of 1934–36. This was significant for two reasons: first, because it helps to explain why many of his later contemporaries in Japan treated his observations on Japanese politics with disdain, and second, because Craigie's experience in the naval talks left him with a deep-rooted personal belief in how Japan should be perceived relative to Britain's global interests. It was this resolutely 'power political' approach, rather than one of espousing a sentimental '*rapprochement* at any price', which was to be the main influence on his diplomatic efforts in Tokyo, and which was to make his position different from the Japanophiles in British circles.

Fundamental to Craigie's assessment of his responsibilities in Japan was the belief that he should do all in his power to neutralize that country in terms of the global struggle for influence with Germany and that, in particular, he should counter Ribbentrop's efforts to win over Japan. As early as January 1936 Craigie was indicating his fear of the consequences of a German-Japanese understanding, and in December of that year, after the signing of the Anti-Comintern Pact, he wrote in response to a criticism of the Eden-Yoshida talks from the then British ambassador to Japan, Sir Robert Clive, that:

> '. . . to rebuff our friends in Japan just at the moment when there much searching of the Japanese heart as to the wisdom of the recent agreement with Germany would be to play the German game.'[3]

This assessment of a potential two-front threat to British interests led Craigie to believe that Britain should be circumspect in its treatment of Japan and, while deploring in private Japan's unprincipled expansionism, avoid any moralistic outbursts which would only have the effect of antagonizing the Japan policymakers. The logical consequence of this attitude was a distinct tendency to play down Britain's regional interests in East Asia for the sake of the larger goal of keeping Japan placid on the global scale.

The most obvious example of this came with Craigie's contention that Britain should adhere strictly to a policy of neutrality in the Sino-Japanese war, on the grounds that Japan was bound to win and that to support the Chinese in any way would antagonize the Japanese needlessly. This was not a popular line to take, as it seemed to ignore the general sentiment that China was deserving of support and the feeling that a Japanese victory would mark the collapse of Britain's considerable economic stake in East Asia. In July 1938 *The Times'* journalist Peter Fleming noted in this respect that:

> His line seems to be to drift in a dignified way into a position where, in a haze of benevolence, we shall be presented by the Japanese with the jackal's share in China (which the poor sap believes will be worth having) . . . [T]hough he may be following what is nowadays often called by the English a "realistic" policy, he almost entirely fails to apprehend the realities in Eastern Asia, however alive he may be to the realities in Europe.[4]

In this analysis Fleming missed the point of Craigie's case, which was that the potential danger of a German-Japanese military alliance meant that the 'realities in Europe' were of vital importance to the formulation of Britain's East Asia policy, and that to concentrate upon defending every aspect of Britain's interests in China would only create grave dangers. The clearest expression of Craigie's views on this subject came in a telegram to the Foreign Office at the height of the Tientsin Crisis, in which he noted caustically:

There has been an open partisanship about our policy which in the circumstances of today does more credit to our heart than to our head . . . I feel
bound to emphasise deadly dangers to which we are heading if we cannot get
back to a position of stricter neutrality.[5]

Another example of Craigie's emphasis on the need to take cognizance of
the global consequences of Britain's policy towards Japan was his reaction to
the debate in Whitehall in 1939–40 over war-time relations with Japan. With
the start of the European war it became even more necessary than ever to iso-
late Japan as a threat, and Craigie felt that Britain could best achieve this by
taking the opportunity provided by Germany and Japan's falling out over the
Nazi-Soviet Pact to improve relations with Tokyo. On 16 November he wrote
forthrightly to the Foreign Office:

. . . I assume it to be of vital importance that Japan should not become an
adversary in the present conflict and, however improbable this may appear
at the moment, we must try to arrest at the start any trend in policy leading
to that direction.[6]

He saw the potential for increasing mutual understanding in a number of
spheres, and argued in particular for a quick solution to the continuing controversy over Tientsin and for Britain to take a lenient attitude towards Japan
over problems arising from the policy of economic warfare against Germany.
The height of his efforts to pursue this policy came, however, in July 1940
when, in reaction to the latest crisis in Anglo-Japanese relations over the
Burma Road, he argued not simply for a solution to that particular issue
but for an altogether wider settlement. He began a telegram on 14 July by
arguing:

In general I agree with the underlying ideas; Powers having possessions in
East Asia should be prepared to make concessions to Japan as a means of pur-
chasing a generous peace for China.[7]

He then proceeded to set out Japan's grievances against the West, and came
to the conclusion that the most effective way in which Britain and the United
States could satisfy Japan's sense of being discriminated against was to allow
her much easier access to raw materials, which he held to be more important
to Japan than territorial aggrandizement. This was a penetrating analysis of
Japan's motives for trying to revise the international system, and can be con-
trasted usefully with Craigie's comments in 1936 about the idea of a colonial
deal with Germany, when he had stated: 'What puts us wrong not only with
Germany but with the whole world is the slogan, when applied to mandates,
of "what we have we hold".'[8] This type of analysis was a logical extension of
his fears of the consequences of imperial over-commitment and showed that
Craigie's thinking was capable of moving beyond the short-term, day-to-day
defence of British interests to a broader understanding that a rigid and inflex-
ible defence of the *status quo* might create the very challenge which one
wanted to avoid.
    To state that Craigie's aim was to avoid war by tailoring British policy to
eschew confrontation does, of course, suggest that his policy was tantamount
to appeasement and that, in terms of his attitude towards China, it involved
all the sacrifice of another nation's interests and moral pejoration that the
word implies. This view can also be supported by reference to the common

claim that Craigie was a 'Chamberlain man', and the widely held but unsubstantiated suggestion that Chamberlain had been responsible for his appointment.[9] In addition, one can point to Craigie's reaction in an embassy memorandum to the Munich Agreement, which was to praise it for its realism and laud it as a check to Hitler's ambitions.[10] In taking such a moralist view, however, one has to be careful, for Craigie's advice by no means always stressed conciliation over confrontation; there was an important element in his thinking of making it clear to Japan that Britain was willing to agree to a reasonable settlement of Anglo-Japanese rivalries but that, if pushed, it was equally willing to see escalation. To choose but one example, during the early days of the Tientsin Crisis, while engaging in efforts to get the Japanese government to accept talks, Craigie was also urging the Foreign Office to set up the necessary apparatus to oversee the initiation of economic sanctions.[11]

There were indeed occasions when Craigie went further than espousing a 'carrot-and-stick' policy, and instead came down strongly in favour of the need for harsh action to be taken against Japan. One example of this can be seen in January 1939 when, following Japan's unilateral abrogation of the Nine Power Treaty and amid rumours of Japanese negotiations with Germany and Italy about a military alliance, Craigie wrote a strident letter to Sir Alexander Cadogan, the Permanent Under-Secretary at the Foreign Office, in which he observed:

> . . . I advocated a policy of conciliation here as long as I felt there was any hope of the Japanese people playing fair with us; but the prolongation of this trouble, the military successes and the eclipse (temporarily, I hope) of more reasonable elements from Japanese political life have necessitated a change of method on our part until such time as the situation here changes for the better.[12]

This sense of disillusionment caused Craigie to propose that Britain should urge strongly on the United States, which had just requested an exchange of views with the Foreign Office on the subject of economic reprisals against Japan, a policy of refusing to purchase gold from Japanese banks.[13] However, the interest of Washington in pursuing a tougher line towards Japan was not to last long, and Craigie was forced to return to his usual cautious stance.

The above incident is significant because it helps to illustrate that Craigie's attitude towards Japan was not constant and that, in particular, it was influenced by two transient factors; first, the position in Japanese political life of a group of policy-makers who were seen by Craigie as moderates and, second, the continuing debate in Washington over whether or not the Roosevelt administration should take a more active role in East Asia and throw off the shackles of isolationism. Of these two factors it is the influence on Craigie of the Japanese 'moderates' which has been the most controversial. As the comment made by Craigie to Cadogan illustrates, the ambassador was convinced that there did exist in Japan a group of politicians and others who were broadly sympathetic to the idea of closer Anglo-Japanese relations, but this was by no means a view shared by many of his British and American contemporaries. The most significant of these critics in this area of debate was the commercial counsellor at the British embassy in Tokyo, Sir George Sansom who, with his long experience in Japan, felt that the 'moderates', if they did exist, only differed in terms of method rather than aim from the 'radicals', and that they were anyway small in number and not very influential.[14] This view was shared by the Far Eastern Department in the Foreign Office and also by Stanley Hornbeck, the adviser on Far Eastern Affairs to the State Department in Washington.[15]

To Craigie this dismissal of the Japanese 'moderates' was overly cynical and lacking in an understanding of the subtleties of the situation. His reaction to one particular episode, in which Hornbeck told Lord Lothian, the British ambassador to the United States, that he entirely discounted the influence of the 'moderates', was to note to the Foreign Office:

> Though every Japanese naturally desires the advancement of his country's fortunes, distinction must be made between moderates who favour gradual economic expansion through the control of vital raw materials and the development of overseas markets as the solution for Japan's organic economic ills, and extremists who, impelled by mystical fanaticism, aspire to world domination.[16]

His belief in the existence and significance of a 'moderate' group can be seen as having its origins in two factors, first the fact that the majority of the Japanese contacts that Craigie had made before his appointment to Tokyo, such as Matsudaira Tsuneo, Rear Admiral Yamamoto Isoroku, Yoshida Shigeru and Nagai Matsuzō, favoured a broadly pro-Western foreign policy and, second, the influence of the military attaché he had inherited in Japan, Major-General F. S. G. Piggott.[17]

IN PURSUIT OF JAPAN'S 'MODERATES'

Piggott's acquaintance with Japan was almost as long as that of Sansom, but his conclusions about the direction of Japanese policy in 1937, when Craigie arrived in Japan, were very different from those of the commercial counsellor. Where Sansom saw only a cause for pessimism, Piggott felt that, if sufficient patience and understanding was shown by both sides, then some sort of *rapprochement* was possible. This attitude, unsurprisingly perhaps, appealed to Craigie more than that of Sansom, for Piggott's thinking seemed to be in line with his desire to counter Germany's influence in Tokyo, and also offered a greater prospect for a personal diplomatic triumph. The result was that Piggott was soon able to develop a close relationship with Craigie, introducing him to Anglophile Japanese and stressing what the 'moderates' could achieve if only given the chance. The ambassador's seeming reliance on the military attaché was anathema to the Far Eastern Department, and indeed to a number of the junior members of the embassy staff, and only helped to underline the impression that Craigie was naive when it came to understanding Japan.

To argue that Craigie's belief in the 'moderates' rested only on the above two factors would, however, be to do him a disservice, and in particular it is too easy to blame his enthusiasms on Piggott. The fact of the matter was that, in the main, it was Craigie's experience of diplomacy in Japan that led him to believe that there was a moderate branch of opinion in the Japanese government. In negotiation after negotiation Craigie found that there were figures, particularly in the Gaimushō, who favoured an amelioration of tensions. His talks with General Ugaki Kazushige in the late summer of 1938, and his meetings with Araki Hachirō over Tientsin in July and August 1939 and over the *Asama Maru* in January and February 1940, seemed to show that with the right sort of approach common ground could be found to overcome even the most difficult of crises.

The inference from these experiences was that, when he was allowed to engage in real diplomacy, progress could be made, but that he was only allowed to negotiate when the Foreign Office had dug themselves in to a new crisis. Even in these circumstances Craigie was only allowed to operate on a very short leash and the Far Eastern Department remained as a constant immovable obstacle to any attempt to strike a more general deal with his Japanese counterparts. The result was a growing sense of exasperation on the ambassador's part, which sometimes boiled over into waspish attacks on the Foreign Office; for example, during the Tientsin Crisis, when Piggott was criticized by the department over his informal meetings with Japanese army officers, Craigie wrote back to London:

> I am left here with the feeling that such efforts as we are able to make here to prevent the state of our relations with Japan from going from bad to worse are viewed with suspicion and misgiving by the Far Eastern Department and that only when we are engaged in our normal duty of protesting and recriminating can you really sleep comfortably in your beds.[18]

However, as noted above, there were times when it appeared clear to Craigie that the influence of the 'moderates' had been eclipsed temporarily and that Japan under the 'extremists' was bent on confrontation. In these circumstances his usual policy was to urge the Foreign Office to follow a more coercive line in the hope that pressure on the Japanese government might lead to a revival of moderate fortunes, or at the very least deter them from escalating tensions further.

It is noticeable that on these occasions Craigie's espousal of a tougher policy was frequently influenced by the simultaneous possibility of Britain receiving diplomatic support from the United States but, even when he seemingly was swept away with enthusiasm at the chances of Anglo-American co-operation, he retained a somewhat jaundiced view of Washington. In understanding Craigie's thinking on America, it is again important to see him as heavily influenced by his diplomatic experience prior to his arrival in Tokyo. His role in the naval talks and his years from 1928 to 1934 as head of the American Department in the Foreign Office had led him to construct his own views on the reliability of the United States, which are best summed up in a letter he wrote to Lord Simon in July 1940:

> . . .   the Americans are for ever inciting us to assume an attitude of utmost firmness towards Japan, only to tell us, when the inevitable crisis comes, that they are of course not in a position to use force. I have been aware of this tendency from the start but the Far Eastern Department of the Foreign Office have been less wary – or perhaps less well-acquainted with American methods – than I have been.[19]

This cynical assessment helped in general to cement even further his belief that Britain should pursue a cautious policy towards Japan, for he felt that, if Britain should confront Japan, there was little chance that America would do more than support Britain with high-sounding rhetoric. This is not to deny that there were various episodes during his time in Tokyo when the United States did appear to be on the verge of collaborating with Britain against Japan, for example in January 1938 and January 1939, but even in these circumstances, when pressed to commit itself, Washington backed down.

In arguing that Craigie's actions as ambassador must be seen against the background of Britain's global security problems, the reluctance of the United States to commit itself to Britain's aid in East Asia, and the complications caused by the factionalism in the Japanese polity, it is possible to see his preferred policy not so much as one of abject appeasement but rather as a practical response to a complex and potentially explosive situation. There may have been occasionally a streak of naivety in his optimism about the good intentions of the Japanese 'moderates', but in the end his view that, as Britain already had enough enemies in the world, it would be foolish to alienate another power needlessly, was fundamentally sound. In the years 1937–40 this was a sensible attitude to take, and Craigie's long-term vision and skill in negotiations acted as a useful counter to a Far Eastern Department which at times seemed hell-bent on propelling Britain into desperately dangerous crises over relatively trivial issues, the most obvious case being Tientsin.

FINAL MONTHS OF PEACE

It is, however, arguable whether Craigie's attitude towards the events of 1941 was as sound as his advice had been in previous years. Before looking at his role in the final months of peace, it is worth noting that from August 1940 Craigie took an increasingly tough line towards Japan. The initial catalyst for this change appears to have been the widespread arrests of British civilians in Japan in late July and early August and the suicide in Japanese custody of the Reuters' correspondent, Melville Cox. Following on from this, the Japanese occupation of north Indo-China and Japan's accession to the Tripartite Pact with Germany and Italy seem to have confirmed in Craigie's mind that the 'moderates' had been swept away by the new Konoe cabinet. In addition, these events caused the Roosevelt administration to conclude that Japan must be resisted, and the subsequent galvanization of America's resources and will seemed to suggest that Britain could afford to take a tougher stance itself. The result was that by 11 October 1940 Craigie was reporting to the Foreign Office:

> The pro-British faction has been driven . . . to ground . . . and is now powerless to exert any influence whatsoever. Japanese foreign policy will continue to be dominated by the extremists until such a time as the Axis powers meet with a decisive reverse in Europe or until the period of an unwanted war with the United States becomes so great that a decisive change in popular opinion begins to make itself felt.[20]

Craigie's pessimism manifested itself in the autumn and winter of 1940-41 in his urging on the Foreign Office the introduction of economic sanctions against Japan, the reinforcement of Britain's military position in South-East Asia, and increased defence collaboration with the Americans; the emphasis was now squarely on containment rather than conciliation.

His backing for the expansion of sanctions, however, began to become more conditional in the spring of 1941, when he feared that restrictions on the sale of foodstuffs to Japan, such as Canadian wheat and copra from North Borneo, might, instead of deterring Japan, drive her into further aggression. On 21 May his fears in this field led him to warn that:

> To extend restrictions on Japanese imports to an extent that would force
> Japan to draw on her reserves on any considerable scale would at present be
> liable to produce those very actions we wish to avoid.[22]

This he saw as the worst possible outcome for a Britain which was still fighting for its very survival against Germany, and he took it as read that Britain
should do all in its power to prevent a war in South-East Asia. In general, it
can be taken from this that he saw the object of sanctions as hurting Japan
and making her rethink her present path, but not as a means of inducing surrender.

Despite these reservations about the direction of British policy, Craigie did
not, however, raise any objections to the Anglo-American-Dutch introduction of a far more comprehensive sanctions policy in late July 1941 following
the Japanese occupation of south Indo-China. In the light of the nature of
the provocation he saw this as a just chastisement of Japan, and this fits in
with the pattern of his support in previous crises for the use of the 'stick' as
well as the 'carrot'. Even with the benefit of hindsight he noted in his Final
Report that this action:

> ... had the merit of removing from the minds of the more responsible
> Japanese leaders the lingering hope that any further southward advance
> could be made without the virtual certainty of war with the United States.[23]

He did, though, begin to express doubts when it became clear in September
that this policy of coercion was not to be balanced by one of rewarding concessions by Japan unless those concessions bordered on a complete surrender
of all the material advantages Japan had gained since 1935. His view of this
apparent lack of desire for a compromise in Washington, which he shared
with the American ambassador in Tokyo, Joseph Grew, was that it would not
deter war but only make it more likely.[24] On 9 September he noted to the
Foreign Office:

> Neither my United States colleague or I are (sic!) suggesting any relaxation at
> this stage of measures our two countries have taken against Japan: but it
> stands to reason that in a confused situation such as exists today in Japan the
> more clearly we can bring home to the Japanese public the advantages of a
> break with Matsuoka's policy the better.[25]

Faced with the resolute refusal of Washington over two months to take a
more positive attitude towards negotiations, Craigie could only hope to remedy the situation by pressing the Foreign Office to intervene in the
Hull-Nomura talks, but here, too, there was firm opposition to even the
faintest glimmer of compromise. It is over this issue that Craigie's reputation
has become most controversial, for in his Final Report it is Britain's failure to
try to influence thinking in Washington that comes in for the greatest criticism. In analyzing this episode, it is crucial to understand that Craigie was as
convinced as ever that his mission was to prevent Britain from being faced
with a second front that would turn the European war into a global conflict
that would fatally overstretch Britain's limited resources. What he failed to
see was that Britain's priorities had now changed; by this stage of the war
Britain had reached full wartime production levels but was still unable to
challenge German domination of Europe, and in Eastern Europe the Soviet
Union in late November 1941 looked to be on the verge of defeat. The result

was that it had become increasingly clear in London that the war could only be won if America not only committed its economic might to the allied cause, but also became a full combatant.[26]

The necessity for the United States to fight alongside the British was so vital to Churchill and his advisers that it outweighed any risks arising from a possible Japanese entry, although of course this perception of relative worth was influenced by the gross underestimation of Japanese military potential. This line of thinking influenced the Foreign Office into arguing that the most dangerous thing they could do in autumn 1941 was to advise the State Department to compromise in its Pacific policy, for such action would raise the spectre of appeasement and perhaps have unfortunate consequences in Congress and on American public opinion.[27]

It can therefore be said that, though Craigie's criticisms of American policy were arguably valid, in that a more flexible policy might have led to war being averted, this cannot be said of his attacks on the Churchill cabinet, as the latter were pursuing the only policy that seemed at that time to offer the prospect of victory, namely, the concerted wooing of the United States. It might be held that, in hindsight, Britain's apparent acquiescence to the path of war proved to be disastrous with the loss of Malaya and Burma and the shaming defeat at Singapore, but even this analysis can be balanced by Churchill's comment on Craigie's Final Report in which he observed:

> It was . . . a blessing that Japan attacked the United States and thus brought the United States into the war. Greater good fortune has rarely happened to the British Empire than this event which has revealed our friends and foes in their true light . . .[28]

It is difficult to escape the conclusion that in 1941 Craigie's previous innate sense of what policy would best serve Britain's global interests deserted him. In a sense this is not surprising; he was after all many miles away from the main theatre of war, and had not returned to London since his first appointment in 1937. In his isolation he adhered to his original orders to keep Japan out of the war at all costs, not realizing that such a policy was now considered expendable.

Craigie was detained after Pearl Harbor and returned to England in the diplomatic repatriation ship in 1942. He went into retirement at the age of 58, but served as UK representative to the UN War Crimes Commission (1945–8) and to the Geneva Conference for the protection of the victims of war (1949).

Craigie's period in Tokyo is thus not an easy one to assess in terms of whether he proved to be a good ambassador or not, and the task is not made any simpler by the continuing partisan debate over the morality of Britain's appeasement policy in the late 1930s. It is important in putting Craigie in context to get away from the idea that he was merely a 'Chamberlain man' with all the connotations that that implies, and instead judge him on his own record and words. The picture that emerges is of a man trapped in one of the most difficult diplomatic missions imaginable; he was set the task of keeping Japan mollified so that there would be no chance of an alliance between Tokyo and Berlin, but at the same time he was supposed to do all he could to protect Britain's interests in East Asia, where virtually insoluble differences naturally led to rising Anglo-Japanese antagonism. In these circumstances it seemed logical to Craigie to try to play down the regional rivalry and instead to concentrate on a low-key, practically-based policy of conciliation; in this he was encouraged by his belief in the Japanese moderates and his lack of trust in the Americans. In the end, however, with the defeat of France and the arrival of a war Britain could not win without American support, Craigie's policy became unsustainable. As American-Japanese antagonism steadily escalated towards war Craigie's line that Britain could take a third position as a mediator was simply not practical; events had passed him by.

PART III

THE POST-WAR YEARS

1945–1972

Sir Oscar Morland (left) with the representative of the Japanese Imperial
Household Agency on the day he presented his credentials in 1959.
Information Councillor, Vere Redman, is to the right.

Introduction

PETER LOWE

The repercussions of the savage conflicts in Asia and the Pacific, between 1937 and 1945, affected Anglo-Japanese relations deeply in the immediate post-war era, examined in the final part of this volume. The surrender of Singapore in February 1942, the sufferings of prisoners-of-war and the hatred engendered by war restricted the opportunities for improving understanding. To this has to be added the fears concerning renewed economic competition, which prevailed in Lancashire and Staffordshire particularly. Equally important was the assertive role now fulfilled by the United States: Britain had forfeited its former prominence and vital decisions determining Japan's fate were taken by General MacArthur in Tokyo and by the Truman administration in Washington, until Japan regained sovereignty in April 1952. After this date, too, American-Japanese relations were far more important than Anglo-Japanese exchanges. This created difficulty for British diplomats used to their country playing a leading part in the affairs of East Asia, as had been the case from the 1830s to the start of the Pacific War in 1941.

Perusing the despatches, telegrams, semi-official letters and minutes in the British Foreign Office files leads the reader to the conclusion that part of the explanation for the critical, negative views towards Japan expressed in these communications resulted from the marginalization of British influence. The principal responsibility for dealing with Japan rested with successive administrations in Washington; Whitehall could exert only limited influence. Perhaps understandably this gave rise to a certain negativism, revealed in the valedictory despatches of British envoys. Sir Esler Dening wrote, in April 1957, that the Japanese had never recovered from the shock of being 'flung overnight from the days of Richard III into the gas-lit end of the nineteenth century'.[1] Dening was not sanguine on the future: a new Japan was starting to emerge from the stage of transition inaugurated in 1945 'and I am not sure that I like the look of it'.[2] Sir Oscar Morland, in September 1963, wrote of the shallowness of democratic practice in Japan and of the inevitable re-emergence of military power.[3]

British envoys in the post-war era came from a more uniform background than had occurred before 1941. Three of the six discussed here had served in the Japan Consular Service – Dening, Morland and Pilcher. With one exception, each was fifty-five years of age upon appointment (Gascoigne was slightly younger). Four had served in Japan before 1941; two were not conversant with Japan before appointment (Lascelles and Rundall). Five came from a similar educational background, as the table below shows:

POST-WAR AMBASSADORS, 1945–72

Gascoigne (1893–1970) [Eton; 6th Dragoons and Coldstream Guards] appointed at age 53
Dening (1897–1977) [Australia; Australian Expeditionary Force] appointed at age 55
Lascelles (1902–1967) [Royal Naval College, Osborne and Dartmouth; Balliol College, Oxford] appointed at age 55
Morland (1904–1980) [Leighton Park; King's College, Cambridge] appointed at age 55
Rundall (1908–1987) [Marlborough; Peterhouse College, Cambridge] appointed at age 55
Pilcher (1912–1990) [Shrewsbury; Clare College, Cambridge] appointed at age 55

It is significant that two served in the armed forces (Gascoigne and Dening) and a third had attended naval colleges (Lascelles). Gascoigne left Eton to join the army before the outbreak of the Great War. Dening, whose father was a distinguished missionary, was educated in Australia and then volunteered for the Australian Expeditionary Force at the age of eighteen. Neither Gascoigne nor Dening attended a university.

The allied occupation of Japan extended from August 1945 to April 1952. The embassy was redefined temporarily as a liaison mission. The head of the latter for most of the occupation was Sir Alvary Gascoigne, known in the Office as 'Joe'. He had served in Tokyo between 1931 and 1934 and had been posted subsequently to Tangier and Budapest. Gascoigne represented British interests effectively during a period of overwhelming American dominance. He established a positive relationship with MacArthur, an essential feature of which was to combine tolerance of the general's monologues with agility in intervening in order to advance British concerns. Gascoigne met MacArthur frequently and conveyed the opinions of Whitehall (or his own) concerning political, strategic or economic matters. Their discussions were usually cordial but there were occasions when MacArthur resorted to shouting when he felt his motives were being questioned too critically. On the whole, however, it may be said that relations between the British mission and the Dai-Ichi building were better than they were between the Dai-Ichi building and the White House. Allowances had to be made for MacArthur's idiosyncrasies but Gascoigne and the Foreign Office believed that he had been a hard-working, conscientious and successful pro-consul. British reservations centred on the extent to which democracy would flourish and survive in the medium to long term. Each of the ambassadors considered in this part held that the occupation had not transformed Japanese society fundamentally and that democratic trends would be modified, as Japan swung increasingly to the right or left (the former was more likely but the latter could not be ruled out). Divergent approaches to waging the Korean war in 1950–1 led to an estrangement between MacArthur and Gascoigne, symbolized in the general's failure to visit Haneda airport when Gascoigne departed to become ambassador in Moscow.

Esler Dening, as Roger Buckley emphasizes, was the most senior and experienced of ambassadors after 1945. Sir Hugh Cortazzi, among others, has written of Dening's formidable character. Dening knew Japan well from his consular service in the inter-war years. In the later stages of the Pacific War, he acted as political adviser to Admiral Lord Louis Mountbatten in SEAC (South-East Asia Command). This entailed dealing with numerous complex matters, often involving differences between British and American approaches. Dening was heavily involved in handling the complications arising from British military intervention in Indonesia in 1945-6. He then returned to London and became an influential official in determining British policy in Asia, relied upon quite heavily by the Foreign Secretary, Ernest Bevin. Following British recognition of the People's Republic of China in January 1950, Dening was apparently destined to become the first ambassador to the new regime but the cool attitude revealed in Beijing, accentuated by the serious problems resulting from Chinese intervention in the Korean war, meant that Dening was instead appointed as last head of the liaison mission and first post-war ambassador to Japan.

The considerable animosity towards Japan, arising from the brutal treatment of prisoners-of-war and the apprehension concerning renewed competition, affecting textiles, shipbuilding and potteries, rendered it more difficult for Dening to establish close relations with the government and Gaimushō. Yoshida Shigeru was an Anglophile, fond of recalling the era of the Anglo-Japanese Alliance, but he was nearing the end of his premiership and he was compelled to place primacy upon relations with Washington. Dening regarded Yoshida's successors with much doubt. Kishi Nobusuke, as Dening observed in his final despatch, was pushing developments in the wrong direction, which was stimulating growing opposition. Anthony Eden, Foreign Secretary and then Prime Minister between October 1951 and January 1957, had little sympathy for Japan, perhaps influenced by his son's death in Burma in 1945.[4] The Conservative governments in Britain pursued a negative policy towards Japan and sought to block Japanese adhesion to GATT. Dening was most industrious and vigorous in stating British policy but he was too heavily influenced by Japan's past record of aggression to view Japanese revival with sympathy.

Sir Daniel Lascelles was related to the royal family and was a noted linguist. He served as ambassador to Ethiopia (1949–51) and to Afghanistan (1953–7) before his appointment to Tokyo in 1957. Dening and Lascelles were bachelors but Dening was helped by his sister in entertaining: Lascelles presided alone. He was evidently a man of some eccentricity, as depicted by Hugh Cortazzi; this is illustrated in his failure to answer dinner invitations and in his preference for travelling around Japan on his own, although he did not speak Japanese. It would appear that he relied substantially upon his staff in compiling reports. Lascelles endorsed Dening's evaluation of Kishi and did not view political trends in Japan with enthusiasm. He served in Tokyo for only a relatively brief period and was then recalled. Since relevant documentation is not available, the reasons have to be inferred, as discussed by Cortazzi. It was an unfortunate appointment and it would have been preferable had Lascelles been sent to a less demanding post to conclude his diplomatic career.

In contrast Sir Oscar Morland was very experienced in the affairs of East Asia, having served in Japan before the Pacific War and dealt with Asian matters in the Foreign Office between 1950 and 1953 and again between 1956 and his appointment to Tokyo in 1959. In the intervening period Morland served as ambassador to Indonesia. He was married to a daughter of Sir Francis Lindley, a former ambassador to Japan. John Whitehead provides a lively portrait of of Morland in this essay. Morland arrived in Tokyo when economic progress was quickening, a trend that was more conspicuous by the time he departed in 1963. He resembled his predecessors in regarding the political system with scepticism. As he observed in his valedictory despatch: 'Spectacular material Westernization had not been accompanied by any significant Westernization in outlook.'[5] Economic advancement would not satisfy the Japanese people; the desire to exercise power in the world would lead to its military concomitant. At present Japan accepted American dominance but if the United States withdrew from the Pacific 'no ideological scruples would prevent them from turning quickly to Russia – or more probably China'.[6] Morland could discern 'little understanding or fear of Communism in Japan'. The only method of ensuring continued Japanese cooperation with the West would be to emphasize Japanese self-interest. Morland argued that Britain enjoyed 'a greater amount of Japanese sympathy and respect than any other Western nation'. This was explicable through the legacy of the Anglo-Japanese Alliance and a certain admiration for 'the British character and way of life'. One cannot help feeling that Morland was, to some extent, deluding himself in this observation. He was on more solid ground in arguing that greater efforts should be made to foster warmer relations by admitting Japan 'into our inner councils': energy expended in the 1960s would produce 'a rich future harvest'.[7] Morland was a competent ambassador but one of his subordinates felt that he lacked 'charisma and push'.[8]

Sir Francis Rundall, known as 'Tony', served as ambassador to Israel between 1957 and 1959 and then worked in Whitehall before his appointment to Tokyo in 1963. He was most conscientious but experienced some health problems. Economic issues were looming larger: the Anglo-Japanese Treaty of Commerce and Navigation was at last signed in April 1963 and Japan adhered to the OECD three moths later. Anglo-Japanese relations were affected by the confrontation between Indonesia and Malaysia. Japan had sponsored the emergence of Indonesia in 1945 and political sympathy, plus economic ambition, influenced the government to favour Indonesia. It was not dissimilar to the situation obtaining during the Falklands War in 1982 when Japan revealed sympathy for Argentina. Rundall endeavoured to persuade the government to appreciate what drew Malaysia, Britain, Australia and New Zealand together. The Olympic Games were held in Tokyo in 1964 and this occupied a fair proportion of the embassy's time. This great event did much to heighten awareness of Japan and appreciation of its growing economic success. Rundall was optimistic over the prospects for encouraging Anglo-Japanese trade, which was assuming considerable significance in the mid-to-late 1960s. In his valedictory despatch, Rundall reiterated the conclusions of Dening and Morland: the Japanese were conspicuous 'pragmatists' and were 'neither militaristic, nor pacific'. Japan essentially supported the West during the Cold War and Britain should do all it could to consolidate this relationship.

Sir John Pilcher had served in Japan before the war. In the 1950s he acted as minister in the British Embassy in Madrid, observing the evolution of

General Franco's regime. He then served as ambassador to the Philippines between 1959 and 1963. On his return to London he was responsible for information work in the Foreign Office before being appointed ambassador to Austria. From there he was transferred to Tokyo in 1967. Pilcher was noted for his sense of humour and lively entertaining. He was rather old-fashioned in having little interest in trade but he tried to become more active in this sphere. Pilcher's term may be described as marking the close of the immediate post-war era in Anglo-Japanese relations, underlined by the state visit to Britain of the Shōwa Emperor (Hirohito) in September 1971. The visit was bound to be rather awkward because of wartime memories and fears of Japanese competition. However, it passed quite successfully; the Emperor was satisfied by the restoration of honours (the Garter) of which he had been deprived in 1942. There was no particular enthusiasm among the British public but no large-scale demonstrations occurred.

For most of the period before the Pacific War British envoys represented the country of greatest significance for Japan; this could not apply after 1945. British power was waning and continued to decline, a trend rendered more obvious or poignant by the decision of Harold Wilson's Labour government to terminate Britain's historic political-strategic role east of Suez. Apart from fulfilling its responsibility in Hong Kong until 1997, Britain could concentrate on its economic and financial activities in East Asia. This change in emphasis is, to some extent, reflected in the essays in Part III. Gascoigne and Dening did not regard themselves as primarily concerned with economic issues. Rundall and Pilcher recognized that trade was assuming growing importance in the career of an ambassador.

Much has been depressing about Japanese politics since 1945 yet the American-patented constitution of 1946-7 has survived largely unchanged; extremism of the right and left has been contained. Japan has enjoyed unprecedented prosperity, despite the setbacks after 1990. Japan has adhered to a quiescent foreign policy. British envoys were deeply sceptical regarding future stability in their final despatches but the qualified optimism of General Douglas MacArthur and John Foster Dulles, as expressed in 1950-1 during the negotiations for a peace treaty, proved more accurate than the qualified pessimism of their critics. Perhaps this is explained by the secondary role played by Britain in the affairs of the Japanese state since 1945.

16
Sir Alvary Gascoigne in Japan, 1946–51

Sir Alvary Gascoigne

PETER LOWE

Alvary Douglas Frederick Gascoigne (1893–1970) headed the British liaison mission (UKLIM) in Tokyo between July 1946 and February 1951. Thus his term of office coincided with the heart of the allied occupation of Japan. Gascoigne arrived less than a year after General Douglas MacArthur assumed responsibility as Supreme Commander Allied Powers (SCAP): he departed two months before President Truman's abrupt dismissal of MacArthur.

Gascoigne served in the sixth Dragoons and Coldstream Guards during the Great War and was mentioned in despatches. He joined the Foreign Office in 1919: his principal appointments before going to Japan in 1946 were as consul-general for Tangier Zone and the Spanish Protectorate of Morocco (1939–44) and as political representative in Hungary (1945–6). He married twice (his first wife, the daughter of an American general, died); he had a son and daughter by his first marriage, the son being killed in action in 1944.

Gascoigne's military experience might be expected to gain more respect than would be the case with a man of more restricted diplomatic background. As a personality Gascoigne was bluff and reasonably direct: he was in no sense an intellectual but evinced a combination of shrewdness and common sense.

It could hardly be said that Gascoigne's appointment to Tokyo was unexpected. Relatively speaking, he had a lot of East Asian diplomatic experience. He had served in China from 1923 to 1925. Later in the politically disturbed years from 1931 to 1934 he served in Japan. Then he was recalled to the Foreign Office to preside at the Far East desk between November 1934 and April 1936, which was again a significant period for Anglo-Japanese relations. Gascoigne, therefore, took up his assignment with a good deal of background experience. He was a diplomat of the old school, of a pre-war vintage.

RELATIONSHIP WITH MACARTHUR

It was essential that the head of the British mission should establish a posi-tive relationship with MacArthur and this required a person who would be patient in listening to MacArthur and who would advance British interests effectively. At the close of the Pacific war the Foreign Office hoped that it would be feasible to achieve a prominent role for Britain in the occupation but by the time that Gascoigne reached Tokyo, it was clear that this would not occur.[1] MacArthur intended to retain as much power as he could in his own hands and the Truman administration did not envisage the allied pow-ers playing a significant part in policy formulation.[2] Maintaining British interests, therefore, necessitated appreciable diplomatic skills combined with a realistic understanding of what could be accomplished: to press too far would antagonize MacArthur and, perhaps, Washington.

It is a measure of the successful relationship that Gascoigne established that MacArthur saw him more frequently than any other official with the sole exception of William Sebald, MacArthur's diplomatic adviser: Gascoigne and MacArthur met on 128 occasions while Sebald and MacArthur met on 138 occasions.[3] MacArthur was not the kind of man to see an official simply as a matter of courtesy. Why, then, did he see the head of the British mission with such frequency? There were two reasons: MacArthur wished to preserve regular contact with the British government in case he needed assistance in disputes with Washington and he respected Gascoigne.

For his part, Gascoigne adjusted readily to the function of listening to MacArthur's monologues, appreciating that this was axiomatic to gaining the general's trust and understanding that much information of interest could be gained in this way. The general was ready to impart his views to a diplomat from an aristocratic background. But the relationship changed dramatically with the outbreak of the Korean War in June 1950: MacArthur was so heav-ily involved in Korean issues that he could not see Gascoigne as he had done formerly and British criticisms of MacArthur's conduct of Korean operations inevitably affected MacArthur's relations with Gascoigne.[4]

MacArthur and the British government shared common attitudes on vari-ous aspects of the occupation while also diverging in certain areas. They were in agreement fundamentally in advocating the implementation of an early peace treaty: once the major reforms sponsored by the occupation had been applied, the United States should take an initiative in starting the process of treaty negotiations and a peace treaty should be signed as soon as practica-ble. MacArthur held that lengthy military occupations were counter-productive because they created unavoidable resentment among the native inhabitants of the occupied country.[5] Britain concurred and felt, in addition, that the Truman administration might succumb, if it had not done so already, to the temptation to allow the occupation to continue, since this was easier than grappling with the many problems inherent in arriving at a peace treaty. MacArthur and the British agreed that the Japanese people required a mixture of firmness and kindness exercised by a proconsular figure: the British thought sometimes that MacArthur erred on the lenient side but, in the main, endorsed his leadership.

In the first two years of the occupation MacArthur enjoyed a great deal of freedom in shaping his policies as he wished: this was the phase of sweeping, idealistic, liberal reform. The situation changed in the latter part of 1947 when he encountered the start of developing intervention from sections of the bureaucracy and big business in the United States. Criticism of MacArthur grew because of a belief that the occupation was not following a correct economic policy and that MacArthur was seized unduly with the supposed merits of radical restructuring of Japanese business. The so-called 'Japan Lobby' in Washington comprising bureaucrats, certain prominent businessmen and journalists, launched a campaign of censure aimed at SCAP.[6]

At the beginning of 1948 Gascoigne reported on speculation that MacArthur might leave Tokyo, in part because 1948 was a presidential election year and it was believed, correctly, that MacArthur was interested in securing the Republican nomination. Gascoigne wrote to Esler Dening in January 1948 that MacArthur appeared to be in good health for a man of his age (he was then 67 years old) and that MacArthur would continue his work in Tokyo unless he was nominated for the presidency.[7]

MacArthur told Gascoigne that big business was gunning for him in the USA and that he might be replaced: this was an exaggerated statement designed to elicit British support in which it succeeded. MacArthur stated that he wanted to reform the zaibatsu and to extend decentralization in the economy but this was disliked by prominent businessmen involved in the Truman administration and by Wall Street. MacArthur's observation met with British sympathy. F. S. Tomlinson of the Foreign Office remarked on the irony of MacArthur '. . . who is ultraconservative at heart' being attacked for following '. . . what American business circles regard as left-wing policies'.[8] Tomlinson found it difficult to believe that the Truman administration would replace MacArthur who possessed such an outstanding record in Japan. Dening entirely agreed, commenting that, 'The prospect of indefinite American occupation without General MacArthur hardly bears contemplation.'[9]

BRITISH PREFERENCES

Gascoigne conversed with George Kennan in March 1948 to emphasize British preferences regarding the future evolution of Japanese industry. Kennan was involved in assessing the overall state of Japan in the context of the growth of the Cold War and his opinions were very different to those of MacArthur and the British Foreign Office.[10] Kennan wished to see the economy revived significantly, reforms cut back, and a peace treaty postponed. Gascoigne indicated that, while Britain assented broadly to the American proposals submitted to the Far Eastern Commission (FEC), Britain supported reparations and these should incorporate industrial assets, shipbuilding with concomitant restrictions on shipbuilding capacity, utilization of Japanese gold deposits and external assets. The Japanese economy should be rebuilt to some extent but it was essential to prevent a renewal of 'unfair competition': reasonable wages should be paid in Japanese factories with the eradication of 'sharp commercial practices.[11]

The Attlee government was preoccupied with the importance of achieving a full employment economy in Britain and with stimulating British exports which would include traditional industries such as textiles and shipbuilding: Gascoigne underlined these points to MacArthur and Kennan but the former was the more sympathetic. Gascoigne believed that it was essential that MacArthur remain in Tokyo from the viewpoint of defending British interests: the appointment of someone aligned with the 'Japan Lobby' would be dangerous.

Accordingly, Gascoigne welcomed the decision of the Republican party to nominate Governor Dewey again for the presidency in June 1948. MacArthur would now remain in Tokyo – 'The General has his faults, in common with all mankind, but there are few, I think, who could have administered this country as well as he has done . . . I trust, therefore, that from the point of view of British interests, the United States Government will not find it necessary to make any change here . . .'.[12] For his part MacArthur told Gascoigne that he regarded his relationship with the British mission and British govermnent as a 'perfect one'.[13] However, as an example in the opposite direction, Gascoigne occasionally experienced stormy meetings with MacArthur and such an occasion occurred on 1 September 1948. MacArthur was incensed at British protests concerning the National Public Service Law as envisaged and Gascoigne was the stoic recipient of MacArthur's wrath:

> My interview with the Supreme Commander was the most painful one which I have yet had with him during my duty in Japan. The mere mention by me of National Public Service draft legislation and of our opinion thereon caused him to shout at me without stopping for one and three-quarters hours. It seemed quite evident that he had already been reprimanded on the subject by Washington.[14]

MacArthur conceded that all administrations made mistakes at times '. . . but to go out of his way to "side with the Kremlin" on the issue was, he thought, the greatest "betrayal of trust" which the British Commonwealth had yet perpetrated in Tokyo'.[15] MacArthur felt that some members of the Commonwealth wished to criticize him because they were jealous of his success in Japan. He made it clear that he had Australia in mind particularly, as he detested Herbert Evatt, the minister for external affairs. He repeated his strong disapproval of the British supporting the Russians in criticizing SCAP but Gascoigne stated that Britain had no intention of supporting the Soviet Union against the United States. MacArthur responded that the Australian representative in Tokyo, Patrick Shaw, should have 'kept his mouth shut' instead of airing grievances as he had done.[16] This is an admirable instance of how MacArthur's wrath could erupt but, as Gascoigne observed, it was by far the most acrimonious encounter he had experienced since his arrival. The storm soon passed and MacArthur reverted to good humour, since he needed British support so as to defend his position against his critics in Washington.

One problem preoccupying Gascoigne at times arose from MacArthur's sensitivity to press criticism. In particular, MacArthur resented the critical tone of some of the reports written by *The Times* correspondent in Tokyo, Frank Hawley. Hawley believed that occupation policies lacked sufficient cohesion and revealed an inadequate grasp of the functioning of Japanese society. MacArthur viewed such criticism as negative and carping and voiced his feelings with characteristic trenchancy to Gascoigne. Gascoigne responded, predictably, that he could not control the press: criticism in the media was often unjust or tedious but had to be tolerated within democracies. MacArthur no doubt understood this point well enough but was not mollified thereby.[17]

ADVANCING THE RETURN OF PEACE

The Foreign Office wished to gauge how Japan would react to the conclusion of a peace treaty and resumption of sovereignty. Gascoigne was asked to give serious thought to the problem and he replied towards the end of 1948, after consulting the counsellor for information, H. Vere Redman. The Japanese wanted the occupation to end in the near future, having secured further economic gains from the USA in the intervening period; differences between the occupying powers would be exploited for Japanese ends. There would be a desire to obtain armed forces once more and the justification for acting contrary to Article 9 of the constitution would be the development of the Cold War and the advance of communism in China. The Japanese would seek to restore Japan's former commercial position, particularly in Asia. Gascoigne also accepted one of MacArthur's favourite themes that the growth of population would necessitate finding areas in which to place Japan's surplus population. Gascoigne was not sanguine regarding the long-term impact of MacArthur's endeavour to democratize Japan:

> The impact of democracy upon the Japanese mind has, as yet, been almost nil, although great play is, of course, made by the Japanese of going through the 'forms' of democratic practice, because they know that during the occupation they can but obey the dictates of the Supreme Commander and that the more they please him (and through him the United States), the greater will be the bounties which will flow from Washington.[18]

The principal priorities, as Gascoigne perceived them, were obtaining guarantees against unfair trading methods and ensuring that government was committed firmly to democracy and was well placed to prevent a swing to the 'totalitarian' right or left.[19] The Foreign Office shared Gascoigne's anxiety and doubted whether the occupation had achieved as much as MacArthur contended when it came to ensuring that Japan was wholly committed to democracy.

Gascoigne discussed the issue openly with SCAP: MacArthur was positively arguing that the benefits of democracy were so conspicuous that it was unlikely that Japan would proceed in a contrary direction when the occupation terminated. In practical terms, Japan would be compelled to rely upon the USA whether this was liked or not. MacArthur recognized the difficulty of anticipating the future but he was far more optimistic than Gascoigne.[20] Gascoigne was always alert to the negative characteristics of the Japanese, as though searching for evidence that would qualify the extent of the changes resulting from the occupation: the same was true of Dening and other British officials. This may be attributed to the cynicism not infrequently seen in world-weary British diplomats but was, arguably, also the product of Britain's exclusion from the centre of policy-making in Tokyo. Given the confusion in American policies towards China and Korea in the later 1940s, it was understandable that doubts should be entertained as to whether the United States was more successful in Japan.

The success of stability within Japan rested in part upon the newly-created institutions, in part on the calibre of political leadership, and in part on the repercussions of the Cold War. One aspect with which MacArthur was less satisfied was the quality of Japanese politicians. MacArthur liked Katayama Tetsu, prime minister in 1947–8, and regretted his loss of office. In a sense,

MacArthur's respect was surprising because Katayama was a socialist; however, he was also a Christian – MacArthur saw Christianity as an enlightening influence in Japan – and MacArthur regarded him as reliable.

Gascoigne discussed the fall of the Katayama government with MacArthur in February 1948. Clearly, he regretted Katayama's resignation and MacArthur did not seem to welcome the prospect of Yoshida Shigeru returning to office. Gascoigne added, '. . . General MacArthur has assured me on several occasions, that, although he has endeavoured for the past two years to unearth a first-class politician and statesman, he has completely failed to do so'.[21] The Foreign Office tended to share MacArthur's reservations about Yoshida. He was experienced in diplomacy but less so in politics. Yoshida was an Anglophile but the British were not convinced that he was capable of dealing successfully with the considerable challenges facing him.[22] In reality, Yoshida was an astute political operator of greater ability and guile than he was credited with possessing by the British and MacArthur.[23] He served briefly as prime minister in 1946–7 and returned in 1948, retaining the premiership until 1954.

Gascoigne viewed Yoshida with more affection than did his UKLIM colleagues. He had known him since 1923 when they were both posted in China and he admired his tenacity and commitment: Yoshida's conservative inclinations no doubt complemented those of Gascoigne himself. Respect for Yoshida grew considerably so that, by the end of Gascoigne's period of office, Yoshida's continued presence as prime minister appeared indispensable.[24] Gascoigne reflected the Foreign Office's newfound interest in trade unionism, explicable through the fact that the foreign secretary, Ernest Bevin, was the greatest British trade union leader of the twentieth century, and urged the advantages of pragmatism upon Yoshida's handling of labour disputes. Gascoigne extolled British methods of conducting industrial relations and commended them for adoption in Japan.[25] Gascoigne viewed the Japan Communist Party (JCP) as a potential menace and applauded MacArthur's action in purging the central committee of the JCP in the summer of 1950.[26] Despite his liking for Yoshida, Gascoigne retained his doubts as to the future direction of Japanese government when Japan regained sovereignty.

BRITISH FRUSTRATIONS

Bevin was frustrated, in the latter part of 1949, by American vacillation over embarking on negotiations leading to a Japanese peace treaty. Dean Acheson assured him that progress would be made soon but this was blocked by the obduracy of the secretary for defence, Louis Johnson, and the Pentagon which opposed a peace treaty because of the deteriorating international situation. Gascoigne spoke to MacArthur in November 1949 when the general talked of having perused drafts sent from Washington. MacArthur told Gascoigne that opinion in the Pentagon favoured rearming Japan:

> For your own personal and secret information the General let slip during the conversation that some of the United States 'service people in the Pentagon wanted to rearm Japan'. He showed, however, later on that he did not think that they would win their case. He described these people as 'sabre rattlers' and from the manner in which he spoke he made it clear that he was not himself of their mind . . .[27]

British concern at the uncertainties surrounding American intentions was fuelled: Bevin sent a trenchant message to Washington on 8 December 1949 emphasizing that he would be meeting Commonwealth prime ministers in Colombo in January 1950 and it would be difficult to report the lack of progress to them – '. . . this question of security is one which very much concerns us all'.[28]

Gascoigne placed more emphasis, in his reports in 1950, on the unfortunate consequence of American failure to provide clearer signals as to where the occupation was going. Gascoigne believed that the Japanese should show due respect to the representatives of the occupying powers and he was always quick to identify examples of truculence or dissent. He reported on 12 June that he had noticed personally, in his discussions with Japanese officials, including governors of prefectures, mayors, and Ministry and Imperial Household officials, that they were prepared to express overt criticism of the prolongation of the occupation and of the absence of a long-term policy. MacArthur's action in relaxing controls in the political, social, economic, and financial spheres accentuated demands for the occupation to be ended.

The security dilemma facing Japan acted as a sobering influence: MacArthur's past reference to Japan as a 'Switzerland of the Far East' was no longer credible and most Japanese desired American protection in an explicit form. Gascoigne believed that the crunch was approaching:

> As was forecast last year, the period of drift in our treatment of Japan which started some two years ago, is now reaching a critical stage, and I feel that if it should continue for much longer we may arrive at a point when either the Japanese will virtually be the masters of the occupation or the occupation will have to take very stern steps against the Japanese, which could indeed be a retrograde step . . .[29]

Gascoigne told MacArthur of his apprehension when they met on 6 June:

> I thought the time had come for me to tell him that I personally felt uneasy about the manner in which the Japanese were now behaving. Public statements and incidents large and small had taken place during these past two months which would never have occurred six months ago. No doubt the Japanese Communists and fellow travellers, by their recent positive actions, roused the latent nationalistic feelings of the ordinary Japanese, who, although they might not, and, in fact, I was sure did not, agree with Communist doctrines, were nationalists at heart and were tired of the allied yoke. I further said that in my opinion the time had come when some impressive demonstration of allied might (a large parade by American forces in the air and on the ground) might well be staged.[30]

MacArthur did not disagree and appeared to accept the force of much of what was communicated by Gascoigne.

The long period of drift over a peace treaty came to an end with the appointment by President Truman of John Foster Dulles as his emissary charged with negotiating a treaty. Dulles possessed tremendous zeal and industry: he was determined to secure rapid progress, appreciating that time should not be wasted and inspired by his own ambition to be the secretary of state in the next Republican administration. Dulles visited Tokyo just before the outbreak of the Korean war and Gascoigne spoke candidly to him:

Psychologically, the effect upon the Japanese of our lack of a policy towards the future of their country was a most unsatisfactory one, and would become more so with the passage of time. I voiced concern lest Russia should take advantage of this state of uncertainty by making a bid for the holding of a peace conference on her own terms, which would be most embarrassing to us.[31]

Dulles questioned Gascoigne about the situation of Australia and New Zealand and how they would view strategic considerations affecting their security. Gascoigne replied that Australia and New Zealand had modified their previous approach and they favoured the conclusion of an early peace treaty with suitable security guarantees intended to defend Japan and to obviate the contingency of renewed Japanese expansion in the future. In response to a question of Dulles concerning the stationing of American troops in Japan once sovereignty was restored, Gascoigne thought that the Japanese should request assistance so that the presence of American troops on Japanese soil was not imposed overtly by the allies; Yoshida would probably react in a positive manner when approached.

As regards the nature of a peace treaty itself, Gascoigne thought that a treaty should be concise and relatively straightforward: he commented that the British would not press for too many restrictions. In this respect it should be noted that British officials were more conciliatory than members of the cabinet as the deliberations in London over a treaty in 1950–1 demonstrated.[32] Dulles emphasized his own potential antagonism to including restrictive clauses engendered by his experience of the Versailles treaty in 1919.

EFFECTS OF THE KOREAN WAR

Gascoigne's harmonious relationship with MacArthur came to an abrupt end in the last week of June 1950. The outbreak of the Korean war marked a watershed in many directions as the Cold War moved into a dangerous phase of becoming a limited 'hot' war. Certainly it was a watershed in relations between Gascoigne and MacArthur: the latter was so dominated by the new responsibilities he assumed on behalf of his own government and of the UN that he could devote only restricted time to Japan. Gascoigne resented the fact that he could not pursue his full exchanges with MacArthur as previously and the tone of Gascoigne's communications with the Foreign Office changed fundamentally. He complained to Bevin on 9 July that all was subordinated to Korean demands: he could not see MacArthur and deprecated his inability to discuss important matters with him. Gascoigne believed that MacArthur now endorsed the necessity to keep American bases in Japan.[33]

Gascoigne's pessimism regarding the future of Japan grew in the second half of 1950. He wrote to Robert Scott in the Foreign Office on 9 October that Japan was likely to move politically to the right after the close of the occupation and that undesirable Japanese practices might re-emerge.[34] Gascoigne wrote to Bevin on 18 November that MacArthur was highly autocratic: 'He certainly remains the complete Dictator and he is enjoying some strong Republican backing in the States.'[35] Gascoigne added that Truman would probably like to see MacArthur departing from his posts in Japan' . . . and there are some who think that one of Truman's main reasons for wanting an early Japanese peace is that it would bring with it MacArthur's exit from Japan'.[36]

In January 1951 Gascoigne accompanied Sir George Sansom to meet
MacArthur. Sansom drafted a brief record in which he was mostly positive
about MacArthur. He was unquestionably impressive, '. . . a great man, whatever his shortcomings'. MacArthur did not say anything notably original or
profound but he advanced his views with vigour and conviction. He was not
noted for strict adherence to the truth and he was ready to amend facts if
necessary:

> His political and military views have a logical coherence and he thinks things
> out very carefully. He may base himself upon some mistaken premises, but it
> would be dangerous to dismiss his opinions as only irrational or prejudiced.
> He has often proved right, and I think his average is fairly high. His trouble
> is vanity.
>   He said (what he has said before) that he did not believe in occupations,
> and thought it was high time that the occupation of Japan came to an end.
> He did not, he said, suppose that the Japanese had become democrats. The
> occupation had merely provided the apparatus which the Japanese could use
> if they desired. He thought that there would be a good deal of change after
> the peace treaties were made, but he did not believe the Japanese would
> revert to unqualified militarism. They could not, even if they wished, so long
> as the Allied Powers could use economic pressure. But in any case he believed
> that there was, since 1945, a growth in the feeling for freedom among the
> Japanese people, and this was bound to play a part in domestic politics in
> Japan in the future.[37]

Sansom's assessment was acute and captured accurately the positive and negative features of the enigmatic MacArthur.

Gascoigne's term in Tokyo drew to a close in February 1951 in consequence
of his appointment as ambassador to Moscow. On 6 February he produced
the customary reflective review of a personal nature customarily drafted by a
British ambassador upon completing his mission. When he had left London
in June 1946 he had been warned that MacArthur could be awkward to deal
with; but he had found him to be amiable and kindly: he was welcomed as a
member of SCAP's 'court'. Gascoigne reviewed the more important reforms
implemented by SCAP including the encouragement given to trade unions,
land reform, and educational measures. With regard to the latter he remarked
that the process of revising textbooks had been protracted and demanding:
he added, presciently, that: '. . . it is not at all certain even today that it has
been successful'.[38]

The greatest success of the occupation was in the economic sphere. The
Americans poured vast sums into restoring the basis of the economy but
inflation loomed as a grave menace in 1948 to the point where MacArthur
professed marked pessimism regarding Japan's future prospects. The Dodge
mission (April–May 1949) combated inflation effectively through emphasizing a balanced budget, ending export subsidies and cutting import subsidies.
The economy recovered substantially between 1948 and 1950 and growth
was further stimulated by the Korean war. Gascoigne remarked that British
commercial interests were flourishing: '. . . and the British commercial community enjoys a respect and exercises an influence quite out of proportion to
its relative importance in the overall commercial and financial field'.[39] In the
social sphere the chief achievement was 'the emancipation ofJapanese wom-
anhood'. The occupation sought to reform the treatment of women: SCAP

aimed to impress on Japanese men the need to regard women far more favourably. Gascoigne commented that it would take considerable time to effect this fundamental reform successfully.

FUTURE PROSPECTS

When Gascoigne had arrived in the summer of 1946 he had discovered a country traumatized by defeat and willing to accept leadership from SCAP. In February 1951 he left a nation of growing self-confidence; supported economically and strategically by the USA, but critical of the extent of American dominance. Gascoigne assessed MacArthur's contribution in balanced fashion:

> MacArthur and his United States satellites have undoubtedly fulfilled their task of furnishing Japan with a democratic blueprint upon which the Japanese can work in the future, they should wish to retain the democratic way of life. But American occupation officials have spoken too long and too loudly about the concrete and positive success of their democratic campaign. In their great enthusiasm they have, many of them, made themselves believe that Japan is already firmly fixed within the democratic fold, and that the teachings which they have been at such pains to disseminate in this country for the past five years have taken firm and permanent root. The occupation has undoubtedly done extremely good work but it is patently obvious that democracy, as we know it, cannot be imposed upon a people during a time of occupation; the democratic way of life can only be attained by years of patience and practice. While I believe that there is hope that the Japanese may retain some of the principles of democracy, they are not likely, I think, to keep the Constitution as it stands. Any future liberalism which may be practised will be modelled from a Japanese pattern.[40]

So far the Japanese had cooperated with the Americans but Gascoigne believed that once Japan regained sovereignty, a reaction would occur against Western methods and there would be a reversion to traditional Japanese principles. It was imperative that a peace settlement with Japan should be reached within the near future. It would not be feasible to stipulate a restrictive treaty and other methods would be required to exert influence in the desired direction. The question of Japanese rearmament was clearly highly contentious: the apprehension felt in Australia and New Zealand must be addressed skilfully.

Gascoigne concluded his report by reflecting on the functioning of the British liaison mission under his leadership. American influence was so all-pervasive that Gascoigne and his colleagues faced an uphill struggle in asserting British interests. Britain's cultural influence was extended through the strenuous efforts of H. Vere Redman, Gascoigne's information adviser, and by Edmund Blunden, his cultural adviser. Gascoigne and his colleagues endeavoured to foster positive relations with the Japanese people, despite the inevitable repercussions of the Pacific War. American officials did not resent the efforts to advance British cultural influence. British nationals in Japan complemented the work of the mission and Gascoigne applauded the efforts of the British community: '. . . who have impressed the Japanese by their skill, enterprise and, above all, by the assurance of the continuity of their efforts'.[41] He felt that the Japanese regarded themselves as closer to the British than to the Americans: he was optimistic on the prospects for a reasonably cordial relationship between Britain and Japan, yet governed by perceptions of mutual priorities.

The urbane tone of Gascoigne's final report was marred by a regrettable dispute over the circumstances of his departure from Haneda airport. Given the nature of the Anglo-American relationship and the length of time Gascoigne had served in Tokyo the British mission expected MacArthur and his senior colleagues to be present at the airport to bid Gascoigne farewell. George Clutton, chargé d'affaires following Gascoigne's departure, wrote to Sir William Strang, the permanent undersecretary:

> Joe Gascoigne's departure from Tokyo was marred, both for him and for us, by the absence at the airport of any American of whatever description. This absence was so painfully obvious that some of us thought that the Supreme Commander in his vindictiveness towards Joe had issued a direction that no one from General Headquarters was to see him off. I am afraid also that it has been impossible to conceal the miserable affair and there has been some indignant comment outside the Mission.[42]

Clutton added that American ideas of courtesy and protocol were peculiar and some allowances had to be made. There was some tension in Tokyo because John Foster Dulles was arriving at Haneda as Gascoigne departed. Clutton stated that he had received an apology from William Sebald. The controversy reached the press in the form of a frank article in an Australian paper, the Sydney Sun: the author of the article appeared well informed and explained that the cause of the problem was that MacArthur had refused to meet Gascoigne on four occasions in order to discuss the course of the Korean conflict. Strained relations between the British mission and SCAP ensued.[43] Clutton wrote to Strang that publication of this article was not inspired by the mission and that the matter should be regarded as closed. Sir Oliver Franks, the ambassador in Washington, spoke to Freeman Matthews of the State Department who was apologetic and said he had known nothing of the circumstances of Gascoigne's departure.[44]

This episode was sad yet, in its way, appropriate for it revealed how sour relations had become between Gascoigne and MacArthur during the Korean War and it was a more accurate indication than the usual diplomatic verbiage covering strained relations. Equally it was misleading as a final note. Gascoigne enjoyed cordial relations with MacArthur from his arrival until the start of the Korean War and Gascoigne's reports of their discussions contain a great deal of importance and interest. Gascoigne discharged his role effectively until matters that he could not influence concerning the waging of war in Korea transformed the situation and destroyed his previously amicable discussions with MacArthur.

While Sir Alvary Gascoigne was not a profound thinker, he possessed an astute grasp of realities and a commonsense approach which was apposite for the kind of situation facing him in Tokyo. It is unlikely that a more forceful approach would have advanced British interests: instead Gascoigne might have experienced between 1946 and 1950 the reactions that he unfortunately encountered in 1950–1. However, between 1946 and 1950 MacArthur and the British government respected each other and were in broad agreement, a very different position to that existing in 1950–1.

17
Sir Esler Dening
Ambassador to Japan, 1951–57

Sir Esler Dening

ROGER BUCKLEY

Esler Dening (1897–1977) was the central figure in British dealings with Japan in the years from the ending of the Pacific War until the mid-1950s. Robust, knowledgeable and with an acerbic streak, Dening had the good fortune to be at the hub of Asian affairs during the war and occupation years; he next had the harder task of running the Tokyo Embassy at a time when British opinion in many quarters was decidedly anti-Japanese. Some material has already been published on aspects of his service, but a synoptic reassessment in the light of newly available official records, covering his entire service in Tokyo, is still lacking. This sketch can only begin to repair this neglect and identify some of his successes and failures in the post-war decade. It will look briefly at Dening's work, and comment on the man who remains the most senior and longest-serving of all British ambassadors to Japan in the post San Francisco Conference era.[1]

Dening achieved professional success the hard way. He began, after enlisting in the Australian forces during the First World War, as a student interpreter in the Japan Consular Service in January 1920. Since he had grown up in Japan, where his father had been a missionary who later lost his faith and turned to writing, this was not a particularly surprising decision. Yet it was hardly a guarantee of preferment when the diplomatic service reserved preference for its own members and may have viewed consular officers as lesser mortals, fated until the Eden reforms of 1943, to remain part of the 'Cinderella Service'.[2] For twenty years Dening criss-crossed north-east Asia working in Seoul, Dairen, Osaka, Kobe and Harbin, until in 1941 he found himself appointed first secretary at the British Embassy in Washington. The outbreak of the Pacific War clearly accelerated his progress and his capabilities were noted firmly in September 1943 when he was made political advisor to Louis Mountbatten at SEAC headquarters. This was Dening's big break and he made the most of it. He may not have always hit it off with Mountbatten or found his own advice welcome to the supreme commander, but the Foreign Office's 'senior officials had a high regard for the abilities and reporting of Dening'.[3]

Dening ended his years in South-East Asia assisting in the making of some rough policy for handling the chaotic situation in the Dutch East Indies. He was sent from Singapore to report and advise on political developments in Batavia following the surrender of Imperial Japan and the arrival of British and Indian troops. Characteristically Demng spoke his mind and was quick to condemn both the returning, vengeful Dutch and the terrorism of the newly proclaimed independent state of Indonesia. As in his activities in Colombo and Singapore, Dening's telegrams had considerable influence in London. But his frank approach could have its disadvantage and many on the Dutch, Indonesian and Allied sides were not unhappy to see Dening posted home in February 1946. His analyses of the confused situation may have been better than his handling of the participants. He found it hard to suffer fools gladly.[4]

DENING AND BEVIN

Still, he was clearly due for further promotion and became assistant under-Şecretary for Far Eastern affairs. It was in this post that Dening did his best work and had the ear of the foreign secretary, Ernest Bevin. The next few years were to prove to be the most rewarding of his entire career. Bevin undoubtedly came to rely on Dening for advice on Asian business at a time when British influence was still sufficiently great for the job to give satisfaction. Dening was trusted by Bevin and given considerable discretion to handle an area of the globe that was already passing rapidly out of the British orbit. The secretary of state had more than enough to cope with in tackling the problems of Europe, the beginnings of what soon became the Cold War, the dilemmas of the Middle East and, above all else, maintaining amicable relations with the United States. If, as Alan Bullock has argued, Bevin's dealings with 'Southern Asia were peripheral', because of divided cabinet responsibilities, the marginal nature of his involvement with East Asia was even greater.[5] All this could only work to Dening's advantage provided he retained the support of his master and colleagues. Dening's record in watching the region and shoring up the British position in occupied Japan led directly to his return to Tokyo in 1951.[6] Herbert Morrison commented to the prime minister, Yoshida Shigeru, at their meeting during the San Francisco peace conference in September 1951: 'We are now sending out as Head of UK Liaison Mission, Sir Esler Dening, a great authority on Japan, who would I was sure promote the interests both of His Majesty's Government and of Japan'.[7] Unfortunately for both countries the secretary of state's sugary expectations proved unfounded. For all Dening's skills and knowledge of things Japanese the 1950s were to be a disappointing decade for Anglo-Japanese ties. We must next see how Dening handled business and ask whether his services in Tokyo were doomed to failure.

RETURN TO JAPAN

Dening was a tough diplomat who knew Japan from pre-war days. He had few illusions about the extent of enforced change that the American occupation might have produced on the newly independent nation. In many cases he was dealing with figures who had been career politicians and bureaucrats in the years before Pearl Harbor. He was sceptical of some of the American claims that Japan had been transformed through defeat and occupation into an example to the rest of Asia. Dening's reporting from Tokyo pulled no punches. On the rare occasion when a British minister did visit Japan it was immediately obvious that 'our ambassador is undoubtedly the commanding figure in the Diplomatic Corps and I have no doubt he is both respected and to some extent feared by the Japanese'.[8] This approach by Dening may not have fitted too easily with the shrunken realities of the British position in East Asia.

Yet most of the strains in Anglo-Japanese relations during Dening's years at the sharp end were beyond his control. All that the ambassador could attempt to do was soften some of the acrimony and press his own government to be slightly less severe in its approach to gaining Japanese understanding. There was little or no prospect of genuine reconciliation in the mid-1950s. The British public's memories of the wartime treatment of its prisoners of war and concern over Japanese economic resurgence were far too strong for any ambassador, however gifted, to counter in dealing with his hosts. It left Dening caught between obviously wishing to improve relations with Japan and having to carry out instructions that were far from forgiving, or in the long-term interests of his own government. At times one senses considerable frustration at what was an unenviable mission to halt deteriorating relations.

Dening, although Japanese officials might deny the fact, was generally sympathetic to the Japanese case; when he felt there was misrepresentation and misunderstanding with British public opinion he said so. Yet evidence of Dening's private views on post-peace treaty Japan is not easy to come by since he does not appear to have kept a diary and little personal correspondence is available. To grasp Dening's vision of Japan and his aspirations for improved Anglo-Japanese relations it is necessary to rely on his voluminous official reportage.[9] Here there is remarkable consistency in his opinions and equally little progress in resolving Anglo-Japanese problems.

ANGLO-JAPANESE SURVEY

In March 1953 in an ambitious survey of Anglo-Japanese ties from the turn of the century onwards Dening argued that 'short of pulling out of the Far East altogether, we must seek to cultivate friendly relations with Japan whether we like it or not'. He criticized the United States for thinking that 'Japan's destinies are to be determined by America alone' and suggested that, since Tokyo wanted to go its own way, there ought to be sufficient room for a British role in Japanese affairs. To achieve this objective, however, Dening was not about to mince his words. The ambassador stated that if 'we are to play this part, we must rid ourselves of some of our antipathies and determine how economic competition is to be met'.[10] On British prejudices he warned that 'just disliking the Japanese may prove an expensive luxury'.[11] He noted that 'If their outlook is materialistic and their policy governed by self-interest, I do not know that this differs very much from other nations with whom we have close relations.'

For Dening the heart of the matter was the economic question. For Anglo-Japanese relations

> The only constant factor which remains from before the War is that of economic competition. Both the United Kingdom and Japan are in the position that they must export to live, and this state of affairs is unlikely to alter at any time in the foreseeable future. Thus Anglo-Japanese relations must be considered on the basis that the two countries will remain competitors in the economic field, and that great care will have to be taken to ensure that economic competition is so regulated as to avoid undue damage to either side.[12]

In an era where British industry still had the edge over Japan at least in third markets Dening pressed the British cabinets of the 1950s to accept the realities of trade competition. Dening argued that this was 'unavoidable', a stance that he had long taken and he maintained Japanese competition 'is only to be met by improving our skills, by increased productivity and better marketing, and not by tariffs and restrictions upon Japanese trade in order to protect industries in which the Japanese are able to compete successfully'.[13] Dening, returning to views that he had shared with Ernest Bevin, stated bluntly that Lancashire could no longer dodge the Japanese onslaught. He admitted that this 'is an unpleasant truth, but nothing to my mind will be achieved by refusing indefinitely to recognize it'.[14]

To reinforce his case that trade friction was better tackled than ducked, Dening widened his perspective and incorporated regional and global factors to buttress his survey. He told Eden that 'if Japan were to range herself on the side of our opponents, the whole position of the Western world in the Far East would be threatened and might prove untenable' and he added, for good measure, the powerful argument that strains between London and Tokyo would upset Anglo-American relations, since US 'energies and resources are directed towards keeping Japan in the western camp'.[15] The paper was a characteristically broad and well-reasoned piece of work, but Dening, for all his advocacy, was out of luck. Relations between Britain and Japan continued to deteriorate throughout the decade.

Anglo-Japanese tension clearly intensified during the Dening years. He found it increasingly hard even to begin to explain the Japanese position as the British governments of the 1950s came under strong political pressure to restrict Japanese products and prevent Japan's accession to international organizations. Dening's difficulties were not helped by the stronger showing now made by the Board of Trade within Whitehall and, therefore, in cabinet submissions. The Foreign Office could no longer count on dominating policy. Public opinion was no longer dormant and both Fleet Street and paperback publishers tended to fuel antagonism. Russell Braddon's bestseller *The Naked Island* kept Japanese wartime brutalities alive.[16]

DEALING WITH A NEGATIVE BRITISH APPROACH

Dening was surely correct to state in his annual report for 1953 that 'there is a growing feeling of coldness and of an unsympathetic attitude on the part of the United Kingdom towards Japan'. Yet by April 1956 little had changed and Dening was obliged to point out once again that Japan's proffered olive branch had still to be accepted by London. He was too experienced a diplomat to endorse suggestions from some Japanese quarters that things might finally be improving; he warned instead that Japanese goodwill was 'tempered by considerable caution as to the prospective response in the United Kingdom to any Japanese advances'.[17] Even the long-anticipated visit of a British minister to Tokyo was something of a disappointment in the autumn of 1956 as the Japanese felt slighted that a more senior figure than the chancellor of the Duchy of Lancaster ought to have been selected. For Japan to have to wait so long and then to have to welcome a minister whose functions were impossible to explain was to invite trouble.

Even the figure sent, Lord Selkirk, admitted to Selwyn Lloyd that he was 'uncertain' whether the visit had accomplished much. Selkirk underlined what Dening had long been pressing on London that the Japanese 'considered they were worthy of a visit from a very senior member of the Government'. He told Lloyd that 'ultimately the Japanese will, however, only respect either strength or real marks of friendship'; pointing out that 'We cannot produce the first, and I am very doubtful whether public opinion is prepared to consider the second.'[18]

Epitomizing Dening's problems was the cabinet's refusal to withdraw British qualifications to Japan's membership of GATT. The cabinet's rejection of the most-favoured-nation clause (Article 35) left his hopes of improving Anglo-Japanese commercial relations without much foundation; it would take more than a decade before the Japanese bureaucracy began to forget this quite intentional slap in the face. What Tokyo found particularly hurtful was the fact that British action was then followed by others within western Europe and the Commonwealth. Selkirk pointed out that the Japanese 'regard the use of waiver as a form of Asiatic discrimination and are, I understand, prepared to pay almost any price in order to get it withdrawn. The fact that it has no practical disadvantage to them at present is irrelevant compared with the question of prestige.'[19] Yet the British public's fears of Japanese export competitiveness in the 1950s were well founded as industry lost ground throughout the decade to renewed Japanese (and West German) manufactured goods, initially in third markets but then also domestically as the post-war battery of import controls and protective mechanisms were scrapped.[20] It may be that the restrictions on Japan's GATT accession did little to stem the economic tide, while doing much to make the diplomats' job in the Tokyo Embassy a daunting task.

Clearly Dening was on a hiding to nothing in matters of trade. Decisions were being taken (or avoided) in London within Whitehall over which he could do precious little. The difficulties and slowness of improving British commercial and financial links would be a headache for his successors in Tokyo. It was after all not until 1962 that a final Anglo-Japanese commercial treaty could be signed and some of the bitterness felt by both sides could gradually subside. Yet making for additional complications was the state of overall political ties between Britain and Japan; here Dening did have a larger role and his record was a mixed one. His pre-war experiences of Japan and his doubts over its post-war behaviour must have irked the Japanese. It is not surprising, for example, that the Foreign Minister, Shigemitsu, was seen by Dening as 'out of touch with world events' and initially at least not 'sufficiently aware of the present day facts of life to make him an effective Foreign

Minister'.[21] Dening's own account to the Foreign Office of his attempts to produce, rather abruptly, an agenda of debating topics for Anglo-Japanese affairs suggests a heavy-handed bid to press Japanese diplomats to accept his views. If, as Dening reports, Shigemitsu was taken aback, then he had good reason.[22] Just occasionally there was a whiff of the nineteenth-century treaty port approach to Japan in Dening's behaviour. By the mid-1950s, and particularly after the Suez fiasco, the hectoring style ought to have been redundant. Indeed, at times Dening's annual reviews read more like a school report on a delinquent pupil than on a nation which could no longer be ignored or casually rebuffed.[23]

Still, most of the time Dening tried to be fair and he was clearly not given all the support that he expected from the cabinet. He had to acknowledge that 'the Japanese, who have found us unexpectedly tough in negotiation, look as a rule in vain for any indications that the United Kingdom is friendly towards Japan'.[24] All he could announce in his annual review for 1955 was that relations 'did not deteriorate quite as much as might have been expected, but there is nothing at present to indicate that they are likely to take a turn for the better in 1956. Indeed, with nationalism and particularly economic nationalism increasing in this country, they might well deteriorate'.[25] The prose and thought was characteristic of the man. (The full text of Dening's Validictory Dispatch is reproduced at Appendix III.)

Dening finally left Tokyo on 1 May 1957. He earned only the briefest of mentions in the subsequent despatch of his successor and after reluctantly undertaking a series of speaking engagements dropped quickly out of the limelight. He continued, fortunately, to follow events in East Asia through his own writings and as chairman in turn of the Japan Society and Royal Central Asian Society. Loaded with honours, including the Order of the Rising Sun, First Class, Esler Dening died at the age of 79 in January 1977.

NOTE
Appendix IV records a conversation with Dening in 1960 which helps to fill out this account of Dening as Ambassador to Japan.

18
Sir Daniel Lascelles
Ambassador to Japan, 1957–59

Sir Daniel Lascelles

SIR HUGH CORTAZZI

The appointment of Sir Daniel Lascelles as British ambassador to Japan was in stark contrast to that of his predecessor, Sir Esler Dening, who had been ambassador for five-and-a-half years, was a former member of the Japan Consular Service and a competent Japanese linguist. Lascelles had had no experience of the Far East before he was posted to Tokyo. He had no knowledge of the Japanese language, people and culture and does not seem to have established any real rapport with the Japanese he came to know in the course of his work. Dening, on the other hand, had unrivalled experience of the Far East having served in various posts in Japanese-controlled Asia before the war and had been political adviser to Lord Louis Mountbatten, C-in-C South-East Asia Command. The Foreign Office apparently wanted – and certainly got – a change of style. Lascelles was recalled after less than eighteen months in Tokyo.

BACKGROUND AND PERSONALITY

Daniel Lascelles was well connected.[1] He was sent to the Royal Naval College at Osborne and then to Dartmouth, presumably with a view to a Naval career, but perhaps because prospects in the Navy after the first war were not promising and because he had an intellectual bent he went to Oxford and became an undergraduate at Balliol. After Oxford he joined the diplomatic service, serving first in Paris, then in Berlin, Teheran (where he learnt Persian), Warsaw, Moscow (where he qualified in Russian), Oslo, and Beirut (where he studied Arabic), He then returned to Teheran and after the Second World War he was in Athens during a very difficult period in Anglo-Greek relations. In 1948, at the age of 46, he was appointed ambassador to Ethiopia. In Addis

Ababa he learnt Amharic. In 1953 he was appointed ambassador to Afghanistan. In Kabul his knowledge of Persian would have been useful.

The record of his service and the comments of those who knew him suggest that Lascelles was an exceptional linguist.[2] Presumably, the Foreign Office believed that he would soon master Japanese, but in 1957 Lascelles was already 55 and it is not easy to learn Japanese late in life. Moreover, Japanese has no affinities with any of the languages which Lascelles had studied. It seems that he resented his inability to master Japanese and was jealous of those members of his staff who had achieved a significant competence in the language.

Lascelles was a bachelor and seemed to some a misogynist.[3] The Foreign Office in selecting him to succeed Dening may have thought that as post-war Japan was very much a male-dominated society, wives and Japanese women did not count. If so, they were mistaken and had also overlooked the valuable role which the wife of a head of mission can play, not only in social relations with local people but also with the wives and female members of the Embassy staff.

Lees Mayall,[4] who succeeded Ralph Selby[5] as Counsellor and Head of Chancery while Lascelles was Ambassador, wrote in his memoir *Fireflies in Amber*[6] '... [Lascelles was] a man of great charm, great intelligence and strong prejudices. He had numerous foibles one of which was never to answer an invitation to dinner though he was punctilious in other social matters ... When I approached Dan [for an answer] he regarded my enquiries as a gross invasion of his personal privacy and would give me an ambiguous or evasive answer.' Not all members of his staff noted his alleged charm and he did not apparently invite the more junior members of his staff to whom he was a very remote figure to help entertain Japanese guests. He does not seem to have shown much sense of humour in dealing with his staff.[7]

Lascelles was essentially a loner and did not make friends easily. He enjoyed fishing, but above all he was happiest wandering off on long walks in the country. He would go off into the country in the ambassador's Rolls and at whatever spot suited his fancy tell the driver to stop and either wait there for him to return or meet him at another spot some way off. Alternatively, he would, according to one member of his staff, take local trains at random, travelling what was then third class and carrying a knapsack. He regarded these trips as opportunities to practice Japanese which he was trying to learn. Mayall recounts:

> On one occasion he told me that he was taking two weeks' holiday, but would not be leaving Japan. As the Minister Bill [later Sir William] Harpham was away on leave this meant that I [Counsellor and Head of Chancery] would be in charge of the Embassy, but since the Ambassador would still be in the country he would still be responsible for it and I would not be Chargé d'Affaires. So I asked if I might have his address while he was away so that I could get in touch with him if necessary. He clearly regarded this request as impertinent but reluctantly gave me the name of a hotel near Osaka where he would be staying. A few days after his departure I thought I should consult him on some minor matter and telephoned to the hotel. They said that Dan had spent the night there four days ago but had left the next morning on a hired bicycle and had given instructions that if he did not return in a fortnight they were to send his luggage back to Tokyo. When he did reappear after two weeks he did not say where he had been and I did not feel like asking him.

Other comments recorded by Mayall suggest further oddities in Lascelles' character and behaviour. One morning, before he left Tokyo on retirement, he asked Mayall to shake hands and after they had done so he asked Mayall if his hand had 'felt scaly or otherwise unpleasant'. Mayall in some surprise reassured Lascelles, who then explained that he was attending a farewell luncheon with the Emperor that day and feared that if he had some kind of rash on his hand this would be unpleasant for anyone with whom he shook hands. Lascelles later told Mayall that the lunch 'had been a complete disaster . . . He was in a wretched state by the time he got back home'.[8]

The circumstances leading to Lascelles' recall are not given in Foreign Office papers released to the Public Records Office. It has been said that there were complaints about him from members of the British community.[9] They do not seem to have liked or respected him. His peculiarities must also have been the subject of comment by visitors to the embassy which no doubt filtered back to the Foreign Office. Members of his senior staff too, when pressed by the Foreign Office for explanations, could not have avoided pointing out the difficulties[10] which they had in operating with Lascelles as their chief. On one occasion he sent a four-page minute to the Chancery about the proper use of a comma. According to Mayall Lascelles only got out of the embassy twenty-four hours before his successor, Oscar Morland, arrived. Lascelles who was 57 at the time of his recall from Tokyo was not given a further post. *Who's Who* reveals nothing about what he did between his retirement and his death.

JAPAN AND BRITAIN 1957–59

Lascelles arrived in Tokyo in September 1957. It seems surprising that he was not asked to delay his departure for Tokyo so that he could be present at the talks in London with Fujiyama Aiichiro, the Japanese Foreign Minister, who made an official visit to Britain from 27 September to 1 October 1957. The talks appear to have covered a very wide range of political topics of mutual interest including relations with the Soviet Union, China, and South-East Asia, Japanese membership of the Security Council. Economic and commercial matters discussed included the Common Market and the European Free Trade Area, shipping policy, outstanding British claims arising from before the war, the possible purchase by Japan of a British-designed nuclear reactor and inevitably the GATT and British invocation of Article 35 against Japan.

The despatches from the British Embassy which were signed by Lascelles and which were printed for circulation in Whitehall and British missions abroad appear to have been almost entirely the work of the competent officials who were members of Lascelles's staff and it is difficult, in the absence of proof through a perusal of the drafts, which have long since been shredded, to note any obvious ambassadorial insertions.

The embassy clearly did not have a high opinion of Kishi Nobusuke, the Japanese Prime Minister while Lascelles was ambassador. The following comment in a despatch of 31 December 1957 about Kishi's second South-East Asian tour, seems to sum up the embassy view and presumably reflected Lascelles' own view:[11]

Mr Kishi is not, from our point of view, at all an attractive character[12] . . . His eye is indeed so firmly on the main chance that he seldom shows any interest in things British, or refers to Her Majesty's Government publicly in any context other than that of nuclear tests.[13]

Unfortunately, Lascelles' did not hit it off with Ohno Katsumi, then vice minister in the Gaimushō and later Japanese ambassador in London. In a letter dated 30 December 1957 to Oscar Morland, then Assistant Under-Secretary in the Foreign Office, Lascelles reported that in a discussion that day about Japanese ships for Indonesia Ohno had at one point 'become distinctly huffy'. Lascelles had been summoned 'at an hour's notice' to meet Ohno at the Gaimushō's social club. Ohno had then read out 'in a very muddled and barely intelligible way, the version of the Indonesian agreement with the Japanese Shipowners Association which had already appeared two or three days before in the press'. Lascelles appears to have irritated Ohno by putting questions to Ohno who complained that Lascelles had shown himself 'ungrateful for his [Ohno's] "kindness in sending for me" (sic)'. Sir Esler Dening, Lascelles' predecessor, cordially disliked Ohno who reciprocated by refering to Dening in speaking to Lascelles as his 'abominable predecessor'.

The Annual Review for 1957 was not sent until 11 March 1958. It was a workmanlike report drafted by Embassy officials with no obvious input from Lascelles. Japan's relations with the United States were a dominant issue for Japan. Relations with the Soviet Union, China and South-East Asia were also themes in the report. On Anglo-Japanese relations the review noted: 'Virtually no progress was made during the year in the negotiations for a commercial treaty.' United Kingdom exports to Japan had risen from £22 million in 1956 to £28 million in 1957.

In 1958 the embassy reported at some length on the progress of Japanese negotiations for a revised US-Japan Security Treaty. In a despatch, which was drafted in the chancery and signed by Lascelles on 7 November 1958, he declared [this was probably the view of Lees Mayall, the Head of Chancery though not of the members of chancery who studied the internal political scene]:

I am indeed coming to have a good deal of sympathy with the *simpliste* American argument which runs:

(1) The Japanese socialists are the avowed enemies of the West;
(2) Sōhyō[14] is the main financial support of the Japanese Socialists;
(3) so to hell with Sōhyō.

According to one member of the chancery Lascelles himself added nothing to what was a report on perhaps the most significant development that year. There is no indication that Lascelles discussed all this with his colleague, the US ambassador in Tokyo.

The annual review for 1958 was once again delayed until 12 March 1959, shortly before Lascelles left Tokyo. This too was a workmanlike report but at 21 paragraphs it was too long and reads as if it was an amalgam of contributions from the various sections in the embassy with minimal editing by the head of chancery or the minister.

The engagement in November 1958 of Crown Prince Akihito [later the Heisei Emperor] to Miss Shōda Michiko [later the Empress] led to this comment:

The Imperial family had always in the past allied itself by marriage with the chief contemporary wielders of real power in the land, and deciding to ally itself on this occasion with the daughter of a millionaire flour-miller it remains essentially true to its tradition.' (But there is nothing in the PRO papers to suggest that Lascelles made any attempt to get to know members of the Imperial family.)

The annual review noted that 'the Government carried on most assiduously with what Japanese newspapers somewhat insensitively describe as "visit diplomacy"'. On Anglo-Japanese relations the report recorded that these 'were superficially better than in the previous year, but they remained somewhat tepid and there is little of major importance to record. . .The Japanese Government's continued failure to make any acceptable offer for the settlement of pre-war claims was the only remaining irritant of importance.'

I have been unable to trace either a 'first impressions' despatch or a valedictory despatch by Lascelles.

CONCLUSION

Lascelles was appointed at a time when British interests and influence in the Far East were at a low ebb. There was probably not a great deal that a British ambassador at that time could do directly to change the Japanese perspective, but he could and should have tried to develop contacts with Japanese politicians and senior officials and to put over the British point of view in speeches and interviews. Lascelles does not seem to have attempted to do any of these things.

In the absence of access to the Foreign Office files of the chief clerk's office about Lascelles' appointment and recall, it is not possible to do more than speculate about the reasons for his recall after such a short time in his post. Did he have some kind of a breakdown or was his behaviour so peculiar that there were fears of a possible scandal? Or was it simply that it had become clear to the Foreign Office that he was simply not up to the job and was not coping with the tasks which fell to him as ambassador? In the absence of evidence one way or another I think we must conclude that those responsible in Whitehall recognized that his appointment was a mistake and that the right course was to recall him.

It is also not clear why Sir Oscar Morland, who was appointed ambassador in 1959 and was both the most senior and the most experienced of the former members of the Japan Consular Service with wide knowledge of Asia, was not appointed to Tokyo in 1957. Perhaps it was thought that he needed more experience in London or that, if he had gone to Tokyo in that year, he would have had to stay for too many years before he was due to retire in 1963. It is also possible that the Foreign Office, having for the first time since the appointment of Sir Ernest Satow to Tokyo in 1895, appointed Sir Esler Dening, an ex-Japan Consular Service officer, to Japan thought that it was time to return to the pre-war practice of appointing a generalist member of the Foreign Service, as the Diplomatic Service was temporarily renamed after the war-time 'Eden reforms'. There was still an element of snobbery among the older members of the pre-war Diplomatic Service who tended to look down on 'mere consuls'. If so, why did the post go to Lascelles rather than someone with experience elsewhere in Asia or at least in the USA which was such an important factor in Japan's relations with the rest of the world? There may have been pressure to give Lascelles, who had a run of tough assign-ments, a good final job involving promotion. None of these arguments should have been allowed to sway the decision in favour of appointing Lascelles.

19
Sir Oscar Morland
Ambassador to Japan
1959–63

Sir Oscar Morland

SIR JOHN WHITEHEAD

O scar Morland (1904–80) was born into a quite wealthy family. His father was one time senior partner of Price Waterhouse. The Morland's lived in Croydon where there was a road named after them. But it was 'new' money and the family were apparently prone to do things which were not quite *'comme il faut'* in the eyes of those who knew that they had already arrived. It was a Quaker family and Oscar was sent to Leighton Park, a Quaker School. There he showed a proficiency in mathematics, which took him up to Cambridge. He went to Kings, a college which also had strong Quaker connections at that time. While at Cambridge he came into contact with Monsignor Lopez, the Roman Catholic chaplain, and before he graduated he had been received into the Catholic Church, which was to remain a major support for the rest of his life. He was very devout and went to mass every day.

On leaving Cambridge, despite the strong accountancy tradition in the family, Oscar tried to join the Diplomatic Service; but like many others he failed the entrance examination and so joined the Far East Consular Service and was sent to Japan. His natural assiduousness and mathematical bent enabled him to learn Japanese to a good competent standard.

MARRIAGE TO ALICE LINDLEY

After postings in Japan and Manchuria he was transferred again to Tokyo in 1931 and became private secretary to the then ambassador, Sir Francis Lindley (see separate essay on Lindley in this volume). Lindley had four daughters and it was not perhaps so surprising that Oscar, then in his late 20s should fall for one of them. Alice was highly extrovert and full of charm and youthful enthusiasm. Despite Oscar's rather more serious nature and his (as they saw it) rather more limited background the relationship prospered.

That it did so, says much for Oscar's determination and tenacity. His boss and future father-in-law was distinctly lukewarm about the affair. As he wrote to his friend Stirling Maxwell:

> Alice is getting engaged to a young man in our Consular service named Morland. I can't pretend I was pleased as it means her living more or less permanently out here, usually at some Post amongst the most uninteresting people. Still, she is 26 and ought to know her mind. Pa Morland is a Quaker . . . and he will settle enough to keep Alice from the dole if the young man hops off. He is very good. Wedding is supposed to be in October.

The 'supposed' suggests a vagueness which had everything to do with the fact that Francis Lindley chose to have nothing to do with the arrangements for the wedding, which were left almost entirely in the hands of Oscar himself. He may have been marrying the boss's daughter but it was clear that he would have to earn his welcome into the Lindley and Fraser[1] families, which would not be lightly given. The lack of pleasure on Lindley's part seems to have had as much to do with the perceived disparity in class as with the feared geographical separation.

But the wedding took place and the couple produced four very able sons who subsequently made their way as a diplomat, a banker, a chartered accountant and a monk. Alice was the member of the partnership who fronted up and waved the flag. Their early years of married life seem to have been unremarkable, Oscar pursuing his interest in playing the cello until he severed a tendon in his wrist as a result of an altercation with a glass door during a black-out in Mukden. They both played bridge to a good standard.

WAR AND RETURN TO JAPAN

When the war came in 1941 Oscar and his young family were all in Tokyo and were promptly interned until the following year when an exchange of internees was arranged off Lourenço Marques. Back in London, Oscar joined the Ministry of Information which did not suit him. So he was transferred to Bletchley where with his mathematical bent he was probably much more effectively used. Soon after the war ended Oscar naturally returned to Japan for a year in the early occupation period. He was by this time a counsellor in the Foreign Service, but all in those days had to hold service rank in Tokyo. Alice in later life would insist that Oscar was a major-general, although this was not the appropriate equivalent; but Alice herself kept up the standard by being loaned a train to take her to Osaka at that time. Oscar was back in London again in 1947 where he became Head of Economic Relations Department in the Foreign Office.

Promoted to under-secretary[2] in the Cabinet Office 1950, he did not have a happy time under Norman Brook,[3] a tough boss and one with whom the chemistry 'was not right'. He survived for nearly three years but it was perhaps partly as a result of this less than successful episode that Oscar was next posted as ambassador to Indonesia, Jakarta then being known together with Jeddah as the two least attractive posts in the Service. Indonesia under Sukarno, still fairly recently independent, was pretty chaotic. But Oscar and Alice rightly took a conscious decision to enjoy their time there. Access, even to the top leadership, was possible but hazardous. On one occasion Sukarno accepted an invitation to lunch but decided at the last moment that he should be accompanied by fifty military officers, which presented certain logistical problems. Unlooked for access was also possible; one evening as the Morlands were quietly dining on their own a 'lady of the night' made a sudden appearance weaving her way in and out of a set of dining-room French windows closely pursued by one of her clients.

Time passed and after three years in Indonesia Oscar again returned to London, this time as assistant under-secretary for Asian Affairs in the Foreign Office, towards the end of which he was told that he should start learning Polish prior to going to Warsaw as ambassador. Fate intervened as a result of a heart attack suffered by one of his senior colleagues and also because of the premature retirement of Dan Lascelles from Tokyo (see Ch. 18). So, at fairly short notice, despite what outsiders might have seen as a natural progression, Oscar found himself almost by chance returning for a final posting to Tokyo as ambassador.

When Oscar, with Alice, arrived at the gates of the British Embassy compound he was greeted unexpectedly by his former driver who said: 'You will need me'. He didn't, but Alice saw a chance and took him on instead. On another occasion shortly after their arrival the Morlands had dinner at the Imperial Hotel. They were so impressed by one of the dishes that they promptly sent the head cook from the residence to the hotel, dressed up in black tie, to find out the details so that he could reproduce it in No. 1 House – an example of quick thinking and early British culinary espionage.

'FIRST IMPRESSIONS' AS AMBASSADOR

In the late 1950s it was customary in the British Foreign Service for heads of mission in their first three months after arrival in post to send a despatch to the Foreign Office containing their first impressions of the country and the government to which they were accredited. Having arrived in Japan in April 1959 Oscar duly sent in his despatch at the beginning of July entitled 'Impressions of Present-Day Japan'.

With long familiarization with Japan spanning more than thirty years on and off Oscar Morland was in a strong position to produce informed views about Japan fourteen years after the end of the war and seven years after the San Francisco Peace Treaty. He was his typical self – modest, somewhat self-deprecating but with generally very clear views strongly held. He knew well what he was talking about while many of those around him were much less familiar with the country or had narrower perspectives. This was a personal despatch as opposed to something which had been submitted to him initially as a draft, although he doubtless had discussions with staff inside the embassy, colleagues outside and with a number of his numerous Japanese friends and acquaintances. He spent much time perusing the Japanese press, having retained his good knowledge of the language, written and spoken, although his reticence, almost shyness, meant that he was not one of those heads of mission who went out of their way to use it. He nevertheless read newspapers and official Japanese communications, and he understood virtually everything that was being said around him; he was therefore no less effective than those who switched to 'send'[4] in Japanese at the slightest opportunity, and he undoubtedly thought seriously and deeply about what he was reading and hearing.

SOUND JUDGEMENT

Above all, he took particular pains over judgement, which paid off since his judgement over his four-and-half-years in Japan was almost invariably sound, with many insights, even though he was inevitably a product of the time that he was writing about. It was a time when the cold war was at its height and the West felt itself under great pressure on many fronts – the Soviet Union's grip on Eastern Europe (Poland and Hungary in particular) had been brutally tightened, when focused Russian technological advance had produced the satellite 'Sputnik', Western difficulties in the Middle East had been exacerbated by the revolution overthrowing King Faisal in Iraq, and American and British troops had gone into Lebanon and Jordan to try to shore up those regimes (all this in the two years before Oscar's return to Tokyo). And while he was in Japan there was the unsatisfactory Kennedy/Khrushchev meeting in Vienna in 1960 which indirectly led in part to the building of the Berlin Wall in 1961 and the Cuban missile crisis in 1962. China under Mao was unpredictable but intransigent, there was regular shelling of Taiwanese islands off the Chinese coast and an uneasy cease-fire on the 38th parallel after the Korean War. Indonesia was in thrall to a repressive military dictatorship and 'confrontation' between the UK and Indonesia started just as Oscar Morland was completing his tour of duty in Japan in 1963. There were the first signs of a build-up in the Russian Pacific Fleet and the situation between North and South Vietnam was beginning actively to go sour with an increasing American involvement on the side of the South (500,000 plus 'advisers' on the ground by 1963).

In the first few lines of the 'Impressions' despatch Oscar was at his disarming best:

> Having lived in Tokyo in the twenties and thirties and up to Japan's entry into the war in 1941, as well as during the first years of the American occupation, I find it difficult to avoid making easy generalizations, based on inadequate recent knowledge of the country. In particular, it is hard not to underestimate the extent to which the changes brought about by the war, the defeat and the occupation can be far-reaching and permanent – there seems at first sight to have been so very little change.

But continuing in his immaculate manuscript, to which there were only rare amendments in his think-pieces, he quickly made his own views crystal clear:

> Newcomers to Japan from the West are, I think, encouraged by their Japanese friends to go to the other extreme, and to believe that in twenty years the character of the Japanese people, as well as their system of government and their attitude to foreign countries, has undergone a profound and permanent alteration. This is certainly a false conclusion: what is undoubtedly true is that the war and its consequences here have accelerated the pace of normal change and development, and have also fostered abnormal developments imported from the West, many of which cannot be acclimatized here and are now disappearing.

He then identified three kinds of post-war change in Japan and took what he called random examples of these: developments hastened by the war, for example, women's Western dress and position in society which had both vastly improved; foreign importations come to stay, such as the directive doing away with absentee landlords which produced a new rural population of fairly conservative-minded, reasonably prosperous peasant farmers which 'would never have happened without the occupation'; and 'foreign importations vanished, or vanishing, because they have no soil here in which to take root' such as the destruction of big business organizations which had 'failed completely' as the pre-war '*zaibatsu*' system quickly came back into its own.

Oscar Morland went on to doubt whether Japan had absorbed much of Western democracy but there had been little strong reaction, since the end of the occupation, against occupation policies – no angry anti-democratic reaction, even in respect of the MacArthur constitution of 1946: 'its inappropriateness is generally recognized, but political disagreement about how to amend it is stronger than resentment against its imposition'. Oscar attributed Japan's rehabilitation since the war to a happy combination of good luck, the unchanged Japanese capacity for hard work, and American wisdom and benevolence. He was impressed by the very small amount of anti-American feeling. The Japanese were free of any feeling of inferiority in their attitude to the Americans, which he attributed to Japanese consciousness of their own much more mature civilization and outlook which enabled them to 'be able to tolerate without rancour what they regard as American childishness or muddling'.

PESSIMISTIC OUTLOOK

He was pessimistic about the outlook for post-war Japanese politics:

'I cannot resist the conclusion that the political scene is returning (for the moment) to something very like its pre-war look. In the thirties the two main parties were controlled by financial (and subsequently military) interests in the background, and the ordinary middle-class Japanese despised politicians as venal and preferred to steer clear of politics, with eventually disastrous results for Japan. At present, under a nominally two-party system of government, the Socialist opposition have no hope of defeating the Conservative Government and their programme and policy are correspondingly irresponsible, while it is extremely difficult to believe that the leaders of the Conservative Party, whether they are members of the Cabinet or heads of anti-Cabinet factions, are not controlled – or, at least, strongly influenced – by forces behind the scenes.

He admitted that Japanese friends had told him that things were not as bad as they appeared – that the younger generation was much more interested in politics, that younger members of the Diet were 'already impatient of that body's fruitless squabbling' and that results from the educational reforms would show through before long. But he was clearly, and rightly, sceptical of these assurances. His initial despatch from Tokyo must stand as one of pure professionalism, sketched out in a succinct bare-bones style of which he had become a master. His judgements after only three months back in Japan have stood the test of time to a remarkable degree.

And his predictions about Japanese foreign policy also continued to give pause for thought. This was a time when Britain, despite Suez, still saw herself as a world power, albeit a declining one, and the Japanese were still in the aftermath period of the war and occupation. Oscar Morland saw feelings in Japan towards the United Kingdom as extremely friendly with a declining 'tendency to think of us as a spent force . . .'

But the Japanese have thoroughly learned one lesson from their defeat – not again to be on the opposite side from American might – and while there is nothing particularly insincere in their profession of friendship with us, I do not think that they would feel it worth their while to go very far, if some difficulty arose, to preserve it.

He saw Japan as 'regaining her confidence in her foreign policy' and as 'beginning to see her role, particularly in the United Nations, as that of an honest broker, essentially on the side of the West against the East, but specially endowed to interpret Arab and Asian views to the West and to reconcile differences of opinion – to her own advantage'. He concluded that Japan, as in the past, would shrink instinctively from close alliances; but he posited a situation in which 'when Chinese consolidation and expansion loom very large she will be forced to identify herself more closely with either camp'. The camps may have changed their character but forty-four years later the general proposition is still one to ponder.

These themes were to dominate Oscar's thinking for the following four years. As it happened, the then permanent under-secretary, Sir Paul Gore-Booth,[5] had served in Japan before the war and had been interned at the outbreak of war. Gore-Booth recognized a missing element in British foreign policy when he wrote: 'It seems to me that, as a nation, we have since the war been abominably slow about Japan . . . The fact is that in Japan by and large we do not count for much, and certainly not as much as we should'. That was written in November 1959. But despite this top-level official recognition and despite our considerable interests in Hong Kong and Singapore as the centre of British interests in South-East Asia, Ministers were preoccupied in the next four years with East-West relations, decolonization particularly in Africa, and an attempt to join the European Economic Community. Oscar Morland went on leave earlier than planned in 1961 because there were tentative plans for Harold Macmillan to visit Japan in the September of that year. But it was not until 1972 that Edward Heath became the first British Prime Minister to 'discover' Japan and it was the 1980s before serious and highly successful efforts were made by both Japan and Britain to set bilateral relations on a firm footing in all respects, commercial, economic, political and cultural.

'REDISCOVERING' JAPAN

Oscar, accompanied by Alice, set about seeing much of Japan and noting the changes. I accompanied them on an extended ten-day trip round Kyushu; more importantly, we were escorted by Aso Kazuko, former Prime Minister Yoshida Shigeru's daughter, who had accompanied her father in London when he was a diplomat there in the late 1930s. She had known the Morlands at that time and had exceptionally been able to arrange for the Morland family to spend part of the summer of 1942 in Miyanoshita in the hills near Mt Fuji at a time when Britain and Japan were at war and the embassy staff were basically confined to the embassy compound. The nine-month internment had had its *longueurs* so the summer break in Miyanoshita was particularly welcome and cemented a relationship which had already been close for some time. Kazuko, whose husband had a large industrial business in Iizuka, just south of Fukuoka in the north of Kyushu, not only knew most people in that part of Japan but proved to be an immensely informative and entertaining guide. She and Alice would josh each other interminably, there was much fun and laughter in which Oscar, despite his reticence and somewhat serious approach, would join with much heaving and shaking of his not very fleshy jowls. The only two problems in the whole trip were Kazuko's certainty that the British Ambassador should stay in the Imperial suites in the best hotels wherever we went, regardless of cost. This didn't sit easily with the still straightened circumstances prevailing in Britain and in government finances. Oscar, after some minor groaning, kept this part of the financial arrangements very much to himself, so how the circle was squared remains a mystery. The other minor hiccup occurred when I was laid low as a result of drinking very cold beer on a very hot day. It was mortifying in those days to upset ambassadorial travel plans even for a short period. It did, however, show me a kind, solicitous and quite amused brace of Morlands in unusual circumstances.

Official trips to Shikoku and Hokkaidō followed, with Oscar continuously making comparison with pre-war Japan: 'the roads are not much better [there was little tarmaced road outside big cities and even inside them the surface was frequently badly broken up] but have you noticed that all the children seem to be wearing shoes?' I hadn't, because unshod Japanese seemed very quickly to have become a phenomenon of the past after the end of the war.

SUMMERTIME AT CHŪZENJI

But the favoured destination in the summer was the ambassador's villa on the lake at Chūzenji above Nikko. The journey could take anything between three and seven hours, the final stretch up a narrow, unpaved, dusty, z-bend bestrewn mountain road requiring a mixture of almost static endurance and dashing hope. But the reward at 4,000 feet lake-level with some mountains of 7,000 feet close by quickly made one forget the car journey as well as the humidity and high temperatures of Tokyo. The eventful journey was not however quite complete. The car had to park several hundred yards from the villa since there was no road to it; the last stage, with luggage, was done by boat – an outsize rowing-boat with one of the servants paddling and steering with a single oar at the back. Here in a quite secluded villa, with beautiful lake and mountain views, Alice Morland took up residence for a good ten weeks each year, while Oscar came and went but made sure he had at least a month's break at some stage. The pace of life and business was comparatively leisurely. But the Ambassador was still in charge. A rather Heath Robinson telephone ensured that there could be intermittent contact between the office and Oscar but this seemed to be used only at times of emergency. The normal run of official papers had to be read, drafts approved and letters and despatches signed. This was the perfect excuse for the private secretary or other members of staff to take a box to the ambassador and to be rewarded with a night or two at Chūzenji, ostensibly while the papers were read or signed.

One lived as part of the family, the welcome was genuinely friendly and warm. Alice was always full of chat as she made her rugs; Oscar significantly quieter. There were regular swims in the lake, which was deep and soon became very black. But his real passion was hill-walking, for which Chūzenji was ideally placed. He would literally race up some of the mountains, sparing neither himself nor those who accompanied him. This was clearly a way for him to burn off much of his nervous energy and for others to imagine

that they were getting fit. Visitors came and went, including on one occasion
John and Delia Pilcher with their daughter Julia, up from Manila where he
was then ambassador (see Ch. 21). They were the greatest fun, even though
much of the time was taken up with a never-ending monologue by John
Pilcher, who had a seemingly endless fund of hilarious and often scurrilous
stories.

JAPANESE CHARACTER

From the two vantage points of the residence in Tokyo (the ambassador at
that stage still worked separately from the office, accompanied only by his
personal assistant and private secretary) and the villa in Chuzenji, Oscar
watched, listened, read and pondered. He had little doubt that, barring
adverse world events, the Japanese would have little difficulty in doubling
their GDP in about ten years as Prime Minister Ikeda promised they would.
But he was concerned about what he saw as a fault-line in the Japanese
national character: 'national characteristics expose the nation now, as in the
decades before the war, to two connected dangers: the danger of tolerating a
bad government out of inertia and dislike of becoming involved in public
affairs, and the danger of acquiescing in the actions of a small but energetic
minority'. This was a recurring theme in his reporting from Tokyo, his comments on 1962 being summed up: 'An uneventful year. Economic recovery
remarkable, but political weaknesses remain . . . Will parliamentary democracy (which he saw as not deeply rooted) be made to work effectively, or will
an alternatively fairly democratic system be adopted before it is overtaken by
a resurgent nationalism?' These were questions for the future and, wisely, he
sought to provide no definite prognosis. But his underlying concern and constant reference to such issues showed clearly that he was troubled on this
score, not only in the light of his own experience before the war but because
of what he saw as weaknesses in the Japanese political system and society.

VALEDICTORY

At the end of four-and-a-half years as ambassador in Tokyo Oscar Morland
summed up his views in a valedictory despatch of September 1963. These
were 'for the sake of brevity . . . expressed . . . dogmatically, but I am well
aware that they are no more than my personal views, unsupported in many
cases by concrete evidence'. Here he was, yet again as with his first impressions, the careful observer with strong views, clearly expressed in his own
style – definite but without rhetorical flourishes – aware that one man's or
one embassy's views were inevitably limited. Unsurprisingly, he had not
changed his 1959 first impressions much. As with all immensely mature cultures radical changes in circumstance of the Japanese had 'done little to
modify their innate characteristics and are likely to remain substantially
unaltered in the future'. The Japanese had continued to profit from ideas and
techniques borrowed from the West but 'spectacular material Westernization
has not been accompanied by any significant Westernization in outlook . . .'.
It would be wrong to 'base our policy on the supposition that Japan will
become gradually occidental in outlook or democratic in a Western sense'.
Japan remained 'convinced of the superiority of her own oriental institutions
and culture'.

The Japanese, in Oscar Morland's view, 'are even less attached to political theory, and even more pragmatic than the British. They have nothing which influences them in their moral conduct and national policies corresponding with our European civilization and Christian tradition, and their ties even with China are more literary and artistic than political. Japan's close relations since the war with America and her recent inclination towards Britain and the free world are based entirely upon self-interest. Western democratic principles and methods have no attraction for the Japanese'.

On relations with Britain he was sceptical about 'threadbare public references to two island nations who must export to live', although he was prepared to concede that we could profit to a marginal degree from 'an instinctive Japanese tendency to admire the British character and way of life' which would 'always serve, if used sparingly, as a lubricant in our relations with Japan'.

As with his first, so with his final, despatch Oscar when writing his own drafts produced a joy of lucidity and brevity. His assessments, for all his self-deprecation, were in general excellent and his proposals eminently sound for the period in which he was writing. There were few in this era who could match him in these respects and the government justifiably and not over generously advanced him to GBE[6] on his retirement.

That he was not advanced a stage further[7] was probably due to two reasons. First, he came from the Consular rather than the Diplomatic Service and although these distinctions were rapidly dying away and there were exceptions to Consular Service officers reaching the very top by way of recognition, some memories lingered in a society which was inclined to delight for no profitable reason in these sorts of distinctions. But second, there was something not completely rounded in Oscar Morland's make-up. On his own he was a superb analyst and his written expositions could scarcely be bettered. But he was an immensely shy man and quite nervous. He smoked almost continuously and one of my abiding memories is of him in his study, cigarette stuck to his lower lip, screwing up his courage to take issue with a member of his staff. It did not come easily to him. A modulated argument required an effort; a rebuke was doubly hard. But even everyday conversation seemed not to come naturally. It was surprising therefore that he picked up as much information and views as he did. Not surprising, perhaps, that he often found it difficult on occasions to give straight answers to his own family. And not at all surprising that as an ambassador in his late fifties he confided little in his private secretary, thirty years his junior.

After retirement Oscar went to live in Thornton-le-dale near Pickering in Yorkshire in what by all accounts was a slightly austere northern house called The High Hall. His main preoccupation until he was seventy was as a Board member of Leeds Regional Hospital with a particular interest in finance. But he would also have been able to indulge in his passion for hill-walking. He died in 1980 aged seventy-six. Alice, his widow, lived on into a ripe old age, varyingly in Thornton-le-dale, Alresford and finally in Yorkshire again, in Ampleforth, where her youngest son was a monk.

20

Sir Francis Rundall
Ambassador to Japan 1963–67

Sir Francis Rundall

SIR HUGH CORTAZZI

Francis Rundall (1908–87), known as Tony Rundall, succeeded Oscar Morland, who had been a member of the Japan consular service before the war. He was in turn succeeded by John Pilcher, the last former member of the Japan consular service to become ambassador to Japan. Tony Rundall had joined the British consular service in 1930 serving in places such as Antwerp and Panama, but had never served before in Japan. Although he had no Japanese expertise he brought other qualities to the post. He had wide experience in political and commercial diplomacy and outstanding ability in administration.

Francis Brian Anthony Rundall, to give his full name, was born in 1908 and educated at Marlborough. From there he went to Peterhouse, Cambridge. He served in Germany after the war with the Control Commission. After a spell as a Diplomatic Service inspector, in 1953 he was appointed consul general in New York, a post whose primary function was trade promotion. In 1957 he was made Ambassador to Israel. From 1959–1963 he was chief clerk in the Foreign Office with the rank of a deputy under-secretary of state in the Foreign Office and was responsible for the administration of the Foreign Service as it was called until the amalgamation between the Foreign Office and the Commonwealth Relations Office.

Rundall was tall, thin and bespectacled. He was courteous, punctilious and highly conscientious. He took his work very seriously, but he knew how to delegate, he never avoided responsibility and was always ready to help his subordinates. He and his wife Mary attached great importance to staff morale (they always spoke of the staff as members of 'the family') and they did all they could to ensure that the mission was a happy one. They were kind and considerate as well as hospitable towards their staff. Where necessary he was firm and would not accept sloppy work.

Rundall and his wife tried hard to learn some Japanese but did not progress beyond simple phrases and vocabulary. Their efforts perhaps inevitably sounded stilted. They also tried conscientiously to learn about Japan and to understand Japanese ways of thought and behaviour, but they were the first to admit that they found the Japanese character difficult to comprehend.

The Rundalls worked hard to perform their responsibilities in entertaining visitors and developing contacts with Japanese and members of the diplomatic corps. But their obviously conscientious efforts to ensure that their guests were looked after properly did not always succeed. Embassy staff, who were rightly expected to help with the guests, would often receive instructions in advance about steering guests to particular sofas and would be summoned to move to other seats after dinner to cope with particular guests.[1]

Rundall suffered from gastric problems while in Tokyo, probably exacerbated by strain as a result of his determination to deal conscientiously with all the issues which he faced as ambassador. His stomach problems inevitably made him tetchy from time to time. He was fortunate in having a first-class and devoted personal assistant in Primrose Winch, who had worked for him previously when he was chief clerk. She helped tactfully and efficiently to steer members of the staff in their relations with their ambassador and to protect the Rundalls when they managed to get away from Tokyo either to the ambassador's house at Chuzenji, which they made available for use by other members of the staff from time to time, or to the little *besso* which they rented on the coast at Akiya. Rundall enjoyed swimming and fishing. In 1967 he decided that he had had enough in a post where he did not find it easy to relax and retired a year early at the age of 59.

After his retirement Rundall helped a variety of companies, including British Electric Traction (BET) in recruitment and management.[2] He suffered less from strain in tasks where his responsibilities were more limited and was able to relax a little.

ARRIVAL IN TOKYO

Sir Oscar and Lady Morland (Alice) left Tokyo in October 1963 and the Rundalls arrived by sea in December shortly before Christmas.[3] They were met by all the senior staff at Yokohama and by 'Jimmy-san' the butler at the residence on whose experience the Rundalls came to rely. Rundall presented his credentials to the Emperor on 16 January 1964. As the road in front of the embassy was a building site, while the final preparations were being made for the Olympic Games held in the autumn of 1964, no state coach could be provided for the ambassador and his staff, but the Japanese provided an imperial Mercedes to convey the ambassador to the imperial palace. The Japanese were reported to be impressed by the fact that the ambassador and the members of the embassy staff who accompanied him for the ceremony were all in diplomatic uniform! Rundall thought that the Emperor was more relaxed than on the occasion of the presentation of credentials by Oscar Morland.

The annual review for 1963 was drafted by Dudley Cheke, the minister. It set the scene for Rundall's mission. Murray Maclehose[4] then assistant under-secretary, commented on the report that 'Japan seems to be paralyzed by a chronic immobilism, anxious for reasons of national prestige to move forward, but not daring to take any step which might anywhere give offence or possibly jeopardise a business opportunity'. British objectives in relation to Japan were, he considered, to bind Japan economically and politically so close to the West that she will be able to resist the draw of communist China and, secondly, to expand trade. Cheke had noted that there were few signs that parliamentary democracy had become firmly rooted in Japan. Japan was suffering from a serious balance of payments deficit and needed to expand exports. The Anglo-Japanese Treaty of Commerce and Navigation had been ratified in April 1963 and Japan had joined the OECD in July of that year.

A POLITICAL PROBLEM – CONFONTATION BETWEEN INDONESIA AND MALAYSIA

Rundall was faced as soon as he arrived by a major political issue namely how to ensure that the Japanese government took a helpful line over the issue of confrontation between Indonesia and Malaysia. Britain still had forces East of Suez and imperial responsibilities stemming from British colonial rule in the Malay Peninsula, Singapore, North Borneo and Sarawak. Rundall was summoned to see Shima Shigenobu[6] at the Gaimusho on 28 December 1963 and was told that the 'The Japanese Government fully shared HMG's view that some of President Sukarno's views could never be condoned' but the Japanese thought the 'temperature needed to be lowered'. Japan 'advocated a selective use of the stick and the carrot'. The British Embassy were given a copy of an analysis, prepared by the Gaimushō's Asian Affairs Bureau, of the issues between Indonesia and Malaysia, which Cheke noted to London contained 'a good many fallacies'. There seemed much wishful thinking in the Japanese assessment.

Rundall paid a courtesy call on Ikeda Hayato, the Japanese Prime Minister, on 22 January 1964. Ikeda then told Rundall that 'he believed Sukarno was now generally looking for a way to improve Indonesia's relations with both Malaysia and Great Britain'. The Ambassador replied that we should need convincing of the sincerity of Sukarno's intentions.

In a despatch sent on 12 March 1964 about Japan and South-East Asia, in preparation for the forthcoming visit to Japan by R. A. Butler, then Foreign Secretary, Rundall noted that there was a lack of direction and coherence in Japanese foreign policy. The events of September 1963 over Confrontation had come as a shock to the Japanese. The Japanese Prime Minister and public opinion tended to favour Indonesia in the Malaysia/Indonesian dispute. Rundall's assessment was confirmed by a message from Prime Minister Ikeda to Sir Alec Douglas-Home, the British Prime Minister, which was handed over when the departing Japanese Ambassador in London, Ohno Katsumi, paid a farewell call on Sir Alec. Ikeda in his message wrote: 'I am very concerned with the development of the Malaysian dispute. President Sukarno seems to be in a dilemma domestically. I am trying to devise a proposal which will save President Sukarno from humiliation internally, but which will still be acceptable to Malysia.' This proposal, termed the Oda plan as it was devised by Oda Takio who had been Japanese ambassador in Djakarta and was shortly to become vice minister in the Gaimushō, was that[7] 'Sukarno should agree to withdraw his guerrillas in return for a unilateral declaration by the Tungku[8] that he would hold a plebiscite in Borneo and Sarawak in five years time.'

Although this plan was temporarily 'pigeon-holed' it was re-presented in a revamped form by Prime Minister Ikeda when Rundall saw him on 21 April 1964. The issue was one of the main topics at the Anglo-Japanese ministerial consultations held in Tokyo in May when R. A. Butler visited Japan. The issue rumbled on for some time as the Japanese continued to attempt to take unhelpful initiatives to mediate in the dispute. Oda was thought by the British to be too close to Sukarno personally and the Japanese police were not thought by the Embassy to have done enough to control pro-Indonesian demonstrations by Indonesian students outside the British Embassy. The problem continued to be a source of friction into 1965. In a despatch[9] of 21 May 1965 about Japan's future role in Asia Rundall drew a critical picture of Japanese policy:

> Japan would like to play an independent role in Asia, but as a bridge between the West and Afro-Asia rather than as a champion of the free world.' He warned that '. . . more positive political activity by Japan might well take the form of unwelcome mediatory initiatives.' Japan, he thought, valued 'her economic ties with the West more highly than her political ones.

THE OLYMPIC GAMES

For Rundall and the embassy perhaps the most important event in 1964 was the Tokyo Olympic Games, which began on 10 October and lasted until the 24th. The Japanese had made huge efforts to improve communications and provide facilities. For the previous three years many Tokyo roads had been hacked up to build underground railway lines and toll roads under and above ground. The huge investment helped to further Prime Minister Ikeda's 'Double the Income' plan and to give Japan a prominent place on the world political and economic map. An account of the 'British Part in the Tokyo Olympic Games 1964' by Dick Ellingworth, our Olympic Attaché, can be found in *Japan Experiences: Fifty Years, One Hundred Views. Post-war Japan Through British Eyes*[10] Rundall, in a lecture to the Japan Society in London in April 1968, quoted in that book, recorded not only his enjoyment of the Games but also the fact that they gave their biggest party with over 900 guests shortly before the Games began 'with the idea that our contingent should have a chance to relax before they had to compete'.

BRITAIN AND JAPAN IN 1964

Rundall, in his annual review for 1964, after recording that Satō Eisaku had succeeded Ikeda as Japanese Prime Minister, commented that 'Political dis-unity remains one of the chief causes of Japan's indecisive role in world affairs'. He thought that policy towards Communist China was perhaps Japan's most significant problem. Turning to trade, which was to become the most important task of the embassy in the coming years, he said that the prospects for Anglo-Japanese trade were good although recent British restric-tive measures had caused disappointment in Japan. He noted that there was persistent Japanese uneasiness over Britain's long-term economic prospects. This was a recurrent theme in his reporting and he made every effort to put over as positive an image of Britain as he could. In his annual review for 1966 he reported that our image had begun to improve.

ANGLO-JAPANESE TRADE

The most important event for Britain in Japan in 1965 was the British exhibition at Harumi in September/October of that year. The exhibition which was primarily a trade fair promoting British exports of capital and consumer goods attracted 775,000 visitors, including most members of the Japanese cabinet and members of the Imperial Family. Rundall acknowledged the particular help given by Princess Chichibu. The exhibition was opened by Her Royal Highness Princess Alexandra of Kent, accompanied by her husband the Honourable Angus Ogilvy. The Princess had charmed all those she met in 1961 when she came out to Japan as the first member of the British royal family to pay an official visit to the country after the war. On this occasion she and her husband, Rundall, recorded, 'lit up every important occasion' and the Japanese responded enthusiastically to their grace and charm.

Douglas Jay, the President of the Board of Trade, came to Japan for the exhibition and for trade talks with the Japanese. In a personal letter to Michael Stewart, then Foreign Secretary, he expressed his gratitude for the way in which the Rundalls had looked after him and his wife. The Ambassador had been tireless in helping him to make the best use of his time. Jay noted the efficiency of the Embassy staff 'whom the Ambassador leads with authority, combined with warm kindness.' Board of Trade officials were generally pleased with the results of the exhibition, and Anglo-Japanese trade moved into rough balance at some £60 million.[11]

Rundall determined, despite the continued Japanese quota restrictions affecting important British products, including whisky and woollen textiles, and numerous tariff and non-tariff barriers, to capitalize on this success. As a former chief clerk he was well aware of he Foreign Office's limited resources, but having been closely involved with the Plowden review of the diplomatic service he recognized that if a good enough case could be made the commercial and economic staff of the Embassy would be augmented. He argued hard for additional staff and arranged for a temporary building, which had been put up on the Embassy tennis court to be used to house the commercial and economic section of the embassy. The building was not made for an earthquake-prone city like Tokyo but it gave the commercial department scope to expand so that it could deal with the increasing flow of business visitors who needed help in what was a difficult and distant market. Apart from providing introductions and market information the department had to look for export opportunities and ways of promoting British products. Under the leadership of Rundall good working relations were developed with the Board of Trade especially with the Commercial Relations and Exports Department and with Trade Fairs and Promotions as well as with the Asia Committee of the British National Export Council (BNEC) under the chairmanship of Michael Montague, Chairman of Valor, which manufactured domestic heaters.

An equally important part of commercial and economic work, in addition to economic reporting and financial issues (as yet no one had been appointed to the embassy from the Bank of England or the Treasury), was to help businessmen cope with tariff and non-tariff barriers.

A major issue for the commercial department was the conduct of the annual trade talks in which we tried to persuade the Japanese to increase quotas for British exports. The talks in 1965 had ended in stalemate and in 1966 and 1967 the Japanese tried to wear down the Embassy staff and visiting officials by insisting on late night sessions and only making concessions of a marginal nature at the last minute. They used similar tactics in the hard bargaining involved in negotiations on civil aviation rights.

Other issues which occupied much time were cases involving copying of British designs and Japanese dumping e.g. of pocket handkerchiefs. We also had to help British industries to work out arrangements with Japanese exporters whose products were, it was claimed, harming British industries. Pottery and fishing reels were examples.

Rundall took a close interest in all commercial and economic work and was always ready to help when needed and gave the department every encouragement, but he was content to leave it to his[12] commercial and economic counsellor to settle priorities and tactics.

In one case, that involving Robert Maxwell,[13] then an MP, Rundall perhaps went too far to help a man who was arrogant, demanding and rude. He had received a letter from the Foreign Office warning him that Maxwell was the sort of man who if he was in the least dissatisfied with the help he was given would complain to Ministers. At the time of his visit he was pursuing the particular interests of Chamber's Encyclopaedia as well as of his publishing empire. He asked for a meeting with the Japanese Prime Minister Satō Eisaku. Rundall agreed to request this.[14] Satō rather surprisingly agreed to meet Maxwell and to receive a set of Chamber's Encyclopaedia.[15] Rundall also gave a reception for Maxwell and the Rundalls accompanied Maxwell to a Japanese dinner given by Tsukasa, the President of the Japanese booksellers Maruzen.[16]

CULTURAL RELATIONS

Rundall rightly urged London to put much more effort into improving cultural relations. In his annual review for 1966 he said that while Anglo-Japanese relations had quietly prospered culturally 'we are not even on the map'. In the cultural field we were 'lagging far behind France and Germany and indeed most other countries, despite the good work of the British Council. It is high time that we mounted a cultural event of real importance.' Unfortunately, neither he nor Mary Rundall had any real feel for Japanese art.

POLITICAL RELATIONS

The main emphasis in political work in Rundall's time as ambassador was on developing exchanges of information and assessments with the Gaimushō. He was also determined to ensure that the arrangement to hold annual talks at ministerial level was maintained as he saw this as an important element in developing close relations between Britain and Japan.

As Rundall could not speak Japanese and there were then very few Japanese politicians with even moderate English, political contacts had to be left mainly to Japanese speakers in the mission. The Liberal Democratic Party (LDP) were firmly in charge. Factionalism continued to dominate the political scene. The Socialist opposition was divided and its anti-American foreign policy was seen by the electorate as unrealistic.

RUNDALL'S SUMMING UP

Rundall sent his valedictory despatch[17] from Tokyo on 6 July 1967. He began by referring to a Foreign Office planning paper which concluded that in Britain's dealings with the Japanese 'we must always remember that their character is such that they require unusually careful and tactful handling'. He had compared his findings with those of Oscar Morland in his valedictory despatch of 1963 and those of Esler Dening in his of 1957:

> The moral of our three despatches is broadly the same. It is that despite all that has happened to them in the last hundred years and in spite of the tremendous changes brought about by the war, the basic national characteristics of the Japanese people have altered very little and that they are still a race apart . . . The Japanese are motivated in their dealings with the outside world by a strong sense of 'national consciousness' or to put it another way by a sense of uniqueness of being Japanese. [The *Nihonjinron* or the myth of Japanese uniqueness which many of us have tried so hard to combat.] The Japanese are convinced that their 'sense of values and way of life are superior to those of other peoples, a somewhat contradictory sense of inferiority – particularly with respect to the West – which makes them awkward and insecure when dealing with foreigners, and a residual if largely latent xenophobia due to their long isolation from the outside world.

This xenophobia, he opined, finds expression in pride in the economic recovery already achieved and in Japanese determination to catch up in sectors where Japan still lags.

Rundall observed that the Japanese were strongly motivated by self-interest noting that in this they were not unique 'but the Japanese as a people seem less concerned about the ethical content of their actions and more adroit at reconciling the unreconcilable to their own satisfaction and advantage than almost any other nation'. He judged that the Japanese had 'become adept at the subtle evasion of their international obligations in the economic field. Apparent concessions are nullified by the fine print of domestic regulations, and where this cannot be done without severe international criticism, there is always the utterly reliable long-stop of "administrative guidance".'

In Rundall's view 'whilst good manners demand an impassive exterior and concealment of one's real feelings, the Japanese are an intensely emotional people.' He drew attention to the Japanese capacity for loyalty and hard work. He found the Japanese 'neither militaristic, nor pacific' and declared they were 'the world's greatest pragmatists'.

Japan had, he wrote, 'become one of the world's strongest powers'. Although per capita income and the general standard of living were 'still well below the highest Western European standards they were determined to catch up quickly'. 'Japan is at present seeking Great Power status by a slow and calculated spread of her economic influence.' There appeared to have been little change in Japanese foreign policy during the last three years. Japan still sought 'the development of the country's economic strength and the promotion of her overseas trade, coupled with the avoidance of any political responsibility or identification with any of the Power blocs to an extent which might lose friends and damage exports.' Japan was 'broadly on the side of the Free World because the majority of her interests lie in that direction, but I do not think that she is ideologically committed in any way and she has kept all her economic pipelines open to all the Communist countries including the Soviet Union and China'. He found 'little nationalism in the pre-war sense'. Japan was unlikely at present, he thought, to assume a greater share of defending the Free World but would do so if military strength at world Power level became necessary to defend Japan's essential interests.

Rundall concluded that 'British policy should aim at showing the Japanese that it is in their interest to remain allied with the West. Our influence is limited but we can build on Japanese gratitude for help given in business and Service matters in bygone years. Japan is about to become the world's third industrial Power and probably our greatest competitor in overseas markets. He thought that in such markets there was a case for seeking their co-operation in joint ventures.'

He recognized that in this despatch he had dealt 'almost exclusively with the less desirable characteristics of the Japanese character, but these are likely, I fear, to be the most important ones in Japan's dealings with the outside world. The Japanese have many more lovable characteristics' including a genuine capacity for friendship, a code of politeness and an almost overwhelming sense of obligation for favours done. The Japanese were loyal to their friends. 'If we can persuade them to accept us as a friendly country and can establish personal contacts at the highest levels, we can exert an influence greater than our strength.'

Rundall's valedictory despatch did not contain any very penetrating insights into the Japanese character and policies, but it was a fair summary of the impressions of a conscientious and experienced diplomatic practitioner who had no previous knowledge of Japan or its culture and little intuitive sympathy with the Japanese with whom he came in contact. Rundall steered his mission with firmness, sensitivity and kindness and deserves to be remembered not least for the emphasis which he rightly placed on the development of Anglo-Japanese trade.

21
Sir John Pilcher
Ambassador to Japan, 1967–72

Sir John Pilcher

SIR HUGH CORTAZZI

John Pilcher (1912–90), British Ambassador in Japan between 1967 and 1972, helped to revive Anglo-Japanese friendship after the Second World War and was long remembered with affection both in Japan and by his friends and colleagues.

John was short and rotund with a balding head. He was witty and amusing with a fund of stories. He was also very well read, an accomplished linguist and a man of broad culture. He was modest, courteous and hospitable. A convert to Catholicism, he was sincerely religious, but he was tolerant and understanding of those who did not share his beliefs. He took a particular interest in Buddhism and appreciated the Buddhist and Shinto elements in Japanese culture. He was an amused observer of Japanese idiosyncracies and his love of Japan was rarely tinged with annoyance at the unpleasant elements which can be encountered there. His second name was Arthur, but in Japan he did not use all three initials, reading JAP, as he knew how sensitive Japanese had become about this abbreviation.

John Pilcher was born in Quetta (now Pakistan) in 1912 where his father, a Royal Engineer, was at that time a lecturer at the Staff College. He was the only child of elderly parents who were very musical. He came to England in 1921. His parents, who lived in Bath in Georgian comfort, encouraged his interest in music and wanted him to become a good linguist. So as a small boy he often stayed with relations in Normandy and spent some time in Italy and Austria. As a result he soon became fluent in French, Italian and German.

His school days were spent at Shrewsbury where he found the regime barbaric and was delighted when he could escape to the civilized atmosphere of Clare College, Cambridge. John had become fascinated by the classical architecture of Bath and he at first wanted to study architecture, but doubted whether he would ever find a sufficiently wealthy patron to pursue what was for him more a hobby than a means of earning his living. He therefore decided to study Spanish and perfect his Italian. Somewhat surprisingly one of his hobbies at Cambridge was beagling.

One of the first Japanese he met at Cambridge was Yoshida Kenichi, the eccentric son of Yoshida Shigeru, Japan's first prime minister after the war. Another Cambridge acquaintance who later became a good friend was Itoh Eikichi, later chairman of Itohchu, the large Japanese trading house. At this stage, John had no idea that Japan would play such a major role in his life.

It was suggested to him that he should join the diplomatic or consular service where his knowledge of languages would stand him in good stead. Although he failed to turn up for the economics paper John was accepted for the Japan consular service.

EARLY CAREER IN JAPAN

Together with another language stddent Tom Bromley, who became a good friend, John made the usual sea journey to Japan, arriving in February 1936 in time to witness the revolt of young turks in the army on 26 February in what came to be called the *Ni-ni-roku jiken*. John later told Peter Martin, who was British Council representative in Kyoto at the time he became ambassador, that he had waded ashore on to a beach from a ship's cutter because the ship would not or could not enter Yokohama. In a lecture entitled 'A Perspective on Religion' delivered at the Nissan Institute on 4 May 1984, John said that the incident in which 'the young military showed their conviction that they alone could properly understand and interpret the will of the revered Emperor' confronted him at once 'by Japanese religious beliefs and their contemporary expression.'

John and Tom Bromley shared the language students' flat which was above the offices but which now forms part of the chancery. They had a maid of all work who had several children by one of the embassy's drivers. When they found their bills escalating they remonstrated with her. In dudgeon she walked out after locking the doors and throwing the keys down the lavatory. Jimmy-san who was later the butler at the residence when John Pilcher became ambassador recalled seeing John climbing up the drain pipe to get into the flat through a window.

John was given the task of acting as private secretary to Sir Robert Clive who was then British Ambassador. He found Clive 'a rather ' pompous old bird' who was getting deaf. Clive was reputed to be having an affair with the wife of the French military attaché. Lady Clive, in a desire to annoy her husband, was said by John to have filled the ambassador's study with birds at whom Clive in frustration would from time to time hurl books.

John Pilcher did not at first take to Japan but his interest in the country was encouraged by George Sansom, the eminent scholar of Japan, at that time commercial counsellor, and his wife Katherine who befriended him. He also became a close friend of Ashley Clarke, who was head of chancery at the time and who later became a distinguished ambassador in Rome. They used to enjoy amateur dramatics and played duets together. His growing interest in Japanese civilization led him back to his European roots and he bagan to take instruction in the Catholic faith.

After Sir Robert Craigie came out as ambassador to Japan, John. who had at one time wondered whether he should ask for a transfer from Japan. persuaded the authorities in the embassy to allow him to go to Kyoto to study away from the distracting pressures of the embassy.

John '. . . was completely bowled over by the beauty of the great Buddhist temples of Nara and Kyoto'.

[He] . . . studied Japanese at the feet of a Zen priest (of Shokokuji, one of the great Zen temple complexes of Kyoto), who was occasionally prevailed upon by the authorities to leave with me thoughts of the National polity, of Shinto inspiration and then much in vogue. The great Suzuki Daisetsu inspired studies in Zen. I had therefore to try to understand the dual principles behind Japanese Life: Shinto and Buddhism and the influence of Confucianism on civic structure.

John had a small Japanese-style house with a tiny Japanese garden near Nanzenji In his lecture of 4 May 1984 John commented that during his two years in Kyoto he lived '. in the grounds of a *Ryōbu Shintō*, establishment, separated from its Buddhist element after the Meiji Restoration. Behind my house was a waterfall under which it was meretorious to stand and pray. I could, therefore, feel the omnipresence of Shintō around me.'

He enjoyed working in the garden and was able to employ a cook who could produce Japanese and Western cuisine and a young maid called O-Haru-san who looked after him very well. He became thoroughly *'tatamisé'* to adapt a Japanese word in the French way. He bought a bicycle and explored Kyoto's temples and gardens. He did not play golf or bridge and was able to concentrate on Japanese culture. He became fascinated by aspects of Japanese language. He particularly enjoyed learning abstruse and grandiloquent terms of address which amused his acquaintances.

His interest in Japanese art was encouraged by the friendship which he developed with Kawai Kanjirō – the famous potter and leading figure in the *Mingei* movement who lived in Kyoto. Through Kawai and the English potter, Bernard Leach, with whom he had a distant family connection, he got to know Yanagi Sōetsu and Hamada Shōji who had founded the movement.

One Japanese scholar whom he saw frequently was Professor Jugaku Bunshō who was translating Dante's *Inferno* and *Paradiso* into Japanese and who was very interested in William Blake. John who could recite long passages of Dante was able to help the Professor.

Jugaku Bunshō's daughter recalls how when she returned from school she would often find John ensconced sitting crosslegged on a cushion. He would join the family for meals and much enjoyed Mrs Jugaku's home cooking and simple Japanese fare. She describes him as going around in a greenish suit and brown soft hat.

Despite the growing militarism in Japan, the Jugaku household remained a haven of free speech and pacifism. Professor Jugaku had an imperial connection and this may have helped to ensure that when John visited them he was not generally troubled by the police or the *Kempeitai* who were highly suspicious of all foreigners in Japan at this time. But John's other Japanese friends who feared that their telephone calls were being tapped were increasingly reluctant to receive visits from him although at times, in order to avoid embarrassment to his friends, he used to leave his bicycle around the corner when making calls.

Professor Jugaku's daughter recalls John's sense of humour and his ability as a mimic. When imitating a Japanese Shinto priest. for instance, he would do an exact copy of the priest's walk. On hot summer days John, when he came to their house, would strip off and wallow in a cool bath. Afterwards he would put on the *yukata* which the household kept for him and then sit on the verandah enjoying the cool of evening.

John was worried that the Jugakus might be in need and kept in touch with them. He managed to visit them in Kyoto in 1948 when lie was on an official tour of the Far East despite the difficulties of travelling in Japan at that time. Mrs Jugaku was delighted to see him again when he returned as British ambassador in 1967. She found that he had not changed and still retained his sense of humour and his knowledge of the language of Kyoto.

PONSONBY FANE

John had known the Ponsonby Fane family in Somerset at their estate at Brympton d'Evercy near Yeovil, and naturally renewed his acquaintance in Kyoto with the eccentric Richard Arthur Brabazon Ponsonby Fane, who always wore '. . . *haori hakama*, surmounted by a decayed woollen scarf with the ravages of moth in evidence on it. It had been knitted for him by the Dowager Empress, widow of the Taishō Emperor'. Ponsonby Fane who 'imbued' John 'with his sense of the fascination of Shinto was '. . . a convinced Anglican and led a dual life as a sage studying Shinto in Kamigamo outside Kyoto and as a cricket-loving country squire in Somerset'.

Peter Martin recalls John's account of Ponsonby Fane's funeral. This was apparently a bizarre affair which was attended by Ponsonby Fane's sister who was described by John as a 'hearty extravert daughter of the shires' who comported herself in nonchalant style throughout her stay in Kyoto. When she visited her brother's house she could not find a chair on which to sit: so she plonked herself down on the *tokonoma* and proceeded to eat a banana from the elegant display set out on a precious dish where she was sitting.

Subsequently, Ponsonby Fane's nephew and niece who came out to wind up his affairs discovered that he had a huge sum in his Kyoto bank account. They tried unsuccessfully to transfer this sum to England. So they drew the money out in cash. The niece then alleged that she was pregnant and was in such a delicate state that she would have to be carried onto the NYK vessel which was to convey them to America. Arrangements were accordingly made, no doubt with John Pilcher's connivance, for her to be taken to the ship lying on a mattress stuffed with yen. As soon as the ship reached US territorial waters she had a miraculous recovery from her pregnancy and managed to convert the yen into dollars with the help of the ship's purser.

TSINGTAO

All good things have to come to an end and in 1939 John was instructed to report to the British consular post at Tsingtao initially for six weeks although in the event he had to stay for over a year. His job was to act as a link between the consulate general, which was normally staffed by members of the China consular service, and the Japanese military authorities who were making life difficult for the British there. Pilcher did not enjoy his time in Tsingtao. The consul general had fortified himself within the compound and John found him an unsympathetic boss. John had been horrified on arriving in Shanghai to see a British woman kick a Chinese rickshaw puller and to discover that the average British resident in China at that time had only learnt enough Chinese to tell their servants to get out. The British residents in Tsingtao who objected to doffing their hats to portraits of the Emperor did not understand the value of politeness. John was accused by the consul general and some residents of being pro-Japanese, but having seen the best of Japan in Kyoto he now saw some of the worst features of Japanese behaviour outside their own country. In 1940 while serving in Tsingtao he was received into the Catholic Church with a German priest officiating.

LONDON, ROME, LONDON

In 1941, before the war with Japan began, John was transferred to London. He travelled home via Manila and the USA. From there he managed to get a place on a flying boat to Lisbon where he made the acquaintance of Norman Douglas, the author and authority on Italy. On his arrival at Bristol from Lisbon the customs officers were very suspicious of John's address-book in Japanese and refused to let him enter Britain until they had confirmed his bona fides with the Foreign Office. The ship on which he was originally to have travelled from the USA was sunk with all his effects on board.

In London John met Delia Margaret Taylor, the Irish Catholic daughter of a retired army officer. John did not participate in the pastimes of the landed gentry such as riding, hunting, shooting or fishing and Delia's family did not approve of the match. So Delia who had been acting as a land girl for the war effort left home and John and she were married privately.

While John worked at the Ministry of Information, Delia joined the Council for Music and the Arts, the forerunner of the Arts Council. One of John's tasks at the ministry was to help cheer up the young students of Japanese from the forces studying at the School of Oriental and African Studies, some of whom were reported to be suffering from stress as a result of the pressures of learning quickly such a difficult language. I was not stressed out but I shall always recall the talk which he gave us in late 1943. He enlivened our day with his humour and his mimicry sitting down on the floor and doing his Kabuki act.

POST-WAR YEARS

The Pilchers found a home in Chelsea. In the immediate post-war period the pressure of work in the information department at the Foreign Office in which John was then working declined and John was able on most days to get home for lunch and a snooze. One day, there was a telephone call from the Foreign Office who were worried because the ceiling in John's office had fallen down and they could not find him! In 1948 I called on John in his office in Carlton House Terrace to discuss a letter which Ron Dore and I had jointly written to *The Times* complaining about the ban imposed by the American occupation authorities in Japan on the sending of books to Japan. In the same year, John was posted to Rome as first secretary information. His excellent Italian and extravert personality made him an ideal choice for the job and the Pilchers greatly enjoyed life in Italy.

In 1951 he was promoted to counsellor and made head of 'Japan and Pacific Department' in the Foreign Office. He thus became responsible for seeing through the ratificaton of the Peace Treaty with Japan, concluded at San Francisco in 1951 (the Treaty came into force in April 1952). This was a difficult period in Anglo-Japanese relations. There was still strong resentment against Japan not least because of the maltreatment of British prisoners-of-war but also because of widespread fears of unfair competition from cheap imports of Japanese-made textiles and sundry goods, allegedly made by sweated labour. John did his best to get ministers to take a more objective view of Japan but it was an uphill task. He used to say that whenever he put up a memorandum on policy towards Japan Anthony Eden, then Foreign Secretary, would simply write on the submission: 'I do not like the Japanese. A.E.'

I was at that time a second secretary in Tokyo and had to spend a great deal of time on negotiations with the Japanese authorities on a United Nations Status of Forces Agreement. This was required to cover bases for UN forces operating in Korea who until the Peace Treaty with Japan came into force had been provided with facilities by the occupation authorities. We received repeated instructions which were increasingly unrealistic to ensure that UN Forces continued to operate 'under the American umbrella'. One day I managed to get a telegram to London approved which inadvertently contained a startling mixed metaphor. 'Surely it is time that we gave up flogging the dead horse of the American umbrella'! This caused ribald mirth in London and John Pilcher sent Arthur de Ia Mare, then head of chancery in Tokyo, a four-page letter in long hand in which there was a mixed metaphor in every sentence. Sadly the letter has not survived.

MADRID, MANILA, LONDON, VIENNA

John's next post was as minister in Madrid, first under Jock Balfour, and then under Ivo Mallet, 'an old acid drop'. John and Delia much enjoyed their five years in Madrid. As Franco was still in charge in those days and his government was generally ostracized, they did not have a single ministerial visit. John did, however, have to deal on one occasion with George Brown who was a Labour MP, later to become Foreign Secretary when John was in Tokyo as ambassador. John was in charge of the embassy which was at San Sebastian where the Spanish government in those days spent the summer months. George Brown demanded an audience with Franco. This was not at all easy to arrange at any time least of all for a 'socialist'. But John knew Franco's confessor and managed to fix the appointment. He felt it desirable to brief George before the audience and asked the Browns to lunch at a famous fish restaurant. Brown commented:'I suppose any old fish restaurant is good enough for an out-of-office socialist.' John pointed out that the restaurant was very exclusive and expensive. George arrived for the lunch rather the worse for wear, but John managed to sober him up in time for the meeting which went reasonably well.

From Madrid John was posted as ambassador in Manila which he had thought from his first visit in 1941 was 'the bottom' in the Far East. In fact, however, he and Delia who were determined to like wherever they went greatly enjoyed the Philippines. They travelled widely in the air attaché's De Havilland Dove and developed a liking for the people and their culture. Their ability in Spanish and the fact that they were both Catholics no doubt helped. They were very hospitable and John coined the phrase (only to be used in strict privacy!) that the recipe for a good party was a mixture of 'Flips and Brits, Dips and shits' (Inevitably this was adapted when John eventually became ambassador in Japan.)

From Manila John returned to London as assistant under secretary in charge of information and culture. This should have been just the job for him, but he found it a frustrating experience as there was never enough money to do anything worthwhile especially in cultural relations. He asked to be appointed as minister to the Vatican but was told that no Catholic could fill this post at the Holy See. Instead in 1965 he was appointed ambassador to Austria. Harold Caccia, then Permanent Under-Secretary, had become fed up with ambassadors who did not enjoy Vienna and wanted someone like John, with his capacity for getting on with people and enjoying life, to go there. Moreover John spoke Austrian German. Once again John and Delia were in their element. They were amused by Viennese society and snobbery and they both adored music. But in 1967 he was told that he was being appointed to Tokyo on promotion to replace Tony (Sir Francis) Rundall who was retiring early owing to ill health. Pileher managed to postpone his departure until after the Salzburg Festival.

AMBASSADOR TO JAPAN

John and Delia arrived in Tokyo in October 1967 and he remained a bassador to Japan until his retirement in the summer of 1972. For John, although he was immersed in European culture, it was great fun to be back in Japan. They soon made an impact on the Tokyo social scene. They entertained widely and became well known for their cultural interests especially their enthusiasm for music. They developed particularly good relations with members of the Japanese Imperial Family, especially Princess Chichibu, and with their diplomatic colleagues. But their circle of friends which included intellectuals, artists, potters and priests, was much wider than that of the normal diplomatic merry-go-round.

They took every opportunity to travel especially to John's beloved Kyoto. They usually stayed at the Miyako Hotel where according to Peter Martin, John 'had great fun addressing the maids ... in ornately old-fashioned Japanese with a wealth of subjunctives, largely incomprehensible to them'.

By his informality and his clear liking for the Japanese and Japanese culture, John Pilcher added a new dimension to Britain's relations with Japan. It would be unfair to his predecesors to imply that they had not worked hard to improve relations but they had generally lacked the personal warmth he displayed. Certainly he helped to interest British ministers in Japan and to improve understanding in Britain of Japan

John did whatever was necessary as ambassador. He enjoyed his work and was conscientious, but he was not a workaholic. He realized that commercial and economic work was becoming increasingly important and as his commercial and economic counsellor I found him always ready to support our efforts even if, as he readily admitted, he did not understand economics (John never made up for the fact that he missed his economics paper when he joined the consular service before the war. Ben Thorne remembers him asking one day, no doubt with his tongue in his cheek, 'What is an economic?') He teased me frequently about the flood of trade missions which we had to look after refernng to them as 'Hugh's peddlers and meddlers', but he greatly enjoyed briefing them about Japan. They were usually enthralled as he explained to them the intricacies of the Japanese language and aspects of Japanese culture. The groups usually called on him before coming on to a reception which I was giving for them and would often arrive late because John would not or (could not) cut short his performance. I would ring through to his study to remind him that my guests were arriving, but John soon got wise to this and simply picked up and put down the telephone receiver. In the end I had no alternative but to arrange the briefings at a different time.

John was also always ready to support our representations for trade-related concessions. One day. I had persuaded him to give a lunch for Raymond Bell, a dour senior official from the UK Treasury whom John found difficult as did we all. The lunch had gone well not least because John had hit it off with, for a Japanese Ministry of Finance official, an unusually cultured individual. At the end having said goodbye to the Japanese guests John turned to Raymond Bell and declared: 'Do you know what Hugh is making me do this afternoon? I have to go with him to see the Minister of the Agriculture to discuss the tariff on biscuits!' He said the word 'biscuits' with much emphasis and contumely. I wondered if John would explode when Raymond Bell replied: 'Well, Ambassador, that is what you are paid for!'

The culmination of our trade promotion efforts was 'British Week in Tokyo' in the autumn of 1969. Every Japanese department store in Tokyo agreed to put on a promotion of British goods at the same time. We had a major exhibition of Britain in the Budōkan and a scientific instrument exhibition at the Science Museum. John was at first rather doubtful about the plans, but when he had grasped fully what was intended and realized the scope for the combination of commerce and culture, he was enthusiastic and active in promoting the success of the week. He insisted on joining many of the planning sessions. Ben Thorne who was in charge of the British Week Office, remembers one occasion when a meeting was called in the ambassador's study in the residence at 9 o'clock in the morning, but the chief information officer from the Department of Trade and Industry, Arthur Savage, had not turned up. Eventually, he arrived clearly under the weather. John determined to adminsiter his favourite remedy. The butler was summoned to bring a glass of dark liquid. This was John's cure-all, Fernet Branca. Arthur was made to drink this foul-tasting potion. He manged to get it down before dashing for the door.

BRITISH WEEK

British Week attracted many VIPs from Britain. Princess Margaret accompanied by Lord Snowdon, was invited to Japan to open the Week and visit the various exhibition sites. John and Delia were in their element although having the Princess and her entourage for a lengthy stay could not have been restful. All went well including the ball which the Pilchers gave when the Princess would not go to bed. Prince William of Gloucester had been sent to work in the embassy and John had allocated him to work under me in the commercial department. Commercial work was not his metier and I gave him the task of organizing his cousin's programme. This caused many problems and I had to have frequent recourse to John Pilcher to sort out royalty!

Another of our VIP visitors for British Week was the then Lord Mayor of

London who was one of the more pompous city gents. He determined to wear his robes and thought himself at least the equal of the Governor of Tokyo even though his 'domain' was a mere square mile. One evening, at a reception at the embassy, the Lord Mayor, finding Pilcher on his right, declared: 'No one stands on my right except the Queen.' John who had suffered much from the man's pomposity stormed back: 'I am the Queen' which, in so far as he was the Queen's representative, was correct.

Shortly after British Week on 28 October 1969, John signed a despatch which had been long in gestation entitled 'The Merry Wives of Ginza: Women's status in Japan'. In the opening paragraph he acknowledged his debt to John Morley, an embassy counsellor, in the drafting of this despatch, but it had all the hallmarks of a genuine Pilcher piece. The despatch begins: 'Japan for the foreigner is a land abounding in optical illusions. One of its most deceptive phenomena is the Japanese woman.' After noting that Japanese men were not good at sex Pilcher asked: '. . . would it be a calumny to add that the congenital inability of the Japanese male to improvize, if projected into the bedchamber, may well deprive his advances of that spontaneous elan which elicits, so they say, the most heartfelt response?' He commented that . . . . there is still about Japanese girls trying to be sexy in public an embarrassingly amateur quality which conjures up the image of some nubile but callow Roedean sixth-former playing Salome'. In conclusion he asked: 'Are they really merry, those wives of Ginza? They still have a profound sense of the sadness of things and of the transience of existence, but at least they would always have agreed with Piers Plowman that "chastity without charity shall be chained in hell".'

Among the many visitors to Tokyo the Pilchers had to look after was George Brown, then Foreign Secretary, and his wife. I realized, when John rang me up on the Sunday evening after they had arrived and asked us to help them over dinner, that despite the episode in San Sebastian recorded above, George was being difficult. He had arrived not in the best of spirits (perhaps because he had already had too much of the liquid sort). George was argumentative and cantankerous. It soon became clear that the only way to deal with him was to stand up to him and not allow him to get away with his bullying.

One visitor who charmed us all was Harold Macmillan. Senior staff were invited to listen to him for an hour or so. He was a great raconteur. He recalled that after the Great Earthquake in Yokohama in 1923 Macmillans, the publishers, had been generous to Maruzen, the Japanese booksellers, allowing them extended credit. Maruzen remembered this generosity and had received Harold Macmillan with great courtesy. John Pilcher also liked another visitor, Arnold Toynbee, whom he took to an audience with the Emperor, with whom he had an extended discussion considerably overstaying the time allowed.

Expo 70 in Osaka was another major event in John's time as ambassador. He had recommended the appointment of John Figgess, whom he had known since before the war, as British Commissioner General. They got on well and had many cultural interests in common. Unfortunately, this could not be said of Pilcher's relations with Robert John, the consul general in Osaka, who had an unerring capacity for rubbing people up the wrong way. In particular Robert John refused to acknowledge the prime significance of Kyoto!

The most important British visitor to Expo 70 was Prince Charles. The Prince of Wales was still a young man in his last year at Cambridge. This was his first official visit abroad. John Pilcher took the Prince round his favourite sites in Kyoto and expounded about Japanese Buddhism and culture. The Prince, who was very impressed by what he was shown, remembered John Pilcher with affection and respect.

STATE VISIT TO LONDON

The highlight of his time as ambassador in Japan was the State Visit by the Emperor Hirohito (Shōwa) and the Empress to London in the autumn of 1971. The Shōwa Emperor, although he was barely 70, walked and talked like an old man and conversation with him was difficult. The Emperor was not received with any warm acclaim in Britain, and the tree which he planted at Kew was pulled up in protest at Japanese treatment of prisoners-of-war; nevertheless, there was none of the rude and intemperate protests which marred the visit of the Heisei Emperor Akihito in May 1998. The Showa Emperor was particularly pleased by the restoration of his banner as a Knight of the Garter and by his appointment as an honorary Fellow of the Royal Society. John Pilcher for his part was awarded the Grand Cordon of the Rising Sun as a member of the Emperor's suite

In advance of the State Visit John sent home a despatch dated 3 March 1971 on the theme 'The Emperor of Japan; Human or Divine?' He answered this question in the following words:

> Officially he is human; in practice his divinity such as it was – and not to be confused with the Christian (or Islamic) concept of one transcendental Godhead – remains. He reports to his heavenly ancestors at Ise and communes with them there. He prays to his deified grandfather at the Meiji shrine, the most popular place of worship in Japan. He carries out in private innumerable rites and ceremonies in his priestly role, traditionally concealed from outside observers. He remains the living link with the past, the unbroken thread in Japanese history (adoption notwithstanding).' [. . .] 'Thus the Emperor is the symbol of what is best in the Japanese character and of what is the worst. He inspires the nation to feats of loyalty and self-sacrifice, but he also sums up their racial, cultural and religious exclusivity which cuts them off from others and makes them so disliked. With no recognition of any scale of values other than their own; with no sense of the divine outside and above the world; with no feeling that their exertions can only be an approximation to that which is right, to that which is perfect, the Japanese are odd men out in the world.

He concluded that the Japanese '. . . have a greater aptitude than the White Queen for believing impossible things, even before breakfast: they positively revel in ambiguity. Hilaire Belloc might have written especially for them the refrain:

> "Oh never, never let us doubt what
> Nobody is sure about."

John's sense of humour rarely deserted him. He also had a quick wit and was an expert in repartee. Few of us can remember for very long witty remarks we have heard, but Brian Hitch, who was head of chancery in Tokyo, recalls one good example. John Pilcher was in the Rolls with the Governor of Hong Kong whom he had just collected from the airport. As they passed the parliament building in Tokyo the Governor asked what it was. John replied 'The Diet'. The Governor commented that he thought that was a way of eating to which John riposted: 'Like the Diet of Worms.'

John liked to shock the prim and there was an element of prep-school humour in him. He used to have fun writing his name in characters which could be read *pe-ru-cha* where *pe* was the character for fart, *ru* meant stop and *cha* meant tea. If he was leaving early in the morning it was always said to be at 'sparrow fart'. He liked to recall, too, the reply of the keeper at the zoo to a question from the Shōwa Emperor on his visit to London in 1971 about why the pandas had failed to mate: 'He mistook the orifice, sir.'

John's child like-qualities appeared in his desire to win at scrabble which he and his guests played at the embassy villa at Chūzenji. Jimmy Abraham, the naval attaché, remembers how John would cheat shamelessly at the game, looking over his opponents shoulders.

He certainly did not believe that 'silence is golden'. Carmen Blacker recalls that '. . . once when invited to Chuzenji for the weekend with Joan Martin they left the Ambassador's residence at 4.30 am and John treated them to an unquenchable flow of anecdotes from then until dusk. He was particularly memorable on the subject of the "long, long scarf' worn [in Kyoto before the war] by old Mr Ponsonby Fane day and night.'

John stayed in Tokyo until after the Queen's birthday party in June 1972 and left with a flourish on Concorde which was on a proving flight in the Far East. (It was destined never to come into conirnercial service other than over the Atlantic.)

On 4 April 1972 shortly before his retirement he wrote a summing-up despatch on the theme of 'Basic Japan and the Shifting Mood 1967–1972'. He began by commenting on Shinto and on the influence of Confucian morality on Japan. He noted the way militarism had deformed the Japanese but thought that the occupation had redressed the balance. Economic man had become the foundation of the new order but the excesses of economic success had brought their own nemesis. A new realism had forced the Japanese to understand the need to curb the upward surge of their exports and adopt orderly marketing. It had also led them to see the need for social expenditure. In his concluding paragraphs he suggested that '. . . we should offer them the benefits of our experience of the welfare state'. He did not anticipate the errors and excessives of the last Labour administration in the 1970s or the need for cutting back on the welfare state, but he was undoubtedly right in urging the Japanese to relax, to take life less seriously and pay attention to the amenities of living.

Turning to foreign affairs he noted that in South East Asia the image was of 'the ugly Japanese'. China, he thought, exercised an excessive fascination for the Japanese. Above all they needed to become more international.

The following are a few key quotations: 'Being a Japanese was – and is – a religion in itself.' '"My country right or wrong" is the very essence of their outlook.' 'In Japanese terms: right is what profits Japan: wrong the reverse. The military had proved themselves to be wrong.' 'Perhaps Japan had succeeded where others had failed in finding a middle way (so dear to Far Eastern minds) between Communist planning and capitalist competition.' 'The old aesthetic is nearly no more and no new set of values has replaced it.

Taste itself, which traditionally in Japan governed so much, has nearly vanished.' But he ended on a more optimistic note: 'Before the war they were blissfully ignorant of their defects; now they are aware of them and will try to correct them.'

RETIREMENT

After his retirement John took on a number of jobs in the city which enabled him to travel widely including to Japan and South America. He particularly enjoyed taking his friends and business associates to Kyoto where he could expound to them on his pet themes and charm them with his wit and erudition. But he was not a bit conceited or pompous. He just wanted everyone to enjoy themselves. He did his duty conscientiously for the societies connected with the countries where he had served. For the Japan Society he did two separate three- year stints as chairman of the council and did whatever he could to further Anglo-Japanese understanding. Unfortunately the *Proceedings* of the Society do not include the texts of his two lectures to the Society as he did not prepare anything in writing. The only piece by him in the Proceedings is one which he prepared for visitors to Japan entitled 'Conservation, East and West' (*Japan Society Proceedings* No. 115, March 1990, pp. 7–12). The flavour of this piece is conveyed by his opening sentence: 'I suspect that we are all brought up on La Rochefoucauld's dictum that "the sole excuse for copying is to show up the faults of the original"'. He concludes by relating how he took some Japanese architectural students to Thaxted: 'Their only comment was that we were primarily concerned with the exteriors and were relatively disinterested in what went on inside. They would tend to view the matter, they said, from the inside out. You may think that there is some validity in their view.'

Sadly, John Pilcher never wrote his memoirs. He could not see why anyone should be interested in what he had done or thought. I hope that in this short piece I have at least proved him wrong in this respect. When he died in 1990, having suffered from Parkinson's disease and a stroke, Japan and John's colleagues lost a good, charming, understanding and amusing friend.

PART IV

SCHOLAR DIPLOMATS

AND CONSULS

Eikoku no yakukan (British offices – i.e., Consulate) in Yokohama, by Kunimasa IV, 1870

Introduction

J. E. HOARE

This section brings together a general account of Britain's Japan Consular Service, from its inception in the 1860s until it was subsumed in the amalgamation of all the Consular Services in 1935, and then in the reformed Diplomatic Service after 1943, and studies of four of its most accomplished members: Sir Ernest Satow, William George Aston, John H. Gubbins and Sir George Sansom. Although the term 'Scholar Diplomats', has been used to describe Satow and Sansom in particular, it would not have been a term used by them or by most of the people who belonged to the Japan Consular Service.[1]

Few of those who joined the Japan Consular Service were ever, strictly speaking, 'diplomats', since the British system drew a distinction between those who were members of Her/His Majesty's Diplomatic Service, and members of the various Consular Services. It was true that by 1900 the aristocratic dominance that had marked the nineteenth-century Diplomatic Service was beginning to fade, and it had never been marked in China or Japan, where movement from the Consular to the Diplomatic branch had begun when Sir Harry Parkes moved from the China Consular to became Minister in Japan in 1865. Yet it was still there, with members of the Consular Service feeling very much part of the 'Cinderella Service' as described by D. C. Platt.[2] To the modern eye, the distinctions between the educational and social levels of those who became diplomats and those who became consular officers in a specialized service such as that in Japan does not seem great, to contemporaries, it clearly mattered. Ernest Satow and A.B. Mitford[3] shared a house and were friends in Japan in the 1860s, but the latter made it clear before the 1870 Select Committee on the Diplomatic and Consular Services that, in his view, interpreters in the China and Japan Consular Services might be of a higher class than those who served in the Levant Service, but that they were not equivalent to diplomatic attachés.[4] They might be experts but they were no match for the generalists who dominated the Diplomatic Service.

For members of the Japan Service, proficiency in the language was deemed essential for confirmation of appointment and for advancement once confirmed. This was especially true in the nineteenth century, but Sansom and others such as Paske-Smith show that high language standards also applied in the twentieth century as well, even though the original main rationale, extraterritoriality, for this had come to an end in 1899 with the entry into force of the 1894 Anglo-Japanese Treaty. It was hard work acquiring Japanese in the early days, with few aids and inexperienced teachers. Few people qualified in the two years allowed, and some took much longer. Esler Dening, who would later note that he was the first British head of mission in Tokyo since Satow left in 1900 to speak Japanese, failed to mention that he had not passed the examinations as a student interpreter after ten years' study.[5] Once candidates had passed, they were not required to requalify, which led some to worry that they would sit on their laurels or 'devote their leisure to dissipation and extravagance', as the Foreign Office's chief official put it in 1874.[6] On the whole, however, the members of the Japan Service proved relatively hard-working and if many tended to coast after qualifying, some acquired a reputation for excellent language skills. As well as proficiency in Japanese, several clearly had a good reading knowledge of Chinese. Some also acquired Korean. Both Satow and W. G. Aston did work on the Korean language, and as Peter Kornicki's essay here shows, by 1881 Aston had acquired fluency in spoken Korean. Aston's identification of the linguistic links between Japanese and Korean is regarded as a major breakthrough in the study of the two languages.[7] When the Korea Branch of the Royal Asiatic Society was established in Seoul in 1900, Aston was one of the three scholars elected to honorary membership of the new society. Later, it was noted in 1912 that Arthur Hyde Lay was the only known Japan Service officer to pass an examination in Korean.[8] By then, however, the need for Korean was already giving way to Japanese as the language required in Seoul.

The rewards for language proficiency were poor. The relatively small field for promotion provided by the Tokyo Legation (after 1902, Embassy) and the consular posts was never quite as large as it seemed on paper. Niigata scarcely functioned as a consular post after the early 1870s, while Hakodate was reduced to a vice-consulate in 1882. The field grew larger with the addition of Tamsui in Taiwan in 1895, Dalian in the Liaotung peninsula in 1905, and Seoul and Chemulpo in Korea from 1910. Chemulpo only functioned spasmodically, however, and closed in 1916. Manila and Honolulu were also staffed from the Japan Service, a somewhat mixed blessing for those who wished to keep up their Japanese. By 1914 promotion rates were already poor; what had taken ten years to achieve in the 1880s now took fifteen. With the coming of World War I, the promotion rate slowed down even more.

To poor promotion prospects were added relatively low salaries, which barely moved in the first sixty years of the Japan Service, and limited leave prospects. No leave at all was allowed for seven years, and then officers went on half pay after the first month. Until 1874, fares were not paid. Thereafter, officers received half fare and dependents one third. Not surprisingly, in such circumstances, some officers rarely took leave. Satow, when Minister in Tokyo in 1899, noted the difficulties that the Consular officers faced, with no private incomes and often with several children.[9]

Living conditions were often not very good. Officers complained of poor offices and residential housing. Modern amenities such as water closets and telephones were slow to be introduced. Staff in Tokyo and Yokohama endured years of cramped and poor quality buildings after the 1923 earthquake.

Many of the posts were isolated, with inadequate communications. Matters improved with the spread of the telegraph system, but the Foreign Office did not encourage overuse of what was regarded as an expensive luxury. The despatch, plus semi-official letters, would remain the chosen method of communication well into the twentieth century. These methods probably did not make for a very heavy workload. Before 1899, extraterritoriality and the administration of justice took up a fair amount of a consular official's time, and the importance of legal work was recognized in the provision of a year's paid leave to read for the bar. After the abolition of extraterritoriality, there was a growing emphasis on commercial work. Two prominent members of the Japan Consular Service who made their mark in this field were Sir Edward Crowe, Commercial Counsellor from 1918–1925, who later went on to head the Department of Overseas Trade, and Sir George Sansom, who succeeded him, and who was to become the doyen of British Japan experts.

Mention of Samson leads onto the scholarly attainments of members of the Japan Consular Service. I suspect that this was not something that mattered a great deal to the powers that be. Sir Charles Eliot's praise of Sansom's 'several valuable linguistic papers and translations' was rare indeed.[10] I cannot now trace the reference, but somewhere in the records of the Foreign Office's Chief Clerk's Department from the 1920s there is a statement to the effect that while it was no doubt a good thing that Mr Paske-Smith wrote books, he had not been sent to be His Majesty's Consul at Nagasaki to do so. Members of the Japan Consular Service were encouraged to prepare official reports as part of their training, or later especially if there was some commercial point to the report, and some of which found their way into print as 'Blue Books' or Parliamentary Papers, and, just occasionally, to the volumes of *Transactions of the Asiatic Society of Japan*,[11] but that was rather different from the scholarly works produced by many members of the Japan Consular Service.

Of course, it was not just these officers who undertook such works. Members of the Diplomatic Service who served in Japan were quite prolific authors, at least in the nineteenth century. The tradition began with Lawrence Oliphant, who accompanied Lord Elgin to Japan in 1858, and who later became Secretary of Legation in Edo (now Tokyo). His *Narrative of Lord Elgin's Mission to China and Japan,* appeared in two volumes in 1859–60. The first British Minister, Sir Rutherford Alcock, produced *The Capital of the Tycoon* in two volumes in 1863, and also wrote on Japanese grammar. Mitford, already mentioned, acquired a good knowledge of Japanese, which he put to good use in writing *Tales of Old Japan*. F. O. Adams, Secretary of Legation in Japan from 1868–72, and Chargé d'Affaires in 1871–72 during Sir Harry Parkes' absence on home leave, produced a two-volume *History of Japan* in 1875. A. H. Mounsey, Secretary of Legation from 1876–78, wrote *The Satsuma Rebellion* in 1878, a contemporary account that still has some value today. Several others were active members of, or produced papers for, the Asiatic Society of Japan.

In the twentieth century, such writings tailed off somewhat. Frank Ashton-Gwatkin, who began as an officer in the Japan Consular Service but who later transferred to the Foreign Office, wrote a series of novels about Japan under the pseudonym John Paris. The most scholarly work to appear until the latter part of the century was *Elements of Sōsho*, by F. S. G. Piggott, published in Yokohama in 1913, when Piggott was a military officer attached to the embassy in Tokyo. It won high praise from Basil Hall Chamberlain, no mean feat.[12] Piggott would later write an autobiography, *Broken Thread*, as would Britain's last pre-World War II ambassador to Tokyo, Sir Robert Craigie, whose *Behind the Japanese Mask*, appeared in 1945. Malcolm Kennedy, also a Military Attaché, wrote a number of books about Japan before and after World War II. Like Piggott, he was often seen as being too sympathetic to the Japanese point of view. Sir Charles Eliot, ambassador from 1920–25, worked extensively on Japanese Buddhism, but his great work was unfinished at his death. Sansom, who completed it, and others felt that it was less than satisfactory.[13] Much later, both Sir Hugh Cortazzi and Sir Sydney Giffard re-established the tradition of ambassadorial works on Japan. Sir John Figgess, an expert on ceramics, carried on the tradition of writings by former Military Attachés.

But it was the output of the members of the Japan Consular Service that was particularly noteworthy. Over the years, much of this output appeared in the *Transactions of the Asiatic Society of Japan*, but papers by members of the Japan Service also appeared in other learned publications, including the *Transactions of the Royal Asiatic Society, Korea Branch,* and, as we have seen, in the journal of the parent body, the Royal Asiatic Society in London. British officials also played a leading role in organizing and running both the Asiatic Society of Japan and the Korea Branch of the Royal Asiatic Society. In the case of the latter body, even today the British Ambassador in Seoul is normally elected Honorary President, in memory of the role of the British Legation and men such as J. H. Gubbins in organizing the founding meeting in 1900.

Consulting the list of contributors and their papers to the Asiatic Society of Japan prepared as Appendix 10 to Douglas Moore Kenrick's centenary history of the society in 1978,[14] shows the large number of papers from members of the Japan Consular Service. Aston, Sansom and Satow lead the field, but they are by no means alone. Gubbins was a regular contributor, with six published papers between 1875 and 1922. John Carey Hall, who ended his career as Consul General at Yokohama in 1914, also published six papers. Arthur Hyde Lay contributed papers in 1891 on Japanese Funerary Rites, in 1902 on the rise of political parties in Japan, and in 1908 on the study of Korean, from the point of view of a student of Japanese. Joseph Longford, who would become the most successful academic of those who served in the Japan Consular Service, contributed papers in 1877, 1878 and 1894. Parkes' nephew, Thomas McClatchie, presented five papers in the 1870s. James Troup wrote four papers, while several others produced one or two papers.

In addition, there were the books by Aston, Gubbins, Longford, Paske-Smith, Sansom and Satow. Longford's works have probably stood the test of time least well. But in the early years of the twentieth century, when he held the chair of Japanese history at King's College London, his publications on Japan and Korea were well-regarded. Of the others, Satow was the most rounded scholar, with interests that were eventually to stretch far beyond Japan; his *Guide to Diplomatic Practice*, which has now undergone a number of revisions at the hands of others, shows a wide breadth of scholarship in international law and practice. Paske-Smith's books are perhaps what would now be described as antiquarian, yet they remain useful quarries of information about the early days of Western involvement with Japan, and the Japanese Christian communities that emerged c. 1870 in and around Nagasaki. Aston's *A Short Grammar of the Japanese Spoken Language* (1869, with several subsequent editions), *Grammar of the Japanese Written Language*

(1872), History *of Japanese Literature* (1899), his translation of the *Nihongi* (1896), and his study of *Shinto* (1905), collectively made him one of the foremost scholars of Japanese at the turn of the nineteenth century.

Writings on the Japanese and other languages were an inevitable off-spin of the training and the job. In the twentieth century, Hobart-Hampden and Parlett collaborated on an *English-Japanese Dictionary of the Spoken Language*. Sansom's first book was *An Historical Grammar of the Japanese Language*, published in 1928, apparently a side product of his work for his *Japan: A Short Cultural History*, which appeared in 1931.

By 1931, the future of the Japan Consular Service was already uncertain. Despite the advantages of a body of Japanese-speaking officers, the problems of a career structure and a promotion ladder were proving impossible to solve. From 1933 onwards, the Japan Service ceased to recruit; thereafter all officers would be part of the General Service. World War II and the 1943 Eden reforms completed the work. The members of the Japan Consular Service were scattered. Many did Japan-related war work, while others found slots in the newly-opened diplomatic world. When peace came in 1945, the Japan Service was no more. But the scholarly record speaks for itself. In its eighty or so years, the members of the Japan Consular Service really had created a tradition of scholar-diplomats of the highest order.

Since the war the Foreign Office has maintained the tradition of training officers in the Japanese language and has insisted that officers so trained should achieve a high level of linguistic competence. In recent years most of the senior posts in the Embassy in Tokyo have been filled by such officers.

22
Sir Ernest Mason Satow in Japan, 1873–84

P. F. KORNICKI

Ernest Mason Satow

Ernest Satow (1843–1929) was a celebrity, the first of the old Japan hands to win the public recognition of a knighthood, membership of the Privy Council, honorary degrees from Oxford and Cambridge, and a caricature in Vanity Fair. He was not unaware that he had a place in history, for in 1921 he published an autobiography covering his early years in Japan which takes some liberties with the historical record and suggests that Satow's own views were more influential than they in fact were. On his death he donated to the Public Record Office the extensive diaries and private correspondence that he had carefully preserved over the years. In Japan he is still a celebrity, partly because of the serialization in the *Asahi shinbun* of a detailed biography, and partly because of the high regard in which he continues to be held as a book-collector and scholar and as an intimate associate of men who led the Restoration movement and controlled the course of Japanese politics up to the end of the century and beyond.

Satow was born in north London to a family with a cosmopolitan flavour. His father was a Swedish merchant who had travelled extensively and finally moved from Riga in Latvia to London in 1825. Perhaps it was from him that Satow inherited his interest in foreign countries and his aptitude for foreign languages. He was undoubtedly quick at his books, for he entered University College, London, in 1859 at the age of 16 and graduated just two years later; when he reached Japan on 8 September 1862 he was not yet 20. While a student at London University, he is said to have attended some of the lectures of James Summers, who was Professor of Chinese at King's College and who launched several short-lived periodicals for the study of the cultures of Japan and China, though he did not set foot in Japan until 1873. Satow claims in his autobiography that his interest was first drawn to Japan by a copy of the account of Lord Elgin's mission to China and Japan which his brother had borrowed from the famous Mudie's Circulating Library. At any rate, Satow came first in the examination for student interpreters to serve in the Consular Service in the Far East and opted for Japan. It was believed at the time that a knowledge of Chinese was a prerequisite for the study of Japanese and so Satow was first sent to the Legation at Peking, where he not only learnt some written and spoken Chinese but also made a start on the study of Manchu. After a few months in Peking he was summoned to take up his duties in Japan.

Satow had left England without any of the few books that had by then been published on the Japanese language and found that those that were to be had in Japan were of little use. After he had insisted that his first task was to learn the language, his superiors allowed him the mornings free of routine consular tasks, such as copying out despatches, in order to work on the language, but gave him no teacher. After a couple of unsatisfactory months he induced the chargé d'affaires to pay for lessons from the Reverend Samuel R. Brown, an American missionary who had just published a work entitled *Colloquial Japanese*, and to pay for the cost of hiring a native teacher. At first it was Brown's lessons that proved more useful, for none of the Japanese teachers knew any English and they did not have an educated understanding of their own language. But then Satow secured the services of a doctor from Wakayama, Takaoka Kaname by name, who 'used to write a short letter in the running-hand, and after copying it out in square character, explain to me its meaning'.[1] After this Satow used to make a translation into English and practise reading the two Japanese versions until he had mastered the whole letter. It was a laborious procedure, but effective as a training in reading handwritten documents. Satow had a succession of other teachers and also took lessons from calligraphy masters: at first he made the mistake of learning a tradesmen's writing style, but after the Restoration of 1868 he took lessons from Takasaki Tanzaki, described by Satow as one of the best half-dozen teachers in Tokyo, and his written Japanese improved markedly in appearance. Cambridge University Library contains some of the notebooks which he used when first reading Japanese texts and some catalogues of his Japanese books which he compiled much later, and the transformation from the awkward, wooden characters most foreigners are condemned to repeat, to the confident, elegant script of the catalogues is remarkable.

In 1864 Satow had the satisfaction of being appointed interpreter to Admiral Kuper on his flagship for the punitive expedition to the Shimonoseki Straits. The domain authorities in Chōshū had been vigorous in their pursuit of an anti-foreign policy and had closed the Straits to foreign shipping. Immediately, two domain samurai, Itō Hirobumi and Inoue Kaoru, who had both participated in the arson attack on the British Legation, in 1861 and who were later to distinguish themselves in government, returned from England, where they were studying to try to persuade their superiors in the domain of the folly of continuing to resist the foreign presence. Satow met them and asked them to convey to the daimyo the determination of the foreign powers to keep the Straits open and to ensure that Chōshū observed the treaties; with the help of one of his Japanese teachers he translated a message to that effect in Japanese and then put them ashore, well knowing that they had imperilled their lives by fraternizing with the enemy. As it happened they were not executed, but their mission was unsuccessful and as a result

Satow saw action. The squadron bombarded the Chōshū shore batteries until they fell silent, and then a strong force of British, French and Dutch troops landed to take the batteries; Satow was detailed to accompany them in case an intepreter was needed and so came under fire. The landing was successful and the batteries were destroyed, and Itō then came back to Satow to state that the daimyo acknowledged his defeat and now wished to sue for peace. This episode marked the beginning of Satow's acquaintance with Itō, an acquaintance that was to prove very useful to both of them in the late 1890s, when Satow was British envoy in Tokyo (1895–1900) and Itō was prime minister (1892–6 and January to June 1898).

Satow's services during the Chōshū expedition made his superiors realize, for the first time, the importance of having someone on hand who could communicate in Japanese without difficulty. Accordingly, early in 1865 he was promoted to the rank of Interpreter at the Consulate in Yokohama and was freed from all other duties. His language abilities were soon put to the test when he had to interrogate a Japanese prisoner prior to witnessing his execution: this was one of the supposed murderers of Lieutenant Bird and Major Baldwin, two members of the British Garrison in Yokohama who had been hacked to death as they were leaving Kamakura in November 1864. Later in 1865 Satow acted as the interpreter for Sir Harry Parkes, the British minister in Japan, and Léon Roches, his French counterpart, during the fraught negotiations in Osaka over the Emperor's ratification of the treaties which the shogun had signed with the foreign powers. The crucial document acceding to the demands of Parkes and Roches was delivered at half past two in the morning, and Satow was immediately summoned to read it out and to make a translation: 'it was a proud moment for me', he wrote, 'when I displayed my knowledge of written Japanese in the presence of the French minister, whose interpreter even could not read a document without the assistance of his teacher'.[2]

Satow was also becoming involved in political journalism at this time. Following the successful conclusion of the negotiations at Osaka, he wrote an anonymous editorial for the *Japan Times* in which he declared that, 'Japan is now for the first time really and legitimately open to foreign trade' and argued that the power of the shogun 'was a shadow and his title a mockery' compared with that of the emperor.[3] In the following year, 1866, Satow published three articles in the *Japan Times* on English policy towards Japan, which were subsequently translated into Japanese, printed and sold on the streets of Kyoto and Osaka. The extensive conversations he had had with the leading daimyo of western Japan and their retainers had already conyinced him that the western powers were wrong to deal exclusively with the shogun and that the real rulers of Japan were the Emperor and a body he called the Confederate Daimyo. The shogun, he argued, had overstepped his authority and was powerless to enforce compliance with the treaties in areas of Japan outside his direct control. So the line he took in these articles was one which was sympathetic to the opponents of the shogunate.

Following the Yokohama fire of 1866, which destroyed his house, Satow moved to a house in Edo. As he described it, 'there was an upper storey where I had my bedroom and apartments for the entertainment of Japanese guests and three staircases provided means of escape in case of attack from the midnight murderer'.[4] Satow's matter-of-fact acceptance of danger reflected the very real possibility of attack by fanatical members of the anti-foreign party.

In 1867 Satow travelled from Osaka to Edo overland in the company of Charles Wirgman, an artist working for the *Illustrated London News*. On the way, they were attacked one night as they slept in an inn, and it was only thanks to the cool bravery of Satow's Japanese retainer, Noguchi, that they all escaped with their lives. Again in 1868, when Satow was in the party accompanying the British minister, Sir Harry Parkes, to his first audience with the young Emperor Meiji in Kyoto, two samurai set upon them with swords. Having missed Parkes, one slashed at Satow only to injure his horse instead: as Parkes coolly remarked, this was 'sensation diplomacy',[5] but it did have the effect of provoking an imperial proclamation calling for an end to anti-foreign sentiment.

On 1 January 1868 Satow became the Japanese Secretary to the British Legation, a position he was to hold for some sixteen years and one which made him responsible for all dealings with the Japanese government. It was in 1868 that the anti-shogunate movement came to a head and throughout the year Satow maintained close contact with Itō and other Japanese acquaintances from the domains. As a result he had an exceptionally clear understanding of the strength of feeling against the shogun. He had already concluded that the use of the expression 'His Majesty' in the treaties to refer to the shogun was mistaken and had established to his own satisfaction that the shogun was subordinate to the Emperor. There was no doubt where his own sympathies lay. In reports that he wrote for Parkes he referred to the shogun as the Emperor's 'rebellious vassal' – but the claim later made by Satow and others that he had swayed Parkes against the shogun and had enabled Britain to support the victorious side does not stand up to close examination. As late as January 1868, when Parkes and Satow were very much afraid that the confrontation between supporters of Emperor and shogun would result in civil war, Parkes was considering how he might mediate between the two parties and was unwilling to commit himself to either side. With the advantage of hindsight, it may seem inevitable that the Restoration forces would not only triumph but also establish a stable form of government, but at the time this did not appear at all certain. In fact Parkes maintained a cautious neutrality until the result of the conflict was no longer in doubt.

Early in 1869 Satow sailed for England for his first home leave since setting foot in Japan. Before leaving he received a gift from the Japanese foreign minister with a letter; 'during your period of service in this country,' he wrote, 'you have spoken our language with extreme facility, and the great services you have rendered to Japan have come to the knowledge of His Majesty'.[6] Satow had lived through a momentous period in the history of Japan, and he wrote much later that, 'those years from 1862 to 1869 were the most interesting portion of my life; then I lived, now I seem to vegetate. The changes that were still to take place in the years between 1869 and 1884, when he was returning from Japan, were also far-reaching, but it was the earlier period that dominated his memories of Japan, and in later life when he wrote his memoirs, *A Diplomat in Japan*, he drew the narrative to an end with his return to England in 1869.

Satow had been under fire several times and had been fully involved in the intricate diplomatic problems of the 1860s, but he had also begun to train himself as a scholar and he was probably the first foreigner to become a serious and well-informed collector of Japanese books. As a bibliographer he was an expert, and as a collector insatiable. There were Japanese bookshops in Yokohama, but they were forbidden to sell maps or *bukan* (lists of daimyo and officials) to foreigners. Satow solved this problem by having his teachers buy materials for him and in this way he managed to acquire a number of manuscripts, including copies of official papers, that were too sensitive to be published or to pass the inspection of the censors. In the Yokohama fire of November 1866 he lost many of his Chinese and European books as well as the notes on Chinese and Manchu which he had made in Peking. In 1868, however, when he was one of the first foreigners to visit Kyoto for several hundred years, he made it his business to head for the bookshops. In the 1880s he was spending large sums of money on early Japanese books, including books printed with movable type in the early seventeenth century and racy fictional works of the later seventeenth century.

He was also buying what Korean books he could find in Japan and sending further sums of money to Korea, presumably by way of his Korean teachers, which were unobtainable in Japan. Like Chamberlain and Aston, he had made efforts to learn Korean in the 1870s and 1880s and had engaged a Korean teacher as well as making use of a manuscript grammar of Korean prepared by Aston. He and Aston often went book-hunting together in Kyoto and Osaka. In 1882 he wrote to Aston: 'the booksellers say that 1,200 yen would secure all there is in Japan of rare editions. I have spent 600 or 700, and so must have about half.'[7] He was clearly exaggerating, but there can be no doubt that his collection was the best ever assembled by a westerner. In later years he gave away or lent large quantities of his Japanese books, to Chamberlain, to Aston and to other former colleagues from his Japan days, and his books are now to be found in London, Cambridge, Bristol, Manchester, Tokyo and several other locations: they carry impressions of the Japanese ex-libris stamp he had made in Japan, and many of them are unique copies of works that have not survived in Japan.

He was no passive collector, for his bibliographical researches on the books in his collection resulted in several articles on the history of printing in Japan and Korea. In fact, he was the first person to establish that movable-type printing in Korea was older than the books that came from Gutenberg's press – by more than a hundred years. He also published, in 1888, a detailed bibliographic study of the Jesuit Mission Press in Japan. This press had printed a number of doctrinal works, together with several works of European and Japanese literature, both in romanized form and in Japanese script, in the late sixteenth and early seventeenth centuries. He owned none of these books himself, for most of these works had survived in only one or two copies, and his researches, which established for the first time the extent of the Jesuits' printing operations in Japan, took him to private and public libraries all over Europe.

In 1884 Satow made the move that was to accelerate his career as a diplomat: he moved to Siam, now Thailand, to take up the position of consul-general in Bangkok. As soon as he arrived he wrote, 'my student days are now at an end',[8] but he continued to buy books voraciously, to study and to write. In 1885 he wrote an article on contacts between Japan and Siam in the seventeenth century, and in 1886 he published a lengthy 'Essay towards a bibliography of Siam', in which many of the items described came from his own personal library and were later to be donated to the Bodleian Library, Oxford.[9] His style as a diplomat differed from that of the irascible Sir Harry

Parkes, and although he found the 'corruption in the native courts, endless delays, equivocation and falseness on the part of native officials' exhausting to deal with, he considered that, 'when one is angry it is very important to be more polite than usual and to have an air of regret at having to remonstrate'.[10] His diplomacy was effective and there were fears in Britain that France's wars in Indo-China might spread into Siam. So in 1885 Satow was promoted to the rank of Minister, which signalled a shift from the more humdrum duties of the consular service to the status and responsibilities of the diplomatic service.

While in Bangkok Satow suffered badly from the climate, and in 1887 he asked to be transferred, and returned to England. During the lengthy period of leave that followed, he completed the legal studies which he had begun earlier and qualified as a barrister; he travelled in Italy, Spain and Portugal in search of books printed by the Jesuits in Japan; and he became a convinced Christian: he was confirmed by the Bishop of London at St Paul's in October 1888.

In that year he was appointed minister at Montevideo in Uruguay. During his four years there he was still accompanied by his Japanese servant, Saburō, who had followed him from Japan to Bangkok. In 1893 he proceeded to Tangier as envoy to Morocco, where in the midst of a succession crisis following the Sultan's death he led the diplomatic community in recognizing the heir rather than a rival known as 'the one-eyed decapitator'. His tact gained him the admiration of the Foreign Office, which wrote, 'you seem to have managed to get your colleagues to work together – a thing which I believe is unprecedented at Tangier'.[11]

After his success in Morocco, which earned him his knighthood, he went on to fill the positions of envoy in Tokyo (1895–1900) and Peking (1900–6). As the head of British missions in Japan and China he fulfilled duties now undertaken by ambassadors, but in more eurocentric days, these states were not regarded as important enough to justify ambassadorial representation. Thus the status and title of ambassador eluded him. His final appointment was as British member of the Court of Arbitration in The Hague, after which he retired to Devon. Satow never married, but there are passages in his diaries that allude to his relationships with Japanese women, and others that have been discreetly papered over. For much of his time in Japan he had a common-law wife and two children.

Satow's appointment as envoy to Japan in 1895 was itself a significant act. In the previous years the foreign secretary, Lord Kimberley, had signed a new treaty with Japan which transformed Anglo-Japanese relations by renouncing the principle of extraterritoriality and making Britons subject to Japanese courts in place of consular jurisdiction. Kimberley was eager for Japan to strengthen its armed forces and hoped for the development of a warm relationship between Britain and Japan, explicitly in order to prevent Russia acquiring a warm-water port on the Pacific. For such purposes no better envoy than Satow could have been imagined, for not only did he have command of the language but among Japanese government leaders of the day were men whom he had known thirty years earlier when they were radical samurai. Satow reached Japan soon after Japan's victory in the Sino-Japanese War and the subsequent intervention of Russia, France and Germany, which forced Japan to renounce some of its gains in the war. The British government was in the midst of a domestic political crisis and in no position to come to Japan's assistance. The general election of July 1895 precipitated a change of government and Lord Salisbury, who now held the offices of prime minister and foreign secretary, was much more sceptical about Japan's capability and reliability than Kimberley had been. Salisbury overestimated Britain's strength in the Far East and saw no need of an ally to help counter Russian expansion. In this he was mistaken, as became only too apparent in the winter of 1897/8 when Britain was powerless to prevent Russia annexing Port Arthur, one of the war gains which Japan had been forced to abandon earlier. Thus the tsar acquired a fortified warm-water port. 'I am convinced,' Satow had already written to Salisbury, 'that the Japanese are ambitious of being a great naval and military power and they are confidently persuaded that they possess the necessary gifts', and he became convinced too that Japan was preparing to challenge the Russian position in the Far East.[12]

Before taking up his position in Peking, Satow returned to England in 1900 for consultations with the Foreign Office and a spell of leave. He was aware that Russian designs on Korea, Manchuria and China were perceived as threatening by the Japanese government, but he believed that Japan would certainly take no action before 1903, by which time her army and navy would have reached their full strength. Even then Japan would only act with Britain's support. During the summer news reached London of the Boxer Rebellion in China, of the dramatic siege of the British Legation and the international relief force. Satow's leave was therefore cut short and in August he set out for Peking.

In Peking Satow's first and most onerous task was to conduct the negotiations between the Chinese authorities and the representatives of the western powers over an indemnity and guarantees for the safety of diplomatic representatives and foreign nationals resident in Peking. Subsequently he followed the growth of Russian activities in Manchuria, which alarmed both Britain and Japan and created the atmosphere in which the Anglo-Japanese Alliance (1902) was conceived. The negotiations took place in London, between the foreign secretary and the Japanese Ambassador, Hayashi, and Satow was not directly involved, but his reports on the fortifications at Port Arthur and the growth of Russian armaments there strengthened convictions in London that war between Japan and Russia was imminent. Satow was not alone in being surprised by the Japanese successes in the Russo-Japanese War, and after the fall of Port Arthur he wrote that, 'they have achieved a wonderful exploit in forcing the surrender of a place so strongly defended by nature and art, when it was still provided with fuels, food and ammunition'.[13] After the terrible losses of the war, from which the European powers learnt so little, Satow had no confidence that lasting peace would follow: 'I give the world', he wrote, 'ten years peace in this part of the world. During that time Japan will recoup her losses and be ready to begin again.'[14] As it happened, less than ten years were to elapse before the outbreak of the First World War.

Throughout his long life Satow read widely and deeply and he wrote on a variety of subjects. His first published writings were two pieces he contributed to James Summers' short-lived journal, *The Chinese and Japanese Repository*, in 1865. One was a description of the various styles of Japanese writing and the other was a translation of the diary of a member of the Japanese mission to Europe of 1862–3. In the early 1870s he had several pieces in Summers' next short-lived journal, *The Phoenix*, and by that time he was contributing regularly to the *Japan Herald* and the *Japan Times*. These contributions included political commentary on current events, accounts of trips made in Japan, and serialized translations of Japanese texts: his translation of *Kinsei shiryaku*, a history of Japan from 1853 to 1869, which he published as a book in 1873, first appeared in this way. He later revised his travel pieces to compile *A Handbook for Travellers in Central and Northern Japan*, which was first published in 1881 and over several editions was the globe-trotter's guide to Japan. He was one of the founder members of the Asiatic Society of Japan and contributed a variety of pieces to the published *Transactions*: some were of an antiquarian nature, such as his articles on the introduction of tobacco to Japan and the use of the fire-drill in Japan, but there were also several important works of scholarship among them, particularly his studies of Shinto and of printing in Japan and Korea.

Unlike Aston and Chamberlain he never made an attempt to compile a grammar of the Japanese language. The nearest he came to doing so was a curious book published in Yokohama in 1873 with the title, *Kuaiwa-hen, Twenty-five Exercises in the Yedo Colloquial*. This consists of sentences in romanized Japanese accompanied by a separate volume of commentary, and it appears that Satow first prepared this work for A. B. Mitford, later Lord Redesdale, when he was posted to Japan in 1866 and wanted to learn some Japanese. He lent it out in manuscript to a number of eager students before deciding to have it printed, and it seems to have enjoyed some success, for a second edition and a French translation were published in due course. He adopted Aston's system of transliteration and made extensive use throughout of Aston's *A Short Grammar of the Japanese Spoken Language*. How useful purchasers really found *Kuaiwa-hen* is difficult to gauge; Satow confessed in the Preface that 'all allusions to Japanese manners and customs which have since become things of the past have been left untouched', which suggests that he saw it as much as a record of patterns of speech as a tool for learning the language.[15] A few years later he joined with a member of the Japanese Foreign Ministry to compile *An English–Japanese Dictionary of the Spoken Language*, which was published in 1876. Here too Satow is explicit about his debt to Aston and follows Aston's system for classifying the conjugations of Japanese verbs. This dictionary underwent a number of revisions over the years, and was still in use during the Second World War, albeit in a much expanded and altered form.

After 1900 Satow wrote very little about Japan, although in 1909 he did write a section on Japan for the *Cambridge Modern History*. The major work of his later years betrayed very little of his knowledge of East Asia: this was his monumental *Guide to Diplomatic Practice*. This was first published during the First World War, in 1917, and at least three further editions were published subsequently, each embodying substantial revisions. Much more than a manual of procedures, it is embued with a feeling for the evolution of European traditions of diplomacy and of the privileges and functions of diplomats. It is immensely rich in its historical and international coverage, and reveals Satow's familiarity with most of the languages of Europe. Japan, of course, had no part to play in the evolution of European diplomacy and was a newcomer to the world of international diplomacy, and it is therefore only to be expected that Japan would not feature prominently in such a work. Nevertheless, it does come as a surprise to find that even in the sections on monarchies and precedence among nations Satow hardly troubles to mention Japan at all. The result is a book which presents diplomacy as a ritual enacted by the great European powers. Part of the blame for this must be attributed to the scholarly, historical approach underlying the book, which is also one of its strengths, but it also suggests that Satow failed to grasp the meaning of Japan's rise to prominence, even after the shock of Japan's victory in the Russo-Japanese War, and failed to appreciate the changing nature of international society in the twentieth century. It was not that he was no longer interested in Japan, but that Japan did not disturb his world view.

Satow's published writings have now all been superseded and are rarely cited. His private papers, which are preserved in the Public Record Office, are disappointingly discreet and betray little in the way of judgements of policy or personality. Nevertheless, they continue to be pored over by historians, for, like John Reed's account of the Russian Revolution in *Ten Days that Shook the World*, they are unique as a record of a non-participant's view of the relatively peaceful Japanese revolution of the 1860s.

FURTHER READING

Bernard M. Allen, *The Rt. Hon. Sir Ernest Mason Satow G.C.M.G: A Memoir*, London: Kegan, Paul, Trench, Trübner & Co., 1933.

Gordon Daniels, 'The British Role in the Meiji Restoration: A Re-interpretive Note', *Modern Asian Studies*, 2 (1968), 291–313.

Grace Fox, *Britain and Japan, 1858–1883*, Oxford University Press, 1969.

N. Hayashi and P. F. Kornicki, *Early Japanese Books in Cambridge University Library: A Catalogue of the Aston, Satow and von Siebold Collections*, Cambridge University Press, 1990.

George Alexander Lensen, *Korea and Manchuria Between Russia and Japan, 1895–1904*, Tallahassee: Florida State University Press, 1966.

E.M. Satow, *A Diplomat in Japan*, London: Seeley, Service & Co., 1921; reprinted 1968.

Nobutoshi Hagihara: *Tōi Gake* Tokyo: Ashai Shinbunsha, 1980.

Ian C. Ruxton (ed.): *The Diaries and Letters of Sir Ernest Mason Satow* (Edwin Mellen Press, Lampeter, 1998).

23
William George Aston and Japan, 1870–88

P. F. KORNICKI

William George Aston
Courtesy National Portrait Gallery

Both to their contemporaries and to several generations of successors, Aston (1841–1911) and Satow and Chamberlain had no equals as scholars of Japan. While Satow and Chamberlain had distinguished public careers, however, one as a diplomat and the other as a professor at Tokyo University, Aston remained in the humbler ranks of the consular service until forced by persistent ill health to retire at the early age of 48. The survival of diaries and letters have enriched our knowledge of the private lives of Satow and Chamberlain, while that of Aston seems destined to remain beyond our reach. On the other hand, it is Aston's writings that have stood the passage of time best, that are still in print almost a hundred years after they were written and that are still extensively quoted and referred to. This is perhaps not so much an irony of fate as the token of a life given up less to a public persona than to scholarship. But the result is that he remains a shadowy figure.

The story of Aston's early years and his career in the consular service is soon told. Aston was born near Londonderry in 1841. In the early 1850s his father, who was a preacher in the Unitarian Church of Ireland, moved to the village of Saintfield to establish a school. Aston grew up in Saintfield and taught in his father's school before matriculating at Queen's College, Belfast, in 1859. His university career was distinguished: he took his BA in 1862 and was gold medallist in classics, and was then awarded a Senior Scholarship in modern languages and modern history for his MA, which he took in 1863. He was, in short, a scholarship boy from the provinces who made good and acquired on the way a thorough if conventional education in classical and modern philology. He had none of Chamberlain's cosmopolitan upbringing or of Satow's more adventurous education, but he was able to expand his intellectual horizons in Japan and in 1882 his old university recognized his achievements as a scholar when it conferred on him an honorary doctorate of literature.

In the summer of 1864 Aston passed the competitive examination for entry to the Consular Service and was appointed Student Interpreter at the British Legation in Edo, where his task was to learn Japanese for the conduct of consular and diplomatic business. In that same year he first made the acquaintance of Kido Takayoshi and other discontented samurai who were later to play an important part in the Meiji Restoration of 1868 and the politics of the new Meiji government. These contacts gave him a good understanding of the political undercurrents in the turbulent years preceding the fall of the Tokugawa shogunate, and the advice of Aston and his contemporary at the Legation, Ernest Satow, was instrumental in ensuring that British policy was well-informed and reponsive during the years of confrontation between the shogunate and its opponents. In the summer of 1867, for example, Aston was on board HMS *Serpent*, first of all in the Shimonoseki Straits reporting on the understanding between Satsuma and Chōshū before moving on to the west coast of Japan in search of a site for an open port on the Japan Sea coast.

In 1870 he was appointed Interpreter and Translator to the Legation and in that capacity was in attendance on the Iwakura Mission during its stay in Britain from August to December 1872: the Mission, which included several senior government ministers, spent the best part of two years examining the constituents of a successfully developed and industralized society in the United States and a number of European countries. In *Macmillan Magazine* in that year Aston published an account of Japan for the occasion: 'the most important embassy that has ever left the shores of Great Japan is now in England, and the moment therefore appears fitting to inquire into the course of events which led to its despatch, and into the present position of the country whence it comes'.[1] Aston made no secret of his sympathy with the desire of Kido and others in the new government to centralize and direct the economic development of Japan, but his reaction to the social changes he had already witnessed in Japan and to the wave of enthusiasm for all things western was bemusement, and he was lost for an explanation: it had all taken place 'by magic'. Aston saw some dangers lying ahead, caused both by the extremely rapid pace of change and by the destabling effect of a leadership composed of revolutionaries, but he saw the visit of the Embassy as a 'golden opportunity' for Kido and the others: 'They can examine our factories, our machinery, and all the various industries for which we are famous, and they can thus learn the source of England's greatness.'[2] There are several strands to Aston's thought here. On the one hand, there is little doubt that Aston was genuinely enthusiastic about Japan's progress and genuinely concerned that it did not lead to instability. On the other hand, his patriotism, and more importantly his loyalty to his own culture, injected a note of condescension into his writing that is apparent here: in the same piece he argued that it was too early to end the extraterritorial privileges enjoyed by British subjects in Japan, as some were advocating, for the new Meiji law codes were untried and it was therefore premature to entrust British subjects to the uncertain mercy of the Japanese courts.

Also in 1872 Aston was one of the founder members of the Asiatic Society of Japan. The Society held regular meetings and published its *Transactions*, and these were a forum along with its German equivalent for enquiry into the history and culture of Japan. Among the other founder members were Brinkley, Dickins, Griffis, Gubbins, Satow and Summers, all of whom were to write extensively on Japan in the years ahead. Aston served as president of the Society from 1888 to 1889 and was a regular contributor to the Transactions: to the first issue he contributed an account of Russian activities in the islands to the north of Japan drawn from manuscript copies of the private correspondence of Japanese officials on duty at Hakodate, and in the issue that appeared just before his death he contributed a short piece correcting an earlier contributor's attempt to locate Takamagahara, the legendary dwelling place of the gods, somewhere in Japan.[3] In 1875 Aston was appointed assistant Japanese secretary at the Legation in Tokyo, and amongst his other tasks at this time were the arrangements for a substantial Japanese presence at the Intercolonial Exhibition held in Melbourne towards the end of the year. In the early 1880s he served several spells as acting consul at Hiogo (Kōbe) and then in 1882 he was appointed consul at Nagasaki.

In August 1882 Aston accompanied Vice-Admiral Willes and his squadron to Korea for negotiations on a trade treaty. The new treaty was closely modelled on the recent American treaty and was signed later that year; but following representations from Sir Harry Parkes, the British minister in Tokyo, about the difficulties it would impose on British traders in Korea, the British government refused to ratify it. In 1883 Parkes and Aston drafted a revised version, and in October Aston met up with Parkes in Korea for further negotiations, which resulted in the Treaty of Friendship and Commerce between Her Majesty Queen Victoria and His Majesty the King of Korea, which was signed at Hanyang (Seoul) in November 1883. In 1884 he was provisionally appointed Consul-General for Korea and took up residence in the house he had selected in 1883 as the best site for a British Legation. The accommodation proved unsatisfactory in the cold winters and difficult to defend from attacks, and at one stage he was compelled to take refuge in the American Legation. It was a difficult year for Aston: he struggled to compile a summary of Korea's foreign trade for the use of British merchants thinking of establishing trading links with Korea, but found that the Japanese consuls had done a better job of gathering statistics than the fledgling Korean customs service; he was not sanguine about the prospects for British traders, and although he did his best to assist Jardine Matheson & Company in their mining and other ventures in Korea, they found the returns insufficient to justify remaining and pulled out of Korea. As the year drew to a close Aston became increasingly convinced that the tension between conservative and reformist elements in the Korean government would only be resolved by a violent clash between the two. In this he was right and in early 1885 was forced by ill health to return to Japan. The dramatic story behind his return to Japan was told after his death by J. C. Hall (1844–1921), one of Aston's sucessors as student interpreter at the Legation:

> In December of that year he [Aston] was one of the guests at the notorious Post-Office dinner when the hosts, led by Kim Ok Kiun, left the table and betook themselves to the work of assassinating their rivals m the government. The guests dispersed in confusion, each finding his way home as best he could. The exposure to the frosty night air brought on a pulmonary attack which nearly cost Aston his life.[4]

It was thanks to Count Inoue [Kaoru], the Japanese foreign minister, who happened to be in Korea at the time, that Aston was able to return speedily to Japan and to expert medical care, and although he planned to return to Korea he proved too unwell to do so.

In 1886 he was appointed Japanese secretary in Tokyo, but chronic trouble with his lungs got the better of him and he retired on a pension in 1889. He first spent some time recuperating in Switzerland and then moved to Beer in Devon, where he spent the rest of his life. The remaining twenty-two years of that life, right up to the time of his death in November 1911, saw the publication of his most important works on Japan. Of his private life during all this time and before, all we know is that he married Janet Smith of Belfast in 1871 and that she died childless in 1908. It seems from Satow's letters that she was an accomplished pianist and from Aston's letters to Sir Harry Parkes that she performed the supremely difficult role of diplomatic spouse in Korea with distinction. During Aston's subsequent illness she was both nurse and amanuensis. Aston dictated his view of recent political upheavals m several letters she wrote for him to Sir Harry. Of the rest, of his political views, of his beliefs, of his friendships and even of his views of Japan, we can only make inferences from his writings. Just as he was a profoundly textual scholar, so he has left us only texts to work on.

His first task in Japan was learning the language and for that he was as well prepared as Satow or Chamberlain. Like both of them he excelled in this and rapidly acquired an enviable mastery of the spoken and written forms of the language. How he accomplished this in the absence of reliable grammars is less clear in Aston's case than it is in Satow's. He may have made use at first of one of several exploratory grammars published in the 1860s for the burgeoning market of foreigners resident in Japan, though it is unlikely that he would have found their attempts to apply European grammatical categories to Japanese very helpful. It appears that one of his principal teachers of classical Japanese and Japanese linguistics was Hori Hidenari (1819–87), a long-forgotten student of the *Kokugaku* (Nativist) school of learning who published several dozens of books concerning the Japanese language and the spiritual values of Japan. If this is the case, however, it is surprising that not one of these books is now to be found in the collection of Aston's books in Cambridge University Library. At any rate, by 1870 he was sufficiently proficient m spoken Japanese to be able to manage interpreting tasks with ease: in that year, when Sir Harry Parkes, then British minister in Tokyo, and his wife visited Wakayama, Aston interpreted for Lady Parkes in her chats with the former daimyo. In the same year some of his translations from speeches made in the forerunner of the Japanese Diet were printed in the Foreign Office Blue Books (Confidential Print).

Aston's earliest publications were closely connected with his mastery of the language. In 1869 he published *A Short Grammar of the Japanese Spoken Language*, which met an immediate need: further editions of it appeared in 1871, 1873 and 1888, and in 1873 a translation of it into French by a French consular official was published in Yokohama. The differences between these four editions reveal fundamental changes not only in the level of Aston's understanding of the language but also in the social setting of language in Meiji Japan. In the first three editions he states that, 'an uneducated Japanese has no word for, nor much idea of, any shorter period of time than one European hour. It is impossible to make him understand what is meant by "five minutes" or "a quarter of an hour"', and that educated speakers use *bunji* or the English word 'minute' to refer to a minute of time; in the fourth edition he states that Japan had now completely gone over to the European system of reckoning time and that the word for minute was *fun*, as it still is now.[5] In all four editions he warns readers against the error of using honorifics when addressing servants or coolies, but his injunction against the use of Malay words in the misapprehension that they are Japanese words is omitted from the fourth edition, which can be taken as an indication of the decline of the pidgin Japanese used in earlier days by the expatriate community. His treatment of the two particles that tax the understanding of students of the language also underwent substantial changes.

In the first edition he describes *wa* as a 'sort of definite article' and *ga* as 'sometimes an indefinite article',' definitions that are so unhelpful as to be demoralizing to the student: as an analyst of the language he was still very much in the dark and at the stage of trying to tie Japanese to the procrustean bed of European grammatical terminology. But in the third edition he arrived at a much better understanding: *wa* is 'a distinctive or separative particle' and it 'has the force of isolating or singling out one object from among a number, or of opposing one thing to another', and *ga* 'often follows nouns in the nominative case'; in the fourth edition these definitions are amplified still further with more examples.[7] The Preface to the first three editions stated that, 'this book is intended for the use of merchants and others who wish to acquire a colloquial knowledge of the Japanese language', and it was therefore an attempt to fulfil a practical end and as such in keeping with his commercial responsibilities as a member of the Consular Service.[8]

The fourth edition, however, has a different preface which points out that the work has been almost entirely rewritten and that, 'more exclusive attention has been paid in it to the Tokio dialect, which now bids fair to become the language of the upper classes of Japan generally'.[9] Among the new material in the book was a warning that categories such as 'noun' and 'verb' were only of limited use for describing the Japanese language because of its fundamental differences from European languages. It is on this work that Aston's reputation as a linguist rests. It was an epoch-making work in that it marked the end of the period in which westerners sought to understand and analyse the Japanese language in terms of the grammar and categories of European languages and constituted the first serious attempt to grasp the internal logic of the Japanese language. As such it remained influential until the end of the century and beyond and set the pattern for subsequent grammars of Japanese, including that of Chamberlain.

Aston's Grammar of the *Japanese Written Language with a Short Chrestomathy* was equally successful, being first published in 1872 and then appearing in subsequent editions in 1877 and 1904. In it he gives a historical and analytical account of the syntax of the classical Japanese written language and appends, for the student to practice upon, a selection of texts reproduced from block-printed Japanese books and notices. It was a more scholarly work and Aston describes it himself as a 'treatise' containing 'the results of a first study of some of the principal works of native writers on Japanese Grammar'.[10] These works, which are listed in an appendix, form an awesome collection of difficult texts; many have now been reprinted in modern annotated editions, but Aston had to work through them in the raw, in the original block-printed editions. As late as 1907 Chamberlain was still recommending it as 'an admirably lucid work embodying all the best results obtained by the native school of grammarians'.[11]

It should be mentioned at this stage that although Aston can be described as a British japanologist, he was by no means as limited in his mental horizons as that term might suggest. In the first place, he took pains to keep himself abreast of European writing on Japan in French and German. In 1871–2 he published several reviews of French translations of Japanese works in which he painstakingly identified errors of interpretation. Regarding *Anthologie japonaise* by Leon de Rosny (1837–1916), appointed the first professor of Japanese at the École des langues orientales in Paris in 1868, Aston admired 'the capital essay on Japanese poetry which forms the introduction', but found de Rosny's philological standards wanting: the translations were 'far from attaining to that degree of accuracy which the student requires'; 'the few grammatical remarks which are ventured upon are rarely correct'; and Aston rightly queries the use of the word 'professeur' to translate the Japanese word *oiran*, which refers to a class of courtesan![12] In the second place, Aston was a scholar of Korean and other languages as well as of Japanese. In 1876 Aston had been one of a party which visited the Loochoo Islands, now known as Okinawa and a part of Japan; the following year he visited Hokkaidō. As a result of these two trips he wrote in 1879 an account of the Loochooan and Ainu languages, concluding that the former was 'merely a dialect of Japanese . . . and contains words which are obsolete in the modern language' and that the latter was quite unrelated to Japanese or Korean.[13] Aston began his much more serious studies of Korean some time in the 1870s, probably using the manuscript manuals which had been prepared in the 1830s by the Japanese interpreters resident in Pusan in southern Korea; Aston's own copies of these manuals are kept today in the Institute of Oriental Studies in St Petersburg. By 1878 he had already acquired some Korean books as well as a collection of Japanese books concerning Korea, and between 1878 and 1883 he wrote an extensive account, making use of Korean as well as Japanese sources, of Hideyoshi's invasion of Korea in the closing years of the sixteenth century.[14] Satow and Chamberlain were also making efforts to learn Korean by this time, and like Aston had Korean nationals resident in Japan as private teachers, but it appears from Satow's letters that it was Aston who made the most progress and achieved fluency in the spoken language by 1881. Aston was clearly well prepared, therefore, for his negotiations with the Korean authorities in 1882 and for his residence there as consul-general later. Of his visit in 1882 he wrote, 'At all the places visited I conversed with large numbers of Coreans, and found them invariably friendly, though sometimes inclined to be unpleasantly familiar. Their desire for information knew no bounds.'[15] He wrote several other articles on Korean literature and language, but his principal achievement in this area was his article, published in 1879 in the *Journal of the Royal Asiatic Society*, comparing the Japanese and Korean languages. This article, in which Aston was the first to demonstrate that the two languages were linguistically related, has been described as a 'breakthrough to the first scientific comparison' of the two languages, and in 1976 the German scholar of Japanese and Korean Bruno Lewin stated that, 'Aston's arguments for the kinship of the two languages are still worthy of consideration even today.'[16]

Although all of Aston's work was based on the most rigorous of philological foundations, in a sense his work in the area of linguistics was a preparation for the literary, religious and anthropological studies with which he occupied himself after his retirement. His earliest published work concerning Japanese literature was a partial translation and summary of the *Tosa nikki*, which he published in 1875.[17] Here, however, his interests were still predominantly philological: his notes touch on such matters as the light which *Tosa nikki* can cast on the nature of colloquial speech in the Heian period, and finally he recommends it as a work with which to begin the study of Japanese classical literature.

Aston is best known today for the three major works of his later life, of which the first was his translation of the *Nihon shoki* (Chronicles of Japan), or *Nihongi*, as he referred to it, which was first published in London by the Japan Society in 1896. It is still the standard translation in English, which is perhaps not surprising given the difficult Chinese, and to a lesser extent Japanese, of the *Nihon shoki* and the later commentaries, and it is still regularly cited. It is indicative of the areas to which his interests were turning and of the audience for whom he was to write more and more, that he declared in the Preface that his object was 'to make accessible to European scholars the very considerable store of material for the study of mythology, folk-lore, early civilization, and manners and customs which it contains'.[18]

Aston's second major work was *A History of Japanese Literature*, which was first published in 1899. This too was a remarkably successful work: it was reprinted several times in England in Aston's own lifetime, and in the United States was reprinted no less than nine times between 1899 and 1937. In the bibliographical note appended to this work Aston acknowledges his 'very considerable obligations' to Mikami Sanji and Takatsu Kuwasaburō's *Nippon bungakushi* (History of Japanese literature) which had appeared in 1890 and had been the first work of its kind to be published in Japan.[19] Aston's own copy of this work is preserved in the Aston Collection in Cambridge University Library and the extensive annotations testify to its usefulness to Aston. But Aston was no slave to it. First, Mikami and Takatsu have nothing whatever to say on the subject of Japanese literature since 1868, whereas Aston devotes his final section to the political novels, new-style poetry and other works written in the years since he first reached Japan. It was this section which was omitted when Aston's work was translated into Japanese in 1908. One of the works he describes in detail in this section is Tsubouchi Shōyō's popular novel, *Tōsei shosei katagi* (The characters of students today), which was serialized in 1885–6 and then published in book form. It appears from Aston's own copy of this work that he bought and read it soon after its publication. He wrote a note in it to the effect that the dialogue was full of vulgar student slang and was not to be imitated, but that did not stop him from using two extracts in the fourth edition of his *A Grammar of Japanese Spoken Language*, which differed from the earlier editions in appending a collection of transliterated passages from works of colloquial fiction. In *A History of Japanese Literature*, Aston describes it as a 'realistic novel', and says that 'it is well written, and contains some graphic and humorous sketches of modern student life viewed from the seamy side, but has little plot, portraiture of character, or dramatic incident'.[20] He gives much less space to Tsubouchi's theoretical work, *Shōsetsu shinzui* (The essence of the novel), which was far less influential at the time than modern scholarship would have us believe, and thus better reflects the climate of opinion in the 1880s.

Second, Aston's emphasis and judgement differ from those of Mikami and

Takatsu, and this is nowhere more apparent than in the section dealing with *ninjōbon*, a romantic genre of fiction popular in the 1830s. Mikami and Takatsu took the view that these works, many of which were set in the demi-monde, were morally exceptionable, but, while recognizing that 'the society into which they introduce the reader is far from select, and the morality sadly defective', Aston's overall estimation of their worth was high: 'The great service rendered by Shunsui and his fellow-composers of Ninjōbon was to recall the attention of writers and readers of fiction to human nature as the proper subject of the novelist's art. Since the time of Murasaki no Shikibu this branch of study had been sadly neglected in Japan.'[21] There are good grounds for supposing that Aston's appreciation of *ninjōbon* and conviction that they represented a literary path worth following were shared by writers and readers in the 1880s, although not by literary scholars. It is only in the last twenty years that *ninjōbon* have been seriously studied in Japan.

Aston's overall estimation of Japanese literature is guarded. Morality is throughout an important consideration, and this prevents him from dealing with Saikaku and his works at any length: 'the very titles of some of them are too gross for quotation'.[22] He had a clear notion of what poetry should be and found Japanese efforts in this direction seriously wanting; he is impatient with classical court poetry and confidently asserts that, 'it would be absurd to put forward any serious claim on behalf of Haikai [haiku] to an important position in literature', though he is prepared to grant that 'it is difficult to see how more could be made of it than Bashō has done'.[23] That is not to say that he sees no merit in any of the Japanese literature he read, but it is true that, although extraordinarily well read in Japanese literature, he tended to see the works of his own literary tradition as norms. On the author of *The Tale of Genji*, for example, he has this to say: 'None, however, but an extreme Japanophile (the species is not altogether unknown) will go so far as to place Murasaki no Shikibu on a level with Fielding, Thackeray, Victor Hugo, Dumas, and Cervantes.'[24]

The last of Aston's major works was *Shinto* (*The Way of the Gods*), which was in 1905. The writing of this book sprang partly from Aston's long-standing interest in early Japanese history and partly from a new interest in anthropology and the study of religion, stimulated in part by his reading of Frazer's *The Golden Bough* and Tylor's *Primitive Culture*. In the Preface he wrote that it was intended, primarily and chiefly, as a repertory of the more significant facts of Shinto for the use of scientific students of religion'.[25] He also wrote a number of articles between 1900 and 1911 for *Man, Folk-Lore and the Journal of the Anthropological Institute of Great Britain and Ireland*, which evince his desire to bring Japanese evidence into debates about the origin of language, primitive religion and other matters. In 1902 he wrote an article attacking the use by 'our most eminent anthropologists', by whom he meant Frazer in particular, of Kaempfer's *History of Japan* as an authority on Japanese religion. He knew no Japanese and 'his ignorance is colossal', wrote Aston, who referred anthropologists instead to some of Satow's articles written in the 1870s and 1880s.[26] He set himself the task of providing an accurate and textually based study of Japanese religion that engaged issues of interest to scholars of the phenomenology of religion, and in this respect one of his greatest contributions, apart from his book on Shinto, was the series of articles he wrote for James Hastings's *Encyclopedia of Religion and Ethics*, encompassing the art and architecture of Shinto, fetishism, adoption and several other subjects.

Aston's *Shinto* is a work based on philological study of the texts rather than on foildore, popular religion or religious practice *per se*: the first chapter is telling in this respect, for it is concerned solely with 'Materials for the Study of Shinto'. As such, it cannot escape the charge that it attempts to see Shinto as a scripturally based and organized religion like Christianity and Islam. As a result, it is not surprising that Aston finds Shinto 'decidely rudimentary in character': 'its polytheism, the want of a Supreme Deity, the comparative absence of images and of a moral code, its feeble personifications and hesitating grasp of the conception of spirit, the practical non-recognition of a future state, and the general absence of a deep, earnest faith - all stamp it as perhaps the least developed of religions which have an adequate literary record'.[27] Although Aston goes on to acknowledge that Shinto 'is not a primitive cult', he is primarily concerned with historical Shinto. Of Shinto in the Japan that he knew at first hand he is dismissive: 'The official cult of the present day . . . has little vitality. . . . A rudimentary religion of this kind is quite inadequate for the spiritual sustenance of a nation which in these latter days has raised itself to so high a pitch of enlightenment and civilization.' And he concludes, mistakenly, 'as a national religion, Shinto is almost extinct'.[28] Inevitably, therefore, his writing on Shinto has long since been superseded.

In most of his writing Aston was almost entirely dependent on his personal library of Japanese books. Like his colleague Satow, Aston was an inveterate collector of books. He and Satow often went book-hunting together in Japan, and even had copies made of rare manuscripts in each other's possession. In later years Satow gave away a great many of his books, some to Chamberlain but the greater part to Aston in 1892 in order to provide Aston with the materials for his research after his retirement to England. In 1911 Aston offered, with Satow's approval, his collection of Japanese books to Cambridge University. He died before the arrangements could be completed, but they were bought from his executors shortly afterwards for £250, which the University rightly considered a very moderate sum. This collection, which contains many rare and unique items, forms an important part of Aston's legacy to his successors in the field of Japanese studies in Britain, but it only contains a small part of his collection of Korean books: the remainder went, at some unknown date between 1900 and 1911, to the Asiatic Museum in St Petersburg and are now preserved in the Academy of Sciences in St Petersburg.

Aston's standing with his contemporaries was high. The great French orientalist Henri Cordier wrote in his obituary notice that, 'Aston formait avec Basil Hall Chamberlain et Ernest Mason Satow ce triumvirat de japonisants qui n'ont pas leur égal dans les autre pays.'[29] It was the view of Haga Yaichi (1867–1927). perhaps the most distinguished literary scholar of his day, that Aston's published work on Japanese literature had done much to create the favourable climate for Anglo-Japanese relations that resulted in the Anglo-Japanese Alliance concluded in 1902. Much later, one of Aston's successors as diplomat-cum-scholar, Sir George Sansom, observed in an address at the School of Oriental and African Studies in London: 'I have noticed that some young students are inclined to dismiss Aston and his judgements as old-fashioned, what they call Victorian'; but he continued to look up to Aston and Satow, for 'their work in their several fields of study was voluminous, accurate and penetrating. It still remains valuable, and I doubt whether it will be excelled.'[30]

From the perspective of the 1990s, three aspects of Aston's work must strike every student of Japan very forcefully. First, Aston worked before the Japanese publishing industry began to produce its flood of secondary literature, annotated editions or even simple movable-type reprints of works of classical literature. He worked therefore sometimes from manuscripts but mostly from block-printed texts, each reproducing a different calligraphic hand and each posing difficulties of decipherment. The philological difficulties he and his contemporaries had to surmount gave them an opportunity for careful textual study as a basis for their future studies. Second, there is Aston's concern not to bury himself as a japanologist but to bring Japan into general debate about language, religion and literature, to take part in a universal, rather than a local, discourse. It is this that drove him to present papers at meetings of the British Association for the Advancement of Science and at the Anthropological Institute and to contribute papers to, and engage in debates in, a variety of journals. Third, there is his conscious membership of a European community of scholars. For de Rosny, it is true, he did not have much respect, perhaps because de Rosny never set foot in Japan and Aston was something of a purist in such matters, but he had very different views about other French writers and German writers, and in particular about Dr Karl Florenz (1865–1939). Before becoming the first professor of Japanese studies at the University of Hamburg, Florenz had resided in Japan as Professor of Philology and German Literature at the Imperial University and had published his own translation of the *Nihon shoki* into German and his own *History of Japanese Literature* in German (1906). Aston frequently acknowledges his debts to Florenz's work, which covered as many different fields as did his own. In each of these respects, his philological mastery, his intellectual breadth and his use of European scholarship, Aston pursued a course that many of his successors have deviated from. As a scholar he had his weaknesses, of course: some of his early ventures in Japanese linguistics were ill-conceived, such as his speculations on Japanese affinity with Aryan languages in 1874 and his attempt to rearrange the order of the Korean alphabet smacks of cultural imperialism, a charge which perhaps few writers on Japan in the nineteenth century can escape entirely. But he passes the acid test: his translation of the *Nihon shoki* and his *A History of Japanese Literature* are still in use, more than ninety years after they were written. No scholar could hope for more.

FURTHER READING

Dictionary of National Biography, Second Supplement 1 (1912) 67–8.
Grace Fox, *Britain and Japan: 1858–1883*, Oxford University Press, 1969.
Toshio Yokoyama, *Japan in the Victorian Mind: A Study of SteQueueotyped Images of a Nation, 1850–80*, Basingstoke: Macmillan, 1987.
N. Hayashi and P.F. Kornicki, *Early Japanese Books in Cambridge University Library: The Aston, Satow and von Siebold Collections*, Cambridge University Press, 1990.
Hugh Cortazzi, *Iwakura* in Britain, *Transactions of the Asiatic Society of Japan*, 4th Series, Volume 16, 2001 (covers Aston as interpreter to the mission)

24
John Harrington Gubbins
An 'Old Japan Hand', 1871–1908

IAN NISH

John Harrington Gubbins

J. H. Gubbins (1852–1929) was an Old Japan Hand. He went out as a member of the Japan Consular Service in 1871 and stayed till 1908. He was Japanese Secretary at the British legation in the great tradition of Ernest Satow, E. M. Hobart-Hampden and Harold Parlett. His greatest contribution to history was in the British response to one of the major issues of Japanese political and diplomatic history in the Meiji period, treaty revision. In retirement he taught Japanese studies in Oxford University, and was the author of several authoritative books. He was the prototype of the scholar-diplomat so often found in East Asia in earlier times who combined a policy-making role with great expertise about Japan. Gubbins was described by a commentator as one of the four (along with Satow, Brinkley and Chamberlain) 'in the firmament of our countrymen who have made themselves masters of the various problems of our Far Eastern Ally'.

Gubbins was born in India, the eldest son of a government officer in the Bengal Civil Service, Martin Richard Gubbins (1812–63). His father was the author of *An Account of Mutinies in Oudh and of the Siege of the Lucknow Residency*, a large book published originally in 1858 and in two later expanded versions. So there was a literary tradition in the family. But his father was forced to leave India and ultimately committed suicide. John Harrington was educated at Harrow. He took the examination for the Far Eastern Consular Service and was sent out to Tokyo in 1871 as student interpreter in the Japanese language. Like one of his predecessors, Ernest Satow (1843–1929), Gubbins became highly proficient in the language and published *A Dictionary of Chinese-Japanese words in the Japanese language* in 1889. In the compilation of this he worked with Okamoto Jun, who held the post described in old Indian Civil Service parlance as 'writer to HBM's legation'.

He became Japanese secretary at the British legation in 1889 to add to his other responsibilities for the language training of new recruits to the legation and the consular service and also to the army and navy language staff General F. S. G. Piggott, himself an army language officer at the time, makes these comments on Gubbins:

> Behind a somewhat austere manner was a fund of kindliness and humour from which many generations of consular and service language students benefited.[1]

Gubbins seems to have formed a special bond with Hugh Fraser, the minister in Tokyo from 1888 to 1894, possibly because of their family connections with India. In a conversation with Fraser's wife, Gubbins showed remarkable modesty. Mary Fraser reported that he had told her that 'though he has been working at [the Japanese language] for seventeen years, though he has translated three dictionaries and is now publishing one of his own . . ., he feels that many life-times would not put him absolutely in possession of the whole language as it is used by the learned Japanese today'.[2]

Like many of his contemporanes in the consular service, he was expected to undertake the exploration of some untrodden paths in Japan. He made one of the early expeditions in 1875 from Aomori to Niigata and paid a visit to the mines of Sado.[3] Gubbins was a competent horseman and included 'riding' as one of his pastimes in his entry in *Who's Who* until his death.

ANGLO-JAPANESE COMMERCIAL TREATY 1894

Gubbins became the legation's chief expert on Treaty revision, the central issue in Japan's foreign policy in the early Meiji period. Japan's desire for the revision of her unequal treaties with the various trading powers was a long-standing issue. Indeed it had been raised by the Iwakura Mission in 1871. Japan's complaint was that the treaties provided for extra-territorial rights for foreigners in Japan and fixed low rates of customs duties, while the treaties could only be revised with the consent of both parties. It was, however, a highly technical, legal subject of the kind which could not be fully grasped by diplomats who came to a posting in Japan for a two-year stint. This played into the hands of those belonging to the Japan consular service, some of whom had been in Japan for decades. In 1886–7 Gubbins served as the 'English Secretary' to the conference for the revision of treaties which was held in Tokyo. During this multi-national conference positive progress was made; but the talks had to be broken off because of an explosion of public indignation against the proposed employment of foreign judges in Japanese courts. From this and other experiences Gubbins drew up countless memoranda giving the past history of negotiations on the topic. It has to be said that it was a profoundly boring subject and the conscientiousness with which he mastered it speaks highly for his patience and tolerance.

Treaty revision came urgently on to the political agenda after the creation of the Japanese Diet in 1890. This was because the new parliamentarians were anxious to find an issue on which they could flay the government. Treaty revision was such an issue; they could at once criticize foreigners from the standpoint of xenophobia and Japanese governments for being too compliant with foreign demands and making slow progress. The risk for Britain was that the new generation of party politicians would put so much pressure on the government that it might just cancel the extra-territorial privileges which were at the core of the treaties and leave the foreign commercial communities throughout Japan severely inconvenienced.

Successive governments raised the subject of treaty revision. The British minister, Hugh Fraser, in responding to one such approach in the summer of 1892 said that he was due to return to London on home leave and suggested a resumption of negotiations there. He added that '. . . Gubbins whose help I should like to have in such a matter, wished to go to England as well as myself and could not fairly be detained after his ten years of continuous residence at his post'.[4] Hence Gubbins who was long overdue for leave was to be found in Britain from December 1892, enjoying a busman's holiday.

But first, Gubbins took the opportunity to get married. In his early days in Tokyo he had met the family of Colin McVean, an *o-yatoi* in the survey department of the Japanese government. Colin had gone out to Japan in association with Richard Brunton in 1868.[5] But the McVeans retired to Killiemore House on the Isle of Mull in 1877. Gubbins on leave from Japan visited them several times and fell in love with their elder daughter Helen. They were married in Edinburgh in April 1893, he being 41 and she 24. They took up residence in Thornton Hill, Wimbledon.

The new Japanese foreign minister, Mutsu Munemitsu, who was in office from August 1892, decided to grasp the nettle of treaty revision and dispose of the commercial treaty with Britain first. He agreed to Fraser's suggestion that, in order to avoid the disturbances which had bedeviled previous negotiations, they should move the venue to London away from the hothouse atmosphere of Tokyo politics. Mutsu decided to depute Aoki Shūzō who had been minister to Berlin since January 1892 to visit London briefly in September 1893 in order to talk matters over with Fraser and Gubbins.[6] He was well qualified for this task since he had earlier as deputy foreign minister negotiated with Britain over treaty revision. Aoki, it was felt, had a good rapport with the two British negotiators. But the outcome was disappointing for Japan as Fraser concluded that she was not ready to make enough concessions. Mutsu had, therefore, to go back to the drawing-board and present fresh proposals. These were approved by the cabinet in November. Mutsu took the precaution also of steering his proposals through the Privy Council before presenting them to Britain. He then instructed Aoki to serve simultaneously in London and Berlin for the purpose of the negotiations.[7]

When the terms reached London, Lord Rosebery as foreign secretary wrote: '. . . who on earth in Britain knows about Japan?' – a question that has gone ringing round the Office over the years. Gubbins was the answer. Fraser led the way in the early discussions with Aoki in December and recommended that Mutsu's proposals were a sufficient basis for negotiations. But he set off to return to Japan in the new year. Gubbins was accordingly seconded officially to Whitehall from February to July 1894, working in tandem with the assistant under-secretary, Francis Bertie. He, therefore, took a major part in the talks which Aoki and Bertie held between April and July. His role was all the more vital because Fraser, having returned to Japan in February, died unexpectedly on 4 June at the height of the negotiations, thus depriving Whitehall of one of the few specialists on the topic.

There was, it has to be said, incredible ignorance on the issue in Whitehall. Some of Gubbins' writings of the time set the scene:

We have nothing to gain in the revision of our Treaties except the goodwill of Japan and the more remote advantage of the establishment of our relations with her on a more satisfactory and in some respects a more permanent footing. The British communities in Japan are quite aware of this essential weakness of our position as regards negotiation, and the mystery, unsought by us, in which negotiations have been shrouded during the last ten years has, not unnaturally, increased the anxiety with which they contemplate any change in existing conditions. Rightly or wrongly they regard Treaty revision, which they understand to be more or less unconditional surrender to Japanese demands, as an abandonment of their interests by Her Majesty's Government.[8]

Gubbins, therefore, proposed that the mercantile community in Japan should be more fully consulted. But he was nonetheless insistent that it was in Britain's own interest to revise these treaties to put an end to the anomalies.

The *imperium in imperio* which extra-territoriality creates wherever it is exercised exists in Japan as elsewhere, and in a country which has borrowed so much of Western civilization and methods its continued exercise engenders constant friction. The foreign merchants who carry on their trade under the aegis of extraterritoriality are tempted to presume upon their privileges, and to assume towards the Government and people of the country in which they reside a high-handed attitude. This is naturally resented by the Japanese, who lose no opportunity of retaliating, and a bitter feeling is thus created on both sides. Moreover, under Treaties so obsolete as are the existing Conventions, encroachments on the part of foreigners . . . are unavoidable . . . Were Japan an Oriental country, moving as slowly as China, this aegis of extraterritoriality, which covers what the advanced patriot in Japan regards as the insidious advance of the foreigner, would not attract so much attention, but in her assimilation of Western ideas she has far outstripped her more conservative neighbours . . . The new proposals lead us . . . further in the direction of concession to Japanese sentiment but it is not easy to see how this can be avoided. Nowhere is *national sentiment* carried to such extremes as in Japan. [my italics][9]

For Gubbins fear of 'national sentiment' boiling over was the main justification for Britain to sign new treaties. He referred to articles appearing frequently in Japanese newspapers dealing with *Yamato Damashii*. It was Gubbins who wrote on 16 June 'Itō is cautious in all things but weak in the face of extremist opinion'.[10] London came to the conclusion that Japan's prime minister of the day, Itō Hirobumi, was a more moderate, trustworthy and cautious prime minister than any Japanese politician who was likely to come to power. This judgement was made largely on the basis of Gubbins' advice. It was on this basis that talks were pursued. The doubts were reinforced when a Japanese soldier attacked a British consul in Seoul just as preparations were under way for signature.

But finally the new Anglo-Japanese commercial treaty and protocol were signed on 16 July 1894. Consular jurisdiction was abolished; the whole of Japan was opened to British traders; and new legal codes would be introduced before the treaty came into force. It was to take effect in five years' time during which much additional negotiation had to take place. Gubbins on his return to duty was appointed as British delegate on the Tariff Commission for negotiating the supplementary convention with Japan which was eventually concluded on 16 July 1896.

Shortly after his return to Japan in the unfamiliar role of a family man, Gubbins was delighted to find that Sir Ernest Satow, one of his predecessors as Japanese counsellor, was appointed as British minister to Tokyo in July 1895. His correspondence with Satow which continued throughout his life shows that their style and intellectual interests were very similar. It was probably Satow who secured for Gubbins in 1898 the award of the order of Companion of St Michael and St George for his work on treaty revision. This was a deserved honour and may have atoned for the frequent complaint of British merchants in Japan that the 1894 treaty had failed and that that failure was due to Gubbins. Even Gubbins in one of his writings stated that 'the new treaty was received with a chorus of disapproval by British merchants in China and Japan'.[11] The British merchant community in the East, deprived of privileges it had enjoyed for a generations was not inclined to see the political advantages.

KOREA AND JAPAN

In 1900, just as he was about to go on home leave, Gubbins was appointed to act as chargé d'affaires in Seoul in the absence of J. N. Jordan of the China consular service. The reasons for this are not wholly clear. Satow on leave in London may have been consulted when the post in Seoul was about to become vacant during Jordan's leave. He may well have recommended that, on account of Japan's increasing interest in the Korean peninsula, it would be appropriate that someone from the Japan consular service should go to Seoul instead of someone from the China service as heretofore. Or again Satow may have thought that Gubbins was in desperate need of a change from Tokyo where he had stayed contentedly since 1871.[12] Revised treaties had come into force in 1899 and Gubbins' presence in the Japanese capital was no longer indispensable.

Gubbins served in Korea from 18 May 1900 to 4 November 1901 when Jordan resumed his position. For the first time in his career he had his own post and was able to report direct to London since Korea was in crisis for most of the time of his tenure. But it was reassuring for him to know that his friend, Satow, was appointed minister to Peking in place of Sir Claude MacDonald who was expected to need a long period of recuperation after the siege of the Legation Quarter there by the Boxers. By a coincidence he was again able to share his problems with Satow.

Gubbins, though he would have liked to stay on in Korea, took a negative view of the country, describing it later as 'an oriental state in complete decay'.[13] He observed the actions of the Japanese and found them to be active in all the aspects of Korean affairs: 'The Japanese legation has the best information in regard to all matters in the peninsula'.[14] He and Jordan fell out over the question of the efforts to be made for British concession-seekers in Korea in imitation of their diplomatic colleagues. Gubbins was distrustful of British merchants and did not want to take an active part in 'the unholy battle of the concessions.[15]

His wife returned to Scotland with her children, another daughter being born there in September 1901. Gubbins followed on leave early in 1902 and they returned to Japan in 1903. He became secretary of legation which meant being transferred from the consular service to the diplomatic service. This entitled him to one of the houses in the legation compound (soon to be given the status of an embassy). Gubbins naturally became the elder states-man and the voice of continuity in the embassy community.

Family life was not particularly easy. Gubbins had returned with a young wife and a household of small children leaving two young sons behind at school in Britain. In order to avoid Tokyo's heat, the family spent the sum-mers at their house in Karuizawa in the hills to the north, an under-policed area where they were liable to attacks from sōshi (unruly elements). On life in Tokyo, his son's biographers report: 'He was incapable of relaxed father-hood, would not brook disturbance when he worked at home and regarded it as his right to shout for silence or service. His inborn irascibility was aggra-vated by tri-geminal neuralgia . . . and recurring rheumatic pains which were the result of rheumatic fever in his youth.'[16]

In 1908, after a five-year stay, the Gubbins family returned to Britain for good, John having passed the retirement age of 55. He had served in Japan for a total of 37 years.

SCHOLARSHIP AND THE WAR

Gubbins had the reputation in Japan of being a formidable scholar. He had been a founder-member of the Asiatic Society of Japan in 1872. He had con-tributed an article entitled 'Jasui Shinhei bemmo, being a treatise directed against Christianity' to its *Transactions* in 1875. He had, as we have seen, compiled a substantial dictionary in 1889 which went into a second edition in the year of his retirement, 1908. He had translated the Civil Code of Japan which was in fact a book but it was published in the *Transactions*.[17]

Gubbins' official retirement began on 10 September 1909. At the instance of Lord Curzon, at that time chancellor of Oxford University who may have been approached by Satow, he was made 'Lecturer in Japanese in the University of Oxford'. Since he had gone straight from school into the Japan consular service, he had never attended a university. He had therefore to be given an honorary Master's degree from Balliol College in order to rectify the position, though he was not listed as a lecturer there.

His book on the *Progress of Japan 1853–71* came out in 1911 from the Clarendon Press in Oxford. He writes in the preface that 'six lectures given in the University of Oxford during 1909–10 are the basis of this book'.[18] They still stand up well in relation to the writings of Satow and G. B. Sansom. At a time when history lecturing was not too rigorous, his approach was rigorous. His study included (in the appendixes) copious translations of Japanese mate-rial which was fiendishly difficult.

But during the next three years the number of interested students declined and the authorities decided to end the appointment. The University decision came as a blow. Gubbins the scholar was well suited to life in Oxford and seems to have spent much time in the Bodleian library. He wrote from his home at 10 Lathbury Road, Oxford on 22 June 1912 to Basil Hall Chamberlain, a companion for decades in Tokyo, who had just retired to Switzerland:

Personally I think Oxford should be represented in Japanese, but it is for them to decide and for me to bow to their decision.

The Oxford decision was clearly a disappointment. Gubbins as for Chamberlain retirement and detachment from Japan were not easy. Their other friend, Satow, who had been less uni-directional in his interests, found it easier:

> Sir Ernest keeps very well and is very busy with local – I had almost said parochial – matters of all kinds. His many-sided-ness comes out in his wonderful adaptation to English modes of life and interests after so many years of foreign experience and official and scholastic activity. I can only look on and admire.[19]

But Gubbins did not have the wide interests of Satow and faced heavy family responsibilities, having two sons and three daughters.

Gubbins had already launched himself on his new book. He told Satow in his Christmas letter for 1912 that he had finished the reading for the first chapter: 'I want to make it a link between old and new Japan, describing the conditions of things politically in some detail, and giving an idea . . . of the international aspect of affairs at the time of the restoration.' But it was to be a decade before it appeared.[20]

When the war broke out in 1914, he took up war work in spite of increasing ill health. He moved to 82 York Mansions, Battersea Park, which he leased for most of the war years. Writing to Satow in December 1915, he said:

> Fortunately for the peace of mind of the War Office I have been able – except for a month in Hampshire – to continue my censorship of Japanese correspondence. Like most work it comes in rushes and during Xmas week my hands were full. It is not always edifying reading. One hears a good deal of sharp comment on English things which one would prefer to criticize oneself.[21]

It is not clear what was meant by this censorship but it raises questions about Britain's confidence in the Anglo-Japanese alliance.

By February 1916 he was complaining of a great increase of censorship work during the previous two months. But shortly afterwards his work appears to change. He put in 'an hour or so every two or three days dictating translations and memoranda to shorthand typists'.[22] His office was however still at the Postal Censorship, Kingsway WC, though Gubbins by special dispensation still did much of his work at home. In March 1917 John Buchan, the novelist, was given the task of centralizing the whole of the 'newspaper work' on behalf of the War Office, the Admiralty and Foreign Office jointly. Press work was, however, jeopardized by delays in the Far Eastern mails on account of the Russian revolution and loss of mails by the submarine menace. By June Gubbins was writing that 'my position as press reader and memo writer is in course of being regularized but I must go to the department [in the War Office] 3–4 hour daily.'[23] It is not easy to tell exactly what his press work entailed but he did comment that he was much worried by the sentiments being expressed in articles in chauvinist journals like *Nihon oyobi Nihonjin*.

Throughout the war, family anxieties increased. Both his sons were at the front. His second son, Colin, who had joined up in the artillery from the start at 18, experienced war on the western front. Gubbins' letters to Satow show that he was very proud of him ('He is really a good lad and has found, I hope, his metier'). But in the same way that he had remained distant from his children in Japan, he still found it hard to show his true feelings. Colin's biographers relate:

Often, when Colin had returned on leave from France, all his father had done was to glance up from his censorship of Japanese correspondence for the Foreign Office, ask 'What are you doing here?' and return to his work. It was small wonder that the son found it difficult to communicate with the father.[24]

Colin Gubbins survived the war, wounded and gassed, but with a Military Cross for bravery; he lived to become head of Britain's Special Operations Executive (SOE) and to be knighted.

LITERARY EFFORTS

In 1917 John Gubbins was invited to write one of the government hand-books on Japan in preparation for forthcoming peace conference. Satow was also involved in the writing of one of these booklets. Dr George Prothero was the responsible editor and it was under his editorial pen from the appropri-ately named Watergate House that they were prepared. The authors gave their services on a voluntary and unpaid basis. Satow's manuscript went in on time, while Gubbins who was fully engaged in war work could not meet his deadline. But the two seasoned authors had a great deal of fun over the good doctor. When the edited version reached him, Gubbins wrote that he felt 'like a school-boy whose exercise is being corrected'.[25] He was able to report to Satow with relief in December 1918 that the draft had been com-pleted. It was ultimately published in 1920 and was a brief and authoritative volume.[26] Like everything that Gubbins turned his hand to, it was a very careful piece of work. It was a very effective summary history, covering a large period of recent history in a relatively short essay. What is important to remember nowadays is that he was writing at a time when libraries on East Asian topics were very poor; and Gubbins had to borrow many of the stan-dard reference books he needed from Satow.

Gubbins had been since 1892 an Honorary Member of the Japan Society of London and occasionally took the chair at its meetings. He delivered to the Society in 1918 an erudite paper entitled 'The Hundred Articles and the Tokugawa Government', giving the findings which were later to appear in his book.[27]

There is a gap of some years in the Gubbins-Satow correspondence at this point. When it was resumed, the discussion was of books and writing. Satow and Gubbins were both publishing major books through the London pub-lisher, Seeley, Service. Satow's book, *A Diplomat in Japan*, was completed in January 1921 and published later in the year. Gubbins produced in 1922 his major work *The Making of Modern Japan*. The Foreign Office tried to prevent the publication of parts of the volume and it required intervention with Lord Curzon, the foreign secretary, before the Office's censors would give way. Responding to Satow's congratulations, he wrote: 'I'm so glad you think I have been just to the Japanese. I have really tried to write with fairness and impartiality but try as one may one does not often succeed.'[28]

1922, however, brought two disappointments. His wife died in Edinburgh in January. Thereafter Gubbins had to follow a solitary existence. He had always rented his houses and found himself with no roots. Instead, he moved from place to place (Jersey, Kent, Edinburgh, Mull), residing where he could find accommodation close to his daughters and seeing them through exceptional patches of ill health and guiding them into adulthood.

Gubbins' sons were dispersed. He lost track of his eldest son who had emigrated to Canada. His second son, Colin, was posted to the army in India. John Gubbins saw little of that family except when Colin's wife and son visited Mull on a visit home in 1925 and Colin joined them in 1926. These were years of serious illness and considerable loneliness as he confessed in letters to Satow, though he did have the consolation of knowing that he was welcome to stay with Colin's family when they returned from India in 1930.

In some ways it was reading and writing which gave John Gubbins the greatest solace. Of these writing – and with it correspondence – appeared to give him the greatest satisfaction. Satow and Gubbins had both published much during their working lives and were equally industrious in retirement. There was only nine years between them in age; and they shared the urge to write. Something of Gubbins' thinking comes out in this comment to Satow:

> I wish Chamberlain would not follow in Lord Acton's footsteps and keep to himself the wealth of information he has acquired. What interesting papers and books he might have written. All his learning will now die with him. It is the greater pity because he can write so well.[29]

During the 1920s Gubbins spent most of his time in Edinburgh where he belonged to an obscure Scottish body called the National Citizens Union. His task was to make notes on the Socialist press for that body. These were written (as he confessed to Satow) 'for the information – I won't say edification – of the Committee of the Edinburgh Branch'. In due course he addressed the branch on the subject and the lecture was published in pamphlet form under the title of 'Socialism and the Socialist Press'. His appealing message was that 'the whole Socialist-Communist movement has spent its greatest force and is now receding like the tide when the ebb sets in. It was his only non-Japanese publication.

John Gubbins died in Buckingham Terrace, Edinburgh on 23 February 1929. Fortunately Colin's wife was around. But his family was dispersed, his three daughters being in Hongkong. Gubbins belongs to that group of Japanese well-wishers who first made contact with Japan at an early age, spent their career there and then for twenty years of retirement continued to study and publish about Japan and the Japanese without re-visiting the country. In three important books – and in a large number of scattered articles in specialized journals – Gubbins had passed on the perceptions of Japan which he had gleaned during many decades of hard labour at the British embassy in Tokyo.

25
Sir George Sansom
Pre-eminent Diplomat and Historian

Sir George Sansom

GORDON DANIELS

Among British historians whose minds and senses have engaged Japan's rich civilization Sir George Sanson (1883–1965) remains pre-eminent. Over seventy years after the publication of his *Japan A Short Cultural History* and about half a century after the completion of his History of Japan, these works remain classics of grace and rigour which set exacting standards for each generation of Western scholars.[1] Yet Sir George Sansom was far more than a historian of formidable and subtle powers. He was a long-serving diplomat, linguist and aesthete who overcame illness and disappointment with epic patience and resolve.

George Bailey Sansom was born in Limehouse on the eastern fringe of London on 23 November 1883. His father was a naval architect who lost most of his savings by investing, unwisely, in his employer's company. As a result Sansom was never to study at a British university and regretted this intellectual loss to the end of his life. Yet within these relatively straitened circumstances Sansom received an education which heightened his cultural sensitivity and refined his linguistic skills.[2] After graduating from Palmer's School, Grays, he moved to the Lycée Malherbe in Caen, and then spent over a year at the Universities of Giessen and Marburg in Germany.

After returning to England Sansom spent some months in purposeful cramming and soon passed the examinations for the Far Eastern Consular Service. In 1904 he sailed for Japan and on arrival immersed himself in a variety of Japanese cultural activities which are rarely embraced by British diplomats. At Nagasaki he joined a *Nō* chorus, began the study of painting and calligraphy; and, more conventionally, began to collect ceramics, screens and other works of art. In these years of diplomatic apprenticeship Sansom also devoted himself to a wide variety of physical pursuits, one of which brought unexpected dangers. Fly-fishing, riding, golf and tennis were conventional diversions from official duties but Sansom also undertook adventurous cross-country hikes. On one of these he was gashed by a poisonous shrub and only a new drug from Vienna saved his life.[3]

Between 1910 and 1914 Sansom served in Yokohama, Tokyo, Chemulpo in Korea and Hakodate in northern Japan, but with the outbreak of war he returned to London and was recruited into the recondite world of naval intelligence. As part of these duties he was despatched to Archangel, and discovered that Russian forces did not lack supplies, but simply the will and organization to remove them from the quayside.

In 1919 Sansom returned to Japan and served as acting Japanese counsellor before assuming a variety of posts in Tokyo and the provinces. The years which followed were to see his reputation rise high within the Tokyo Embassy and in 1925 the ambassador, Sir Charles Eliot, evaluated him as follows:

> For intellectual brilliance Mr Sansom is generally admitted to stand first in the Japanese Service. He is an extremely good Japanese scholar – he has also published several valuable linguistic papers and translations. He is a very good draftsman in English, is well informed on all political and social questions and has specially studied commerce and financial matters. At present he is greatly handicapped by ill health.[4]

At this evaluation it suggests Sansom's relationship with Sir Charles Eliot was close and friendly. What is more, it extended well beyond the narrow confines of professional diplomacy. Both men were committed scholars who were deeply interested in Japanese Buddhism and its rich and subtle intellectual heritage. From these shared interests stemmed a close rapport which continued after Eliot's retirement to Nara.

By 1926, Sansom had begun work on his first important historical work, a cultural history of Japan. In this he was aided by a diplomatic life which retained some of the relaxed ambience of Victorian days. During the summer long periods were spent in the hills near Lake Chūzenji, and weekends and evenings were rarely disturbed by diplomatic work. This regime was especially conducive to Sansom's method of historical research, which differed markedly from much library-based historical enquiry. Sansom visited temples and shrines in Kyoto, Nara and Ise, and even travelled to Korea to examine sites and museums which illuminated the origins of Japanese art and architecture. Even more important was his creation of a sophisticated network of Japanese informants whose help he always acknowledged in later years. This group included Professor Anesaki Masaru, the great authority on religious history; Professor Fukui Rikichiro, a renowned scholar of Japanese art; and Professor Yashiro Yukio, who possessed a deep knowledge of both Japanese and European art. Later Sansom recalled the preparation of his cultural history with great warmth and enthusiasm:

> I was in a state of continuous excitement. I had spent a decade or more in the society of Japanese artists scholars, collectors, archaeologists, monks, museums, directors, actors, farmers and fishermen. There is very little mentioned in the book with which I was not familiar – paintings, sculptures, buildings, landscapes, mountains and rivers.[5]

Even before he completed this labour of love Sansom had published his first major book, which was in part a by-product of his historical enquiries.

Though his *Historical Grammar of Japanese* was chiefly 'a work of reference' for advanced students of Japanese, it was also 'designed to provide material for study of the affiliations of the Japanese language – for inquiry into the origins of the Japanese race'.[6] This pioneering work continued to be reprinted for forty years after its publication in 1928.

Japan: A Short Cultural History was finally published in 1931.[7] Despite Sansom's later achievements this event may have marked the highpoint of his Japanese experience. The book's preface mentions Japan's 'brave and lovable people', a description which would have been unlikely in the years following the Manchurian Incident of September 1931. However, the Manchurian Crisis focused Western attention upon Japan to an unprecedented degree, and may have contributed much to the *Cultural History's* success in Europe and the United States. Despite its scholarly strengths, the *Cultural History's* reception was not uniformly enthusiastic. *The Times Literary Supplement* acknowledged the author's 'erudition and painstaking research' but continued:

> . . . candour compels the observation that the general reader is likely to find it more instructive than stimulating. His procession moves in stately fashion through the eventful centuries, compelling our respect: but it compels our regrets also, in that it moves without banners or beating of drums, giving but little hint of those dramatic elements, of that romantic quality, persistent throughout the darkest periods of Japanese history.[8]

This was scarcely the view of discerning Japanologists.

Arguably, the writing of the *Cultural History* may have posed less difficulties for Sansom than his next scholarly undertaking, the preparation for publication of Sir Charles Eliot's unfinished manuscript 'Japanese Buddhism'. Not only was Eliot's manuscript a draft, but it lacked a section on the major Japanese Buddhist leader Nichiren. In 1935 Sansom completed a final chapter on Nichiren's life and thought, and the book was published; but as he later confessed, 'adding a chapter to a book written by a genius is a terrible job . . . your heart sinks as you take the pen'.[9]

Although *Japan: A Short Cultural History* may now appear the most lasting product of Sansom's pre-war years, his diplomatic writing and reporting was of great contemporary significance. From 1926 to 1939 his principal role was that of commercial counsellor, at a time when trade was a central issue in Anglo-Japanese relations.

Sansom later claimed that he had accepted this position as it permitted him remarkable freedom and independence, but this rationale never detracted from his commitment to the post or the professionalism which characterized his economic reporting. Indeed, Sansom's observations on Japanese economic development was often prescient and prophetic. He perceived Japan's transition from a pre-modern to a modern economy before many others, and in 1932 concluded 'Japan is rapidly passing out of the imitative phase and is developing into a powerful industrial and commercial state.'[10] Long before the British textile industry had recognized the true dimensions of Japan's competitive power, he was attempting to persuade Lancashire industrialists to 'look upon Japan as a modern industrial country. In fact an able competitor'.[11] Sansom's perceptive analyses of international trade also led him to note the negative influence which Western protectionism could exert on Japanese foreign policy. Despite his antipathy towards Japan's Manchurian adventure in November 1932, he could still write:

> ... the Japanese, if they find themselves, as they well may, driven out of one foreign market after another by tariff measures directed against them, are likely to be confirmed in their present mood of hostility. They can argue that the very Powers which reproach them for their conduct in Manchuria are forcing them to desperate measures by closing other markets against them. This argument is not without foundation, for the past few years Japan has had to contend with tariff increases – some of which were aimed specifically at her – in India, Australia, South Africa and the United Kingdom; while she is now confronted with the possibility of further increases in the United States, the Philippines, Java and India, at a time when she is suffering severely from the boycott and depressed condition in China.[12]

These cogent opinions failed to dissuade Britain and her Commonwealth partners from taking 'legitimate defensive measures against Japan but the notion that trade lay at the centre of most international relationships – including those between Tokyo and the West – was to form an important motif in Sansom's diplomatic thinking.

Despite Sansom's understanding of Japan's economic difficulties he had no sympathy for her continental expansionism or the populist chauvinism which shaped her politics in the 1930s. His detestation of ultra-nationalist fanaticism was a natural product of his humane values but it was further deepened by his loss of close Japanese friends in the political assassinations of the time.[13]

In these years of increasingly exacting work Sansom still retained his broad cultural and intellectual vitality. In 1929 the Indian 'poet-sage' Tagore visited Tokyo, and Sansom and his wife Katharine met him to discuss 'literature and language'. Four years later George Bernard Shaw spent some days in Japan and Sansom escorted him to the Nō, to meet Prime Minister Saito and, more improbably, to confront the ultra-nationalist Araki Sadao, a bizarre battle of wits. Sansom's meetings with Tagore and Shaw probably helped him to keep abreast of recent literary trends, as did his encounters with Peter Fleming, W. H. Auden and Christopher Isherwood, all of whom visited Tokyo on literary pilgrimages to the Far East. Sansom's intellectual vitality was also apparent in his next ambitious plan for historical research. In 1934 he began active work on a major study of the impact of Western thought on Japan. However, the final manuscript *The Western World and Japan* would not be published for a further sixteen years.[14]

By 1934 Sansom's reputation as a historian was so well established that he was invited to give a series of lectures on Japanese culture at Columbia University in New York. He happily accepted this invitation and arrived in New York in September 1935. To his surprise he was greeted like a Japanese scholar returning from distant lands. Dr Evarts Green, the head of the Japanese department at Columbia and Tsunoda Ryūsaku, professor and librarian, waited at the quayside, accompanied by two students, who were to act as porters. In New York and Boston the Sansoms were honoured and feted in ways which would have been unimaginable in Tokyo. Perhaps the highlight of Sansom's stay was an invitation to speak at the prestigious Pilgrims dinner. He chose this occasion to advocate the expansion of oriental studies in American universities and concluded:

All over the Far East important movements are shaping, which will presently affect our own lives in one way or another. The least we can do is to study them and I am convinced that all such study must be based upon a foundation of pure learning. Great progress has been made of late in Oriental Studies in this country – less in my own I am ashamed to say – but 1 wish to plead for still greater effort.[15]

Soon after Sansom rejected the offer of a permanent post at Columbia, but his exhilarating stay in New York had persuaded him that a stay in an American university would form an agreeable postscript to retirement.

In 1936 Sansom returned to Japan to find its politics more violent and volatile than before. These developments not only depressed him, they brought many practical difficulties to his work. As xenophobia suffused Japanese ministries, officials increasingly restricted foreign diplomats' access to information. This inevitably slowed the compilation of Sansom's annual economic reports.[16]

In 1937 overwork and the outbreak of the undeclared Sino-Japanese War further deepened Sansom's depression and an ulcerated stomach now added to his anxieties. Even worse, the new British ambassador, Sir Robert Craigie, knew little of East Asia or Japan and took scant notice of Sansom's expert knowledge and advice.[17] Craigie's indifference did allow Sansom more time to relax at his summer house in Kita Kamakura, but this was little consolation when Japan's government seemed set upon a course of authoritarian rule and military expansionism.

By 1939 these many depressing circumstances had persuaded Sansom to leave the Foreign Office and accept a new invitation to spend a term teaching at Columbia. In May he left Japan for London and on arrival quickly handed in his resignation.[18] Unfortunately, events moved too quickly for Sansom to escape easily to academic pastures. The outbreak of the war with Germany increased the Foreign Office's world-wide burdens and Sansom was recalled to official service. After some months working in London he was again despatched to Tokyo to work alongside his less-than-favourite ambassador, Sir Robert Craigie.

In Tokyo Sansom reflected on the complacency which had characterized British policy in the previous year. Recalling his own research he lamented the 'steady if almost imperceptible deterioration which overcomes a society or a class which will not accept or adjust itself to change'.[19] He continued, 'That has been our trouble. The defence of the status quo isn't necessarily immoral or mistaken but it always tends to be a losing battle unless it is conducted along with a more positive aim.' The condition of Japan in 1940 gave further cause for lamentation as many of its day-to-day felicities were giving way to coarseness and petty crime. On 27 July 1940 he wrote, 'It is infuriating to see the rude, tough kind of Japanese in the ascendant and to know that all the time in this country there are immense reserves of decency and kindliness and the essential things of civilization.'[20]

Having completed his temporary mission to Tokyo Sansom was free to spend the winter semester at Columbia. As before, his lectures on Japanese history were warmly received, and American friends, Louis and Jean Ledoux, provided generous hospitality at Cornwall-on-Hudson. Unfortunately, the harsh realities of Britain's position soon interrupted Sansom's academic idyll. On a visit to Washington he offered his services to the British Ambassador

Lord Halifax, who suggested creating a post which would permit Sansom to do 'Far Eastern things'. Unfortunately, before such a post materialized the Far Eastern crisis worsened, and Sansom was needed in Singapore.

In the spring of 1941 Sansom sailed from Los Angeles to take up his new position as advisor to the Far Eastern Mission of the Ministry of Economic Warfare. Despite its title this post involved political rather than economic duties; more specifically the collection of information concerning 'events and psychological movements in Malaya, South China, Thailand, Burma and . . . Singapore Island'.[21] Sansom was also appointed to be the civilian representative on the Singapore War Council and appears to have shocked his superiors by clearly stating that a Japanese attack was inevitable. Indeed, Sansom's forecast, that the war would begin 'about the end of November' was extremely accurate, for the attack on Pearl Harbor came a mere week later. Sansom also transmitted a message to Washington warning that Japanese forces in Indo-China were preparing to advance into Thailand and Malaya.[22]

By January 1942 it was clear that the fall of Singapore was inevitable and Sansom was ordered to Java to join General Wavell at his new headquarters. At Bandung he acted as political and diplomatic adviser to General Headquarters and provided news and information to British and foreign journalists. On 15 February Singapore finally fell to Japanese forces and the Sansoms escaped from Batavia to Melbourne on a Dutch liner. After these months of stress and exhaustion in the tropics Sansom was again weak and ill and was compelled to spend some weeks convalescing in Australia.

In the late spring of 1942 the Sansoms recrossed the Pacific, and in May arrived in New York. During the summer they recuperated in the cool air of the Catskills, and in September the scholar-diplomat accepted a specially created post in the British Embassy in Washington. Sansom now became minister to deal with Far Eastern questions, a position which left him free to visit many colleges and universities to lecture on British policy and Far Eastern problems.

Seven months later Sansom was appointed to a new position in the British Embassy – liaison officer between the Foreign Office and the Combined Chiefs of Staff. In this capacity he was to liaise with American leaders regarding the shaping of policy towards defeated Japan. The Foreign Office hoped that Sansom would monitor and perhaps influence American thinking, but Sansom 's views were often at variance with those of American planners.[23] These differences are hardly surprising for they stemmed from profound cultural and philosophical differences. Sansom always found American academic life and hospitality highly congenial, but his political views were very different from those which dominated Roosevelt's America. In short Sansom was a self-confessed 'old Tory' while New Deal conceptions of active government and social engineering increasingly dominated plans for the occupation of Japan. These differences were clearly apparent in a triangular conversation between Sansom, Hugh Borton and George Blakeslee on 28 July 1943. On this occasion Sanson lent his support to notions of economic recovery and an early peace, but showed himself hostile to ideas of radical reform. Hugh Borton summarized these elements in Sansom's thinking as follows:

In general Sir George was opposed to the enforcement by the United Nations of changes in the Japanese Constitution and Government as such enforcement would be practically impossible if the Japanese themselves were not convinced of the need for these changes. Specifically, he felt it extremely inadvisable to depose the emperor. The supervision from the outside of the Japanese educational system would be quite impossible. The enforced adoption by Japan of a bill of rights would have little meaning as the ordinary Japanese is little aware of the real significance of personal liberties.

Sir George believed that the military occupation of Japan, unless it came about as a result of hostilities, was both unnecessary and unwise. He believed that the future air strength of the United Nations would be sufficient to protect any disarmament commissions that might be sent to Japan to supervise the enforcement of the terms of surrender.[24]

No-one can doubt the sincerity of Sansom 's views for they were consistently held throughout the war, but they were a significant obstacle to close Anglo-American co-operation. Furthermore, Sansom's conservatism may have contributed to the British government's tardiness in beginning discussion of Japan's future. In fact, Whitehall did not turn its formulated attention to these issues until May 1945 by which time most American policies had been formulated. On 28 May an official in the Department of State showed Sansom a draft of its plans for occupied Japan which envisaged a first phase of severe American military administration. Not only was this concept contrary to Sansom's non-interventionist views but 'the United States Government did not intend as yet to inform other Governments of their views or invite participation'.[25]

Soon after Sansom returned to London and drafted a critique of American policy which emphasized Japan's economic weakness and rejected the need for 'a costly machinery of *internal* controls'. Despite their realism and practicality, Sansom's views were not accepted by the Foreign Secretary, Anthony Eden, who feared any friction with Washington. Yet in one important respect Sansom's views anticipated the realities of the Occupation which was to come: he always favoured working through the Japanese government rather than attempting the complexities of direct military administration.

Despite Sansom 's presence in London in these crucial weeks, his role was surprisingly restricted. He was not selected to accompany the British delegation to Potsdam and he attacked the Potsdam Declaration as 'really a poor document'. In a letter dated 30 July he sadly lamented his situation:

> I have been seeing various old friends who all think I should have gone to Potsdam, and I thought so myself. But . . . it would have been churlish to object. Also they all feel I should have been Ambassador to Japan before the war and think even now that I should be. But I have no ambition of that kind.[26]

Despite these morose reflections Sansom was selected to represent Britain on the Far Eastern Commission, the Allied body established to 'oversee' the Occupation of Japan from Washington. Before the Commission established itself in the American capital, it paid an exploratory visit to Japan in January and February 1946. Sansom took this opportunity to renew links up with many of his long-standing Japanese friends.

As before Sansom was critical of many aspects of American policy, in particular the notion of destroying the major industrial and financial groups, the *zaibatsu*. He also exhibited a disdain for aspects of American society which had been elevated to the status of blueprints for the new Japan. After a meeting with members of MacArthur's Civil Information and Education Section,

he wrote acidly, 'education in the United States today is not of such a quality as to encourage one in feeling that it provides a model for any other
country'.[27]

Yet for all his dislike of the radicalism and inexperience of many of
MacArthur's aides, he recognized the Supreme Commander's own charisma
and the overwhelming nature of American power. Before meeting any of his
old Japanese friends, he felt it necessary to ask the Supreme Commander's
permission. Even more striking was his tactful rejection of an invitation to
meet the emperor after consulting General McCoy the American chairman of
the Far Eastern Commission.[28]

Following his return to London Sansom's knowledge and judgement
appear to have been more highly regarded by the new foreign secretary,
Ernest Bevin, than by his predecessor Anthony Eden. He was frequently consulted on important issues of Far Eastern policy, and received the GBE 'in
recognition of the valuable services' he had 'rendered to the state'.[29]

From May 1946 to October 1947 Sansom spent much of his time in
Washington serving as both minister in the Embassy and United Kingdom
representative on the Far Eastern Commission. In view of his long experience
as commercial counsellor it was perhaps natural that he was now appointed
chairman of the Commission's Committee on Economic and Financial
Affairs. In this capacity Sansom saw uncertainty as a major threat to Japan's
economic recovery, and repeatedly emphasized the importance of setting levels of industrial production which Japan would be permitted to achieve.
Unfortunately American power and obstructionism left little scope for British
diplomats to assert their influence, and Sansom could achieve little during
his time in Washington.[30]

In the autumn of 1947 Sansom finally left the Foreign Office and satisfied
his long-held desire to return to academic life. Twelve years after his first lectures at Columbia he became the first director of its Far Eastern Institute.
Sansom was now 63 and had little appetite for university administration;
however, most routine tasks could be safely left to his assistant, Hugh Borton.
Freed from day-to-day duties Sansom had ample time for reflection and
research.

Despite his fragile health Sansom still continued his transatlantic journeys
and spent his summers at his home, Chandos Lodge at Eye in Suffolk. During
these stays he strengthened his friendships with British writers on Asia such
as Victor Purcell and Guy Wint, and consulted G. C. Allen on aspects of
Japan's social and economic history. In particular, Sansom was troubled by an
American tendency to apply the epithet 'feudal' to Tokugawa and modern
Japanese society. In a letter to G. C. Allen he wrote:

> I think you would agree that many of Japan's troubles which are now attrib-
> uted to feudal ideology, are in reality quite ordinary phenomena in a modern
> capitalist state, and may well in many cases represent a departure from feu-
> dal standards, thus being more Western than Eastern.[31]

Yet despite Sansom's advanced interpretation of Japan's economic development, he remained sceptical of American policies of democratization. He
saw democracy as an essentially Western phenomenon and in 1949 wrote of
the Japanese: 'Why . . . should it be expected that a people whose social and
political history has not prepared them for such a process, can be induced –

spontaneously and indigenously? – to depart from the own tradition by precept or even by example, offered by their conquerors?'[32]

Despite his obvious dislike of aspects of American thought and action Sansom found Columbia a sympathetic and creative environment. In 1950 he completed *The Western World and Japan*, his first major book since 1931. This not only analysed the history of Europe's impact on Japan from the sixteenth to the nineteenth century, but anticipated much later scholarship. Sansom's new work clearly focused on the theme of 'Westernization' or 'modernization', which was to preoccupy both American and Japanese scholars in the 1960s and 1970s.[33] Furthermore, Sansom's assertion that 'some at least of the causes that produced the industrial revolution had been operating . . . in parts of Asia, particularly Japan, long before the ships of the foreigners came to Japanese shores' unconsciously anticipated T. C. Smith's later analysis of the 'agrarian origins' of Japan's modern development.[34]

In October 1950 Sansom set off on his Far Eastern travels again. His first destination was Lucknow where he attended the Institute of Pacific Relations conference and met Prime Minister Nehru. Of greater interest was his subsequent visit to Japan where he met the Emperor and lectured at the University of Tokyo. These lectures, later published as *Japan in World History*, demonstrated a generosity of spirit which was rare among contemporary visitors to Japan. In contrast to many Occupation personnel Sansom showed a deep admiration for Japanese culture and scholarship which must have impressed his Japanese hosts. In his first lecture he declared: 'I have no right to pose . . . as an authority upon Japanese history and no foreigner can hope to achieve the depth of knowledge and understanding which we expect from Japanese scholars. . . . We must regard ourselves as pupils not as teachers.'[35] Yet more impressive was Sansom's emphasis on Japan's broad significance in 'the history of the aggregate of human societies' – particularly at a time when many Westerners saw Japanese as a uniquely delinquent people; of little relevance to the history of Western or Asian humanity.

Despite the beginnings of Japan's economic recovery, life in Tokyo in 1950 was still harsh and austere. Weakened by cold and discomfort Sansom succumbed to double pneumonia and was unable to leave Japan for several weeks. He finally returned to Suffolk after convalescing in the dry, warm climate of the American west.

Sansom remained at Columbia until his retirement in 1954. During these years he lectured *twice* each week to undergraduates and, with the support of the Rockefeller Foundation, embarked upon another major project, a three-volume *History of Japan*. For a man who was physically frail and already 71 this was a vast heroic enterprise.

At this time the cold and humidity of New York and Suffolk winters increasingly threatened Sansom's health and he sought a drier and milder refuge for his retirement. Fortunately, two friends from Singapore days now enabled him to settle in California. Two Australians, John Galvin and Stanley Smith, had worked with Sansom in 1942 and offered to build him a house on the campus of Stanford University. In this calm and exquisite setting Sansom was able to consult the Oriental Collection of the Hoover Institution, and meet distinguished Japanese scholars who were invited to Stanford. Among these was his old friend from the 1920s, Yashiro Yukio.

At Stanford Sansom confessed to being 'less given to enthusiasm, less capable of sustained effort and more cynical' than in earlier times, but within four years he completed the first volume of his new *History*.[36] Although Sansom made little use of post-war Marxist writing, he drew upon many original documents to describe the history and eclipse of the Heian Court. Even more striking was his fastidious account of Heian aesthetics and sensibilities, which was based upon a profound knowledge of literary sources.[37]

In preparing the second volume of his History, which analysed the years from 1334 to 1615, Sansom again drew upon many original sources as well as the knowledge of distinguished Japanese historians. For several months he worked 'at the same desk side by side' with Professor Toyoda Takeshi, and also corresponded with Fukui Rikichiro.[38] By 1961 the new volume was complete, and within four years Sansom published the third and final section of his *History*. Although John Whitney Hall regretted the 'modest proportions of this concluding volume he acclaimed it as the work of a 'master craftsman', which succeeded in 'capturing the interplay between the [Tokugawa] system and its enemies'.[39]

In these final productive years Sansom received a series of well-merited academic honours and distinctions. In 1954 Columbia awarded him the honorary degree of Doctor of Laws. Soon after he became Honorary Consulting Professor at Stanford. In the 1960s Mills College and Leeds University added further honorary degrees.

Sir George Sansom died on 8 March 1965 in Tucson, Arizona. His ashes were laid in a mountain canyon.

Sansom's greatest achievements were those of a historian who combined courage, humanity and scholarly refinement. As a diplomat he pioneered the serious study of the Japanese economy – when few Westerners understood its modernity or its crucial significance. Ironically, the achievements of this remarkable Englishman owe most to friends and institutions beyond the seas. Without John Galvin and Stanley Smith, Stanford and Columbia, his health and creativity would have been much impaired.

More recent works about Sir George Sansom include Ian Nish 'Sir George Sansom, Diplomat and Historian' in *Collected Writings of Ian Nish, Part II*, pp. 179–99, and Ian Nish, 'G. B. Sansom and his Tokyo Friends' in *Transactions of the Asiatic Society of Japan*, Vol 14 (1999), pp. 87–100.

26
Britain's Japan Consular Service, 1859–1941*

J. E. HOARE

Entrance to Tozenji temple, site
of Britain's first legation in Japan,
c. 1860

At the time of the 'opening' of Japan in the 1850s, Britain had three British Consular Services. A general service operated in most of the world, primarily for the protection of trade. It was the oldest and least organized service. Theoretically reformed in 1825, it was not held in esteem.[1] Better regarded was the Levant Service, covering parts of the Near and Middle East. Its origins, too, lay in trade but its officers also had political and judicial functions. Formally organized as a separate service only in 1877, its origins went further back, to the foundation of the Levant Company. The company was wound up in 1825 and its consular establishments passed to the crown. Its staff were systematically recruited, properly paid and exercised jurisdiction over their countrymen.[2]

By 1858, the China Consular Service resembled the Levant Service rather than the general service. Until the abolition of the East India Company's monopoly over China trade in 1834, Britain had left the protection of its citizens to the company. There followed a disorganized period until the 1842 Treaty of Nanking opened five ports for trade and residence, with a consulate at each. At first these posts were filled by anybody available, and no knowledge of Chinese was expected. Gradually, a professional Chinese-speaking service emerged. It was well-paid, and its members, unlike diplomats, were not expected to have a private income.[3] This was the model for the Japan Service.

THE EARLY YEARS

By 1858, the China Service had developed a structure which lasted until the 1940s. Candidates were recruited specifically for a career in China. Knowledge of Chinese was required for the conduct of business and in 1849, Palmerston laid down that this was essential for promotion.[4] After an initial group of recruits drawn from military and merchant backgrounds, the net was widened to include university graduates and others with a good education. By the late 1850s, the principle was accepted that outsiders would not fill senior positions; those who qualified as interpreters would fill such slots as they became available. As in the Levant Service, rules against trading were strictly enforced. There would be proper salaries and allowances during an officer's employment and a pension at the end.[5]

In 1854, in preparation for the opening of Japan, Clarendon, then Foreign Secretary, wrote to several university colleges seeking nominations. Those selected went to Hong Kong as 'supernumerary interpreters'. It is not clear if any of them took up appointments in Japan. Certainly none was ready in 1859.[6] Instead, the foreign secretary assigned A. J. Gower, private secretary to the Superintendent of Trade, Sir John Bowring, to Japan '. . . as I understand that during his employment . . . he has directed his attention to Japanese'.[7]

As in China, consular officers were to report to the senior diplomatic representative in the country. This was Rutherford Alcock, former consul at Canton. Sent out as consul general, he soon became envoy extraordinary and minister plenipotentiary, with detailed instructions on the management of the new service, and was enjoined to strict economy in selecting consular premises.[8] Salaries for the new service were relatively generous, though less than in China. The consul general would receive £1,800 (raised to £2000 in February 1860); consuls £800; vice consuls £750; interpreters £500; assistant interpreters £405 in Edo and £324 elsewhere; and student interpreters £200. Later, consuls received £1000. The posts were at Edo, a vice consul, an assistant, a Dutch interpreter and two students; Nagasaki, a consul and a Dutch interpreter; Hakodate, a consul and a Dutch interpreter; and Kanagawa (soon to be replaced by Yokohama), a consul and such staff as could be spared from Edo. Consular officers received free quarters, medical attention and, in the case of the single men, free messing.[9]

The earliest appointments were mixed. Some came from the China Service, others caught the attention of the Foreign Secretary. None was particularly well-qualified to live in the tense atmosphere of Japan. Within a few months, Alcock reprimanded G. S. Morrison, transferred from China to Nagasaki, for his behaviour to the Japanese authorities. Morrison was to retire early in 1864, angry at being passed over for promotion and convinced there was a plot to kill him at Nagasaki.[10] C. Pemberton Hodgson, consul first at Nagasaki and then at Hakodate, was also aggressive towards the Japanese, his servants and the British community, failed to keep accounts and drank heavily. He admitted that he was sometimes drunk, but said he was not always so, and claimed mitigating circumstances for his other faults. It was to no avail and he was dismissed.[11] Captain Vyse, consul at Kanagawa/Yokohama, was forced to resign in 1866, following the robbery of Ainu bones for 'scientific' purposes.[12]

There were also difficulties with interpreters and language training. Because the Dutch maintained a trading post at Nagasaki from the mid-seventeenth century, Dutch was the only Western language widely known in Japan. Britain, therefore, at first employed Dutch speakers in Japan. There was perhaps some optimism about the extent of knowledge of Dutch in Japan, but the use of Dutch was only a short-term measure until staff were trained in Japanese. Four Dutch interpreters were selected in London: A. Annesley, C. F. Myburgh, F. M. Cowan and Richard Eusden. Martin Dohmen, a supercargo on a Dutch ship, later joined them. Another Briton, J. J. Enslie, was appointed in 1861.

Cowan died in the autumn of 1860, Myburgh in 1869. The others stayed, even though it was obvious that officers who understood Japanese would be required. As early as 1861, Alex von Siebold, was employed as a supernumerary interpreter because he knew Japanese. Ernest Satow, joining the legation in 1862, found that Eusden, 'The Japan Secretary', knew not a word of Japanese, yet was supposed to provide language supervision for the students. This lasted until 1867, when a consular post was found for Eusden, and Satow himself took over as Japanese Secretary. The others served on. Enslie acquired sufficient Japanese to pass an oral examination in 1878. Annesley, denied promotion, eventually left, becoming consul at Reunion and then at Portland, Maine, before retiring in 1885. References to Dutch interpreters disappeared in 1872.[13]

Extraterritonality, provided for in the 1858 treaty, also brought problems. British subjects were to be tried under British law by British officials, an obligation Britain took seriously. At first Britain operated a system of consular jurisdiction. Consular officers had the power to try cases, with assessors drawn from the local community in more serious matters. Appeals were to the Minister. But often neither consul nor minister had legal training, and the result was botched cases. One remedy was to encourage consular officers to undergo legal training, but that took time. To improve matters, an Order in Council in 1865 replaced the British Minister as the supervising and appellate authority by a chief justice in Shanghai, with a judge at Yokohama. The British courts were now circuit courts under the control of the supreme court m Shanghai. Consular officers still lacked legal training, but they had a legally trained officer to whom they could apply for help, while appeals would be heard by a trained judge in Shanghai. The Order in Council also gave the British Minister law-making powers to meet situations not otherwise covered in British law.[14]

LANGUAGE TRAINING

Whatever A. J. Gower' s language abilities, they were no match for the reality of Japanese in practice. He was widely regarded as a good sort, but was no good at either running the Legation or learning Japanese. He retired in 1874 with everybody's good wishes.[15]

Language training was deemed vital to the Japan Service, but it was not systematically organized. Satow, recruited in 1861, was sent to China initially, since Alcock believed that knowledge of Chinese would help him to acquire Japanese. Urgent need cut short the experiment, and Satow, R. A. Jamieson and Russell Robertson set out for Japan in August 1862. Jamieson left at Shanghai to become a newspaperman. The other two went on to begin language training.[16] On arrival, they found that there were no arrangements for teaching them, Western books on Japanese were few, out of date and not easily obtained in Yokohama. There were no teachers, and no funds to pay for them. They had to devise their own methods of learning. At first they worked on their own, but were eventually allowed to employ an American missionary for two hours a week at public expense. A Japanese teacher was also provided at public expense. They paid for a second one themselves. The Japanese were in no sense qualified teachers, which created its own difficulties. There was also the problem of time for study. Satow had it in writing that his task was to learn Japanese, but his seniors in Japan shared the general view that the best training for those embarking on a diplomatic or consular career was to learn about current issues by copying. It took much effort to persuade them otherwise.[17]

They learnt spoken and written Japanese by puzzling out the language with books and a Japanese teacher, and Satow remained wedded to this method for the rest of his life.[18] By June 1863, he could provide an adequate translation of a Japanese document. (Robertson had gone home on health grounds, but resumed his studies later.) In 1865, on the recommendation of the new Minister, Sir Harry Parkes, he was appointed as 'Interpreter for the Japanese Language,' with a salary of £400 per annum, double that of a student, but less than the senior Dutch interpreter. Eusden finally moved in 1868. Satow became the Japanese Secretary, with a salary of £700, ranking with, but after, the diplomatic second secretaries. By then, he had a circle of Japanese friends and acquaintances who were to be useful in the years to come.[19]

The need to study Japanese was clear. Few Japanese had any knowledge of English, at least in the 1860s and 1870s, and the consular officers had to conduct business in the local language. Passing the interpreters' examination, and thus moving on to an assistant's post, however, was itself no easy task. It was never achieved in the two years allowed. Even though copying gave way to typewriters and carbon, to the end of the Japan Service, there were always other requirements which took the student interpreters away from their main task.[20] Yet, having passed the examination, officers were not required to requalify, and there was some concern that they would sit on their laurels or 'devote their leisure to dissipation and extravagance'.[21]

OTHER TRAINING

There was little attempt at other training. Officers learnt on the job. Copying was still seen as the best way to understand current issues. Concern was expressed in London in 1885 when it was found that the constables were doing it, rather than assistants. The Minister, Francis Plunkett, argued that it gave the constables something to do, and allowed assistants the time to keep up their Japanese.[22]

The exception to the general lack of training was that officers were encouraged to read for the bar. If the minister agreed, then an officer with five years' service was allowed an extra year's leave on full pay to qualify as a barrister. Several did so, including both Satow and Russell Robertson. But the acquisition of barrister status did not automatically result in promotion, and there was resentment and at least one resignation at this failure to reward hard work.[23]

THE ESTABLISHED SERVICE

Early recruitment was haphazard, but from 1862 onwards, more systematic arrangements were in operation. At first, Clarendon's practice of writing to selected schools and universities for nominations continued. Requirements for China and Japan, and later Siam, were similar, and candidates were recruited together until 1902. There were even occasional exchanges after the initial appointment.[24] From 1860 onwards, candidates were also certified as qualified by the Civil Service Commissioners.

From the late 1860s, nominations were no longer sought for recruitment. Instead, those who had enquired since the last examination were invited to

apply. In 1872, the specialist consular services were opened to all by adver-
tisement. This was eventually considered too egalitarian, and after 1907, it
was again necessary to secure the Secretary of State's nomination before taking the examination. Applicants had to be natural-born British subjects, of
good health and education, between 18 and 24 – or 29 if they were already
in the Foreign Office – and unmarried. They sat obligatory examinations in
English composition, arithmetic, French, Latin and law, and could offer
optional Italian, German and geography.[25]

This produced a standard of consular officers higher in ability and social
status than in the general service. A. B. Mitford said in 1870 that student
interpreters in China and Japan were of a higher class than 'dragomen' in the
Levant: '. . . young gentlemen who come out principally from the Irish universities'. Asked if they were of the same class as diplomatic attachés, Mitford
replied that they were not. The First Civil Service Commissioner put it more
gently in 1914. Recruits for the Far Eastern Services were like diplomats 'but
not so highly qualified'.[26] In fact, the social origins of entrants to the Japan
Service were firmly middle to upper class. Mitford's 'Irish universities' and
Irish schools were well represented. Many were sons of the clergy. Those from
Ireland included J. J. Quin, consul at Nagasaki; J. H. Longford, who was
another consul at Nagasaki and later became professor of Japanese at King's
College, London; J. C. Hall, consul general at Yokohama; W. G. Aston, who
like Satow acquired a considerable reputation as a scholar and became the
first consul general in Seoul; and H. S. Wilkinson, a noted lawyer. Those from
Scotland included L. W. Kuchler, appointed a student interpreter in 1878.[27]
Satow, educated at University College London, was the son of a merchant.
Russell Robertson, consul at Yokohama, was the son of Sir Daniel Brooke
Robertson, the first consul at Canton, and a friend of Parkes. Parkes's
nephews, H. P. and T. R. McClatchie, who joined respectively the China and
the Japan Services, were the sons of a missionary. J. H. Gubbins, another
scholar and the chief British negotiator of the 1894 revised treaty with Japan,
was a nephew of the Duchess of St Albans. His father had been in the Indian
Civil Service. E. M. Hobart Hampden, a student at Brasenose College, Oxford,
who joined in 1888, was also from an ICS background.[28]

THE WORK

After two years, students became assistants. There were three assistant grades,
at £300, £350 and £400 respectively. In addition, an allowance of £100 was
paid to up to six officers who had passed the interpreter's examination.
Parkes drew up a training scheme in 1870 under which third class assistants
spent one year at the court at Kanagawa (Yokohama), for legal training, and
one year at a consulate for practical experience.[29] In practice, assistants were
often called upon to do more advanced work before completing formal training. Henry Bonar found himself acting consul in 1882 with no legal training
and no previous consular experience.[30]

Office hours could be long, five or six hours a day minimum, and an assistant's lot was not exciting. Apart from the ubiquitous copying, there was
much translation. Parkes discouraged the Japanese from writing in English,
and it was not until his departure that such communications were generally
accepted. Plunkett, Parkes' successor, noted in 1885 that a first assistant kept
accounts, prepared despatches and letters to the Japanese authorities, kept

the land and other registers and undertook notarial acts. In addition, if the consul was absent, he acted as judge. The junior assistants looked after the Japanese-language archives, translated from Japanese, registered claims, and copied most of the outward letters and despatches.[31] Each assistant level took two to three years. An officer then become a vice-consul, or, if good at the language, assistant Japanese Secretary. Another three or four years would take him to consul. It was normally at least ten years before a man became consul. Some took longer, but periods as acting consul softened the blow of delayed promotion.[32]

There were two main strands of work. The best linguists went to the Japanese Secretariat in the legation. There, two or three officers were in charge of the Japanese language work of the Legation, and supervised the next generation of language students. Satow was the doyen of Japanese Secretaries, but successors included W. G. Aston and J. H. Gubbins, both also prominent scholars. For other officers, their normal career was as consular or judicial officers at the open ports or cities. After the opening of Hyogo (Kobe), Niigata, Osaka and Tokyo in 1868–9, no more Japanese ports or cities were opened to foreign trade or residence until after 1899. There were at first consulates at all the open ports and cities. British interests were small at Osaka and Tokyo, which were left to vice-consuls. They were non-existent at Niigata and after 1871 the British consulate functioned only occasionally. Hakodate, the most northerly of the treaty ports, was reduced to a vice-consulate in 1882.[33]

Work at the consular posts was straightforward. Notarial duties became heavier as the communities grew. But they were outweighed by the demands of the Merchant Shipping Acts. The signing on and off of crews played a big part in most consuls' lives. By 1879, there were some 15,000 seamen passing through Yokohama each year, and there were some 3000 residing ashore at any one time. The majority of these were British or on British ships. Yokohama was also a minor centre for shipbuilding, and therefore for registration.[34] Even Hakodate enjoyed a new lease of life in the 1890s, with the development of the pelagic seal trade. Henry Bonar noted in 1896 that 'The sealers have kept me busy morning noon and night.'[35]

Commercial work was also important, especially the provision of commercial information and the protection of merchants' rights. Consuls were not, however, expected to push specific British trade interests, nor to be advocates for a particular company or product. As late as 1914, the London Chamber of Commerce complained that it was still necessary to persuade consuls to abandon prejudices against supporting trade.[36] The provision of information was also not without difficulties. The main method was an annual consular report, which was then published in a regular series. According to the treaty port press, most British merchants found the Japan reports lacking. In 1880, the Japan Gazette said that the Hakodate report was late and that, instead of an incisive analysis of trade, '. . . we are treated to lengthy dissertations upon the disastrous fires . . . [at] Hakodate, written in terms which would have been appropriate [from] . . . a cheerful old lady addressing friends at home . . .'[37] The *Japan Mail* defended the reports, arguing that they were prepared by people with considerable knowledge. But even it felt that they were too stereotyped to be of real use.[38] In due course, a new attitude began to develop towards trade promotion and consuls became more willing to identify market opportunities.

Most important was the legal work. The courts handled large numbers of cases; even at the end of the 1860s, Yokohama handled two to three hundred legal cases a year, and even a small post might have twenty or so. Theoretically, all were handled by men with legal training. Britain, alone of all the countries operating extraterritoriality, tried to make reality match the ideal. Joseph Longford, a former consul, claimed that 'no crime committed by a British subject in Japan ever failed to be visited with its proper legal penalty . . . nor did any civil claim against a British subject ever fail to be equitably adjudicated', and Satow said much the same in private.[39] But the 'exigencies of the services meant that consular officers had to act in legal proceedings without training or experience. Satow, knowing neither how to register a birth nor to conduct a case, was a consular officer, and found himself filling an unexpected gap at Tokyo.[40] The Chief Justice at Shanghai put it to Clarendon that it was as if 'your lordship insisted upon appointing me chief surgeon to a London hospital'.[41]

Not surprisingly, there were criticisms over poor judgements which continued to the very end of extraterritoriality.[42] Yet the system worked and there were few serious mistakes. Even at the end, the British arrangements were working well. Japanese objections to extraterritoriality hinged on the basic unfairness of the system, rather than to individual miscarriages of justice.[43]

CONDITIONS OF SERVICE

Salaries remained at the 1859 levels, supplemented by allowances. Some allowances stopped when an officer went on leave. Housing was supplied, or an allowance in lieu, but not furniture until the twentieth century, and staff suffered losses each time they moved. Housing was a mixed blessing. The Yokohama consulate surpassed the Shanghai club for the title of the ugliest building in the east, while the Nagasaki consul's house was uninhabitable in 1885. Although the wells were tainted, the Treasury refused to pay for the piped water for the Yokohama consulate. Houses were hot in summer, cold in winter.[44]

To casual visitors, Japan seemed cheap. But living in European style was not, and the salaries of the Japan Service remained lower than those in China.[45] The need to import many goods, the small market for Western-style foodstuffs and other items made Japan expensive. It was argued that servants were essential. Insurance was difficult to obtain – impossible at Hakodate in the 1870s – and costly when it came. Health care was not cheap. Children had to be sent home for schooling at an officer's expense; local schools were thought unsuitable for European children.[46] Leave, especially local leave, was difficult to arrange. The total number of officers available was about 25, and frequent absences on sick leave reduced the pool. Officers had to wait seven years for home leave, and that, too, was often postponed. Before 1874, fares were not paid. Thereafter, officers received half fare, dependants a third. Full salary was paid for the first month; thereafter, officers were on half salary. Inevitably, those on leave from Japan spent most of it on half salary and there were occasionally protests. J. C. Hall, unable to take home leave for 16 years, persuaded the Treasury in 1907 that half pay was not fair in such circumstances. He received an ungenerous five-eighths salary for part of his leave.[47]

Japan was a difficult place to live, and not just in the early years. It was remote and there was the constant fear of assassination. Morrison was not the only man to feel threatened, though most coped better. Russell

Robertson's marriage broke down because of his wife's drinking.[48] Even when assassinations ceased in the early 1870s, there were other strains. Hakodate and Niigata were remote and ships were few and far between. Local communities were small and faction ridden, and there was a widespread sense of claustrophobia. Consular officers found themselves the targets of local jealousies and tensions, to which they sometimes contributed.[49] There was much sickness and a number of officers and family members died prematurely – four officers and a wife, for example, between 1866 and 1869. Others died soon after retirement. There were also mental breakdowns. Kobe (Hyogo), Nagasaki, Niigata and Yokohama were all counted as unhealthy posts, and attracted added years for superannuation purposes. Most officers left well before the official retiring age of 70 – later 65 – with few questions asked about the medical reasons offered.[50]

THE TWENTIETH CENTURY

In 1899, when extraterritoriality ended, the Japan Consular Service was forty years old. It was to survive another forty. When Britain first considered treaty revision in the early 1880s, it was assumed that eventually British consular officers in Japan would become general service officers. But while such views found occasional echoes in subsequent years, nothing happened.[51]

Language training continued to dominate. Although as early as 1910, the Japanese Secretary argued for better teachers, new recruits found that they were left without guidance and expected to teach the teachers how to teach, just as in the 1860s. Satow, in retirement, argued that there was no other way, as did George Sansom, the commercial counsellor, and W. B. Cunningham, the Japanese Secretary, in 1933. London thought this was complacent. It was true that the language skills of many in the service attracted praise and ambassadors argued the need to keep up both the supply of students and the high standards. Officers such as Colin Davidson and Sansom were widely admired for excellent Japanese. Yet others found difficulty in meeting the standards. Esler Dening had not passed the examination after ten years. Not all kept up the language after qualifying. No new system had been devised by 1941 and nobody drew any lesson from the fact that British language students, after four years, were failing to reach a standard others did in two.[52]

After 1900, additional posts were added to the Japan Service. The process began with the Sino-Japanese War of 1894-95, and Japan's acquisition of Taiwan, where Britain had a consulate at Tamsui. Dalian (Dairen) in the Liaotung peninsula was added in 1905, and Seoul and Chemulpo in 1910. Manila (1903) and Honolulu (1904) were also added to the Japan Service, partly to improve career prospects. They were nevertheless something of a mixed blessing. It was not easy to keep up Japanese in either, and different terms of service applied. One new post in Japan was Shimonoseki, opened in 1901.[53]

The cost of living went up steadily after the Sino-Japanese War. Salaries, however, essentially remained the same, though a system of local and occasional *ad hoc* allowances made things easier. Eventually, in 1913, Edward Crowe, the commercial attache, prepared the case for across the board increases. The Treasury was not happy, arguing that some posts had received additional allowances as recently as 1912, but in the end accepted the arguments. The increases were nowhere spectacular – the Japanese Secretary got

£100, the Yokohama consul general £50, while Manila and Honolulu received nothing – but were nevertheless welcomed.[54] Another grievance was the steady build up of a promotion blockage. Officers still retired early, on health and other grounds, as in the past. But there was also a core of relatively young or apparently immovable senior officers, and by 1913, the ten years minimum of the 1880s had become fifteen years.[55]

The First World War intensified such problems. Leave could not be taken. Some officers left to join the forces, and others were detached for long periods of war work. One resigned because of a German family background. Recruitment stopped. The cost of living soared. Maintenance and construction work halted, even on essential works such as lavatories at Shimonoseki. When peace returned, it took much effort to prise staff out of their wartime slots, and some never returned. Cost-of-living claims and salary increases had to take their turn with those from elsewhere. Recruiting proved particularly difficult. An approach to the War Office failed to produce a single recruit, and it was decided that the universities might produce a better response.[56]

The immediate crisis passed, but the basic problems remained. Promotion continued to be slow. Staff shortages meant posts were left empty or seriously undermanned. Seoul suffered particularly badly.[57] As in the past, pressure took its toll in mental illness, drink and premature retirement. Economic constraints in the 1920s and 1930s hit hard, both in reductions in salaries and in the poor physical environment in which staff worked. The consular premises at Yokohama, destroyed in the 1923 earthquake, were not rebuilt until the late 1920s, and the consular residence not until 1937. There were long delays in providing new accommodation in Tokyo after 1923. At Kobe, the poor state of the consulate was a standing joke. There were battles over minor improvements such as telephones, electric fans and other amenities. Officers in Japan looked with longing eyes on China, where the number of posts seemed to expand and the rewards were high, or on the general service, where promotion seemed faster and more assured. London argued that such impressions were false, but they remained. The Japan Service seemed to be creaking to a halt.[58]

It was not alone. Similar problems existed in all the specialized services. A series of reports and committees in the 1920s and early 1930s concluded that the solution was amalgamation, a decision implemented in 1932. China remained outside the amalgamated service, because of the continued existence of extraterritoriality. Elsewhere, after 1934, all consular staff would be recruited to one service. These arrangements had barely begun to produce results when a new war threw everything into chaos.[59]

When peace returned, there were many changes. The Diplomatic and Consular Services were combined in 1943. Japan was under occupation for several years. In 1952, when it regained its independence, consular posts were re-opened at Tokyo, Yokohama and Osaka, but staffed on a new basis. Many former members of the Japan Consular Service enjoyed successful careers in the amalgamated service, some in Japan. In retrospect, the Service's high reputation for linguistic skills and Japanese scholarship owed more to a few bright stars than to the mass of its members. What killed it, however, was not lack of talent, but the problems of managing a small, highly specialized cadre in a rapidly changing world.

APPENDIXES

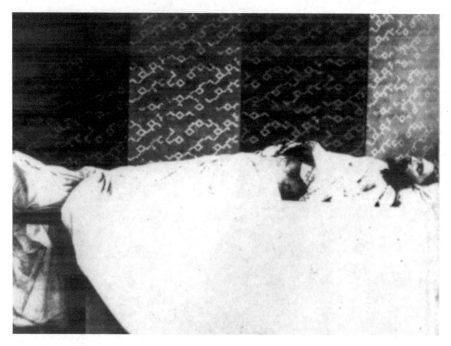

'The body of Mr Richardson', September 1862

The British Bombardment of Kagoshima, 1863
Admiral Sir L. Kuper and Lt Colonel Neale

SIR HUGH CORTAZZI

Admiral Sir L. Kuper

Admiral Sir Augustus Leopold Kuper (1809–85),[1] whose ancestry was German, joined the Royal Navy in 1823. In 1841 he was promoted to Captain and was engaged during the first China war (1840–2) including the operations which led up to the capitulation of Canton. In 1842 he was made a Companion of the Bath (CB). In 1861 he was promoted to Rear-Admiral and in 1862 he succeeded Admiral Sir James Hope as Commander-in-Chief, East Indies and China. In 1864 he was in command of the British fleet involved in the steps taken to reopen the Inland Sea and the Straits of Shimonoseki. Kuper was made a Knight of the Bath (KCB) in 1864 'in acknowledgement of his services at Kagoshima'. He was in due course made a GCB and promoted to the rank of Admiral.

PREPARATIONS

Although the actual attack did not take place until August 1863 Lt Colonel Edward St John Neale, the British Chargé d'Affaires in Japan, prepared in April that year a letter to 'the Prince of Satsuma' i.e. the daimyo, setting out the British demands for reparation for the murder of Charles Lennox Richardson and the injuries sustained by Woodthorp Clarke and William Marshall at Namamugi on the Tōkaidō near Yokohama on 14 September 1862 as a result of an attack on them by retainers of Shimazu Hisamitsu of Satsuma, father of the daimyo and the leading figure in Satsuma. Neale, after setting out the facts, declared that 'This event filled with great and just indignation the British Government and people'. He had exercised 'forbearance' in not taking immediate military action and left it to the Tycoon's Government to arrest and punish the murderer. The 'orders and decrees' of the Japanese Government had been disregarded by the Satsuma authorities. The culprits had not been arrested and no redress had been obtained. He was demanding an apology from the Tycoon's government and the payment of a considerable penalty for permitting the murderous attack by Satsuma retainers on British subjects. The British Government had also decided to make direct demands on the Prince for the immediate trial and capital execution in the presence of one or more naval officers of the chief perpetrators of the assault and the payment of 25,000 pounds sterling to be distributed to the relations of the murdered man and to those who had escaped death. Neale went on to declare that if these demands were not immediately met 'the Admiral commanding British forces in these seas will adopt such coercive measures, as he may deem expedient, to obtain the required satisfaction and redress'. This letter was to be delivered by the commander of a British ship sent to Kagoshima. In fact, it was only delivered after the British fleet reached Kagoshima on 11 August 1863 and was redated 1 August 1863.

Before Admiral Kuper's fleet left Yokohama for Kagoshima Neale[2] told the *Bakufu* of the British intentions. He was promptly asked in writing to postpone the project. This letter was followed by a visit from a Vice-Minister who, however, instead of using further arguments against the project told Neale that the *Bakufu* proposed to send a steamer with a senior official on board to accompany the fleet. However no steamer appeared.[3]

NEGOTIATIONS AT KAGOSHIMA

The British fleet, which consisted of Her Majesty's Ships *Euryalus* (screw, frigate, 35 guns) *Pearl* (screw corvette, 21 guns), *Perseus* (screw sloop, 6 guns), *Argus* (paddle, sloop, 6 guns), *Coquette* (screw, gun vessel, 4 guns), *Racehorse* (screw, gun vessel, 3 guns), and *Havoc* (screw, gun vessel, 2 guns), left Yokohama on 6 August 1863. Neale, who was accommodated on Kuper's flagship *Euryalus*, was accompanied by most of the members of the Legation, whose 'more or less proficiency in the Japanese language'[4] was thought and proved to be 'highly useful'. They were divided between the various ships.

The fleet, 'under easy steam and sail' reached Kagoshima on 11 August and anchored in deep-water. Early the following morning a boat with two officials came alongside and asked a number of questions about the fleet and its intentions. A few hours later the squadron moved further into the bay and 'cast anchor off the batteries of the town'. A second boat then approached and asked about a letter which Neale was reported to have addressed to the daimyo. They were handed the letter described above with a supplementary letter announcing the Admiral's arrival and Neale's own presence on board. These letters were taken on shore and a few hours later the Satsuma officials informed Neale that the daimyo was not in Kagoshima but 'at a residence about fifty miles distant'. They requested that Admiral Kuper and Neale should go on shore 'where a building for the reception of foreigners' had been especially arranged for the interview. 'Great anxiety was evinced that we should accede to this proposal; and they urged that it would be impossible to commit to writing all that might be discussed.' Kuper and Neale replied that the only business, which had brought them to Kagoshima, had been fully set forth in the letter, which had been already handed over, and declined to go on shore. 'The officials departed much disconcerted.' Neale and Kuper assumed that 'treachery and violence' would have followed if they had acceded to the Satsuma demands.

On 13 August several Satsuma officials, including one of 'superior rank', came alongside the flagship. They were accompanied by 'numerous two-sworded adherents[5] in several boats'. A long parley ensued in which they sought Neale's agreement to receive the 'high official' and asked that he should be accompanied by at least forty of his adherents. The Admiral agreed to this, but instructed a guard of marines with fixed bayonets to stand facing the gangway. When the Satsuma retainers came aboard they were disposed in single file along the line of guns. The high official then came on board and was received by Neale accompanied by the Admiral. 'He exhibited the utmost agitation and confusion; he was speechless.' One of his attendants then stated that the high official was charged to speak for his chief and was bearing a written reply to Neale's letter, but they 'had some serious matters to add'. Hardly had the meeting begun than a boat, waving a flag, reached the ship and a message passed to the Satsuma official. He informed Neale that a mistake had been made in the written reply from the Satsuma authorities which must be rectified and he hurriedly left the flagship.

Meanwhile, the batteries on shore, which were constantly manned and within range, had their guns pointed at the ships in the fleet, especially at the flagship. The Admiral decided to shift the anchorage of the squadron 'to as convenient a position, though still partially within range, as the extreme depth of the water would admit'.

To Neale's surprise the high official returned to the ship late in the evening and delivered the reply from the Satsuma authorities. The letter, signed by Kawakami Tajima, Minister of the Prince of Satsuma, began with a conciliatory statement that 'It is just that a man who has killed another should be arrested and punished by death, as there is nothing more sacred than human life'. They had endeavoured to secure the murderers, but it had been impossible to do so 'owing to the political differences at present existing between the Daimios of Japan, some of whom even hide and protect such people'. The murders were not ordered by Shimazu Hisamitsu and if offenders could be detected and after examination found guilty they would be punished and British naval commanders would be informed so that they could witness the execution of the culprits. After noting that the provincial authorities were subordinate to the government in Edo the reply disingenuously, stated: 'We have heard something about a Treaty having been negotiated in which a certain limit was assigned to foreigners to move about in; but we have not heard of any stipulation by which they are authorized to impede the passage of a road.'

The next paragraph not only showed total ignorance of the position in foreign countries but was bound to infuriate Neale: 'Supposing this happened in your country, travelling with a large number of retainers as we do here, would you not chastise (push out of the way and beat) anyone thus disregarding and breaking the laws of the country? If this were neglected Princes could no longer travel.' 'The insufficiency' of the government in Edo 'is shown by their neglecting to insert in the Treaty (with foreigners) the laws of the country (in respect of these matters) which have existed from ancient times.' 'To decide on this important matter' a high official of the government in Edo and of the British government 'ought to discuss it before you, and find out who is in the right. After the above question has thus been judged and settled, the money indemnity shall be arranged. We have not received from the Tycoon any

'The bombardment of Kagoshima.' *The Illustrated London News*, Nov. 7, 1863

orders or communications by steamer that your men-of-war were coming here.' The reply also declared that 'Our Government acts in everything according to the orders' of the government in Edo.

Neale, when he saw the translation, deemed it 'utterly unsatisfactory'. He and the Admiral were highly suspicious of Satsuma behaviour. They feared that the retainers of the daimyo might attempt to take over the flagship. The Admiral was no doubt also unwilling to delay action for long while time-wasting arguments were exchanged. Neale accordingly[6] requested the Admiral 'to enter upon such measures of coercion, by reprisals or otherwise, as you may deem expedient and best calculated to awaken the Prince of Satsuma to a sense of the serious nature of the determinations which have brought Her Majesty's squadron to this anchorage.'

THE NAVAL ACTION

Kuper recorded[7] on 17 August 1863 the action which he had taken in response to Neale's request. He had immediately directed Captain Borlase of HMS *Pearl* to proceed with part of the squadron to a bay to the north of Kagoshima, seize three steamers[8] there belonging to the Prince and bring them to the squadron's anchorage. Borlase was to 'avoid, as much as possible, all unnecessary bloodshed or active hostility'. This service was 'executed with much zeal and discretion by Captain Borlase' and the three steamers arrived in the forenoon at the anchorage lashed alongside three of HM ships. However, at noon the Japanese batteries opened fire with shot and shell. 'In vindication of the honour of the flag, and as a punishment for the outrage' the fire was returned, but as the squadron's operations were hampered by the three Japanese steamers Kuper ordered that they should be set on fire and destroyed. Kuper went on:

> The squadron, then as you are aware, proceeded to engage the batteries on Kagoshima, advancing in line of battle (the *Euryalus*[9] leading) from the northernmost battery, along the whole line, and finally attacking the southernmost or spit battery,[10] after which I deemed it advisable, in order to ensure the safety of Her Majesty's ships, to direct them to seek an anchorage; the weather, which had been threatening for a gale, becoming at this time most unfavourable, and, as night was approaching, the signal was made to discontinue the action, and the squadron returned to an anchorage under Sakurajima.
>
> It was impossible to ascertain precisely the extent of the injury inflicted upon the batteries; but considering the heavy fire which was kept up from the ships, at point blank range, the effect must have been considerable, many guns were observed to be dismounted, the batteries were several times cleared, and the explosions of various magazines gave evidence of the destructive effects of our shell; one half of the town was in flames and entirely destroyed, as well as a very extensive arsenal or factory, and gun-foundry, and five large Loo-Choo [Ryūkyū] junks, the property of the Prince, in addition to the three steamers already described.
>
> A heavy typhoon blew during the night, and the conflagration increasing in proportion to the height of the storm, illuminated the entire bay.

On the following afternoon, the gale having moderated, Kuper decided to move the squadron to a safer anchorage, having observed the Japanese at work erecting batteries on the hill above the little bay where the small vessels were at anchor. They weighed anchor and 'passing in line between the batteries of Kagoshima, steamed out and anchored to the southward of the Island'. They took the opportunity to shell the batteries on Sakurajima and also the daimyo's palace which Kuper thought had been destroyed. The fire in the town of Kagoshima was still burning[11] and he believed that 'the entire town of Kagoshima is now a mass of ruins'.

Kuper having received from Neale an expression of his satisfaction with the extent of these operations proposed to return with the squadron, 'immediately the partial refit which is now in progress shall admit of our putting to sea'. These final words in Kuper's letter to Neale indicated the damage and casualties which Kuper's squadron had suffered as a result of firing from Satsuma batteries.

An account of the battle, based largely on Kuper's despatches to the Admiralty is contained in an essay, which also covers the bombardment of Shimonoseki in 1864, entitled 'The Long Arm of Seapower: The Anglo-Japanese War of 1863–64' by Colin White.[12] The British casualties were high for what was a minor operation involving so few ships. 'The final list was eleven killed and fifty-two wounded, of whom two later died of their wounds.' Kuper's flagship the *Euryalus* was damaged and Kuper was lucky not to have become a casualty himself. 'A roundshot killed Captain John Josling and Commander Edward Wilmot[13] as they stood behind Kuper on the bridge; a shell exploded in the gun port of No. 3 Gun on the main deck, killing seven men outright and wounding a further twelve. The starboard boom boats . . . were destroyed by another shell, sending up a shower of lethal wooden splinters which killed two men and wounded four more. Finally, and possibly worst of all because of its effect on morale, the breech-loading Armstrong gun[14] on the forecastle blew out its breech piece, knocking down its entire crew and concussing them severely.' Other ships were also damaged. The *Racehorse*'s engines failed and in the strong winds drifted on to the shore 'under the guns of the "North Fort". Luckily, the fort had suffered the most from the concentrated fire of the heavier ships and so was almost silenced but even so, the *Argus* – which together with *Coquette* came to the rescue of their consort – lost her mainmast before finally at 6.00 p.m., the *Racehorse* was refloated.' Only the *Havoc* escaped completely without loss.

According to Colin White:

> Tactically, the battle was also open to much criticism. The British squadron had been caught unprepared, which was inexcusable in view of the mounting tension of the previous three days. It is obvious that Kuper had not formulated any proper form of attack, since his ships simply scrambled into action in order of seniority. This left the smaller and weaker vessels at the end of the line, where they would be very exposed if any accident occurred – as happened in the case of the *Racehorse*. The ships had also gone in too close to the batteries.

Colin White was also critical of the fact that it took nearly two hours for the squadron to form line of battle and clear for action. 'Such a long wait at such a crucial moment seems inexcusable.'

'Kuper realised how close to failure he had come. He had been greatly shocked by the heavy loss of life and especially by the deaths of Josling and Wilmot.' 'The Kagoshima batteries were not permanently disabled, merely temporarily silenced by the deaths of their gun crews.' From this he learnt an important lesson, which he bore in mind during the attack on Shimonoseki in 1864, that 'bombardment had to be supported by a landing in force.'[xv]

Graphic accounts of the bombardment of Kagoshima were given by Satow[16] and Willis.[17] Pictures of the battle in the form of engravings were included in *The Illustrated London News*.[18] Satow noted that two prisoners from the *Sir George Grey* transferred to the *Euryalus* were two Satsuma men who were to become famous in the Meiji era. One was Godai Tomoatsu, a businessman,the other was Matsuki Kōan, who was later known as Terajima Munenori and who became Minister in London and Foreign Minister. Satow thought that 'differences had arisen' between Neale and Kuper, 'the former of whom interfered too much with the conduct of the operations. No doubt the etiquette was for him to remain silent after he had placed matters in the hands of the Admiral, but this the impetuosity of his nature would not permit him to do.'

A JAPANESE VIEW

A report[19] on the bombardment from a Japanese point of view by a Commander Okuda, a Satsuma man who had been present in Kagoshima at the time of the attack, provides some interesting further facts and comments. When on 11 August 1863 the alarm was given in Kagoshima, the batteries were manned and ammunition supplied, 'as prearranged'. The Satsuma Headquarters were at Sengeji temple at Nishida. The Satsuma commander was Komatsu Tatewaki and Okubo (Ichizō, later known as Toshimichi) was the officer in attendance on the daimyo. The senior staff officers were Orita Heihachi, Ichiji Masaharu and Oyama Tsunayoshi. Other Satsuma men who later achieved eminence in the Meiji era and who were part of the Satsuma defending forces included Itō Shirozaemon and Tōgō Heihachirō; both later became Admirals of the Fleet. Saigō Takamori (Kichinosuke) was not present as he was still in exile. The batteries consisted of 87 guns. The envoys sent to Admiral Kuper's flagship were Orita Heihachi and Ichiji Masaharu, described as 'War Councillors'.

Commander Okuda notes that the Satsuma envoy knew that the Shimazu Prince would not accept the British demand, but 'feigning ignorance of his master's intentions' said, 'As the daimyo is now at the hot-springs of Kirishima, and communications with him will take several days, I am afraid that your [Neale's] desire cannot be complied with.' 'The daimyo considering the demands both to be unjust and unreasonable, preferred to fight rather than accede. He repeatedly asked the minister and others to come ashore, but the Minister [i.e. Neale], knowing the hot-tempered men of Satsuma and thinking that the matter could not be settled by negotiations, prudently remained on board.' The Satsuma samurai 'became excited and furious . . . and decided on this stratagem:

> As a forlorn hope 73 desperate men[20] were to go off in boats, disguising themselves as tradesmen and taking with them in the boats eggs and vegetables as if for sale; they were to divide themselves into 7 parties, each party going in one boat, and each boat to go alongside one British ship respectively. When on board they were at a given signal previously arranged to all simultaneously draw their swords and slay the British officers and men.

Thereupon the coast batteries were to open fire, thus forts and boarding parties working together the British ships would be captured.

The British ships, apart from the *Euryalus*, 'suspecting them', refused to allow them on board. 'The *Euryalus* allowed a few men to come on board but these few were so closely watched, they could do nothing.'
According to Commander Okuda: 'The daimyo prohibited any rash action on the part of his hot-tempered Samurai, and ordered them not to commence battle until the order was given.' When the order was finally given the Tempōzan fort was the first to fire. 'It was not the British squadron which took the initiative but the Japanese. The British fleet was taken by surprise but did their best under the circumstances. The weather became worse, the air was misty and a heavy sea was running.' The *Perseus* suddenly coming under fire, in much confusion, 'slipped her cables and left her anchors, then came into battle formation with the remainder. The Japanese Samurai when they saw her do that all laughed heartily.'
Commenting on the battle Okuda wrote:

> The fort itself was hit by many projectiles, as nearly all the guns were put out of action, the gun's crews lay down on the ground, not to escape the hail of shot, but, thinking that the bluejackets of the *Racehorse* would land and storm the fort, they intended to remain hidden and then suddenly rush out and slay the Englishmen.

But no landing was made and the *Racehorse* was towed out of danger.
Commander Okuda declared that 'The Casualties of the Satsuma force were only one man killed and six wounded.[21] The British suffered an undreamt of defeat. Their defeat may have been partially due to the storm, which made the manoeuvring of the fleet difficult, but was also due to the bravery and valour of the Samurai of Satsuma.'[22]

REACTIONS IN LONDON

When reports of the bombardment and the destruction of Kagoshima were received in London the attack was sharply criticized in Parliament. Satow[23] noted that 'The Admiral in his report, which was published in *The London Gazette*, took credit for the destruction of the town, and Mr Bright[24] very properly called attention to this unnecessary act of severity in the House of Commons; whereupon he wrote again, or Colonel Neale wrote, to explain that the conflagration was accidental. But that I cannot think was a correct representation of what took place, in face of the fact the *Perseus* continued to fire rockets into the town after the engagement with the batteries was at an end, and it is also inconsistent with the air of satisfaction which marks the despatch reporting that £1,000,000 worth of property had been destroyed during the bombardment.' Grace Fox[25] records that although Neale had expressed his regrets over the destruction of the Satsuma capital and the Queen's speech at the opening of Parliament had reported the Queen's 'regret' that the coercive measures needed to bring Satsuma to terms had 'led incidentally to the Destruction of a considerable Portion of the Town of Kagoshima', Kuper's action was hotly debated in the House of Commons. Charles Buxton, the member for Maidstone 1859–65, introduced a motion, 'That this House, while only imputing to Admiral Kuper a misconception of the duty imposed on him, regrets the burning of the town of Kagoshima, as being contrary to those usages of war which prevail among civilized nations and to which it is the duty and policy of this country to adhere.' Grace Fox noted that: 'in tearful tones he [Buxton] pictured the seven British men-of-war throwing shells broadcast into a city of 180,000 people and the consequent suffering of women and children, the aged and the infirm. Lengthy indictments of all British policy in Japan followed.'

Other members,[26] however, 'maintained that the slaughter of Englishmen could not be ignored. Britain had to prove her power to exact reparation for injustice in order that Japan should treat her with justice.' Palmerston, who was Prime Minister while Russell was Foreign Secretary, intervened to declare that the 'entire government . . . approved Russell's instructions and Kuper's fulfilment of them. The destruction of the town was incidental to the action of the Japanese batteries in a violent gale. Regrets had been expressed.' At the conclusion of the debate the motion was withdrawn, but *The Quarterly Review*[27] was highly critical of 'English foreign policy towards the weakest powers. In principle it is overbearing, exacting, pushing every right to the extremest limit, and where the very existence of a right is doubtful, cynically throwing the sword in the balance. In execution these principles are carried out with no diplomatic courtesy; and with no consideration of the feelings or the wounded honour of those to whom they are applied, but rather with ostentatious insolence.' This theme was taken up by Richard Cobden[28] who was a stern critic of British sabre-rattling under Palmerston. 'Booklets and pamphlets burned with indignation based on ill-founded facts.' Neale, attempting to correct misconceptions, explained in a letter read to the House of Commons on 14 March 1864 that the population of Kagoshima had never exceeded 40,000 and that the citizens of the town had withdrawn before the British attack.[29] Neale, noting that Satsuma had since voluntarily paid the indemnity (see below), believed that 'the agents of Her Majesty displayed a degree of caution and moderation duly appreciated by those most deeply interested.'

AFTERMATH

On 9 December 1863, envoys from Satsuma who called on Neale[30] in Yokohama suggested to him that the 'money which they were about to pay . . . should be considered in the light of a deposit, the absolute payment of which might take place hereafter . . . These obstacles and objections, pertinaciously urged during some hours, were utterly rejected by me, and as good-humouredly one by one abandoned by the Envoys. The indemnity money was brought to the Legation and the sum of 100,000 dollars duly paid, that sum being the equivalent of 25,000 pounds sterling at the current rate of exchange.' While the money was being counted Neale 'received from the Envoys a written engagement[31] in respect of the pursuit, and execution when arrested, of the principal murderers of Mr Richardson'. This document was 'countersigned by two of the Tycoon's officers as attesting witnesses. The agents of Satsuma now expressed a desire that I should furnish them with a written promise to facilitate the purchase of a ship of war in England. I saw no material objection to this . . . and I accordingly furnished them with a memorandum . . .' Neale thus felt able to 'report the final accomplishment of my instructions.' He could 'not resist the expression of the satisfaction I have derived at the accomplishment of my unabating endeavours to avert even a partial or momentary cessation of our commercial relations with Japan throughout these difficulties'.

Soon after the Satsuma envoys had departed Neale 'received a congratulatory despatch from the Tycoon's Ministers, accompanied by words of goodwill and promises for the future. Neale remained doubtful about how far these promises could be relied on, but 'the knowledge that a military force within certain limits had been rendered available' to him and 'the presence of the squadron sufficiently ensures the communities against all dangers of violence'.

ASSESSMENT

Grace Fox[32] recorded that the instructions given to Neale for reparations were not drawn up solely by Russell and the Foreign Office:

> Queen Victoria, herself, fully aware that war with Japan could result from British action, insisted that 'the opinion of the whole cabinet be ascertained before the country is committed to demand a reparation which the Government of Japan have no power to enforce.' The resulting consensus seems to have followed Alcock's[33] advice and the opinion of the Duke of Somerset, then First Lord of the Admiralty: Britain should punish the daimyo who were hostile to foreigners, especially Satsuma, to whom Richardson's assassins belonged; his port should be blockaded and his capital probably shelled. Thus he and his people could be embarrassed without any general interference with British-Japanese trade. If the central government was weak and unable to afford Britain redress, it was Britain's responsibility to convince these daimyo that they must suffer personally for their misdeeds. The cabinet advised a short operation which would concentrate the attack on Satsuma, 'disclaiming any hostility to the nation, but even, all things considered, to the State.'

Palmerston, as Prime Minister, was thus forced to be more restrained than he was on other occasions when he was Foreign Secretary. British 'gun-boat' diplomacy would not be acceptable today, but in those days, with no United Nations and a Japanese government incapable of ensuring the maintenance of order and the safety of foreign residents, British opinion in Victorian times would have demanded some firm action, but was the action taken commensurate and effective?

Kuper cannot escape censure for the way in which the operation against Satsuma was handled. The British suffered a serious loss of life and damage to RN ships.[34] Kagoshima was destroyed partly by British fire (the strong winds caused the *Euryalus* to rock and as a consequence the guns often fired low) but Satsuma casualties had been limited. Satsuma, which claimed a victory, quickly recognized that they could gain more from friendship than from enmity with Britain. So the *Satsuei sensō* (war between Satsuma and Britain) led to British friendship with Satsuma.

As Commander Okuda's report shows Neale was right to be suspicious of Satsuma intentions. He was on the whole restrained and his firmness paid off in the end.

Appendix II

The Naval and Military Action at Shimonoseki

SIR HUGH CORTAZZI

Vice Admiral Sir A. Kuper reported[1] on the action from his flagship HMS *Euryalus* in the Straits of Shimonoseki on 15 September 1864. The allied fleet, which amounted to a formidable force, consisted of:

British (all wooden ships): *Euryalus* (screw frigate, 35 guns), *Tartar* (screw corvette 14 x 8inch guns 4 x 40 pounders), *Conqueror* (2nd rate battleship, screw, 40 guns), *Barrosa* (screw, corvette, 21 guns), *Leopard* (paddle, frigate, 18 guns) *Argus* (paddle sloop, 6 guns), *Perseus* (screw sloop 6 guns), which had joined the fleet at the entrance to the Bungo channel towing a large collier from Shanghai, *Coquette* (screw, gun vessel, 4 guns), which had joined the fleet from Nagasaki, *Bouncer* (screw, gunboat, 2 guns) and a battalion of Royal Marines.

French: *Semiramis* (screw, 35 guns, flagship of Rear-Admiral Jaurès), *Dupleix* (screw, 10 guns), *Tancrède* (screw, 4 guns), despatch vessel.

Dutch: *Metalen Kruis* (screw, 16 guns, senior officer's ship). *D'Jambi* (screw, 16 guns), *Amsterdam* (paddle, 8 guns), *Medusa* (screw, 18 guns).

United States: *Takiang* (a US chartered steam-vessel[2] with an officer, a party of men, and a gun of the United States corvette *Jamestown*).

The squadron assembled at the island of Himejima in the Inland Sea and steered for the entrance to the Straits of Shimonoseki anchoring in the afternoon of 4 September out of the range of the shore batteries. Vice-Admiral Kuper and Rear Admiral Jaurès 'reconnoitred the position of the batteries' and agreed that action should begin next day 'as soon as the tide served'. At 2 pm the signal was given for the ships to take up their positions:

As soon as this was accomplished the action was commenced from the bow gun of the *Euryalus*, and the fire was smartly returned and kept up with much spirit by the Japanese batteries. At about 4.30 pm the fire from Nos. 4 and 5 batteries evidently slackened, and shortly afterwards ceased altogether; and by 5.30 batteries Nos. 6, 7 and 8 were also silenced. The day was now too far advanced to admit the landing parties being disembarked, but the *Perseus* and the Dutch corvette *Medusa*, being very close to battery No. 5, and it being too dark to signalize for instructions, a party of men from the two ships gallantly landed, spiked most of the guns in that battery, and returned to their ships without casualties of any sort'.

In the attack the allied force seem to have cooperated efficiently. The advanced squadron under the command of Captain Hayes RN which con-sisted of the *Tartar*,[3] *Dupleix*, *Metalan Kruis*, *Barosa*, *D'Jambi* and *Leopard*, concentrated on batteries Nos. 3 to 9. The two flag ships *Euryalus* and *Semiramis* also fired on the same batteries. 'The light squadron, under Commander Kingston consisting of the *Perseus*, *Medusa*, *Tancrède*, *Coquette* and *Bouncer* were directed to take the batteries in flank.' The *Argus* and the *Amsterdam* which had been kept in reserve initially were later 'ordered to close and engage'. The *Conqueror* which had the battalion of Royal Marines on board was, because of the 'difficult navigation, directed to approach only sufficiently near to admit of her Armstrong guns bearing on the nearest bat-teries. During this operation the *Conqueror*[4] grounded twice on a knoll of sand, but came off again without assistance and without sustaining any dam-age. The *Takiang* also fired several shots from her one Parrot gun, doing good service.'

At daylight on 6 September 'No. 8 battery again opened fire upon the advanced squadron, doing some damage to the *Tartar* and the *Dupleix*.' But the battery 'was soon silenced'. The landing parties, which consisted of small arms companies from the *Euryalus* and *Conqueror*, the battalion of marines and other marines of the squadron plus 350 French and 200 Dutch seamen and marines, were then distributed in the boats of the squadron and towed to the opposite shore. Kuper recounts:

> [The landing] was effected without accident . . . and the force proceeded, under my personal directions to assault and take possession of the principal batteries, which was accomplished with only trifling opposition. All the guns, having been dismounted and spiked, carriages and platforms burnt, and magazines blown up and deeming it inexpedient, from the very rugged and almost impenetrable nature of the country, to retain possession of any post on shore during the night, I directed the whole force to re-embark at 4 pm.

Unfortunately, this was not the end of the engagement. After the French and Dutch contingents were already in their boats, the Naval Brigade, sta-tioned at No. 5 battery, was suddenly attacked

> . . . by a strong body of Japanese assembled in the valley in the rear of the battery. Colonel Suther's battalion of marines coming up at this moment, a joint attack was immediately organized, and the enemy driven back upon a strongly placed stockaded barrack, from which they were dislodged after making a brief but sharp resistance, leaving seven small guns in our posses-sion . . . The whole force having been ordered to embark, reached their ships without accident, notwithstanding the violence of the currents, which pres-ents serious obstacles to any operations in these Straits.

The British suffered a number of casualties in this engagement.[5]

The *Perseus*, whilst covering the landing 'was driven on shore by a strong eddy of the current, and, resisting all efforts to get her off' remained fast until midnight on 7 September, 'when having been considerably lightened, she was towed off' by the paddle steamer *Argus*.

Batteries Nos. 1 to 8 were now entirely in allied possession and working parties were landed on 7 September to embark the captured guns. On 8 September Kuper, in company with Admiral Jaurès, transferred his flag to the *Coquette* and accompanied by the *Tartar, Metalen Kruis, D'Jambi* and *Dupleix* moved to open fire on batteries Nos. 9 and 10. Their fire was not returned, parties were landed to destroy the batteries and embark the guns. In all the allies took 'sixty-two pieces of ordnance, of various sizes.'

Kuper noted that since the conclusion of the operations he had satisfied himself, 'by personal examination of the entire Straits, that no batteries remain in existence on the territory of the Prince of Choshiu, and thus the passage of the Straits may be considered cleared of all obstructions.'

The Admiral, although he had been enjoined not to enter into negotiations with the Prince, concluded his despatch with an account of talks with an envoy from the Prince of Chōshū and a letter from the Prince. Kuper commented with a note of self-satisfaction:

The very satisfactory character of the Prince's written communication, and its humble tone, afford, in the opinion of Rear-Admiral Jaurès and myself, reasonable grounds for the presumption that apart from the brilliant success achieved in a military point of view, and the great extent of the injury inflicted upon the Prince of Choshiu, his power and prestige (advantages of an important nature in a political sense) may very possibly result from the presence of the allied squadrons in these Straits.'

Admiral Kuper in his despatch mentioned the gallantry of many officers and men in his force and expressed his appreciation of the services of Messrs Lowder and Satow[6] who had been lent to him by Alcock. He also recorded his sincere thanks to the senior officers of the allied forces. In particular he praised the 'hearty co-operation and cordial goodwill displayed by Rear-Admiral Jaurès, during the preparations for and the progress of these operations'.

Alcock[7] duly reported to the Foreign office the success of the operation. He noted without further comment that the Prince had undertaken that:

1. All ships should 'freely navigate the Straits, be treated in a friendly manner, and allowed, if necessary, to coal and purchase provisions'.

2. The batteries would 'not be repaired or rearmed, and no new ones built'.

3. 'A ransom shall be paid for the town of Shimonoseki, which has been spared, although it [sic] fired upon the ships, and therefore might have been destroyed. The Prince had further engaged to pay the whole expenses of the expedition.'

Alcock did not have the official return of casualties but reported that 8 British had been killed and 51 wounded while the French and Dutch losses were 4 killed, 1 missing and 5 wounded.

'Assault on the lower battery at Simonoseki.' *The Illustrated London News*, Dec. 24, 1864

AFTERMATH

Despite the fact that the Foreign representatives in Yokohama had specifically enjoined the naval force commanders from making any demonstration of force in the vicinity of Osaka Kuper[8] reported from the *Euryalus* at sea on 30 September 1864 that 'it having been considered advisable by Rear-Admiral Jaurès and myself that the whole force should proceed through the Inland Sea to be prepared to resist any attempt that might be made by hostile Daimios to obstruct the passage of that sea in the neighbourhood of their respective territories, the squadrons accordingly proceeded by that route. A few batteries were passed, but no symptom of hostility was anywhere displayed,[9] and the squadrons, having appeared off Hiogo [sic, now Kobe] and Osaka, left the Inland Sea on the 27th instant [September] by the Kii channel.' They had no great difficulty except in the vicinity of Awajishima 'where two tides meet, and which requires to be more carefully surveyed, as many knolls of mud have been thrown up'. The *Conqueror* unfortunately grounded for about twenty-four hours and had to be towed off by the *Leopard* and the *Argus*.

Kuper added that he had left in the Shimonoseki Straits until 5 October HMS *Barrosa*, the French ship *Tancrède* and the Dutch ship *D'Jambi* to prevent any infractions of the convention.

COMMENTS

Kuper certainly interpreted flexibly his instructions from Alcock. He was not supposed to enter into negotiations with the Chōshū authorities and he was told not to make a show of force near Osaka. He disobeyed but may have been right to do so. His ships were not attacked during their voyage through the treacherous waters of the Inland Sea. The bombardment of Kagoshima and of Shimonoseki, in which some British ships ran aground, at least temporarily, demonstrated the need for more accurate surveys of Japanese coastal waters.

Cohn White,[10] naval historian, has pointed out that although the batteries defending the Straits of Shimonoseki 'constituted one of the strongest systems of fortification in Japan' they had some significant weaknesses:

> Although the sides of the Straits were steep and high, none of the batteries had been built on top of them – from where they would have been able to fire plunging shots onto any ships below. Instead, they had been built on low ground close to the shoreline, where they were on much the same level as any of the attacking ships. Worse, many of them had been placed on the *foot* of the sheer cliffs so that any enemy shot of shell which went over simply hit the solid rock face and rebounded into the middle of the gunners, or exploded, sending down showers of lethal splineters. Second, although the batteries were capable of delivering concentrated fire to their front, none of them had been designed to support their fellows with flanking fire and so it was possible to capture them one by one. Finally and most important of all, the Daimyo of Buzen, whose lands were on the southern side of the Strait refused to help Nagato [Chōshū] in his fight, which meant that the allied ships were able to hug the southern shore and did not have to contend with crossfire.

White noted: 'Every important feature of the operation – the range of 1000 yards, the special outflanking squadron and the strong landing force –

demonstrated how well Kuper had learned the lessons of Kagoshima.' The
Conqueror which had grounded on uncharted shoals was 'the last of the old
"wooden walls" ever to fire her guns in anger.' The fire from the Japanese batteries 'were as furious and accurate as at Kagoshima and all the allied ships
were hit several times, although nearly always at a very long range. In the
Barrosa, for example, there were six hits on the quarterdeck alone but no one
was killed or wounded.' 'On the other hand, thanks to Kuper's careful posi-
tioning of his ships, the Japanese were subjected to a withering crossfire and
earned the admiration of their foes by the way in which they stood to their
guns.'

White reminded his readers that 'It was one of the last occasions when a
full squadron of the old-stye "cruisers" [all still made of wood and not steel]
– frigates, corvettes and sloops – went into battle and it is intriguing to see
how those half-mechanical, half-sailing ships performed. The teething troubles of the Armstrong guns caused much investigation at the time and led,
eventually to the abandonment of the new breech-loaders for another twenty
years'. White also noted that the ships 'had not proved very efficient. On the
way to Kagoshima, the squadron had found it easier to keep in company
under sail than when steaming.' The *Racehorse*'s engines [a screw gun vessel[11]
with 3 guns] had failed at Kagoshima while the *Perseus* had been unable to
combat a fast crosscurrent at Shimonoseki. The problems of navigating
wooden ships combining engines and sail in poorly charted waters around
Japan were underlined by the loss of HMS *Rattler* off Cape Soya in September
1868.

White thought that the main interest of the war was 'the classic use of
ships in conjunction with landing forces at Shimonoseki'. He wondered
'what might have happened at the Dardanelles in 1916 if similar tactics had
been employed there.'

Appendix III

Sir Esler Dening's Valedictory Despatch, 24 April 1957

Sir Esler Dening to Mr Selwyn Lloyd (Received April 24, 1957)

(No. 37. Confidential)　　Tokyo,
Sir,　　　　　April 18, 1957.

I do not find it easy to write a valedictory despatch which must take into account not only the five-and-a-half years I have spent as head of this mission, but also the fact that for the whole of the thirty-seven years I have spent in the Foreign Service, I have never ceased to be concerned with Japan, whether in the country or out of it, in peace or in war, or even when my responsibilities covered a far wider area.

2. A British Member of Parliament referred to Japan not very long ago as a psychiatrist's paradise, and I fear this is only too true. Apart from the fact that the Japanese, through centuries of isolation, became a nation of introverts, what is really the matter with them is that they were flung overnight from the days of Richard III into the gas-lit end of the 19th century and have never wholly recovered from the shock. The feudalism which prevailed until the Restoration of 1868 was, at its worst, as brutal as our own feudal age; at its best it displayed a certain paternalism of which the traces have not yet wholly disappeared. The results of Japan's passion in the ensuing years to adopt Western ways and Western ideas deceived a great many people. Material progress has been spectacular and industrially Japan to-day still ranks first in Asia. But the Western ways and the Western ideas, apart from material progress have been by no means assimilated, and one constantly comes up against characteristics in the Japanese people which can only be explained by their so recent feudalism.

There are a few Japanese who are really Western in outlook, but they are totally unrepresentative, and for the rest there has been little change in the mental outlook of the bulk of the people. It is still, generally speaking, not polite to say what you think, and the Japanese language, which is inadequate to the requirements of to-day, is so constructed that it is easier to be vague than precise. To ask a Japanese what he thinks is usually to be sure that he will not tell you. Someone a few years ago wrote a letter to a newspaper saying that nobody hated or distrusted a Japanese more than another Japanese, and this again is a characteristic of the feudal background, for the family and the retainers of the overlord were potential friends and everybody else was a potential enemy. To-day one sees that while Japanese are exquisitely courteous to those whom they know they are very offhand with those whom they do not know, and of civic manners they have none at all. The obligations and restrictions of feudal life were, if anything, enlarged in the Meiji era, for in addition to obligations to the family, to the employer (who replaced the overlord) and to the Throne, additional obligations were incurred at school and in the university. Thus it has been said that almost from birth upwards the Japanese are under such a load of obligations that they are never free to follow an independent course. It is for this reason that it is almost impossible to get an immediate decision from an individual; he must always consult first with all the people to whom he has obligations in the matter.

3. These, nevertheless, are the characteristics of the nation with which we have to deal to-day, and in spite of the war and the occupation and a superimposed democratic Government, they have not changed very much in the years I have known this country. Such changes as there are, are superficial and material, but the outlook of the people is much what it was. Contrary to popular belief the Japanese people in the main are both timid and docile. They thus give every opportunity for the bully to flourish and authoritarianism to prosper, even though the casual visitor might suppose that the people

of the country are freer than they used to be. The only difference is that authority is rarely exercised publicly; nevertheless, at a given moment everyone says and does the same thing and those who disagree remain silent. An example is to be found in the recent agitation over the hydrogen bomb tests at Christmas Island. Government and Press and Communists all speak with the same voice, but it is perfectly clear that the people as a whole are not particularly interested or agitated. On the other hand, if they are told to give vent to emotion on the subject they will do so because they are accustomed to doing what they are told, and in the process work themselves up to a point where, as a Japanese once told Basil Hall Chamberlain in relation to *Bushido*, they say 'We believe it, though we know it is not true.'

4. This is not a healthy state of affairs and it means, in effect, that Japan can be a beneficent influence in the world only if it has a good Government. If it has a bad Government it can become an evil influence again, or with an ineffective Government it may have no influence at all. Since the Peace Treaty came into force this country has had a succession of ineffective Governments until now, when the Kishi Government seems to be exercising an unhealthy influence in the wrong direction. It is too early to say whether this Government will continue, or whether its influence will remain unhealthy. At the moment the excuse can be made that a new Prime Minister is seeking to consolidate his position by placating widely divergent interests, and that once he feels secure in power he can change his ways. But the methods he is adopting to placate his opponents are in the direction of neutralism and pacificism and contrary to the

interests of the United States and the United Kingdom. It can be no accident that all the organs of public opinion reflect this attitude, which has a certain attraction for the Japanese because it creates a sense of independence and thus appeals to nationalism and because it fosters a natural dislike for expenditure on defence. Thus we find the strange phenomenon that, with a Conservative Government in power, the party line on certain issues is more akin to that of Moscow than to that of Washington or London.

5. It is conceivable that the Japanese Prime Minister, if he succeeds in consolidating his position, will reverse this tendency, but the longer he goes on doing and saying what he is now doing and saying, the more difficult it will become. He has certainly been astute in the way he has acquired the premiership, since what he forecast some two years ago has come to pass (though rather earlier owing to the illness of Mr. Ishibashi than even Mr. Kishi himself may have expected.) But it has yet to be proved that his political acumen goes beyond an ability to appreciate the intricacies of internal political intrigue. There is as yet no evidence of statesmanship, and statesmanship is what Japan sadly lacks. It must be admitted that if Mr. Kishi proves not to be a statesman, there is no other statesman on the horizon.

6. Whether it is better to have an ineffective Government which just drifts, or a Government which rallies the nation to lead it in the wrong direction, is a matter of opinion, but at the moment of leaving this country I confess that I would feel happier with the first alternative than with the second. It is true that an indefinite series of ineffective Governments can do harm to the country but not, I think, as much harm as can be done by more vigorous leadership if it leads in the wrong direction, for I hope I have said enough to show how easily the Japanese can be led. Two things are possible: one that Mr. Kishi will consolidate his position and reveal virtues which he has not so far disclosed, and the other that the opposition to him will grow with the passage of time and yet another change will take place. One should not therefore be too pessimistic, but the immediate outlook is not a favourable one. Japan, in short, is only to be trusted when she has a good Government, and she has not got a good Government now.

7. I feel that the Japanese people on the whole deserve a better fate than they get. With their capacity for hard work, they have staged a remarkable economic recovery which would have been unbelievable when I came to Japan five-and-a half-years ago. They may overreach themselves, and some people are beginning to sound notes of warning about renewed inflationary trends, but as yet the signs are not patently unhealthy and there is a good prospect that economic prosperity may continue though the rate of growth may be slowed. But it is dependent on a number of factors some of which, such as the general state of world economy, are not under Japanese control. With a population still increasing at roughly the rate of 1 million a year, there is always likely to be a certain precariousness about Japan's economy, but in so far as the people are able to influence the course of events themselves they have the qualities and the capabilities to prosper. Wealth is badly distributed, and labour conditions are far from what they should be in the small industries. There are indeed many things which could be better, and it is conceivable that

they will be bettered with the passage of time, but even as things are
the state of the Japanese people is
probably much better than it is in
any other country in Asia.

8. In the last resort, however, it is
the politics of this country which
may make things go wrong, and on
this I am not at the moment optimistic, though I hope that the future
may prove me to be wrong. It so
happens that the five-and-a-half
years I have spent here have been a
transition period, and the real Japan
– if there is such a thing – is only
now beginning to emerge. I am not
sure that I like the look of it.

9. I am sending copies of this
despatch to Her Majesty's
Ambassador, Washington, the
Commissioner-General in Singapore
and the Governor of Hong Kong.

I have, &c.
ESLER DENING.

Appendix IV

Record of a Conversation on 6 February 1960 between Richard Storry, Geoffrey Hudson and Sir Esler Dening (Head of UKLIM and British Ambassador to Japan, 1952–57)

HUDSON   What were the principal issues between Britain and Japan during the time that you were at the Tokyo Embassy?

DENING   Very few really. There are no longer any political issues of significance. The first issue, an aftermath of the war, was the hostility in this country of ex-prisoners of war towards the Japanese; and there was a great deal of fuss in Parliament about the compensation to the POWs under Article 16 of the Treaty, which said that although there were no reparations Japan agreed to pay compensation, out of funds deposited in neutral countries, to people who suffered while they were POWs.

   In my recollection the Japanese funds in neutral countries such as Thailand, Sweden and Switzerland (which had the largest sum) were to be divided as a form of reparation to POWs. The Japanese were fairly slow to implement that. There was a good deal of agitation here. Questions were asked in Parliament. There was a POW association. This was a pressure group in a way. Towards the end of 1954 Mr Yoshida, the then Prime Minister, was coming to England. I was to meet him here. Eventually, through politics in Japan his journey was delayed. I went back, and we met in Vancouver, where I represented to him the views of Her Majesty's Government on the implementation of Article 16. Yoshida took action and was very fair. Sir Norman Roberts was sent to Tokyo to negotiate the actual settlement and Yoshida managed to implement it just before he fell from power. The POWs said that they would stop agitating once the terms were satisfied and they did so. Thus that particular source of friction was removed.

Then there was the rather ridiculous case of the two sailors. This caused a great deal of agitation both in Japan and here. In 1952, two drunken sailors of the Royal Navy beat up a taxi driver and stole 1,000 yen. The Treaty was then in force, but there was no agreement about jurisdiction over United Nations forces as opposed to the American forces. The Americans had their agreement, we did not. There was a sort of gentleman's agreement with the Japanese Prime Minister, in the shape of an exchange of letters to the effect that incidents were to be settled amicably. The incident took place in Kobe.

Both the Japanese authorities on the spot and the British consul were rather dilatory in reporting to Tokyo. The men were sentenced by a Japanese judge to five years hard labour. This was considered rather a savage sentence. Jurisdiction was still in question, and we would not concede the right of Japanese courts to sentence British servicemen before agreement was reached. There was an uproar in England. The incident aroused a certain amount of nationalistic reaction in Japan. It was settled in a typically Japanese way. The Japanese in Tokyo were actually quite cooperative. An appeal was made, and the sailors apologized for their conduct. The judge reduced the sentence to three years, which meant that, under Japanese law, it could be suspended, which it was. The sailors were then released.

It was an unsatisfactory case from the official point of view, because these sailors certainly should have been punished. They were treated rather too well by the Japanese: they were shown press-cuttings about themselves and the trial, and given cigarettes. They were 'Bush Lawyers' enough, as they say in Australia, to plead, when they were had up before their captain, that having been tried once they could not be tried a second time for the same offence – the old principle of '*autre fois* convict'. It was an absurd 'storm in a teacup', and it shows how sensitive all countries are over jurisdiction.

In the recent negotiations on the Antarctic treaty in Washington, I found the Japanese negotiater was Mr Shimoda, whom I knew well. The United Kingdom proposed an article on jurisdiction in the treaty, and I got the consent of the Japanese to quote the Two Sailors' Case to show how important it was to have an agreement about jurisdiction.

The third issue was the copying of designs, and in particular textiles and pottery. Our pottery people sent out the president or secretary of their federation to Japan to have a talk with the Japanese pottery industry. As a result there was much better understanding between the two. As to textile copying, progress was rather slower. When I was in England on leave in 1954, I went to Manchester and talked to the people there. Both sides encouraged the idea that the only way was for the industries to discuss the issue direct rather than through governments. Governments are not the experts in such matters. If the Japanese were willing to try to put an end to this kind of thing, the best thing was for the two industries to get together. The result was that the Japanese first went to Manchester and were rather put on the spot. After that a British mission went to Japan. There was no government intervention. The result on the whole has been a fairly happy one. The Japanese set up a council rather similar to the one that exists in Manchester, where all designs are put in so that the council is able to check whether or not a design is being copied. Certainly the agitation in Manchester against the Japanese cotton industry has very largely died down, though the Japanese habit of copying foreign designs in other fields of industry has by no means been entirely eliminated.

And then finally the Peace Treaty obliged Japan to express her willingness to include new treaties of commerce and navigation with the signatories of the Treaty. The Japanese said that they wanted one. In those days HM Government's view was that one could not see the pattern of post-war trade and that one should not hurry these things. The reluctance in the first place was perhaps rather on the United Kingdom side. The Japanese were rather sensitive about this. Negotiations are still in progress. (They were concluded in 1962.) Under the GATT treaty any member nation can say that it will not apply the provisions of GATT to a certain country. It does not have to give reasons. There are in fact about 13 of the GATT countries who invoke Article 35 in respect of Japan. The reasons are, from the point of view of United Kingdom industry, that the Japanese, being a low-cost country, can so quickly disrupt a market by flooding it with low-cost goods. There is no visible remedy under GATT or under anti-dumping legislation that can deal with it. The Japanese have not denied the possibility outright nor have they provided a complete answer. There was a GATT meeting in Tokyo last October where the Japanese were rather anxious to put pressure upon the powers who were assembled there, not to continue to invoke Article 35. Curiously, they found themselves heavily attacked by the US for their restrictive practices against foreign trade. The view was put forward that if one wanted to get some world-wide agreement to admit goods freely from low-cost countries, there must not be a situation where low-cost countries themselves imposed highly restrictive practices on other people. From the point of view of prestige, there seems to be little doubt that the Japanese are the people holding up commercial negotiations because of this one matter of GATT. Until we cease to invoke Article 35, they will not be willing to finalize a commercial treaty.

The views on Japanese competition do not seem to be as strongly held as they were. It is possible that feeling is somewhat exaggerated. Japan would have to put forward some definite gentleman's agreement, I think, whereby if some sort of disruptive action took place she herself would place a curb on it. I think it is getting to be realized in Japan that to upset a market is not the best way to trade with it. That is a comparatively new realization.

HUDSON   What about the Japanese reaction to our atomic tests?

DENING   Though it was alleged to be spontaneous, it was in fact an artificially stimulated agitation in which the Communists played an active part. I believe that those who oppose tests in this country are far more sincere. The Japanese have for many years past been experts in staging demonstrations. I discovered some of the techniques involved in all this. For example, a Japanese housewife will immediately subscribe to an appeal in order that she can get on with her housework so that it is easy to collect a large number of signatures. No person in the government or any officials ever mentioned the Christmas Island tests to me personally during the whole of the agitation up to the time I left, though, of course, there was a formal governmental *démarche*. There are people who feel genuinely; but the horror of the atom bomb was only discovered in Japan long after Hiroshima.

It began when American medical teams came to examine the after-effects of the bomb. They set up those very admirable institutions at Hiroshima and Nagasaki. The Japanese then discovered that many Americans had a guilt complex. There is nothing more delightful for a defeated nation than to discover a sense of guilt in the conquerors. They exploited this to the maximum. For example, when I visited Hiroshima I was presented with a roof tile by the mayor as a souvenir of the atomic explosion. They give these tiles as presents, but they must have exhausted the supply of original tiles a long time ago.

The Hiroshima explosion has been very considerably exploited, but it is not a good thing to mock at these things in public. The whole of the Japanese agitation is artificial. When I was there, it was clear that the Japan Council for the Abolition of the Atom and Hydrogen Bomb had among its members a number of extremely respectable names, but its inspiration was and is Communist. A number of the agitations were caused by the Communists.

During the time that I was there, the Egyptian ambassador and the Indian ambassador were invited to address one of these Communist-inspired mass meetings. It was just after the Suez business. The Egyptian ambassador went and made a very discreet speech. He could have exploited the situation; but he didn't. The Indian ambassador was told he might attend but might not speak. The Japanese Prime Minister sent a message of goodwill to the meeting. I asked the Vice Minister of Foreign Affairs why, when the meeting was inspired by the Communists, the Government sent a message of goodwill. I thought it rather curious.

At the last Hiroshima meeting in 1959 to which messages were sent by J.B. Priestley and Bertrand Russell, etc., the Westerners eventually walked out because it was so Communist. The Government also began to withdraw its patronage. The anti-bomb campaign lacks spontaneity and genuine emotion, and it is exploited for political purposes. That is not to say that the population cannot be worked upon by artificial means to a degree of genuine agitation which has little relationship to the original cause.

The Japanese are extraordinarily cynical about death and about the deaths of other people. Many Japanese say that Japan has not yet got a national conscience about the sufferings of others. I would gravely doubt if the Japanese were profoundly moved by the casualties of the Hiroshima and Nagasaki disasters at the time they occurred. I think it is largely artificial. In 1957 some 250 people were drowned when a coastal vessel sank, yet the incident was hardly headline news in the afternoon press, and was almost forgotten the next day. This is not being cynical; I just think that the Japanese have not got to that form of emotionalism yet. The Japanese were more or less shamed into sending a note of protest to the Russians about the exploding of nuclear weapons in the Soviet Union. They had never protested before to the Russians, who exploded their bombs when the wind blew from west to east and carried the radio-active cloud over Japan. Yet when we exploded our bomb in the Doldrums some 6,000 miles away, where there was no danger of a radio-active cloud coming their way, as there was no wind, we received a note of protest. Having finally nerved themselves to protest to the Russians the Japanese were reticent about the reply which they received, though it is understood that it amounted to a complete and very curt rejection. In general the Japanese found it more profitable to protest to the US and the UK.

STORRY   Wasn't there very genuine agitation at the time of the Bikini atom test among the fishermen – over the fish?

DENING   That was quite natural. The Japanese eat tuna. A number of the fish were found to be infected. All the fish markets of Japan for a few days went into a panic. That is understandable.

HUDSON   Were the fish from around the Equator?

DENING   Yes, some of the tuna in the vessel affected by radio-active fallout were found to be infected. It was rather like the mass panic after the 1923 earthquake in Kantō, when there was the massacre of Koreans. The Government did nothing to stop the massacre. The rumour had spread that Koreans were poisoning the wells. 8,000 Koreans were murdered during that massacre and the Government took no action to contradict the rumours or to protect Koreans. Similarly, they took no action to damp down agitation over the infected fish.

DENING   No, they did not. On the ambassadorial level I think we both – Allison and myself – took great care to make it clear that we were not exploitable as against each other. I would not say at lower levels that it did not happen, particularly in the services. I think the Japanese at Government level have a fairly intelligent appreciation that it is one of those genuine differences; that it does exist, and is not exploitable. I think, without doubt, that they agreed with our point of view; on the other hand they knew which way their 'bread was buttered'.

HUDSON   What was the attitude to the Russians when you were there?

DENING   Quite different to the attitude towards China. It was the Russians who made the first move. In 1954 something was put out in Moscow while I was on leave. It was the first move in either direction. The Japanese made no move towards Russia. It was not until 1956 that the Soviet Union suggested treaty negotiations. I think the Japanese are very interested in Russia. Lots of Japanese learn Russian as people do in this country. There is an interest, but no enthusiasm. In all respectable circles there is profound suspicion. It is quite different from the attitude towards China where many Japanese live in what I would call a 'dream world'. There is no real feeling of wanting to get closer to the Russians. There is fear and suspicion. There is a strange lack of fear of the Chinese, who are really the greater menace to Japan.

STORRY   When considering the preparation of the Peace Treaty, did the British Government at one time have plans to restrict Japanese ship-building?

DENING   From the point of view of Japan it was an advantage that the Treaty was not signed until 1951. At the first Commonwealth conference in Canberra to discuss a peace treaty in 1947, which I attended, the views were fairly tough. In this country the shipping industry, and therefore the Board of Trade, and the Ministry of Transport, would have liked to have imposed some restriction on Japanese ship-building. By 1950, 1951, the matter was still viewed with alarm, though there were no restrictive clauses in the Treaty. At a later stage there was some trouble over Mitsui who were suspected of having secret subsidies. I said to the Japanese officials at the time that there must be an orderly re-emergence of Japanese shipping in world trade. If one disrupts a country's shipping that country will become hostile. By and large they have been fairly orderly. The Japanese Ambassador here told me the other day that they only build shells, and that we in fact get far more profit from our shipbuilding orders. Whether this is true or not I do not know. With a big tanker I believe, they build the hull and not much more. They do not get profits from the rest.

STORRY   That ship-building capacity must supply a great proportion of Japan's foreign exchange?

DENING   I should imagine so; it must play a big part. One of the things is that they carry much more in Japanese bottoms. That is essential to their economy.

STORRY   I should be grateful if you would go back over the matter of Dulles and the Treaty.

DENING   The US invited Britain to be joint sponsors of the Treaty. There was consultation among the principal Commonwealth powers about the terms of the treaty. But as joint sponsors we were very closely concerned with the drafting of it. About May or June 1951, Dulles came across to the UK to discuss the terms with the Labour Government. The Government expressed the view that they thought it would be unwise for the former allies to seek to dictate to a Japan, which would become free on the coming into force of the treaty, the terms on which it should re-establish its relations with neighbouring countries such as China and Russia.

Nationalist China said that it would not sign because of the reparation clause. Russia actually came to San Francisco but did not sign. Some months before the San Francisco Conference, an agreement was drawn up between the UK and USA that Japan would be free to choose which of the two Chinas she would recognize. The agreement was never published. Dulles's general attitude afterwards was that the Senate, which had to ratify the treaty, would create difficulties. One must recall that the Democratic party was on the way out. Dulles was a Republican, and he was invited by Acheson to undertake the 'spade work' of the peace treaty. He took the view that the senators' feelings about Japan being free to have a choice between the two Chinas, would create such difficulties that they might not ratify the treaty. My answer then and now, would be that since the US was the architect and sponsor of the treaty, for the Senate not to ratify would create such a ridiculous situation that it was untenable.

The US was largely the winner of the Pacific War. The Senate had been kept informed throughout the course of the negotiations. To have gone back on the treaty at the moment of ratification was unbelievable. In the event, in defiance of the agreement, Dulles went over to Japan and bullied the Japanese Government, which was not yet independent, to enter into negotiations with Chiang Kai-shek. That has been the whole source of the complex: the feeling of agitation and so forth, over Japan's relations with China and with the US though of course it has never been publicized by the Japanese for obvious reasons.

HUDSON   Do you think that, if they had been free to choose, they would not have actually recognized the Peking Government?

DENING   I think that it is likely that they would have been coy about recognizing either government for a number of years. They made no move themselves in the case of Russia. They could have been willing to have informal relations with both Chinas. They would have argued probably that it was all very difficult, and they would have procrastinated as long as they would to get the best of both worlds. But they would not have been able to blame any of the ex-victors of the war in the end. That was in my mind at the time that all this came up. One cannot forecast how the Japanese will go. They should not be able to blame something on one of the victors. And it seems to me that that is precisely what is happening in the relations between Japan and the US. Most Japanese blame the US for the quandary in which Japan is placed.

HUDSON   Are they influenced at all by the example of India? Do they consider that India gives any kind of lead?

DENING   No, I think that there is a curious lack of love between the Japanese and the Indians. The Japanese have a certain contempt for the Indians, and the Indians find this intolerable. Most of the Indians feel that the Japanese have not changed at all, and that they are just as bad as ever they were. Considering the Indian nationalist association with Japan during the war, this is rather curious. They just don't get on. They have goodwill visits, but they don't really get on. One thing is that Japan never concedes any kind of moral leadership to India.

STORRY   Somebody once told me – a Japanese in Tokyo – that during the war General Terauchi, when he was told on some occasion that the army must cease to treat the Indian nationalist army as a purely puppet force, had replied that his father, as Governor-General of Korea, had never had much time for colonial independence movements and that he felt the same way.

DENING   When the Duke of Gloucester came to Japan in 1929, the Japanese asked us to communicate to them the names of Indian nationalists in Japan who might cause trouble, and to our amazement the authorities threw them all into jail. They thought they might cause trouble. We would have watched them and taken precautions, but we would not have locked them up.

STORRY   What happened to Rash Behari Bose? He must have died?

DENING   Yes, I think he must have, and that it must have been from natural causes.

HUDSON   Have the Japanese since the war kept up any connections with their former factions in South-East Asia? Are their past connections with Indonesia and Burma entirely obliterated?

DENING   I think completely. The only attraction to the locals was that they wanted independence, and thought that the Japanese might get it for them. So much so that the Indonesians who appeared terribly pro towards the end of the war, seem to be more anti-Japanese than most today. I am told by people who have been to Indonesia more recently that the resentment against the Japanese is very strong. I can understand the resentment of the Filipinos but there were no battles in Indonesia or fighting in which they were actually killed.

HUDSON   The Japanese do not regard Indonesia as, so to speak, a sort of god-child?

DENING   They would love to, I think. But the Indonesians have not responded.

HUDSON   Of course, the Indonesians would never have got their independence but for Japan. The Japanese armed them in Java.

DENING   They got all the arms. But everybody got all the arms everywhere – Malaya, Burma, Indo China, and everywhere else. It is a curious thing that the Japanese are not an affection-inspiring people outside of their own country, and even in their own country as far as aliens are concerned, unless one takes trouble. There is a superficial geniality, but it goes no further. One has to dig deep to find the attractive qualities. To me personally, the Japanese have character. Very often it is bad character. I find the Japanese are very interesting. Sometimes I am extremely fond of them. At other times they madden me more than any other people I know. There is nobody who could drive me to a greater state of exasperation and irritation. It is all evidence of character.

HUDSON   I suppose that they have been more thrown back on themselves in recent years. They have been subjected to a new period of Western influence, but at the same time, being turned out of all these countries and for a long time unable to travel abroad, they must feel tremendously bottled-up.

DENING   Most of the Japanese going abroad now are the wrong people. We are always told that the Ministry of Finance is very strict about allowing money for travel, but thousands of the wrong type of Japanese wander around, MPs etc. They see practically nothing of the countries they go to, except the night clubs, etc. They are the bane of every Japanese Embassy. There is no money for the student and people like that, who might derive some benefit. Even the Japanese press criticizes this.

STORRY   I suppose Siam is the country where they were least disliked during the war?

DENING   The Siamese fooled the Japanese. They have a tremendous sense of humour. The Siamese hid our 'cloak and dagger' people right in the centre of the capital, in the Chulalong Korn University. Pridi once told me that our 'cloak and dagger' people built an airstrip somewhere. Then some Japanese colonel got suspicious about this and decided to go and investigate. However, the Siamese wined and dined him so well that he caught dysentery, and in the end he never did get there. Because the Siamese pulled the legs of the Japanese they perhaps did not feel so strongly about them as other Asians.

STORRY   Another interesting thing is the way that the Japanese are strongly hated in Korea, whereas, I gather, the feelings in Formosa are rather different. Perhaps it is the result of the Nationalists going back to Formosa?

DENING   The first Chinese general who went back was a bad lot. But, I think the Formosans themselves are in a sense expatriates from China. They have not the strong sense of Formosan nationality which the Koreans have always had as regards Korea. I remember some American woman journalist, some ten years ago, telling me that she would have said that about one third of the people of Formosa would like to link up with Japan again. How she could possibly get an idea of the numbers I don't know. The link would be more for the sake of their economic future. Some Japanese contemplate the sort of link that exists between Great Britain and Northern Ireland.

HUDSON   I must say that the older generation in Taiwan speak either Japanese or Hokien. Yet the younger generation speak Kuo-yu. The younger generation must feel much more Chinese than the older generation. On the other hand, recent events in China probably have made them very glad that they are not included in the mainland.

DENING   The Chinese abroad always had strong links with the home country. They were not political links by and large in the old days. They were Confucian links – family and so forth. As for the Koreans theirs is a virulent nationalism which nothing can kill. Look at the way that Korea was ruled by everybody in the last 150 years. They quarrel with each other, yet everything is distinctly Korean – speech, individuality, writing and even their pottery is very interesting. Everything about them is Korean.

STORRY   Were you in Tokyo when General MacArthur left?

DENING   No. I visited Tokyo at the time when I was a roving ambassador. I called on the General in 1950, when I was taken to see him by Sir Alvary Gascoigne. I was back in London when he left. Of course he was accepted by the Japanese because he was authoritarian and the Japanese needed authority – that was my theory during the occupation period. One dictorial regime was overthrown and another took its place. It was probably a good thing that there was a MacArthur at that particular time. Where, I think, the Americans went wrong was that they believed that the Japanese really liked it.

I believe that the Japanese have the gift of telepathy much more than any other people I know. If you hear one Japanese talking to another and they know one another very well, very often they have only to say one word, a noun or something, not a sentence, or sometimes they only look at each other, and the rest is then immediately grasped. One of the things when I was in Southeast Asia Command when the Armistice came, was that suddenly this fierce Japanese army turned into an army of lambs. They did exactly what they were told with great speed and efficiency. This knocked our South-east Asia Command over. They could not understand it. I said that it was a defeat drill. Before, it had been an aggression drill. They were told – though there were no written orders – that they had to obey our discipline, and therefore they did everything they were told. Throughout the whole of Japan precisely the same thing happened. They thought that if they did this everything would be over much more quickly. They looked as if they liked it, and the Americans took it all in. One never finds any document to indicate that the Japanese people were instructed in their behaviour, and this supports my theory of telepathy. I had a servant and I only had to say the operative word and he did exactly what I wanted without my having to complete the sentence. He had studied my ways, and he knew what I wanted. It is an extraordinary quality.

STORRY   To go back to the Japanese surrender – you must have met Terauchi?

DENING   Terauchi had already had a stroke. We were told that he had had a stroke when we set out in August 1945 in a party for Rangoon to discuss the Japanese surrender. The Japanese party consisted only of the Chief of Staff – Numata, a rear admiral and an astonishing lieutenant-colonel, who was in military terms 'O' 'A' 'Q' & 'I'. He had one of those little typically Japanese briefcases in which were all the answers. Major-General Denning who was our principal administrator, told me afterwards that he was astounded. This lieutenant-colonel had an answer to everything right at his finger tips. It was amazing, considering the size of our party and the size of the Japanese party.

It was I who suggested that they should be allowed to wear their swords as they had not yet surrendered. They came into the room with their escorts, and we came in afterwards. Browning, who was Chief of Staff, made a curt speech and told them to get on with it. Then Numata got up and took my breath away because he said 'First of all I would like to thank you very much for your courtesy in allowing us to wear our swords, and secondly I should like to congratulate you on your splendid victory.' This staggered me, especially after the years in Manchuria and elsewhere where I had seen the arrogance of the Japanese army.

We went on negotiating. A signal came in from MacArthur while we were negotiating the surrender in Rangoon, saying that no surrender was to take place in any theatre until he himself received the surrender of the entire Japanese armed forces in Tokyo Bay on 3 September 1945. It so happened by sheer chance that the Southeast Asia Command was on the very verge of an attack on Malaya when the Armistice came and was well equipped therefore to deal with any situation. MacArthur was going to Japan with initially small forces and anything might have happened. The decision was no doubt wise, but it was most disconcerting for us who were arranging the surrender in Southeast Asia.

Perhaps rather foolishly I said that we should have to explain to the Japanese that this was to be a sort of staff exercise, and that the real thing would take place in Singapore on 9 September. Then the Japanese got suspicious and began to 'dig in their toes'. They could not understand. I suggested that I should meet the General alone with the interpreters, and that we talk this over. Boyce was our interpreter, and the Japanese had two very good ones. And so we had a two-hour session. In the end it was agreed that the Japanese would sign the surrender document. There was a sort of ceremony in the ballroom with photographers, etc. I attended the formal ceremony in Singapore on 10 September.

STORRY   MacArthur suggested that the surrender should take place in Tokyo. How did the Singapore surrender fit in?

DENING   He said that no surrender should take place until after the surrender of the Japanese Imperial Forces in Tokyo. The regional surrenders followed that event.

HUDSON   What about the terms which were imposed in the first surrender about the handing over of arms and prisoners to other people? There was no punishment when they did in fact hand over prisoners to the Indonesians and gave the Indonesians arms.

DENING   On the other hand they also fought the Indonesians on our instructions. Nothing else could be done about it. The only people there were the Japanese. A battle ensued between the Japanese and the Indonesians.

HUDSON   Many of the Dutch were killed after being handed over to the Indonesians. Were the Japanese told originally that they would be held responsible?

DENING   They were, but nothing could be done about it. It was disobeying orders and it may have been brought up afterwards. They always walked out in too much of a hurry. In Rangoon they evacuated the city before we managed to get [there]. The result was that the whole of Rangoon was looted. The same thing happened in Singapore, where every refrigerator and every lavatory pan was taken. We afterwards had to buy them back again from the shops.

STORRY   Wasn't there an incident in Indo-China where they fought under our orders?

DENING   There may have been. Norman Brain might know about that. I did not go there until much later. There was a large amount of stirring up of mischief in Indonesia. There was a Japanese major-general who at one time had been at Sandhurst, and while he was there he met General Christison who was then Adjutant and they met later in Indonesia after the war. This Japanese said to Christison, probably as a parting shot, 'Well, we have stirred up plenty of trouble for you in Indonesia as you will find to your cost.' So I think a good deal of it was originally instigated, and the rest of it was due to Indonesian lack of discipline.

When Mallaby was murdered and Dutch women and children slaughtered, Soekarno went down to Soerabaya but could not control the mob. We put in a division and there was a battle. There were alleged to be a number of Japanese in that battle. I think it was quite possible because their fire was more accurate than the Indonesians were capable of. The net result of it all is that the resentment against the Japanese seems to be stronger than anywhere else except perhaps the Philippines, where they did of course slaughter numbers of Filipinos.

STORRY   Did the Australians object to the draft treaty very strongly?

DENING   No, they did not. We had a Commonwealth Committee in London of which I was the official level chairman, so we were aware of the attitudes of various Commonwealth countries. At the time Dr Evatt was still Minister and it was he who said that the Australians did not want any reparations. That rather surprised me at the time, in view of the strength of Australian feeling about Japan.

STORRY   I suppose the Anzus Pact really was a sort of *quid pro quo* for the Australians?

DENING   It was, I suppose. Australia and New Zealand wanted it as a safeguard and the Americans were willing. That was the American attitude. The real threat from Asia nowadays is Communism. Politically the Pact was considered vital in Australia. There was a great fuss as to whether the UK should join. I thought our ties with Australia were sufficiently close for it not to matter, but there was some feeling in England at our not being a party. There is no part really that the UK can play in the defence of the S. Pacific region once it is attacked. If the S. Pacific was threatened it would be a paramount issue for the US, and it would be the US and not the UK who could defend it in force. At present Australia, New Zealand and the UK are linked by a common interest in the defence of Southeast Asia, to which the US is also a party.

Appendix V

Index and biographical details of diplomatic names associated with Japan

PART I

Biographical details of selected members of the Diplomatic Service and Japan Consular Service who served in Japan 1859–1945, apart from those covered by individual biographical portraits.

ADAMS, Sir Francis Ottiwell, KCMG, CB (died 1889). Secretary of Legation in Japan January 1868. Chargé d'Affaires at Tokyo from May 1871–May 1872. Secretary of Embassy at Berlin 1872, Paris 1874. Minister to Switzerland 1881. His book, *The History of Japan*, in two volumes, was published in 1875 in London. In 1868 he was on board HMS *Rattler* when the ship foundered off Cape Soya in Hokkaidō while reconnoitring the area to determine the nature of the Russian presence. Wrote an extensive report about Japanese sericulture.

ALSTON, Sir Beilby Francis, GBE, KCMG, CB (1868–1929). Counsellor/ Minister at Tokyo and Chargé d'Affaires 1919–20, Minister to China 1920–22, to Argentina and Paraguay 1923–25. Ambassador to Brazil 1925–29.

ASHTON-GWATKIN, Frank (1889–1976), CMG. Japan Consular Service, 1913–19, served in the Foreign Office from 1920. Wrote novels with a Japanese setting under the pseudonym of John Paris. See biographical portrait by Ian Nish in *Biographical Portraits, Vol. I*, 1994.

BARCLAY, Sir George Head, KCSI, KCMG, CVO (1862–1921). First Secretary, later Councillor [sic] of Embassy at Tokyo 1902–05, Minister to Persia 1908–12.

BONAR, Henry Alfred Constant, CMG (1861–1935). Student interpreter in Japan 1880, served in consular posts in Japan and the Legation at Tokyo. Became assistant judge of HM Court in Japan. Consul General at Kobe 1908. Transferred to Seoul 1909. Retired 1912.

BOOTHBY, Sir Brooke, Baronet (1856–1913). First Secretary, later Secretary of Legation at Tokyo 1901–02. Minister to Chile 1907–13.

BUCHANAN, RT. HON. Sir George William, GCB, GCMG, GCVO (1854–1925). Second Secretary at Tokyo from 1879–1882. Ambassador to Russia 1910–18 and to Italy 1919–21.

BUNSEN, RT. HON. Sir Maurice William Ernest De, Baronet, GCMG, GCVO, CB (1852–1932). Secretary of Legation at Tokyo 1891 where he acted as Chargé d'Affaires from June 1892–February 1894. Minister to Portugal 1905, Ambassador to Spain 1906, to Austria 1913.

CHALMERS, Arthur Morrison, CMG (1862–1949). Student interpreter in Japan 1882. Served in various consular posts in Japan. Consul General at Seoul 1912, at Yokohama 1914. Retired 1920.

CHEETHAM, Sir Milne, KCMG (1860–1938). Second Secretary at Tokyo from 1899–1902. Minister to Switzerland 1922, to Greece 1924 and to Denmark 1926. Retired 1928.

CLARKE, Sir (Henry) Ashley, GCMG (1903–94). First Secretary at Tokyo 1934–38. Ambassador to Italy 1953–62.

CROWE, Sir Edward Thomas Frederick, KCMG (1877–1960). Student interpreter in Japan 1897. Served at various consular posts in Japan and Taiwan. Commercial attaché at Tokyo 1906, Commercial Counsellor 1918. Transferred to the Department of Overseas Trade 1924, Comptroller-General 1928. Retired 1937.

CUNNINGHAM, Wilfred Bertram, CMG (1862–1960), Joined the Japan Consular Service 1906. Japanese Counsellor at Tokyo 1930–41.

DAVIDSON, Sir Colin John KCVO, CIE (1878–1930). Student interpreter in Japan 1903, Private Secretary to Sir Claude MacDonald. Served in various consular posts in Japan. Consul General Seoul 1927. Attached to the staff of the Prince of Wales for his visit to Japan 1924. Also to the Garter Mission,1929. Japanese Counsellor 1927–30.

DODD, Charles Edward Shuter (1891–1974). Counsellor at Tokyo 1934–35 where he also served as Chargé d'Affaires. Minister to Panama 1939–43.

DODDS, Sir James Leishman, KCMG (1891–1972). Counsellor at Tokyo 1938–40, where he also acted as Chargé d'Affaires. Minister to Bolivia 1940–43, to Cuba 1944–49, Ambassador to Peru 1949–51.

DORMER, Sir Cecil Francis Joseph KCMG, MVO (1883–1979). Counsellor at Tokyo 1926–29, where he also acted as Chargé d'Affaires. Minister to Thailand 1929, to Norway 1934, Ambassador to Poland (government in exile) 1941–43.

ENSLIE, James Joseph (died 1896). Student interpreter in Japan 1861. Served at Hakodate 1861–1868, then at other consular posts in Japan including Kobe where he died.

EUSDEN, Richard (died 1904). Dutch interpreter at Edo 1859. Japanese Secretary and interpreter to the British Legation 1860. Served as Consul at Hakodate from 1867. Retired 1882.

FLOWERS, Marcus Octavius (died 1894), Dutch interpreter at Edo 1861. Served at various consular posts in Japan. Consul at Nagasaki 1868, Hyogo (Kobe) and Osaka 1877. Retired 1882.

FORSTER, Ralph George Elliott, CMG (1865–1931). Student interpreter in Japan 1886. Served at various consular posts in Japan. Japanese interpreter to Admiral Sir E.Fremantle on the outbreak of war between Japan and China in 1894. Consul General at Kobe 1914. Retired 1926.

GORE-BOOTH, Sir Paul Henry (later Baron) GCMG, KCVO (1909–84) Third Secretary Tokyo 1937–41, Ambassador to Burma 1953–56, High Commissioner to India 1960–65, Permanent Under-Secretary, FCO 1965–69.

GOWER, Abel Anthony James (died 1899). Private Secretary to the Governor of Hong Kong and assistant in the British Consulate at Canton. Assistant to the

British Consul General in Japan 1859. Present at both the 1861 and 1862 attacks on the British Legation at Tōzenji in Edo and at the British bombardment of Kagoshima. Consul at Nagasaki 1864 and at Kobe 1868. Retired 1886.

GURNEY, Sir Hugh, KCMG (1878–1968), Counsellor at Tokyo 1920, Minister to Denmark 1933–35, Ambassador to Brazil 1935–39.

HALL, John Carey, CMG, ISO (1844–1920). Student interpreter in Japan 1867. Served at various consular posts in Japan and as acting Japanese Secretary at Tokyo 1884–86. Acting Judge of HM Court in Japan in 1888–89. Consul General at Yokohama 1903. Retired 1914.

HANNEN, Sir Nicholas John (died 1900), Deputy Judge at Yokohama 1871, Judge of HM Court for Japan 1881. A British delegate to the Tokyo conference for the revision of the treaties December 1886–July 1887. Chief Justice of the Supreme Court for China and Japan 1891.

HARRINGTON, Thomas Joseph, CMG (1875–1953). Student interpreter in Japan 1896. Served at various consular posts in Japan, and Taiwan and at Honolulu. Consul General Manila 1920. Retired 1935.

HARRISON, Sir Geoffrey Wedgwood, GCMG, KCVO (1908–90). Counsellor at Tokyo, 1935–37. Ambassador to Brazil 1956–58, to Persia 1958–65, and to the Soviet Union 1965–68.

HENDERSON, RT. HON. Sir Neville Meyrick GCMG (1882–1942), Second Secretary at Tokyo 1909–12. Ambassador to Yugoslavia 1929–35, to the Argentine 1935–37, and to Germany 1937–39.

HOBART-HAMPDEN, Ernest Miles, CMG (1864–1949). Student interpreter in China 1888, transferred to Japan 1889. Served at various consular posts in Japan and Taiwan. Japanese Secretary 1909. Retired 1919.

HODGSON, Christopher Pemberton (died 1865) served as acting Consul in Nagasaki in 1859 and as Consul at Hakodate from 1859–61. His account of his time in Japan was published in London in 1861 under the title *A Residence at Nagasaki and Hakodate in 1859–1860 with an account of Japan Generally.*

HOHLER Sir Thomas Beaumont, KCMG (1871–1946). Second Secretary, at Tokyo 1901–05. Minister to Chile 1924–27, and to Denmark 1928–33.

HOLMES, Ernest Hamilton, CMG (1876–1957). Student interpreter in Japan 1897. Served at various consular posts in Japan and Korea. Consul General at Yokohama 1920. Retired 1935

KENNEDY, Sir John Gordon, KCMG (1836–1912). Secretary of Legation at Tokyo 1878. Chargé d'Affaires there from October 1879 to January 1882. Minister to Chile 1889. Minister to the King of Roumania 1897. Retired 1905.

KIRKWOOD, William Montague Hammett, was crown advocate for Japan from 1882–5. Legal adviser to the Japanese Government 1885–1902.

LAMPSON, Sir Miles Wedderburn (later Baron Killearn), GCMG, CB, MVO (1880–1964). Member of the Garter Mission to Japan, 1906 and of the mission to the funeral of the Meiji Emperor 1912, Second Secretary Tokyo 1908–10. Later Ambassador to Egypt and High Commissioner for the Sudan, Special Commissioner in South East Asia 1946–48.

LAY, Arthur Hyde, CMG., FRGS (1865–1934). Student interpreter in Japan 1887. Served in the office of the Japanese Secretary in Tokyo and at various consular posts in Japan and Korea. Consul General at Seoul 1914. Retired 1927.

LAYARD, Raymond de Burgh Money, CMG (1859–1941). Student interpreter in

Japan 1881. Served at various consular posts in Japan and Taiwan as well as at Honolulu. Consul General at Manila 1908 and at Kobe 1909. Retired 1913.

LOCOCK, Sidney (died 1885), Secretary of Legation at Edo 1865. Transferred to The Hague 1868. Minister Resident and Consul General to the republics in Central America 1874, Minister Resident in Servia 1881.

LONGFORD, Joseph Henry. Student interpreter in Japan 1869. Served in various consular posts in Japan. In attendance on Prince Akihito at the Coronation of King Edward VII in 1902. Retired 1902.

LOWTHER, RT. HON. Sir Gerard Augustus, Baronet, GCMG, CB (1858–1916). Secretary of Legation at Tokyo 1894 where he acted as Chargé d'Affaires from May to July 1895 and from May to November 1897. In 1898 transferred to Budapest. Minister to Chile 1901–04, Minister at Tangier 1904–08, Ambassador to Turkey 1908–13. Retired 1913.

LOWTHER, Sir Henry Crofton, GCVO, KCMG (1858–1939). Councillor [sic] of Embassy at Tokyo 1906 where he also acted as Chargé d'Affaires. Minister to Chile 1909–13, to Denmark 1913–16.

MCCLATCHIE, Thomas Russell Hillier (died 1886). Student interpreter in Japan 1870. Served in various consular posts in Japan. His translation of some Japanese dramas appeared as *Japanese Plays (versified)* in Yokohama in 1879.

MITFORD, Algernon Betrtram Freeman, Lord Redesdale KCVO, CB (1837–1916). After serving in the Foreign Office, at St Petersburg and Peking was posted to Edo in 1866 and appointed as a Second Secretary. He left Tokyo in 1871 and resigned from the Diplomatic Service in 1873. He was Secretary to the Commissioners of Works and Public buildings from 1874–1886 and M.P. for Stratford from 1892–95. His *Tales of Old Japan* was published in two volumes in London in 1871. His accounts of Japan at the time of the Meiji Restoration and his other writings on Japan have been collected and edited by Hugh Cortazzi in *Mitford's Japan*, first published in London in 1985 and republished by Japan Library in a revised edition with new material in 2002.

MORRISON, George Staunton (died 1893), After long service in China was Consul at Nagasaki from December 1858 to 1 January 1864 when he retired. He was seriously wounded in the attack on the British Legation at Tōzenji in Edo in July 1861.

MOUNSEY, Augustus Henry, FRGS (died 1882). Secretary of Legation at Tokyo 1876. Transferred to Athens in 1878, Minister to Colombia 1881. His book *The Satsuma Rebellion* was published in London in 1877.

MYBURGH, Francis Gerard, MD (died 1868). Interpreter to the consulate in Nagasaki 1859. Transferred to Edo in 1860, acting Japanese Secretary 1861, Chargé d'Affaires at Edo from April to July 1861. He was then acting Consul at Nagasaki and Yokohama.

NAPIER AND ETTRICK (William John George Napier) Lord. Secretary of Legation at Tokyo 1888, where he was briefly Chargé d'Affaires in 1889. In 1891 placed *en disponibilité*. Succeeded as the 11th baron in 1898.

NORMAN, Herman Cameron, CB, CSI, CBE. (1878–1930). Attached to the special mission sent to the coronation of the Emperor 1915.

OLIPHANT, Lawrence FRGS (1829–88). Was Private Secretary to the Earl of Elgin on his special mission to China and Japan in 1858 about which he gave an account in his *Narrative of Lord Elgin's Mission to China and Japan*, published in two volumes in Edinburgh in 1859–60. Appointed Secretary of Legation at Edo in early

1861. In the first attack on the British Legation at Tōzenji in Edo in July that year he was severely wounded and invalided home. For an account of Oliphant's life and personality see Laurence Oliphant and Japan, 1858–88, by Dr Carmen Blacker in *Biographical Portraits Volume II* Japan Library 1997.

PAGET, RT. HON. Sir Ralph Spencer, KCMG, CVO (1864–1940). Third Secretary at Tokyo.1893. Acted as Chargé d'Affaires there from June to August 1894. Transferred to Cairo in 1899. Minister to Denmark 1916–18 Ambassador to Brazil 1918–20

PALAIRET, Sir Michael KCMG (1882–1956). Counsellor at Tokyo 1923 where he also acted as Charge d'Affaires. Minister to Roumania 1929–35 to Sweden 1935–37, to Austria 1937–38, and to Greece 1939–42, Ambassador to Greece 1942–43.

PARLETT, Sir Harold George, CMG (1869–1945). Student interpreter in Japan 1890. Served at various consular posts in Japan and as acting Japanese Secretary in Tokyo 1902–03. Appointed Japanese Secretary 1919 with the local rank of Counsellor. Retired in 1927.

PASKE-SMITH, Montagu Bentley Talbot, CMG, CEB (1886–1946). Student interpreter in Japan 1907. Served in various consular posts in Japan and at Manila. Minister to Colombia 1936–41.

PETERSON, Sir Maurice Drummond, GCMG (1889–1952). First Secretary at Tokyo 1925. Minister to Bulgaria 1936–8, Ambassador to Iraq 1938–39, to Spain 1939–40.

ROBERTSON, Russell Brooke, CMG, FRGS (died 1888). Student interpreter in Japan 1860. Served at various consular posts in Japan. Acting Judge for Japan from 1881–83. Died at his post.

ROYDS, William Massy (1879–1951). Student interpreter in Japan 1902. Consul General at Kobe 1926–31, at Seoul 1931–34.

RUMBOLD, RT. HON. Sir Horace George Montague, Baronet, GCB, GCMG, MVO (1869–194). Councillor [sic] of Embassy at Tokyo 1909–13, Chargé d'Affaires Tokyo 1909, 1911 and 1912–13, Ambassador to Turkey 1920–24, to Spain 1924–28, to Germany 1928–33.

SAUMAREZ (James St.Vincent), Lord de, after service in the Grenadier Guards, joined the diplomatic service. Second Secretary at Tokyo 1875. Transferred to Rome 1880. Resigned 1885. Succeeded to the peerage 1891

SIEBOLD, Alexander von (died 1911) was son to the outstanding botanist, geographer and Japanologist Philip Franz von Siebold. Supernumerary interpreter to the British Legation at Edo 1859. Accompanied the Shogun's brother Prince Tokugawa Mimbutaiho from Japan to Paris in 1867 and on his visits to other European countries. Resigned in 1870.

SNOW, Thomas Maitland, CMG (1890–1997), Counsellor at Tokyo 1930–33 where also acted as Chargé d'Affaires. Minister to Cuba 1935–37, to Finland 1937–40, Minister, later Ambassador to Colombia 1941–45, Minister later Ambassador to Switzerland 1946–49.

SPRING-RICE, RT. HON. Sir Cecil Arthur, GCMG, GCVO (1859–1918). Assistant Private Secretary to Lord Granville 1884–85. Appointed to Washington 1886 and transferred to Tokyo as a Second Secretary in 1891. Employed at Washington from March 1891 to February 1892 and transferred there in 1893. Minister to Persia 1906 and to Sweden 1908. Ambassador to the USA 1913.

TROUP, James (1840–1925). Student interpreter in Japan 1863. Served in various consular posts in Japan. Consul General at Yokohama 1896 and assistant Judge of HM Court in Japan. Retired 1898.

VYSE, Captain Francis Howard (died 1891). Vice-Consul at Edo 1859, Consul at Yokohama from December 1860 to December 1862. Consul at Hakodate December 1862 to 1865 when he was transferred to Nagasaki. Resigned 1866.

WATSON, Robert Grant (died 1892) after service in the Indian army, became an attaché in 1859. Secretary of Legation at Tokyo 1872 where he was Chargé d'Affaires from May 1872 to March 1873. Transferred to Washington 1874. Retired 1880.

WHITEHEAD, Sir James Beethom, KCMG (1858–1928). Secretary of Legation at Tokyo in 1898, where he also acted as Chargé d'Affaires from May to November 1900 and May to October 1901. Transferred to Brussels 1901. Minister at Belgrade 1906. Resigned 1910.

WILKINSON, Sir Hiram Shaw (1840–1926) (not to be confused with Wilkinson, Hiram Parkes (1866–1935) who was a Judge in China, Korea and Siam). Student interpreter in Japan 1864. Called to the bar in 1872 and held various judicial appointments in China, Korea and Japan. Judge of HM Court in Japan 1897–1900. Retired 1903.

WHITE, Oswald, CMG (1884–1970). Student interpreter in Japan 1903. seved at various consular posts in Japan. Consul General Seoul 1927, Osaka 1931, Mukden 1938, Tientsin 1939–41.

WILLIS, Dr William (1837–1894). Doctor and assistant to the British Legation in Japan from 1862–69. Vice-Consul in Edo 1868–69. Established a teaching hospital in Kagoshima where he resided from 1870–77. For details of his life in Japan see *Dr Willis in Japan, British Medical Pioneer 1862–1877*, by Hugh Cortazzi, London 1985.

WINCHESTER, Dr Charles Alexander (died 1883). Was a medical officer in Hong Kong and China where he assumed consular duties. He moved to Hakodate in 1861 and to Yokohama in 1862. He was Chargé d'Affaires at the British Legation in Japan from March to May 1862 and again from December 1864 till July 1865. Transferred to Shanghai as Consul 1965. Retired 1870.

PART 2
Ex-Japan Consular Service officers who attained at least Counsellor rank in the post-war Foreign (from 1966 Diplomatic) Service.

BRAIN, Sir Henry Norman, KBE, CMG (1907–2002), Minister at Tokyo 1953–55, Ambassador to Cambodia 1956–58 and to Uruguay 1961–66.

BROMLEY, Sir Thomas Eardley, KCMG (1911–1987), Ambassador to the Somali republic 1960–61, to Syria 1962–64, to Algeria 1964–65, to Ethiopia 1966–69.

CHEKE, Dudley John, CMG (1912–93), Consul General Osaka/Kobe 1956–58, Minister at Tokyo 1963–67, Ambassador to the Ivory Coast, Niger and Upper Volta 1967–70.

DE LA MARE, Sir Arthur James, KCMG, KCVO (1914–94) Ambassador to Afghanistan, 1963–65, High Commissioner, Singapore 1968–70, Ambassador to Thailand, 1970– 73.

FOULDS, Linton Harry, CBE (1897–1952). Minister to the Philippines 1946–51.

GRAVES, Sir Hubert (Ashton), K.C.M.G. (1894–1972), Minister to Vietnam, Laos and Cambodia 1951–54, Ambassador to Vietnam 1954–55.

HAINWORTH, Henry Charles, CMG (1914–), Minister at Vienna 1963–68, Ambassador to Indonesia 1968–70, UK Representative to the Disarmament Conference, Geneva, 1971–74.

KERMODE, Rev Sir Derwent, KCMG (1898–1960), Ambassador to Indonesia 1950–53, to Czecho-Slovakia 1953–55.

LLOYD, John Oliver, CBE (1914–82), Consul General Osaka/Kobe 1965–67, Ambassador to Laos 1970–73.

MACDERMOTT, Sir Dermot, KCMG, CBE (1906–89), The MacDermott, styled Prince of Coolavin, Minister to Romania 1954–56, Ambassador to Indonesia 1956–59, to Thailand 1961–65.

SAWBRIDGE, Henry Raywood, CBE (1907–90), Consul General at Yokohama 1949–53, Chargé d'Affaires in Korea 1950.

TOMLINSON, Sir Frank Stanley, KCMG (1912–94), Consul General New York 1964–66, High Commissioner to Sri Lanka 1966–69, Deputy Under-Secretary FCO.

WATTS, Ronald George Henry, CBE (1914–93), Consul General Osaka/Kobe 1958–63, Paris 1966–67.

PART 3

List of Japanese Language Officers who served at Tokyo between 1946 and 1972 and attained senior rank.

BAKER-BATES, Merrick Stewart, CMG (1939–), Counsellor (Commercial) Tokyo 1971–82, Consul General Los Angeles, 1992–97.

BENTLEY, Sir William, KCMG (1927–98), Ambassador to the Philippines 1976–81, High Commissioner to Malaysia, 1981–83, Ambassador to Norway 1983–87.

COOPER, Robert Francis, CMG, MVO (1947–), Head of Planning Staff, FCO 1989, Minister at Bonn 1996–98, Seconded to European Commission in Brussels.

CORTAZZI, Sir (Henry Arthur) Hugh, GCMG (1924–), Minister (Commercial) at Washington 1972–75, Ambassador to Japan 1980–1984.

DIMOND, Paul Stephen (1944–), Counsellor (Commercial), Tokyo 1989–93, Consul General Los Angeles, 1997–2001, Ambassador to the Philippines 2002– .

ELLIOTT, Mark, CMG (1939–), Ambassador to Israel 1988–92, to Norway 1994–98

FIELD (Edward) John, CMG (1936–), Minister at Tokyo 1988–91, High Commissioner to Sri Lanka, 1991–96.

GIFFARD, Sir (Charles) Sydney Rycroft, KCMG (1926–), Minister at Tokyo, 1975–80, Ambassador to Switzerland 1980–82, Ambassador to Japan 1984–86.

GOMERSALL, Sir Stephen (John), KCMG (1948–), Deputy UK Representative to the UN in New York 1994–98, Ambassador to Japan, 1999–

GREENWOOD, James Russell, LVO (1924–93), Counsellor Information at Tokyo 1968–73, Consul General at Osaka 1973–77.

HITCH, Brian, CMG, CVO (1932–), Minister at Tokyo, 1984–87, High Commissioner to Malta 1989–91.

HUMFREY, Charles Thomas William, CMG (1947–), Minister at Tokyo, 1995–99, Ambassador to Korea, 2000–2003. to Indonesia 2003–

HODGE, Sir James, William, KCVO, CMG (1943–), Counsellor (Commercial) Tokyo 1982–85, Minister at Peking 1995–96, Ambassador to Thailand, 1996–2000, Consul General, Hong Kong 2000–03.

McCARTHY, Nicholas Melvyn, OBE (1938–), Consul General at Osaka 1985–90, Ambassador to Cameroon 1995–98.

SLATCHER, William Kenneth, CMG (1926– 97) (originally studied Chinese), Consul General at Osaka 1977–80, High Commissioner to Guyana 1982–85.

SPRECKLEY, Sir Nicholas, KCVO, CMG (1934–94), Ambassador to Korea 1983–86, High Commissioner to Malaysia 1986–91.

THORPE, Adrian Charles, CMG (1942–), Minister at Tokyo 1991–95, Ambassador to the Philippines, 1995–98, to Mexico 1998–2002.

WATSON, Richard E. G. Burges CMG (1930–), Minister Commercial and Consul General at Milan1983–86, Ambassador to Nepal 1987–90.

WESTLAKE, Rev Peter Alan Grant, CMG, MC (1919–), Minister at Tokyo 1971–76.

WHITEHEAD, Sir John (Stainton), GCMG, CVO (1932–), Minister at Tokyo 1980–1984, Ambassador to Japan 1986–92.

WILLIAMS, Nigel Christopher Ransome, CMG (1937–). Ambassador to Denmark 1989–93, Permanent Representative to the UN at Geneva 1993–97.

WRIGHT, Sir David (John) GCMG, LVO (1944–), Ambassador to Korea, 1990–94, Ambassador to Japan, 1996–99, Group Chief Executive, British Trade International 1999–2002.

PART 4

Officers who served at Tokyo in the rank of Minister or Counsellor between 1945 and 1972 who were neither former members of the Japan Consular Service or Japanese Language Officers.

ASHE, Sir Derrick (Rosslyn), KCMG (1919–2000), Minister at Tokyo1969–71, Ambassador to Romania 1972–75, to the Argentine 1975–77, to the Disarmament Conference at Geneva 1977–79.

CHADWICK, Sir John (Edward), KCMG (1911–1987), Commercial Counsellor at Tokyo 1953–56, Ambassador to Romania 1967–68, to the OECD 1969–71.

CLUTTON, Sir George (Lisle), KCMG (1909–1970), Minister at Tokyo 1950–52, Ambassador to the Philippines 1955–59, to Poland 1960–66.

FIGGESS, Sir John, KBE, CMG (1909–97), Military Attaché at Tokyo 1956–61,

Information Counsellor, Tokyo, 1961–69, Commissioner General for the UK at Expo 70 in Osaka. See biographical portrait by Hugh Cortazzi in *Biographical Portraits* Volume III, 1999.

HALFORD (later Halford-MacLeod), Aubrey Seymour, CMG, CVO (1914–2000), Counsellor and Head of Chancery at Tokyo 1953–55, Political Agent Kuwait 1957–59, Ambassador to Iceland 1966–70.

HARPHAM, Sir William, KBE, CMG (1906–1999), Minister at Tokyo 1956–59, Ambassador to Bulgaria 1964–66.

HARRIS, Colin Grendon, CMG (1912–92), Counsellor Commercial at Tokyo 1963–66.

JOHN, Robert Michael (1924–80), Consul General at Osaka 1967–71, Ambassador to Panama 1974–8.

LINGEMAN, Eric Ralph, CBE (1898–1966), Economic Minister at Tokyo 1947–50, Minister (Commercial) Rome 1950–51, Ambassador to Afghanistan 1951–55.

MAYALL, Sir (Alexander) Lees, KCVO, CMG (1915–1992), Counsellor and Head of Chancery at Tokyo 1958–61, Vice Marshall of the Diplomatic Corps 1965–72, Ambassador to Venezuela 1972–75.

McGHIE, James Ironside, CMG (1915–92), Second Secretary at Tokyo 1954–57, Minister (Commercial) at Tokyo 1973–75.

OLDHAM, Alan Trevor, CBE (1904–71), Consul General at Osaka 1952–56.

PINK, Sir Ivo Thomas Montagu, KCMG (1910–66), Counsellor at Tokyo 1948–49, Ambassador to Chile 1958–61.

REDMAN, Sir Vere, CMG (1901–75), Counsellor Information at Tokyo, 1946–61. See biographical portrait by Hugh Cortazzi in *Biographical Portraits* Volume II, 1997.

ROBERTS, Sir Norman Stanley, KBE, CMG (1893–1972), Minister (Commercial) at Tokyo (later Minister), 1950–53.

SELBY, Ralph Walford, CMG (1915–97), Counsellor and Head of Chancery at Tokyo 1956–58, Ambassador to Norway 1972–75.

SHAW, Thomas Richard, CMG (1912–89), Ambassador to Ivory Coast, Niger and Upper Volta 1964–67, Minister at Tokyo 1967–69, Ambassador to Morocco 1969–71.

THORNE, Benjamin, CMG, MBE (1922–), First Secretary Commercial at Tokyo 1968–69, Commercial Counsellor at Tokyo 1973–79.

TRENCH, Sir Nigel (Crosby) (later 7th Baron Ashtown), KCMG (1916–), Counsellor and Head of Chancery at Tokyo 1961–63, Ambassador to Korea 1969–71, to Portugal 1974–76.

WAKEFIELD, Sir Peter (George Arthur), KBE, CMG (1922–) Economic and Commercial Counsellor (later Minister) at Tokyo 1970–73, Ambassador to the Lebanon 1975–78, to Belgium 1979–82.

WARNER, Sir Edward (Redstone), KCMG, OBE (1911–2002) Minister at Tokyo 1959–62, Ambassador to Cameroon 1963–66, to Tunisia 1968–70.

Notes

PART I. INTRODUCTION

1. Professor W. G. Beasley in his study *Great Britain and the Opening of Japan* (London 1951) surveyed the history of British interest in Japan from the time of the British trading post in Hirado to the Elgin Mission of 1858.
2. See J. E. Hoare, 'Captain Broughton, HMS *Providence* and her Tender and Japan, 1794–98' in *Biographical Portraits Volume III*, Japan Library, 1999
3. See W. G. Aston, 'H.M.S. *Phaeton* at Nagasaki' in *Transactions of the Asiatic Society of Japan First Series Volume VII*, 1879 pp. 323–36.
4. The text is contained in Appendix A to W.G.Beasley's *Great Britain and the Opening of Japan,* London 1951
5. See appendixes to G. A. Lensen, *The Russian Push towards Japan*, Princeton 1959.
6. See W. G. Beasley, *Select Documents on Japanese Foreign Policy 1853–1868*, London, 1955.
7. A detailed account of the mission of Lord Elgin to Japan is contained in Laurence Oliphant's two-volume '*Narrative of the Earl of Elgin's Mission to China and Japan in the years, 1857, '58, '59*, Edinburgh and London, 1859.
8. W. G. Beasley, *Britain and the Opening of Japan*, page 190
9. Hugh Cortazzi, *Dr Willis in Japan, British Medical Pioneer*, London, 1985, page 28.
10. The Diplomatic Corps in Edo and Yokohama was tiny. At first the only missions were the Americans, the British, the Dutch, the French and the Russians. Even at the end of the nineteenth century the corps was small in comparison to what it would become in the twentieth century.
11. Ernest Satow, *A Diplomat in Japan,* London, 1921, page 156 et seq.
12. *Mitford's Japan*, edited by Hugh Cortazzi, 2nd edition, Japan Library, 2002, page 31.
13. H.J.Jones, *Live Machines, Hired Foreigners and Meiji Japan*, Tenterden, 1980
14. Ernest Satow, *A Diplomat in Japan*, London, 1921.
15. *Mitford's Japan*, edited by Hugh Cortazzi, 2nd edition, Japan Library, 2002.
16. Mrs Fraser, *A Diplomat's Wife in Japan*, edited by Hugh Cortazzi, Weatherhill, 1982.

1. SIR RUTHERFORD ALCOCK

1. Alexander Michie, *The Englishman in China during the Victorian Era as Demonstrated in the Career of Sir Rutherford Alcock KCB DCL, Many Years Consul and Minister in China,* Edinburgh and London, 1900, Vol. I, p. 135.
2. See 'William Keswick, 1835–1912, Jardine's Pioneer in Japan' by J. E. Hoare *Biographical Portraits Volume IV* (pp. 111–117), Japan Library, 2002.
3. Hugh Cortazzi, *Dr Willis in Japan, British Medical Pioneer, 1862–1877*, London, 1985, p. 33.

4.   *Mitford's Japan*, edited by Hugh Cortazzi, London, 1985, p. 11.
5.   Sir Rutherford Alcock, *The Capital of the Tycoon: A Narrative of Three Years' Residence in Japan*, London, 1863, Vol. I pp. 166–81.
6.   Dr William Willis was in due course appointed to fill the post of medical officer and legation assistant, but he did not arrive until after the first Tōzenji incident. If Alcock had not himself had experience as a surgeon the Legation would have suffered even more than it did in the 1861 attack.
7.   Matsumai was the name of the Japanese fief which was responsible for the whole of Yezo, i.e. the present Hokkaidō.
8.   Alcock's 'imperialist' interests continued after his retirement from the post of Minister at Peking. He became chairman of the British North Borneo company in 1881 and remained in this post until he resigned in 1893. K. G. Tregonning, *Under Chartered Rule (North Borneo 1881–1946)*, Singapore, 1958.
9.   For details of Oliphant's experiences see *Episodes in a Life of Adventure*, New York, 1887, pp. 174–86. George Alexander Lensen in his book *The Russian Push towards Japan, Russo-Japanese Relations, 1697–1875*, New York, 1971 puts the episode in a different perspective. He asserted that (p. 448) 'The surveying of the Tsushima coast by an English warship in 1861 strengthened the Russian conviction that the British, who had been prevented by the Russo-Chinese treaties of 1858 and 1860 from gaining a naval station on the Asian continent between the Amur River and Korea, might try to annex Tsushima and ultimately bottle up Russian expansion at this point. Consul Goshkevitch informed the Shogunate that the British had designs on the island, and urged the Japanese to make adequate defence preparations, offering Russian assistance in supplying Tsushima with cannons in constructing suitable gun emplacements. The Japanese declined his offer. Nevertheless a Russian man-of-war soon arrived at Tsushima and the Russians appeared to be about to take over the island.'
10. Alcock, *Art and Art Industries in Japan*, London, 1878, pp. 15, 237 and 292.

2. LT. COLONEL EDWARD ST JOHN NEALE

I should like to thank Professor Nakasuga Tetsuro for many helpful suggestions and valuable insights.

Official despatches to and from the Foreign Office are in the Public Record Office file FO 46 and as published for Parliament. A selection of relevant documents, especially on the Japanese side, covering plans to expel foreigners and the Namamugi Incident can be found in W. G. Beasley: *Select Documents on Japanese Foreign Policy 1853–1868*, Section V pp 222–256.
1.   The Foreign Office lists in the nineteenth century did not give dates of birth or details of education. Neale was clearly born before the compulsory registration of births. I have tried various sources in an effort to trace his date of birth but without success. The Central Registrar's overseas records could not trace a death certificate. Burke's Landed Gentry recorded various Neales, but not Edward St John Neale. I also tried the baptismal records in Madras in case he had been born there but this search yielded nothing. We can probably assume that as he joined the army in Spain in 1832 he was at least 20 by that time. This suggests that he was born somewhere between 1805 and 1812 and was getting on towards 60 when he died. Foreign Office reports in the PRO (FO45/47 and 48) record that Neale's death was reported by C. Smith, Vice Consul at Guayaquil, in a despatch dated 23 December 1866 'after an illness of only 48 hours'. He had instructed Neale's son, Henry St John Neale who was with his father in Quito, to deposit the archives of the Legation for safe-keeping with the US or French Legation. Neale, as he reported in his despatch from Quito dated 4 Jan 1866, had arrived at Guayaquil on 4 December 1865. He recorded that that the roads from Guayaquil to Quito were in 'so impassable a condition' at that season that 'even the Indians had for a while ceased to travel over them'. However, feeling that if he waited longer he might not be able to reach Quito he set out and 'after a harassing journey of eleven days' reached Quito on 4 January 1866. His predecessor at Quito, a Mr Fagan,

had left Quito and taken another road to Guayaquil; so they never met. Fagan had left the archives of the Legation with the French Chargé d'Affaires. Neale sent home on 5 December 1866 a despatch on the situation in Ecuador (which had been known as Equator). On 15 December a despatch signed by Henry St John Neale to Lord Stanley, the Foreign Secretary, reporting his father's death added that he had indeed handed the archives of the Legation for safe keeping to the French Chargé d'Affaires. He recorded that he had had his father's remains embalmed and would proceed with them to Europe for burial. FO records include a protocol expressing the condolences of Neale's diplomatic colleagues in Quito and 'the painful impressions produced by the opposition of the ecclesiastical authorities to the passage of the remains within the precincts and under the disposition of the Catholic Church'. There is also in FO records a note from the Minister of Ecuador in Quito to the Foreign Secretary dated 15 December 1866 which expresses condolences and notes that Neale 'died of a serious complaint against which the efforts of science were unavailing.'

2.   See Hugh Cortazzi's biographical portrait of Alcock in this volume.

3.   Foreign Office despatch to Lt Col Neale, 10 November 1863.

4.   *The Illustrated London News*, 27 February 1864.

5.   Page 133 of The Foreign Office List for 1867. I have been unable to find confirmation in the Army Lists for 1832–1838 of Neale's service in the British army.

6.   The will, dated 9 November 1857 when Neale was HM Consul at Varna in Bulgaria, mentions his wife Adelaide, his daughter Adelaide Harriet Eliza and his two sons Henry St John Dudley Neale and William Buchanan Neale, as well as his brother William Trevor Neale. The executor who proved the will in 1867 was his cousin Major Henry Clarinbold Powell. When probate was granted on 20 April 1867 the 'Effects' of the deceased were declared to be under £10,000. A note adds that this was 'resworn at the Stamp Office under £9,000 in July 1869'. Under the will if any of his children who were beneficiaries became Roman Catholics or entered a convent or monastery they were to lose their inheritance.

7.   Hugh Cortazzi *Dr Willis in Japan, British Medical Pioneer in Japan 1862–1877*, 1985,(page 48). Willis described Winchester as being 'as fat as a pork butcher. He is a very good man and easy to get along with, with no pride or nonsense about him. He is passably clever, will do what he is ordered and nothing more'. Mrs Winchester, according to Willis, was a mischief maker. She was 'an immensely big woman six feet high and about nineteen stone. She has the lord and master all under her thumb and, indeed, she is the Chargé d'Affaires.' Because of her size she was nicknamed 'Daiboots' after the Daibutsu at Kamakura.

8.   For an account of the Legation at Tōzenji and the two Tōzenji incidents see Hugh Cortazzi 'The First British Legation in Japan 1859–1874' in Japan Society *Proceedings* No 102, page 25 et seq

9.   In a letter to the Foreign Office dated 7 June 1862 he protested about the costs of his move.

10. There was in fact only one 'assassin'. He was Itō Gunbei (1840–62) of the Matsumoto fief (*Han*). He had been angered by the rough and arrogant behaviour of some foreigners and was concerned by the strain on the finances of the Matsumoto fief in meeting the costs of providing guards for the British Legation. He seems to have thought that if he killed a British guard the Matsumoto fief would be absolved from providing guards for the Legation. After he had killed two guards he returned to the fief's yashiki in Edo, confessed to his colleagues what he had done and forthwith committed suicide.

11. Matsudaira Mitsuhisa (1832–92) was the daimyo of Matsumoto in the province of Shinshū (now Nagano prefecture). After the first Tōzenji incident in 1861 his fief had been appointed together with the Ogaki and Kishiwada fiefs to provide a guard for the Legation. It consisted of about 535 men.

12. For a graphic account of this incident through the eyes of Dr William Willis see Hugh Cortazzi *Dr Willis in Japan*, 1985, pp 23–27.

13. The senior officials of the *Bakufu* consisted of four to five *rōjū* and three to four

wakadoshiyori plus a number of *bugyō* (governors). After the Treaties were concluded in 1858 up to ten *gaikokubugyō* and two to three Kanagawa *bugyō* were appointed. Members of the *rōjū* also performed duties as ministers for foreign affairs.

14. Vice Admiral Hope in a despatch to the Admiralty from Shanghai dated 2 August 1862 noted that 'The position of the present Legation House for defence is so bad, it being situated in a narrow dell with wooded banks, that it is difficult to afford adequate protection . . .'

15. In a despatch to the Admiralty on 27 August 1862 Vice Admiral Hope took a bellicose line. He recommended that once the new Legation on Gotenyama was ready the former residence at Tōzenji should be razed to the ground, the area kept bare and a monument put up 'to the perpetual remembrance of the detestation' caused by the recent incident. He called for a blockade of the ports of Edo, Nagasaki and the Inland Sea if the Japanese authorities do not take adequate measures against the daimyo responsible including payment of a 'heavy fine'. These recommendations did not find favour in London.

16. Shimazu Hisamitsu (1817–87) was the father of Shimazu Tadayoshi (1840–97), nominally the daimyo of Satsuma, but was the real power in Satsuma. He had come to Edo with an imperial emissary Ohara Shigetomi (1801–79) leading about 1000 men and had had an audience with the Shogun Tokugawa Iemochi (1846–66). He had demanded various reforms including a relaxation of the *sankin kōtai* sytem (whereby the daimyo were forced to spend part of the time in Edo and to leave their families there as hostages when they returned to their fiefs). This was the first time in the history of the Edo *Bakufu* that one of the tozama (outer fiefs) daimyo had attempted to intervene in the affairs of the government in Edo and underlined the weakness of the *Bakufu*.

17. Neale to Russell, 15 September 1862.

18. Memorandum dated 28 November 1862.

19. Howard Vyse was lucky not to have been sent home on the next ship for his disloyalty to his chief, but Neale was short of staff. Vyse was moved to the consulate at Hakodate in December 1862 and to Nagasaki in May 1865. He resigned in 1866.

20. For a brief account of the discussions in London leading up to the issue of these instructions please see final section of Appendix I on the British bombardment of Kagoshima.

21. According to Japanese records Richardson was cut down by an expert swordsman Narahara Kizaemon (1831–65) and was despatched by Kaeda Nobuyoshi (1832–1906)

22. Neale to Russell, 12 December 1862.

23. Neale to Russell, 15 January 1863.

24. According to Japanese records the arson attack took place in the middle of the night of 31 January/1 February. The twelve perpetrators from the Chōshū fief included Takasugi Shinsaku (1839–67), Kusaka Genzui (1840–64), Itō Shunsuke (later Hirobumi) (1841–1909) and Inoue Bunta (later known as Kaoru) (1835–1915). They had originally planned to attack the settlement at Yokohama.

25. Neale to Russell, 10 February 1863.

26. Three weeks before Neale wrote this despatch, on 16 January 1863, following the visit of the imperial emissary Ohara Shigetomi to Edo, another imperial emissary Sanjō Sanetomi (1837–91), accompanied by the daimyo of Tosa Yamanouchi Toyonori (1846–86), and others had handed to the shogun an imperial rescript demanding the expulsion of the foreign barbarians. The *Bakufu* had agreed to break off relations with the foreign powers and had said that they would confirm when action would be taken during the Shogun's planned visit to Kyoto. The Shogun Tokugawa Iemochi, accompanied by the *rōju* and some 3000 men reached Kyoto on 21 April, 1863. This was the first time in 229 years since the time of Tokugawa Iemitsu that a Shogun had visited Kyoto and underlined the weakened position of the *Bakufu*.

27. Neale to Russell, 29 March 1863.

28. On 6 June 1863 Tokugawa Yoshinobu (Keiki) (1837–1913) told the Emperor

Kōmei, in the name of the Shogun, that the date for action on the imperial demand
would be 25 June. On the following day he informed all the daimyo of this decision,
but Keiki did not himself believe that the expulsion of the foreigners could be accomplished.
29. Neale to Kuper , 24 June 1863.
30. Described as Ogasawara Jewsio no Kami i.e. *Ogasawara Zusho no Kami* Nagamichi
(1822–91). At the same time as the reparations for the Namamugi incident were paid,
the foreign representatives had been handed a note calling for the closure of the ports
of Yokohama, Nagasaki and Hakodate and the withdrawal of foreign residents. This
had been sent to comply with the orders received from the court in Kyoto.
31. Translation from Dutch translation from the Japanese. Neale also included translations from the Japanese made by von Siebold and by Satow, but the purport did not
differ materially.
32. Letter from Neale to the Minister dated 24 June 1863.
33. An Ambassador today could never hope to receive a despatch in a similar vein. It
has to be remembered that it took up to four months to receive a reply from London
in those days.
34. On the same day 3 July 1863 Sakai Tadamasa (1816–76), one of the *wakadoshiyori*,
handed to the British and French Chargé d'Affaires and to the commanders of their
fleets a letter assigning to them the defence of Yokohama.
35. Neale to Russell, 29 July 1863.
36. Neale to Russell, 31 October 1863.
37. Neale to Russell, 16 November 1863.
38. Neale to Russell, 29 January 1864.
39. The attack took place at the instigation of the anti-foreign faction in Chōshū led
by Kusaka Genzui and Takasugi Shinsaku following the *Bakufu*'s notification to the
court that the date for executing the court's instructions for the expulsion of the foreigners would be 25 June 1863.
40. Neale to Russell, 13 July 1863.
41. Neale to Russell, 11 September 1863, enclosing reports by Mr Consul Winchester.
42. Japanese exports consisted largely of primary products such as raw silk, tea,
marine products, copper and lacquer. The sudden increase in demand had a serious
inflationary impact on the Japanese economy. This in turn undermined the *Bakufu*.
43. Neale to Russell, 14 October 1863.
44. Neale to Russell, 1 March 1864.
45. Ernest Satow *A Diplomat in Japan*, London 1921, page 53 and 54.
46. Ernest Satow pages 61–62.
47. Ernest Satow pages 69–71.
48. 'Old gentleman' suggests that Neale was at least in his late fifties.
49. Hugh Cortazzi *Dr Willis in Japan*, pp 30 and 36.

3. ALCOCK RETURNS TO JAPAN, 1864

Despatches quoted are from papers presented to parliament covering correspondence
respecting affairs in Japan in 1864/5. See also PRO FO 46. See also *Select Documents on
Japanese Foreign Policy 1853–1868*, W. G. Beasley, Oxford University Press 1955, Section
VI, pp. 257–289.

1.   The wording of this despatch suggests a compromise between officials in the
Foreign Office and the Admiralty to reflect the views of all parties!
2.   Lord Russell to Alcock of 26 July 1864 referred to the 'considerable burden' of the
squadron and declared that it was not 'easy to perceive' how a war 'would enable Great
Britain to reduce her present expenses. The invasion of the interior would of itself be
a most costly undertaking, and the enforcement of a new Treaty by the establishment
of forts and garrisons in Japan would entail a very large permanent burden'
3.   Russell to Alcock of 8 August 1864.

4.   Alcock to Russell. 25 May 1864, received in London on 2 August 1864.
5.   Russell to Alcock, 18 August 1864.
6.   Kuper to the Secretary to the Admiralty, 23 July 1864.
7.   Alcock to Kuper, 22 July 1864, Yokohama.
8.   Alcock to Russell, 28 September 1864.
9.   Alcock to Russell, Yokohama, 28 October 1864. The French in the convention concluded in early 1864 in Paris but which had not been ratified by the Shogun's government had agreed to accept 140,000 dollars for the Japanese attack on the Kienchang. This set a precedent for payments to the other powers whose ships had been attacked. Payment of the indemnity was still an issue between Britain and Japan at the time of the Iwakura Mission in 1872
10. Alcock to Russell, 15 October 1864.
11. Alcock to Russell 19 November 1864.

4. SIR HARRY PARKES

1.   Quoted in 'The Pestilently Active Minister' by Sir Hugh Cortazzi. *Monumenta Nipponica*, Vol. XXXIX, No. 2 (1984), p. 148.
2.   H. Cortazzi, *Dr Willis in Japan: Bntish Medical Pioneer 1862–1877*, London: The Athlone Press, 1985, p. 67. (Hereafter referred to as *Willis*.)
3.   Grace Fox, *Britain and Japan 1858–1883* Oxford: Clarendon Press, 1969, p. 160. (Hereafter referred to as Fox.)
4.   Isabella Bird, *Unbeaten Tracks in Japan*, London, 1880, p. 22.
5   *Willis*, p. 206.
6.   *Willis*, p. 206.
7.   *Willis*, p. 80.
8.   S. Lane Poole and F. V. Dickins (eds.) *The Life of Sir Harry Parkes*, 2 volumes, London, 1894, Volume II, p. 357. This deals with Parkes in Japan (Hereafter referred to as Dickins.).
9.   Dickins, p. 358.
10. Dickins, p. 169.
11. Fox, p. 160.
12. Dickins, p. 169.
13. Dickins, p. 337.
14. Dickins, p. 355.
15. H. Cortazzi (ed.), *Mitford's Japan, The Memoirs and recollections of Algernon Bertram Mitford, the first Lord Redesdale*, London: The Athlone Press, 1985, p. 22. (Hereafter referred to as Mitford.)
16. *Willis*, p. 77.
17. Mitford, pp. 110–12.
18. Sir Ernest Satow, A Diplomat in Japan, London, 1921, p. 141. (Hereafter referred to as Satow.)
19. Mitford, p. 30.
20. *Willis*, p. 68.
21. *Willis*, p. 79.
22. Satow, p. 141.
23. Satow, p. 233.
24. Mitford, p. 22.
25. *Willis*, pp.71/2.
26. Satow, p. 260.
27. Satow, p. 332.
28. Satow, p. 398.
29. Dickins, p. 354.
30. See footnote No. 67.
31. Fox, p. 596.
32. Basil Hall Chamberlain, *Things Japanese*, London and Tokyo, 1890, p. 267.

33. Mitford, pp. 82–4.
34. Satow, p. 141.
35. Satow, p. 158.
36. *Willis*, p. 123.
37. Dickins, p. 354.
38. Fox, p. 161.
39. W. E. Griffis, *The Mikado's Empire*, New York, 1876, p. 577.
40. Fox, p. 176.
41. Fox, p. 214.
42. Fox, pp.224/S.
43. Fox, p. 543.
44. W. G. Beasley, 'Sir Harry Parkes and the Meiji Restoration', *Transactions of the Asiatic Society of Japan*, Third Series, Vol. 12, December 1975, p. 33.
45. Ibid, p. 35.
46. Ibid, p. 36.
47. W. G. Beasley, *The Meiji Restoration*, Stanford: U.P., 1972, p. 310.
48. Ibid, p. 344.
49. *tozama daimyō*, literally 'outer lords' in contrast to the *fudai daimyo˜* who were related to, or close supporters of, the Tokugawa.
50. Fox, pp.179, 423/4.
51. Satow, p. 160.
52. Fox, pp.248/9.
53. Fox, p. 487.
54. Fox, p. 493.
55. Fox, p. 494.
56. G. Daniels, 'Sir Harry Parkes and the Meiji Government, 1868–83', in *Proceedings of the Japan Society*, 115 (March 1990), p. 20. (Hereafter referred to as Daniels.)
57. Hazel Jones, *Live Machines: Hired Foreigners and Meiji Japan*, Tenterden: Paul Norbury Publications, 1980, pp. 148–9. (Hereafter referred to as Jones.)
58. R. H. Brunton, *Building Japan, 1868–76* (edited by Sir Hugh Cortazzi), Folkestone: Japan Library, p. 9.
59. Fox, p. 375.
60. Fox, p. 544.
61. Jones, p. 61.
62. Daniels, p. 24.
63. Dickins, p. 319.
64. Dickins, p. 322.
65. Fox, p. 477.
66. Daniels, pp.22/3.
67. Daniels, p. 24.
68. Jones, p. 182, quotes from a letter from Okuma Shigenobu 'that it was a pity that the Japanese always tended to heap the blame upon the English and former Minister Parkes in particular. Parkes' contributions were quickly forgotten'
69. Daniels, p. 25.
70. Fox, p. 435.
71. Dickins, p. 278.
72. Dickins, p. 279.
73. Dickins, p. 273.
74. Fox, p. 267.
75. Daniels, p. 25.
76. Dickins, p. 343.
77. Basil Hall Chamberlain, *Things Japanese*, London and Tokyo, 1890, p. 267.
78. Daniels, p. 26.

5. SIR FRANCIS PLUNKETT

PRINCIPAL SOURCES. FO files in the Public Record Office covering Plunkett's time in Japan (FO 46 and FO 262 series), Foreign Office lists, *Dictionary of National Biography*, *The Times* as quoted and the *Japan Weekly Mail* for 1886 and 1887.

1.   DNB entry for Francis Plunkett by Thomas Henry Sanderson.
2.   *Embassies in the East* by J.E.Hoare, Richmond: Curzon Press, 1999, page 115.
3.   *Sir Harry Parkes, British Representative in Japan, 1865–83* by Gordon Daniels, Richmond: Japan Library, 1996, pages 160/1.
4.   Plunkett's account of his journey in August 1875 in HMS *Frolic* has been preserved at the PRO (FO 46 193)
5.   Papers preserved in the PRO are quite voluminous.
6.   *Embassies in the Far East* by J. E. Hoare, Richmond: Curzon Press 1999, page 117.
7.   Quoted in the *Life of Sir Harry Parkes* by F. V. Dickins and Lane Poole, Volume II, London: 1894, page 221.
8.   In relation to Consular jurisdiction as set out in the 1858 Treaties.
9.   See page 5 of a paper by Ian Ruxton of the Kyushu institute of Technology on 'The Ending of Extraterritoriality in Japan' for The History, Political and International Relations section of the 9th triennial conference of European Association of Japanese Studies at Lahti, Finland in August 2000. This paper also provides useful additional background on the Treaty Revision negotiations.
10.   For a fuller account of this conversation see Ian Nish's paper entitled 'Japan's Modernization and Anglo-Japanese Rivalry in the 1880s' in *Bruno Lewin zu Ehren: Festschrift aus Anlass seines 65. Geburtstages* Band II Japan. Universitaetsverlag Dr.N.Brockmeyer. Bochum. 1989.
11.   *Japan Weekly Mail*, Aug 7, 1886.
12.   Satow Papers (PRO 30/33 1 / 2)
13.   *The Diaries and Letters of Sir Ernest Mason Satow, 1843–1929, a Scholar Diplomat in East Asia*, edited by Ian Ruxton, 1998, Lampeter: Edwin Mellen Press, page 214.
14.   Nigel Brailey of the University of Bristol who has made a particular study of Satow especially during his time in Bangkok is the source for this information.
15.   See Ian Nish's biographical portrait of Gubbins in *Biographical Portraits*, vol. II, Richmond: Japan Library, 1997 reproduced in this volume.
16.   In his essay on the 'The Era of Unequal Treaties' in *The Political-Diplomatic Dimension 1600–1930*, edited by Ian Nish and Yoichi Kibata, Palgrave, 2000, Jim Hoare wrote of Francis Plunkett that he 'was a more easy-going man, less given to hectoring. But he had been Parkes's Secretary of Legation in the mid-1870s, and naturally continued something of that approach'. I have not found direct evidence to support Dr Hoare's comment.

6. HUGH FRASER

Sources include: PRO Records in FO 46 for 1889–1894, *The Japan Weekly Mail*, 1889–1894, Mary Fraser: *A Diplomatist's Wife in Japan; Letters from Home to Home* (first published in 1899 by Hutchinson and Co and republished as *A Diplomat's Wife in Japan; Sketches at the Turn of the Century* (edited by Hugh Cortazzi Weatherhill, Tokyo and New York, 1982); Mary Fraser: *Reminiscences of a Diplomatist's Wife in Many Lands*, 1911; Mary Fraser: Further Reminiscences, 1912.

1.   *A Diplomat's Wife in Japan: Sketches at the Turn of the Century* is the title of the edition which I made in 1982 and which was published by Weatherhill, Tokyo.
2.   Eton College Records.
3.   *Further Reminiscences*, published in 1912, includes more comments on Hugh Fraser's career and character than are contained in either of Mary Fraser's other books.
4.   For background on Mary Crawford please see the introduction to my edition of *A Diplomat's wife in Japan.*

5.   In her three books listed above.
6.   *A Diplomat's Wife* page 89.
7.   *A Diplomat's Wife* page 224.
8.   *A Diplomat's Wife* page 334. Three strawberries (*fraises*) were part of the Fraser coat of arms ('azure trois fraises argent')
9.   The Treaties concluded in 1858 with their provisions for extraterritorial jurisdiction over foreign residents as well as their trade provisions were increasingly resented by the Japanese who had made strenuous efforts to modernize their country. They limited Japanese sovereignty and extraterritoriality came to be seen as insulting. Various attempts had been made in the 1870s and 1880s to get agreement from the Powers to revised treaties. One proposal had been for the establishment of mixed courts but this aroused a furore of protest and the Japanese position gradually hardened. The Japanese recognized that at this stage in the nineteenth century an agreement with Britain was the key to revision of the other treaties, but they also saw that benefits might be had by trying to seek agreement first with other Powers e.g. the USA and Germany, thus putting pressure on Britain to make concessions.
     The foreign communities, of which the British were by far the largest, while wanting to be able to travel freely outside the Treaty ports and resenting Japanese restrictions on their freedom to trade desired at the same time to retain their privileged position (consular rights, leases etc). They were highly critical of Japanese justice and vigorously opposed concessions often accusing those involved in the negotiations of not standing up for the 'rights' of foreigners in Japan.
     Background on the Treaties and on some of the other personalities involved can be found in Ian Nish's biographical portraits of Aoki Shūzō and J. H. Gubbins in *Biographical Portraits*, Vols II and III (Japan Library for the Japan Society, 1997 and 1999). See also essays by James Hoare 'The Era of the Unequal Treaties 1858–99' and by Inouye Yuichi 'From Unequal Treaty to the Anglo-Japanese Alliance, 1867–1902' in Volume I of *The Political-Diplomatic Dimension, 1600–1930*, edited by Ian Nish and Yoichi Kibata, 2000.
10. Despatch No 97.
11. See Dr Carmen Blacker's essay 'Two Piggotts ...' in *Britain and Japan, 1859–1991, Themes and Personalities*, edited by Hugh Cortazzi and Gordon Daniels and published for the Japan Society in 1991.
12. *Biographical Portraits*, Volume II, 1997.
13. *Biographical Portraits*, Volume II, 1997.
14. *Despatch* No 144.
15. See biographical portrait of 'Josiah Conder (1852–1920) and Meiji Architecture' by Dallas Finn in *Britain and Japan, 1859–1991, Themes and Personalities*, edited by Hugh Cortazzi and Gordon Daniels, London 1991.

7. POWER HENRY LE POER TRENCH

1.   Trench's entry in FO List.
2.   According to The Life of Sir Harry Parkes by F. V. Dickins and S. Lane-Poole, London 1894, page 344 Trench accompanied Sir Harry at a farewell audience with 'the Mikado' on 25 August 1883.
3.   His friends in the Tokyo Club gave an elaborate farewell dinner for him at the Rokumeikan on 27 March 1889. The entremet's, perhaps inevitably, included 'Pouding Diplomate'.
4.   Later Sir Francis Ottiwell Adams, KCMG, CB, ended his career as Minister in Berne. He died in 1889.
5.   Paget (1864–1940) became The Right Hon. Sir Ralph Spener Paget KCMG, CVO. He was Minister to Siam and then Belgrade before becoming the first British Ambassador to Brazil (at Rio de Janeiro). He seems to have suffered from ill-health in Tokyo as he was allowed leave of absence from Tokyo on health grounds in late 1894 returning to Japan in the early spring of 1895. Hugh Fraser died in 1894, Trench suf-

fered a stroke in 1895 and Paget was sick in 1894. The British Legation in Tokyo in
these years does not seem to have been a healthy one.
6.   *Japan Weekly Mail*, 25 August 1894.
7.   According to Count Mutsu's memoir *Kenkenroku* (translated by Gordon Mark
Berger and published in 1982 by the University of Tokyo Press) the Russian Minister
was Mikhail Khitrovo.
8.   *Kenkenroku* page 130.
9.   From late February 1895 Lowther signed despatches for Trench. On 5 March he
received a note from Mutsu to the effect that following Trench's illness the Secretary
of State for Foreign Affairs had requested through the Japanese Minister in London
that the Foreign Minister communicate in future with Lowther.
10. An account of these incidents was given in *The Japan Weekly Mail* for 10
November 1894.
11. Lowther (1858–1916) became The Right Hon. Sir Gerard Augustus Lowther Bart
GCMG, CB. He was Minister to Chile and Tangier before becoming Ambassador to
Constantinople (1908–13). Baroness d'Anethan, the English wife of the Belgian
Minister, recorded in her diary (*Fourteen Years of Diplomatic Life in Japan*, London,
1912) that on 31 January 1985 'half Tokyo came to the Legation [Belgian] to meet Mr
Gerard Lowther and his sister'. 'They seemed extremely charming.'
12. Baroness d'Anethan refers twice to Trench in her diary. On 2 January 1895 she
records that Trench was a member of their party when they visited Atami 'some in
chairs, some on foot, some in *kagos*'. They had good weather and enjoyed the scenery
of what the baroness referred to as 'the Japanese Riviera'. Her second reference was on
1 March when she called to inquire after Trench's health. 'We received a by no means
reassuring account.' Lady MacDonald wife of Sir Claude MacDonald who took over as
Minister in Tokyo from Satow in 1900 was appalled by having to occupy a residence
which had been in the charge of bachelors [Trench was a bachelor and Satow nominally one]. ' She would not attempt to describe the drawing room paper chosen by Mr
Trench.' Quoted in *Embassies in the East* by J.E.Hoare, 1999, page 121.

8. SIR ERNEST SATOW

1.   It will be assumed that readers know something of Satow's previous posting in
Japan, having read *A Diplomat in Japan* (Seeley, Service & Co. London, 1921) about the
years 1862–69. See also Peter F. Kornicki's chapter on Satow in Cortazzi and Daniels
(eds), *Britain and Japan, 1859–1991* (Routledge, London and New York, 1991) reproduced in Part IV of this volume, and Ian C. Ruxton (ed) *The Diaries and Letters of Sir
Ernest Mason Satow* (Edwin Mellen Press, Lampeter 1998).
2.   Diary, 17 May 1895. Satow's private diaries are in the Satow papers beginning at
PRO 30/33 15/1–17 (1861–96), continuing in PRO30/33 16/1–12 (1896–1912) and
ending at PRO 30/33 17/1–16 (1912–26 and various travel diaries 1879–1906).
3.   See Brailey, N. (ed.) The Satow Siam Papers, vol. 1, The Historical Society,
Bangkok, 1997.
4.   In a letter to his former Japan colleague and friend W.G. Aston, provisionally
appointed Consul-General in Korea, dated 27 June 1884 Satow wrote enviously: 'The
work must be very interesting, and you have a teachable people to deal with.' Satow
Papers, PRO 30/33/11/3
5.   The long leave was the low point in Satow's diplomatic career, but he made good
use of his time, visiting family and friends (A.B. Mitford, William Willis), reading in
libraries (in Oxford, Rome, Madrid and Lisbon) and getting confirmed in the Anglican
faith on 29 October 1888.
6.   See Dr. H. Temperley's entry on Satow in *Dictionary of National Biography, 1922–30*
(Oxford: Oxford University Press, 1963).
7.   Ian Nish, *The Anglo-Japanese Alliance*, (London: The Athlone Press, 1966) p. 11. In
Japan there had been growing pressure for repudiation of the old treaties, so that the
process of renegotiation may have been an attempt by the Western Powers to keep

Japan within the 'comity of nations' and prevent her sliding back into '*sakoku*' – isolation (see N. Brailey, 'Ernest Satow and Japanese Revised Treaty Implementation', a paper delivered at STICERD on 9 July 1999).

8.   For more detail, see Mutsu Munemitsu, *Kenkenroku: A Diplomatic Record of the Sino-Japanese War, 1894–1895.* (trans. Gordon M. Berger. Tokyo: University of Tokyo, 1982.) See also Beasley, W., *Japanese Imperialism 1894–1945* (Oxford: Clarendon Press, 1991); Lone, S., *Japan's First Modern War: Army and Society in the Conflict with China, 1894–95* (London: Macmillan, 1994).

9.   From Lensen, G. A. (Translated and ed.) *The d'Anethan Dispatches from Japan, 1894–1910* (Tallahassee, Florida: The Diplomatic Press, 1967). p. 53.
For more excerpts from Satow's diary see also Lensen, G. A. (ed.) *Korea and Manchuria Between Russia and Japan, 1895–1904, The Observations of Sir Ernest Satow* (Tallahassee, Florida: The Diplomatic Press, 1966). Henceforth this latter work is cited as 'Lensen'.

10.   It was quite common for Japan to be described as Britain's 'natural ally' by shrewd observers on both sides in the 1890s. (Nish, p. 11, quoting S. Gwynn (ed.), *The letters and friendships of Sir Cecil Spring Rice*, 2 vols, London, 1929, volume i, pp. 145–6, Rice to Ferguson, 28 May 1893: 'In England we regard [Japan] as a practical joker . . . The general feeling in Japan is that England is her natural ally.')

11.   Satow Papers, PRO 30/33/5/2

12.   Satow to O'Conor (private), 3 September 1895, Satow Papers, PRO 30/33/14/8

13.   Diary, 20 September 1895, PRO 30/33/15/17.

14.   Satow had expressed the same view in a letter dated 18 April to his friend F. V. Dickins before leaving Morocco, when he had likened it to cutting through a mouldy cheese. Satow to Dickins, 18 April 1895, PRO 30/33/11/6.

15.   PRO 30/33 14/11

16.   See 'Aoki Shūzō (1844–1914)' by I. Nish, Ch. 12, *Britain and Japan: Biographical Portraits* vol. 3 (ed. J. Hoare, Japan Library,1999).

17.   PRO 30/33 14/11

18.   Fukuba Bisei (1831–1907). After the Meiji Restoration he entered the Office of Shintō Worship (Jingikan) and worked to promote Shintō. Appointed to the *Genrōin* in 1881 and later served in the *Kunaishō* and the House of Peers. Elsewhere Satow calls him the 'dwarf Shintoist' Diary, 14 August 1895.

19.   PRO 30/33 16/1

20.   Diary. PRO 30/33 16/2

21.   Diary. PRO 30/33 16/3

22.   Some consular staff were disgruntled at being moved from Japan to Formosa. One example is Ernest Alfred Griffiths who was moved from Hyogo to be first assistant at Tainan in 1896, and did not return to Japan until 1903. (Enslie to Satow, 12 March 1896, and Satow's reply to Enslie refusing to reconsider the transfer dated 16 March. PRO 30/33 5/8).

23.   PRO 30/33 5/5.

24.   Diary. 2 February 1897. See also *Shades of the Past* by H.S. Williams (Tuttle, 1984) for a journalistic piece on the Carew case which was controversial.

25.   Gembei mura was where Satow rented a house for use at weekends to see his family, and research and cultivate plants and bamboos. It is also called Totsuka or Takata or just 'the suburbs' in Satow's diary. (S. Nagaoka, *A-nesto Satō Kōshi Nikki*, vol. 1, p. 165; Tokyo: Shinjinbutsu Ōraisha, 1989). This was a different house to the one that stood until the 1960s at Fujimi-cho 4–chome, in Tokyo's Kudan district which Satow bought and paid for while on leave from Bangkok on 7 November 1884 for Takeda Kane and their two sons to live in, the site of which is between the present Hōsei University library and Yasukuni shrine, now marked by a plaque.

26.   He frequently walked up from Arai's Hotel at Nikkō to the lake at Chūzenji, and also enjoyed the walks in the area. On 19 September 1895 he 'saw Mrs. Bishop at Kanaya's'. This was the married name of Isabella Bird (1831–1904) the intrepid lady traveller.

27.   Diary. 3 February 1899.

28. Diary. 1 August 1895.
29. Diary. 23 October 1896.
30. Diary. 12 January 1897.
31. Lensen, pp. 21–24.
32. Published in the Transactions of the A.S.J. Vol. 27, Part 2, 1899.
33. Published in the T.A.S.J. Vol. 27, Part 3, 1899.
34. William Kirkwood was appointed legal adviser to the Japanese Ministry of Justice in 1885, and when a Foreign Ministry judicial review committee headed by Inoue Kaoru was set up on 6 August 1886 he was appointed to it with G. E. Boissonade. Kirkwood offered opinions on Boissonade's proposed legal codes and translated a large part of Japanese law into English. His employment terminated on 31 July 1901 and he returned to England, having been awarded the Order of the Rising Sun, 2nd class, in recognition of his services to Japan. (source: *Rainichi Seiyōjin Jiten*, edited by Hiroshi Takeuchi, Tokyo: Nichigai Associates, Inc. 1995)
35. See 'Thomas Wright Blakiston (1832–91)' by Sir H. Cortazzi, Ch. 5, *Britain and Japan: Biographical Portraits* vol. 3 (ed. J. Hoare, Japan Library,1999).
36. Yet when Satow discussed the possibility that he might be transferred to Peking with H. S. Wilkinson he said 'that nothing in the world would induce me to ask for a post of such difficulty, but we agreed that if it were offered I could hardly decline'. (Diary, 25 July 1899).
37. He would have to leave his Japanese family, but had shared actively in the formative teenage years of his sons. He saw O-Kane and Hisayoshi again on his last visit to Japan in 1906, and on his way home visited Eitarō who was farming in Denver for health reasons. Hisayoshi, later Dr. Takeda shared his interest in botany and studied in England from 1910–16. There is no indication that Satow ever fell out of love with O-Kane, and on 26 January 1916 he noted in his diary that Hisayoshi should return because his mother was lonely and he could no longer afford to pay him an allowance of £200 a year.

PART II. INTRODUCTION

1. J. E. Hoare, *Embassies in the East*, Richmond: Curzon, 1999, pp. 130–3.
2. *Collected Writings of Ian Nish*, Part II, ch. 21; and Lindley to Stirling-Maxwell, September 1931, in Stirling- Maxwell papers, Hunter Library, Glasgow.
3. Sansom to wife, July 1928 as quoted in *Collected Writings of Ian Nish*, Part II, p. 181.

9. SIR CLAUDE MACDONALD

1. J. A. S. Crenville, *Lord Salisbury and Foreign Policy: The Close of the Nineteenth Century*, London, 1964, p. 305.
2. T. H. Hohler, *Diplomatic Petrel*, London, 1942, p. 65.
3. P. D. Coates, *The China Consuls: British Consular Officers, 1843–1943*, Hong Kong, 1988, p. 166.
4. Shiba Gorō, *Pekin rōjō* [Siege of Peking], Tokyo: Heibonsha for Tōyō Bunkō, 53, 1965, pp. 20–2; Suyematsu Kenchō, *The Risen Sun*, London, 1905, p. 45.
5. MacDonald to Salisbury, 24 Sept. 1900 in British Foreign Office Records (Public Records Office, Kew, London) FO 405/94–5. See also Coates, *China Consuls*, p. 365.
6. MacDonald's semi-official letters are to be found in FO 800 (Lansdowne, Grey etc.) and among the correspondence of Sir Charles Hardinge at Cambridge University Library, Sir John Jordan and Sir Ernest Satow at the Public Records Office, Kew. Jordan who was a close friend wrote the entry on MacDonald for the *Dictionary of National Biography*.
7. I. H. Nish, *Anglo-Japanese Alliance: The Diplomacy of Two Island Empires, 1894–1907*, London, 1966, pp. 144–53.

8.   FO Japan 577, MacDonald to Campbell, 18 Feb. 1904. A.M. Pooley (ed.), *Secret Memoirs of Count Hayashi*, London, 1915, pp. 121–4.
9.   See e.g. Itō to Katsura, 6 Dec. 1901, from *Itō Hirobumi Kiroku*, no. 35 translated in Nish, op.cit., pp. 385–6.
10. F. S. G. Piggott, 'Ethel, Lady MacDonald, DBE, RRC', in *Trans. Proc. Japan Society of London*, 37 (1939–41), xxii–xxiii.
11. Hugh Cortazzi (ed.), *Mitford's Japan: Memoirs and Recollections, 1866–1906*, London, 1985, pp.195-237. I. H. Nish (ed.), *British Documents on Foreign Affairs*, Part I, series E, Vol. 10, doc. 19, 'Mr Lampson's private diary of the Garter Mission to Japan, 1906', pp. 61–100.
12. MacDonald to Grey, 11 May 1907, in Grey Papers, FO 800/29.
13. MacDonald to Campbell, private, 4 Nov. 1907, FO 371/272.
14. Rumbold diary, 1 Dec. 1910, quoted in M. Gilbert, *Sir Horace Rumbold: Portrait of a Diplomat, 1869–1941*, London, 1973, p. 87.
15. 'The Reminiscences of Sir George Sansom', Oral History Research Office, Columbia University, New York, 1957, p. 7.
16. D'Anethan to Davignon, 23 June 1910, in G. A. Lensen (ed.), *The D'Anethan Dispatches from Japan, 1894–1910*, Tokyo: Sophia, 1967, pp. 254–5.
17. MacDonald to Grey, 5 April 1991, in G. P. Gooch and H. W. V. Temperley (eds), *British Documents on the Origins of War, 1898–1914*, Vol. 8, no. 417.
18. Ibid., no. 420.
19. Ibid., no. 445.
20. G. Feaver, *The Webbs in Asia: The 1911–12 Travel Diary*, London, 1992, pp. 111–12.
21. MacDonald to Grey, 28 Sept. 1912, in FO 410/61[38854].
22. *Meiji Hennenshi*.
23. Gilbert, Rumbold, p.95.
24. C. M. MacDonald, 'The Japanese detachment during the defence of the Peking lega-tions, June–August 1900', in *Trans. Proc. Japan Society of London*, 12 (1913–14). pp. 1–20.
25. Hohler, *Diplomatic Petrel*, p. 65.
26. Gilbert, *Rumbold*, p. 81.
27. Piggott, 'Lady MacDonald', *Trans. Proc. JSL*, 37 (1939–41), p. xxv.
28. MacDonald to Lansdowne, 24 Oct. 1905 in Lansdowne Papers, FO 800/134.
29. Nish (ed.), *British Documents on Foreign Affairs*, Part I, series E, Vol. 9, 'Annual Reports on Japan, 1906-13'.
30. *Jiji Shimpō*, various dates, Oct.–Nov. 1912.

10. SIR WILLIAM CONYNGHAM GREENE

1.   For a lucid analysis of the situation during the 1890s, see I.R. Smith, *The Origins of the South African War* (London, 1996).
2.   Ibid., pp. 136–7.
3.   Ibid., p. 367.
4.   Ibid., p. 351. For further evidence of the discussions between Greene and Smuts, see Keith Hancock and J. van der Poel (eds), *Selections from the Smuts Papers* vol. I (Cambridge, 1966), pp. 201–4, 266–8, 283–305.
5.   Smith, pp. 379–80.
6.   See Ian Nish, *The Anglo-Japanese Alliance: the Diplomacy of Two Island Empires, 1894–1907* (London, 1966) and *Alliance in Decline: a Study in Anglo-Japanese Relations, 1908–23* (London, 1972) for an authoritative survey of the alliance from its origins to its demise. See also Peter Lowe, *Great Britain and Japan, 1911–15: a Study of British Far Eastern Policy* (London, 1969).
7.   See M. B. Jansen, *The Japanese and Sun Yat-sen* (Cambridge, Mass., 1954).
8.   See Ian Nish, 'Sir Claude and Lady Ethel MacDonald', in Ian Nish (ed.), *Britain and Japan: Biographical Portraits* (Folkestone, 1994), pp. 133–45, reproduced in this volume as ch. 9.
9.   Greene to Grey, 12 September 1913, FO 405/212, pp. 130–2, Public Record Office, Kew.

10. Lowe, p. 113.
11. Ibid., p. 120.
12. Greene to Grey, 14 December 1913, FO 371/1621.
13. Letter from Greene to Sir Walter Langley, Assistant Under-Secretary of State, Foreign Office, Langley papers, FO 800/31.
14. Lowe, pp. 161–2.
15. Enclosure in Greene to Grey, 3 March 1914, FO 371/1941.
16. Greene to Grey, 10 and 12 June 1914, FO 371/1942.
17. Letter from Greene to Langley, 22 February 1914, Langley papers, FO 800/31.
18. Greene to Grey, 10 August 1914 (two telegrams), FO 371/2016. For a stimulating assessment of Japan's response to participation in the First World War, see F. R. Dickinson, *War and National Reinvention: Japan in the Great War, 1914–1919* (Cambridge, Mass., 1999). Dickinson provides a favourable assessment of Katō Takaaki, arguing that Kato was pursuing a policy of traditional imperialism, analogous to that reinforced by the Occidental powers in China during the nineteenth century. He portrays Kato as wishing to assess the control of foreign policy by the political parties with the exclusion of the influence of the *genro*.
19. Ibid.
20. Grey to Greene, 11 August 1914, FO 371/2016.
21. Lowe, p. 190.
22. Greene to Grey, 25 January 1915, FO 371/2322. See Dickinson, pp. 84–116. I am not persuaded by Dickinson's highly sympathetic portrayal of Katō Takaaki. While Katō was able, courageous and very experienced, he seriously underestimated the problems he faced in simultaneously expanding Japan's role in China, compelling Yuan Shih-k'ai to comply, inducing the western powers to acquiesce in Japanese aims, marginalizing the *genro* and controlling the army. Katō was very capable and tenacious – but he was not a Bismarck. Katō made serious mistakes in 1915 which damaged his standing as a diplomat and his ambitions as a party leader.
23. Greene to Grey, 10 February 1915, FO 371/2322.
24. Ibid.
25. Lowe, p. 235.
26. Letter from Jordan to Alston, 2 February 1915, Alston papers, FO 800/248.
27. Letter from Alston to Jordan, 19 March 1915, Jordan papers, FO 350/14.
28. Letter from Greene to Rumbold, 10 May 1915, cited Lowe, p. 256.
29. Letter from Greene to Langley, 9 September 1915, Alston papers, FO 800/247.
30. Nish, *Alliance in Decline*, p. 198. See also Dickinson, pp. 117–53.
31. Greene to Balfour, 18 January 1917, cited Nish, *Alliance in Decline*, p. 199.
32. Ibid., p. 200.
33. Ibid., p. 206.
34. Greene to Langley, 30 August 1917, cited ibid., pp. 220–1.
35. Ibid.
36. Ibid., pp. 236–8.
37. Ibid., p. 250.
38. Greene to Cecil, 2 November 1918, cited ibid., p. 262.
39. Ibid.
40. Ibid., p. 300.
41. Cited Lowe, p. 309.
42. Nish, *Alliance in Decline*, pp. 310–12.

11. SIR CHARLES ELIOT

1. Major-General F. S. G. Piggott, *Broken Thread*, Aldershot, 1950, p. 204.
2. Sir Harold Parlett, 'In Piam Memoriam', in Sir Charles Eliot, *Japanese Buddhism*, London, 1935, xvii. Parlett's affectionate memoir is the fullest account of Eliot's personal life, although it says little of his activities as ambassador.
3. Thomas Preston, *Before the Curtain*, London, 1950, pp. 123–4.

4.   Ian H. Nish, *Alliance in Decline: A Study in Anglo-Japanese Relations 1908–1923*, London, 1972, pp. 310 and 312–13, Eliot's first dispatch is Eliot to Curzon, 17 June 1920, Documents on British Foreign Policy 1919–1939 (hereafter cited as DBFP), XIV (52).
5.   Curzon to Eliot, 28 July 1921, DBFP, 1, XIV (350), note 1.
6.   Eliot to Curzon, 13 January 1922, DBFP, 1, XIV (548).
7.   The suggestion that Eliot thought of resigning but was persuaded to stay on to ease the transition in Anglo-Japanese relations is found in Captain M. D. Kennedy, *The Estrangement of Great Britain and Japan 1917–35*, Manchester, 1969, p. 66.
8.   Eliot to A. J. Balfour, 29 June 1922, F.O. 371/8052 (F 2493/2493/23).
9.   Curzon to Eliot, 17 February 1922, F.O. 371/8042 (F 654/1/23).
10. Eliot to Curzon, 1 May 1922, Lloyd George papers, F/56/4/3.
11. *The Times*, 17 March 1931.
12. Eliot to Balfour, 30 July 1922, F.O. 371/8047 (F 2800/426/23).
13. Eliot to Balfour, 29 June 1922, F.O. 371/8052 (F 2493/2493/23).
14. Eliot to Austen Chamberlain, 14 November 1924, F.O. 371/10961 (F 28/28/23).
15. Eliot to J. Ramsay MacDonald, 3 May 1924, F.O. 371/10391 (F 1968/1968/23).
16. See Dennis Smith, 'The end of Japan's Siberian adventure: withdrawal from the maritime province, 1921-1922', *Proceedings of the British Association for Japanese Studies* 11(1986), pp. 13-19.
17. Eliot to MacDonald, 3 May 1924, F.O. 371/10391 (F 1968/1968/23).
18. Eliot to Balfour, 30 July 1922, F.O. 371/8047 (F 2800/426/23).
19. Eliot to MacDonald, 17 July 1924, F.O. 371/10303 (F 2435/14/23).
20. Eliot to MacDonald, 8 February 1924, MacDonald Papers, F.O. 800/219.
21. Dennis Smith, 'The Royal Navy and Japan in the aftermath of the Washington Conference 1922-1926', *Proceedings of the British Association for Japanese Studies*, 3 (1978), 2, pp. 69–86.
22. Eliot to MacDonald, 3 May 1924, F.O. 371/10319 (F 1968/1968/23).
23. Eliot to Austen Chamberlain, 14 November 1924, Austen Chamberlain Papers (Public Records Office), F.O. 800/256.
24. Eliot to Chamberlain, 3 September 1925, F.O. 371/10939 (F 4370/190/10).
25. Minute by V. A. A. H. Wellerley, 13 September 1924, F.O. 371/10244 (F 3099/19/10).
26. Eliot to Chamberlain, 15 January 1925, Eliot to Sir E. Crowe, 29 January 1925 and Eliot to Chamberlain, 4 April 1925, F.O. 800/257; Eliot to Chamberlain, 20 October 1925 and Chamberlain to Eliot, 24 November 1925, F.O. 800/258.
27. Katharine Sansom, *Sir George Sansom and Japan: A Memoir*, Tallahassee 1972, especially p. 77.
28. *DBFP*, 1A, II, pp. 953-4.
29. Sir F. Lindley to Arthur Henderson, 23 July 1931, DBFP, 2, VIII (495). Lindley was troubled by the deteriorating status of cricket in Japan.

12. SIR JOHN TILLEY

1.   Sir John Tilley, *London to Tokyo* (London: Hutchinson, 1942), p.23.
2.   Ibid., pp. 79–84. Sir John Tilley and Stephen Gaslee, *The Foreign Office* (London & New York: G. P. Putnam's Sons Ltd., 1933), p. 84.
3.   *London to Tokyo*, p. 96.
4.   Ibid., p. 135.
5.   Ibid., p. 138.
6.   J. E. Hoare, *Embassies in the East* (Surrey: Curzon, 1999), pp. 130–1.
7.   *London to Tokyo*, p. 145. Hara Takeshi stated in his *Taishô Tennô* [Emperor Taishô](Asahi Shimbunsha, Asahi sensho, 2000) that stress made the Emperor insane.
8.   Public Record Office, Foreign Office papers, FO371/12524, F3611, from Tilley. No. 155, 15 Mar. 1927.
9.   Please also see Harumi Goto-Shibata, 'Anglo-Japanese Co-operation in China in the 1920s' and Ian Nish, 'Echoes of Alliance' in Nish and Yoichi Kibata (eds.), *The*

History of Anglo-Japanese Relations, vol. 1 (London and Basingstoke: Macmillan, 2000), pp. 224–278.

10. F. S. G. Piggott, *Broken Thread* (Aldershot: Gale & Polden Ltd., 1950), pp. 199, 204. Katô was the minister and then ambassador to Britain, served four times as the Foreign Minister, and finally became the Prime Minister from June 1924 to January 1926.

11. Ibid., p. 226.

12. Shidehara Kijūrō, *Gaikō 50 nen* [50 years in diplomacy] (Yomiuri Shimbunsha, 1951), pp. 38–42, 247–250.

13. FO371/13965, F3909, from Tilley, no. 271, 2 July 1929. Piggott, *Broken Thread*, p. 184.

14. FO405/260, F1035, Chamberlain to Tilley, no. 127, 18 March 1929.

15. *London to Tokyo*, pp. 143, 162. FO371/12518, F5040, from Tilley, no. 249, 25 April 1927.

16. FO371/13164, F200, from Tilley, no. 623, 12 Dec. 1927; FO371/13965, F5593, from Tilley, no. 426, 2 Oct. 1929.

17. FO405/256, F203/7/10, Tilley to Chamberlain, 15 Dec. 1927.

18. Prince and Princess Chichibu, *Ei bei seikatsu no omoide* [Memories of our lives in England and the United States](Bunmeisha, 1947), pp. 105, 124, 166.

19. FO371/13964, F17, from Tilley, no. 490, 29 Nov. 1928.

20. *London to Tokyo*, pp. 176–8.

21. Eric Hobsbawm and Terence Ranger (eds.), *The Invention of Tradition* (Cambridge University Press, 1983). See also Takashi Fujitani, *Tennō no peijent* [Pageant of the emperor] (Nihon hōsō shuppann kyōkai, NHK books, 1994).

22. *London to Tokyo*, p. 179.

23. FO371/12523, F2068, from Tilley, no. 35, 31 Jan. 1927.

24. FO371/13964, F17, from Tilley, no. 490, 29 Nov. 1928. *London to Tokyo*, p. 180.

25. FO371/13964, T21, from Tilley, no. 499, 5 Dec. 1929.

26. FO371/12520, F4345, from Tilley, no. 177, 23 Mar. 1927.

27. FO371/13968, F1767, from Tilley, no. 100, 13 Mar. 1929.

28. *London to Tokyo*, pp. 176–8.

29. Nish, 'Echoes of Alliance', p. 270.

30. Katharine Sansom, *Sir George Sansom and Japan* (Tallahassee, Florida: The Diplomatic Press, 1972), p. 35.

31. FO371/13968, F1767, from Tilley, no. 100, 13 Mar. 1929.

32. FO371/14754, F958, from Tilley, no. 1 Confidential (1/13/30), 3 Jan. 1930; FO371/14756, F2622, from Tilley, no. 150 (1/237/30), 26 Mar. 1930

33. Both Makino and Chinda were diplomats. Makino served at the Japanese Embassy in London for about three years from 1880. He was the Foreign Minister from February 1913 to April 1914, and one of the Japanese representatives at the Paris Peace Conference held in 1919. Chinda became the ambassador to Britain in June 1916. He also represented Japan at the Paris Peace Conference.

34. *London to Tokyo*, p. 136, 146, 168, 180–2, 197.

35. See Takie Sugiyama Lebra, *Above the Clouds: Status Culture of the Modern Japanese Nobility* (University of California Press, 1993).

36. FO371/12525, F8585, from Tilley, no. 541, 13 Oct. 1927. Tokugawa Iyesato was one of Japanese representatives at the Washington Conference of 1921–22.

37. *London to Tokyo*, pp. 75, 148.

38. Nish, 'Echoes of Alliance', p. 265.

39. *Foreign Office*, p. 258.

40. *London to Tokyo*, pp. 143, 149.

41. Ibid., p. 136.

42. FO371/14756, F2622, from Tilley, no. 150 (1/237/30), 26 Mar. 1930.

43. FO371/13964, F1400, from Tilley, no. 69, 20 Feb. 1929; F1757, from Tilley, no. 80, 2 Mar. 1929.

44. FO371/12522, F1322, from Tilley, no. 17, 10 Jan. 1927; FO371/13968, F1767, from Tilley, no. 100, 13 Mar. 1929; FO371/14756, F2622, from Tilley, no. 150 (1/237/30), 26 Mar. 1930.

45. *London to Tokyo*, pp. 206–7.
46. Ibid., pp. 153, 187.
47. FO371/14752, F2188, from Tilley, no. 134(1/224/30), 18 March 1930.
48. *London to Tokyo*, p. 140. FO371/12524, F3611, from Tilley, no. 155, 15 Mar. 1927; F6510, from Tilley, no. 365, 28 June 1927. FO371/13246, F186, from Tilley, no. 616, 7 Dec. 1927.
49. FO371/12522, F9438, letter from Tilley to Mounsey, 5 Nov. 1927. FO371/13250, F6542, from Tilley, no. 453, 31 Oct. 1928.
50. FO371/13250, T13282, from Tilley, no. 247(R), 24 Nov. 1928; FO 371/14756, F6549, enclosure, from Snow, no. 556 (69/22/30), 22 Oct. 1930. *London to Tokyo*, pp. 175, 183, 195.
51. *London to Tokyo*, p. 197.
52. Ibid., p. 140.

13. SIR FRANCIS LINDLEY

1.   I. H. Nish, 'Jousting with Authority: The Tokyo Embassy of Sir Francis Lindley, 1931–4' in Japan Society of London, *Proceedings*, 105 (Dec. 1986), 9–19. Also 'Sir Francis Lindley (1872–1950) and Japan' in H. Cortazzi (ed.), *Biographical Portraits*, vol. 4 (Richmond, Japan Library, 2002), pp. 89–100 of which this essay is a revised version, though truncated.
2.   J. E. Hoare, *Embassies in the East* (Richmond: Curzon, 1999), p. 136
3.   Lindley to Stirling-Maxwell, 24 July 1931 in Papers of Sir John Stirling-Maxwell (1893–1932), Glasgow City Archives, Mitchell Library, T-PM 122/1/38 [Hereafter cited as Maxwell Papers]
4.   Lindley to Dawson, 2 Sept. 1931 in Papers of Geoffrey Dawson, Bodleian Library, Oxford, 76; *Documents on British Foreign Policy, 1919–39*, second series, VIII, no 495 [hereafter cited as 'DBFP']
5.   Letter to the author from Capt. Malcolm Kennedy, 15 Oct.1977
6.   *DBFP*, ii/VIII, no 495
7.   Lindley (Tokyo) to Maxwell, 1 Nov. 1931 in Maxwell Papers, T-PM 122/1/38. Yoshizawa Kenkichi, *Gaikō 60-nen* (Tokyo: Jiyu Ajiasha, 1958), ch. 6 deals with his half-year as foreign minister without mentioning Lindley.
8.   Lindley to Horace Rumbold, 30 March 1932 in Papers of Sir Horace Rumbold, Bodleian Library, Oxford, 39
9.   Lindley to Maxwell, 27 March 1932 in Maxwell Papers, T-PM 122/1/39.
10.   Joseph C. Grew, *Turbulent Era*, 2 vols (London: Hammond & Hammond, 1953), vol. ii, p.23
11.   Lindley (Chuzenji) to Maxwell, 21 August 1932 in Maxwell papers T-PM 122/1/39
12.   Lindley to Simon, 15 March 1933 in *DBFP*, ii/XI, no 453, fn 5
13.   Lindley to Simon, 24 Feb. 1933 in *DBFP*, ii/XI, no 371
14.   *DBFP*, ii/XX, no 4
15.   Ibid
16.   R. Bassett, *Democracy and Foreign Policy*, London: Cass, 1968, pp. 513–16
17.   *Nihon Gaikō Bunshō*: Showaki II/2/2, p. 724ff
18.   *Nihon Gaikō Bunshō*: Showaki II/2/2, p. 781ff
19.   DBFP, ii/XX, nos 1 and 39, p. 75. Philip Bell, *Chamberlain, Germany & Japan, 1933–4* (London, 1996). FSG Piggott, *Broken Thread* (Basingstoke: Palgrave, 2002), p. 226 for Whitehall's reactions to Lindley's reports.
20.   K. Sansom, *Sir George Sansom and Japan* (Tallahassee: Diplomatic Press, 1972), p. 70; *DBFP*, ii/XX, nos 41 and 68
21.   The Amō Declaration is to be found in *Nihon Gaikō Nempyō narabi Shuyō Bunsho*, ii, pp. 284–6, including Hirota's discussion with Lindley on 26 April.
22.   C. G. Thorne, *Limits of Foreign Policy* (London: Hamish Hamilton, 1972), p. 99 quoting Royal Archives

23. Lindley to Dawson, 26 May 1934 in Dawson papers
24. M. Morland to the author, 22 March 2000, quoting *The Times* (London), 11 June 1994. I am grateful to Mr Morland.
25. Speech at the Japan Society's dinner on 19 June 1935
26. K. Sansom, *Sansom and Japan*, p. 95. Transcript of the Sansom-Nevins interview in Columbia University, New York, Oral Archive
27. H. Cortazzi, 'Japan Society' in Cortazzi and Daniels (eds.), *Britain and Japan* (London: Routledge, 1991), pp. 36–40 passim. For later aspects of Lindley's career, see Nish, 'Sir Francis Lindley' in Cortazzi (ed.), *Biographical Portraits*, vol. 4, pp. 96–100.

14. SIR ROBERT CLIVE

The author acknowledges the permission of Her Majesty Queen Elizabeth II to use material from the Royal Archives at Windsor Castle'

1. See in particular A. Trotter, *Britain and East Asia, 1933–1937*, (Cambridge University Press, Cambridge, 1975).
2. See Ian Nish's essay on Lindley in this volume and my own 'Sir Robert Craigie as Ambassador to Japan, 1937–41' in I. H. Nish (ed.), *Britain and Japan: Biographical Portraits*, (Japan, Library, Folkestone, 1994) reproduced in this volume.
3. C. Hosoya, C., '1934-*nen no Nichi-Ei fukashin kyōtei mondai* [The Problem of the Anglo-Japanese Non-Aggression Pact in 1934]. *Kokusai Seiji*, 1977, pp. 69–85, and G. Bennett, 'British Policy in the Far East 1933–1936: Treasury and Foreign Office', *Modern Asian Studies*, 1992, vol. 26, pp. 545–68, and Trotter, *op. cit.* pp. 97–107
4. Trotter, *op. cit.* p. 120.
5. PRO FO262/1891 Clive (Tokyo) to Wellesley (FO) 12 October 1934.
6. Royal Archives Windsor, PS/GV/P510/68 Clive to Wigram 8 November 1935.
7. PRO FO371/19359 F1090/483/23 Clive to Simon 7 January 1935.
8. PRO FO371/19359 F1090/483/23 Vansittart (FO) minute 2 March 1935, and CAB24/254 CP80(35) 'The Far East' Simon note April 1935.
9. Cadogan papers, Churchill College Cambridge, ACAD1/3, diary 19 November 1935.
10. Royal Archives Windsor, PS/GVI/C/053/JAP/3 Clive to Wigram 26 March 1936.
11. PRO FO371/21029 F570/28/23 Clive to Eden 27 January 1937.
12. Knatchbull-Hugessen papers, Churchill College Cambridge, KNAT2/55, Clive to Knatchbull-Hugessen (Nanking) 14 April 1937.
13. Chatfield papers, National Maritime Museum, CHT4/8, Little (C-in-C China) to Chatfield (FSL) 6 July 1936.
14. Kennedy papers, Sheffield University Library, 4/31, diary 3 March 1936.
15. PRO FO371/19364 F4680/4680/23 Clive to Vansittart 25 July 1935.
16. PRO FO371/20279 F7400/89/23 Clive to Eden 6 November 1936.
17. PRO FO371/21044 F5093/5093/23 Ashton-Gwatkin (FO) minute 5 August 1937.
18. PRO FO371/21024 F2568/597/61 Clive to Eden 25 March 1937.
19. PRO FO371/21040 F2388/414/23 Clive to Orde (FE Dept) 22 March 1937.
20. Trotter, *op. cit.*, p. 35.

15. SIR ROBERT CRAIGIE

1. For recent critical judgements of Craigie, see K. Satō, 'The Historical Perspective and What is Missing', in K. Satō, *Japanese and Britain at the Crossroads, 1939–1941*. A Study in the Dilemmas of Japanese Diplomay. (Tokyo: Senshu Univ. Press, 1986), pp. 207–8, and S. Olu Agbi, 'The Pacific War Controversy in Britain: Sir Robert Craigie Versus the Foreign Office', in *Modern Asian Studies*, Vol. 17, pp. 489–517.
2. For recent broadly favourable assessments of Craigie, see D. C. Watt, *How War Came: The Immediate Origins of the Second World War, 1938–1939*. (London: Heinemann, 1989), p.350; P. Calvocoressi, G. Wint and J. Pritchard, *Total War. The*

Causes and Courses of the Second World War. Vol. 2: The Greater East Asia and Pacific Conflict (London: Penguin, 1989), pp. 256–7; and P. Lowe, 'The Dilemmas of an Ambassador: Sir Robert Craigie and Japan', in *Proceedings of the British Association of Japanese Studies*, Vol. 1, no. 2, 1977, pp. 34–56.

3.   Sir R. Craigie minute 24 December 1936, on Sir R. Clive to A. Eden, 24 December 1936, in Public Record Office Kew (PRO) Foreign Office 371/20279, F7963/89/23. (Hereafter cited as FO.)

4.   P. Fleming to Sir A. Clark Kerr, 12 July 1938, in Inverchapel Papers, Bodleian Library, Oxford, General Correspondence 1937–8.

5.   Sir R. Craigie to Lord Halifax, 18 June 1939, in *Documents on British Foreign Policy*, Series 3, Vol. IX, no. 227. (Hereafter *DBFP*.)

6.   Sir R. Craigie to Lord Halifax, 16 November 1939, in F0371/23534, F11946/6457/10.

7.   Sir R. Craigie to Lord Halifax, 14 July 1940, in F0371/24925, F3465/23/23.

8.   Sir R. Craigie minute 22 December 1936, on Sir R. Vansittart memorandum, 'The World Situation and British Rearmament', 16 December 1936, in F0371/19787, A9996/9996/51.

9.   Behind these rumours lies the suggestion that Chamberlain and Craigie were close personal friends; the lack of any letters from Craigie to Chamberlain in the latter's papers deposited in Birmingham University Library would, however, suggest that this relationship may have been exaggerated.

10.   Sir R. Craigie to Lord Halifax, 15 June 1939, in F0371/23399, F5883/1/10.

11.   Sir R. Craigie memorandum, 5 October 1938, in F0262/1978, 8/234/38. I am indebted to the late Anthony Haigh for initially putting me on to the trail of this memorandum.

12.   Sir R. Craigie to Lord Halifax, 30 January 1939, in F0371/23555, F2215/76/23.

13.   See Sir R. Craigie to Lord Halifax, 1 January 1939, in *DBFP* 3 (VIII), no. 382.

14.   On Sansom, see G. Daniels, 'Sir George Sansom', in Sir H. Cortazzi and G. Daniels (eds), *Britain and Japan 1859–1991: Themes and Personalities* (London: Routledge, 1991), pp. 227–38 reproduced in this volume.

15.   For Hornbeck's views, see Lord Lothian to Lord Halifax, 9 December 1939, in F0371/23551, F12625/4027/61.

16.   Sir R. Craigie to Lord Halifax, 1 January 1940, in F0371/24708, F297/193/61.

17.   On Piggott, see C. Blacker, 'The Two Piggotts', in Cortazzi and Daniels (eds), *op. cit.*, pp. 118–27.

18.   Sir R. Craigie to R. Howe, 30 June 1939, in F0371/23485, P8566/372/10.

19.   Sir R. Craigie to Lord Simon, 1 August 1940, in Simon Papers, Bodleian Library, Oxford, Mss Simon 86.

20.   Sir R. Craigie to Lord Halifax, 11 October 1940, in F0371/24737, F5295/626/23.

21.   On the issue of Canadian wheat, see Sir R. Craigie to A. Eden, 11 March 1941, in P0371/27918, F1836/122/23. On copra see Sir R. Craigie to A. Eden, 30 May 1941, in F0371/27895, F4964/18/23.

22.   Sir R. Craigie to A. Eden, 3 June 1941, in P0371/27895, F4810/18/23.

23.   Sir R. Craigie to A. Eden, 4 February 1943, in P0371/35957, P821/821/23.

24.   For Grew's arguments at this point, see W. Heinrichs, *American Ambassador: Joseph C. Grew and the United States Diplomatic Tradition.* (New York: Oxford University Press, 1966), pp. 345–50.

25.   Sir R. Craigie to A. Eden, 9 September 1941, in F0371/27883, P9172/12/23.

26.   For the global situation in November 1941, see W. Heinrichs, *Threshold of War: Franklin D. Roosevelt and American Entry into World War II* (New York: Oxford Univ. Press, 1988), p. 213.

27.   On the issue of appeasement, see R.J. Grace, 'Whitehall and the Ghost of Appeasement: November 1941', in *Diplomatic History*, Vol. 3 (1979), pp. 173–91.

28.   W. Churchill to A. Eden, 19 September 1943, in P0/371/35957, F2602/751/23.

PART III. INTRODUCTION

1.   Dening to Selwyn Lloyd, 18 April 1957, FJ1016/16.
2.   As 1 above.
3.   Morland to Lord Home, 26 September 1963, FJ 1015/18.
4.   Hugh Cortazzi, *Japan and Back and Places Elsewhere*, Global Oriental, 1998, p. 76
5.   Morland to Home, 26 September 1963, FJ1015/18.
6.   As 5 above.
7.   As 5 above.
8.   Hugh Cortazzi, *Japan and Back* . . . pp. 100–101.

16. SIR ALVARY GASCOIGNE

1.   See R. W. Buckley, *Occupation Diplomacy: Britain, The United States and Japan, 1945–1952* (Cambridge, 1982), pp. 41–53. See also Buckley, 'Working with MacArthur: Sir Alvary Gascoigne, UKLIM and British Policy towards Occupied Japan, 1945–52' in Ian Nish (ed.), *Aspects of the Allied Occupation of Japan*, International Studies (STICERD, LSE), 1986/4, pp.1–14.
2. For two comprehensive and illuminating accounts of MacArthur's work in Japan, see D. Clayton James, *The Years of MacArthur*, vol. III, *Triumph and Disaster, 1945–64* (Boston, 1985) and R. B. Finn, *Winners in Peace: MacArthur, Yoshida, and Postwar Japan* (Oxford, 1992).
3.   Clayton James, III, 693.
4.   For a discussion of British views towards MacArthur during the Korean war, see Peter Lowe, 'An Ally and a Recalcitrant General: Great Britain, Douglas MacArthur and the Korean War, 1950–1', *English Historical Review*, vol. CV (July 1990), 624-53.
5.   See Douglas MacArthur, *Reminiscences*, paperback edition, (Greenwich, Conn., 1965), p.323.
6.   See H. B. Schonberger, *Aftermath of War: Americans and the Remaking of Japan, 1945–1952* (London, 1989), pp. 134–60.
7.   Gascoigne to Dening, 9 January 1948, FO 371/69885/1368, Public Record Office, Kew.
8.   Minute by F. S. Tomlinson, 28 January 1948, ibid.
9.   Minute by M.E. Dening, 29 January 1948, ibid.
10. See G. F. Kennan, *Memoirs, 1925–50* (London, 1968), pp. 384–94.
11. Foreign Office to Tokyo, 18 March 1948, FO 371/69885/4213.
12. Gascoigne to Bevin, 30 June 1948, FO 371/69911/7609.
13. Tokyo to Foreign Office, 1 July 1948, FO 371/69911/9266.
14. Tokyo to Foreign Office, 1 September 1948, FO 371/69823/12111.
15. Ibid.
16. Ibid.
17. See Sir John Figgess, 'Japan under Occupation: A Personal Reminiscence', in *Proceedings of the Japan Society*, 121 (1993), 120.
18. Gascoigne to Bevin, 18 December 1948, FO 371/76178/7527.
19. Ibid.
20. Ibid.
21. Gascoigne to Bevin, 13 February 1948, FO 371/69819/3508.
22. Minute by Tomlinson, 17 February 1949, on dispatch from Gascoigne to Bevin, 2 February 1949, FO 371/76179/2420.
23. For a valuable assessment of Yoshida, see J. W. Dower, *Empire and Aftermath: Yoshida Shigeru and the Japanese Experience, 1878–1954* (London, 1979), pp. 273–492.
24. Conversation between Gascoigne and Yoshida, 22 January 1951, FO 371/92521/4.
25. Gascoigne to Bevin, 2 February 1949, FO 371/76179/2420.
26. Gascoigne to Younger, 12 June 1950, FO 371/83831/93.
27. Gascoigne to Dening, 21 Novemb~ 1949, FO 371/76214/23G.
28. Foreign Office to Washington, 8 December 1949, ibid.
29. Gascoigne to Younger, 12 June 1950, FO 371/83831/93.

30. Ibid.
31. Gascoigne to Bevin, 22 June 1950, FO 371/83831/97.
32. See Peter Lowe, 'Great Britain and the Japanese Peace Treaty, 1951', in Peter Lowe and Herman Moeshart (eds), *Western interactions with Japan: Expansion, the Armed Forces, and Readjustment, 1859–1956* (Folkestone, 1990), pp. 91–104.
33. Gascoigne to Bevin, 9 July 1950, FO 371/83832/103.
34. Gascoigne to Scott, 9 October 1950, FO 371/83834/148.
35. Gascoigne to Bevin, 18 November 1950, FO 371/83816/63/G.
36. Ibid.
37. Record of interview between Sansom and MacArthur, communicated in Gascoigne to Scott, 22 January 1951, FO 371/92521/3.
38. 'Trend of Events in Japan from July 1946 to February 1951', in Gascoigne to Bevin, 6 February 1951, FO 371/92521/5.
39. Ibid.
40. Ibid.
41. Ibid.
42. Clutton to Strang, 13 February 1951, FO 371/92657/4.
43. Clutton to Strang, 17 February 1951, FO 371/92657/2, enclosing typed extract from *Sydney Sun*, no name or date.
44. Franks to Strang, 26 February 1951, FO 371/92657/5.

17. SIR ESLER DENING

1.   Reference to separate parts of his career can be found in Philip Ziegler, *Mountbatten*, London, 1985; Peter Dennis, *Troubled Days of Peace*, Manchester, 1987; Christopher Thorne, *Allies of a Kind*, London, 1978; Alan Bullock, *Ernest Bevin*: Foreign Secretary, London, 1983; Roger Buckley, *Occupation Diplomacy: Britain, the United States and Japan, 1945–1951*, Cambridge, 1982; Peter Lowe, *The Origins of the Korean War*, London, 1986. On the Tokyo Embassy years, see Buckley 'From San Francisco to Suez and beyond: Anglo-Japanese relations, 1952–1960', in Warren Cohen and Akira Iriye (eds), *The Great Powers in East Asia* (New York, forthc4oming).
2.   The phrase is the title of D.C.M. Platt's work, *The Cinderella Service: British Consuls since 1825*, London, 1971. Nothing comparable to P. D. Coates's splendid work, *The China Consuls: British Consular Officers, 1843–1943*, Hong Kong, 1988, yet exists for its Japan counterpart.
3.   Thorne, *Allies of a Kind*, p. 548n.
4.   See Buckley, 'Responsibility without power: Britain and Indonesia, August 1945 to September 1946', in Ian Nish (ed.), *Indonesian Experience: The Role of Japan and Britain, 1943–1948* London: LSE, 1979. A falling out with Australia's Macmahon Ball precluded Dening from winning the job of the Commonwealth's representative on the Allied Council for Japan. This post was filled by McMahon Ball. The two men had clashed over Indonesian policies.
5.   Bullock, *Ernest Bevin*, p. 153.
6.   I am grateful to Lord Henniker for discussions on the professionalism of Dening and Bevin's trust in his work.
7.   Morrison to Yoshida, 8 September 1951, in Morrison papers, FO 800/639.
8.   Chancellor of the Duchy of Lancaster (Lord Selkirk) to Selwyn Lloyd, 24 October 1956, FJ 1054/45A (FO 371/121048).
9.   Records from official Japanese sources are beginning to trickle out for this period. For information on abortive Japanese attempts to join international organizations and the negative British response, see the *Japan Times*, 16 October 1989.
10. Dening to Eden, 24 March 1953, FJ 1051/21 (FO 371/105374).
11. Dening was not immune from such attitudes. In the same despatch he wrote, 'the Japanese, physically unprepossessing and lacking the superficial charm of many other oriental nations, are, in my experience, if no better certainly no worse than many other Asians with whom we have to deal. Provided they do not once again come under

the direction of a totalitarian regime, they are at least as likely to honour obligations into which they have freely entered – and this is an important qualification – as other oriental countries'. Dening to Eden ibid.

12. Ibid.

13. Ibid.

14. Ibid. Dening, deploying his usual bluntness, wrote that it has 'been obvious for the last 25 years to my knowledge that, even without dumping or commercial mal-practices or sweated labour, the Japanese cotton industry can compete successfully with Lancashire'.

15. Ibid.

16. Braddon's article in the *Daily Express* for 25 November 1955 was headlined, 'They'll Get You Yet! Beware those Japs'. Commentary on Emperor Shōwa's death and funeral suggests that the approach still continues.

17. Dening to Foreign Office, 18 April 1956 FJ 1052/3 (FO 371/121046). Dening clearly endorsed the Japanese doubts that the visit to London by Japanese Dietmen had made any substantial difference to British thinking.

18. Selkirk to Lloyd, 24 October 1956.

19. Ibid. See also CAB 128/29 (1955) and CAB 129/77 (1955).

20. For discussion of the worsening trade picture, see A. R. Prest and D. J. Coppock (eds), *The UK Economy: A Manual of Applied Economics*, London, 1974, cli. 3.

21. Dening to W.D. Allen, 25 January 1955, FJ 1051/4 (FO 371/11523).

22. ibid. Dening's suggestion seemed rather to alarm him, and he said that was a very serious subject, to which I retorted that we need not discuss it as seriously as all that'. After Dening had made his pitch he felt the 'response to what I said was virtually nil'. This might have had something to do with Dening's approach and the lack of prepa-ration from a nation that likes to come prepared.

23. Dening's remarks on American foreign policy in the region were equally harsh. He had more than a few differences with US officials, including Dulles, though his rela-tions with the US ambassador, Allison, in Tokyo were cordial.

24. Dening to Selwyn Lloyd, 'Japan: Annual review for 1955', FJ 1011/1 (FO 371/121030).

25. Ibid.

18. SIR DANIEL LASCELLES

1. Lascelles was the family name of the Earl of Harewood who married Mary, the only daughter of King George V and became Princess Royal. Sir Frank Lascelles was ambassador at Berlin from 1895–1908.

2. There are not many people, however able in foreign languages, who can claim to have mastered as many difficult languages as Lascelles would seem, from his record, to have done.

3. c.f.footnote 9.

4. Lees Mayall who became Vice-Marshall of the Diplomatic Corps in London. Was made a KCVO as well as CMG. His final post was as ambassador to Venezuela.

5. Ralph Selby's last post was as ambassador to Norway. He was appointed a CMG.

6. Published in Salisbury by Michael Russell (Publishing) Ltd in 1989.

7. When a visit by the then Archbishop of Canterbury was being planned Lascelles reacted with irritation to a comment by one member of the chancery that the visit by the Archbishop would be of similar interest to the Japanese as that of a Shinto High Priest to the UK would be to the British public.

8. For Mayall's account of what happened at the luncheon and after it was over see pages 574–575 of *Japan Experiences: Fifty Years, One Hundred Views. Post-War Japan Through British eyes, 1945–2000*, Japan Library, 2001.

9. Dorothy Britton (later Lady Bouchier) who was born in Japan and lived there since shortly after the end of the war was asked to join Lascelles at a performance of Britten's *Turn of the Screw*. The British Council representative and his deputy, some-what oddly in the circumstances, left Dorothy to look after Lascelles. She found him

charming. She added: 'Shortly, thereafter, he invited me and my mother to a most delightful dinner and musicale with a group of cultivated European ambassadors and their wives. My mother and I were utterly charmed by Sir Daniel and looked forward to entertaining him at Hayama [where they lived] but very soon after he left Japan.'

10.   After his return to Britain Lascelles asked for some papers consisting of exchanges of letters with the Foreign Office about his recall, which he had left with other personal items in his office bookcase.

11.   PRO papers do not indicate that Lascelles was ever received by Kishi, although presumably they may have met at a reception.

12.   Sir Esler Dening in his valedictory despatch of 18 April 1957, para 6, had commented that 'it has yet to be proved that his [Kishi's] political acumen goes beyond an ability to appreciate the intricacies of internal political intrigue'.

13.   British nuclear tests at Christmas Island had aroused vocal protests in Japan and demonstrations before the British Embassy in Tokyo. These had culminated in a demonstration by over 10,000 students on 17 May 1957 (para 3 of annual review for 1957).

14.   Sōhyō was the left-wing federation of mainly public-sector unions.

19. SIR OSCAR MORLAND

1.   Lady Lindley was a Fraser.

2.   Under-secretary in the Cabinet office was the equivalent of an assistant under-secretary in the Foreign Office.

3.   Sir Norman Craven Brook, later Lord (Baron) Normanbrook, 1902–67, Cabinet secretary and later chairman of the BBC.

4.   John Whitehead has commented: 'Whether one is discussing French, German, Arabic, Japanese or whatever , there are those who prefer to switch into the language at the slightest opportunity and those who don't necessarily do so. Sometimes it is a natural hesitation on the latter's part, sometimes not. But whatever the reason it should not necessarily be taken as a lesser degree of proficiency in the understanding of the language. In the case of Oscar Morland I suspect his natural shyness led him to open up in Japanese rather less than some others. But it did not reflect on his ability to understand what was being said, nor on his ability in the language generally'.

5.   Later Lord Gore-Booth (baron) GCMG, KCVO 1909–84. .

6.   GBE is short for Knight Grand Cross of the Order of the British Empire.

7.   Editor's comment: He might have been advanced in the order of St Michael and St George to GCMG (Knight Grand Cross of the Order) . The order of St Michael and St George takes precedence over the Order of the British Empire. It has traditionally been the highest honour for members of the diplomatic service although a limited few were in the past made Privy Councillors or peers. The distinction between the two awards is probably only understood by a small number of *cognoscenti*.

20. SIR FRANCIS RUNDALL

This account is based on FO and FCO files preserved in the Public Record Office and from my own memory of service under Rundall when I was First Secretary and Head of Chancery from 1963 to mid-1965, and as commercial and economic counsellor from mid 1966 until Rundall retired

1.   I remember one dinner party when I was conversing with a Japanese official and was summoned to talk with the Finnish Ambassador, a porcine and somnolent gentleman who clearly would have preferred to be able to doze off!

2.   He told me that he had been appalled by the lack of proper personnel assessment systems in the British companies he helped.

3.   See *Japan Experiences: Fifty Years One Hundred Views. Post-War Japan through British Eyes, 1945–2000*, Japan library, 2001, pages 579–582.

4.   Later Lord Maclehose of Beoch, KT, GBE, KCMG, KCVO, Governor of Hong Kong 1971–1982.

5.   PRO file FO 371/176005 (FJ 1022).
6.   Later Japanese Ambassador in London
7.   Letter from Rundall to Maclehose of 26 March 1964.
8.   Tungku Abdul Rahman was the Prime Minister of Malaysia.
9.   FO 371/181073.
10. *Japan Experiences*, Japan Library, 2001 pages 217–219.
11. In 1969 when a 'British Week' was held in Tokyo this had risen to around £100 million.
12. Rundall asked for me to return to Tokyo, although I had been less than a year in London as commercial and economic counsellor in succession to Colin Harris who was much senior to me.
13. Captain Robert Maxwell, MC. Was of Czech origin. He built up a commercial empire which included various publishing companies and *The Daily Mirror*. He kept many of these going by fraud and when it all began to crumble he disappeared at sea.
14. I thought that this request was unjustified and that it was a mistake to press for a meeting as it used up limited goodwill, but I understood Rundall's wish to avoid a row with London
15. I accompanied Rundall and Maxwell on this call and thought that I detected a wry smile on Satō's face. He recognized Maxwell as another go-getting politician.
16. I heard that Maxwell behaved badly on this occasion treating Mrs Tsukasa as if she were a geisha
17. FCO 21/258.

21. SIR JOHN PILCHER

Note: I am indebted to Delia Pilcher and other friends for information about John Pilcher. I am also grateful to the Foreign Office for allowing me to see some of his despatches before they were released under the thirty-year rule rate and to quote from them.

PART IV. INTRODUCTION

1.   E. g. Ian Ruxton, editor, *The Diaries and Letters of Sir Ernest Mason Satow (1843–1929): A Scholar-Diplomat in East Asia*, (Lewesiton, New York; Queenstown, Ontario; and Lampeter, Wales: The Edwin Mellen Press, 1998).
2.   D. C. M. Platt, *The Cinderella Service: British Consuls since 1835*, (London: Longman Group, 1971). Chapter 5 deals with the 'Far Eastern Service', though there was never in fact one Far Eastern Service; rather, there were separate China, Japan and Siam (Thailand) services.
3.   A. B. Mitford who later became the first Lord Redesdale (baron) was a considerable linguist and acted as interpreter during the visit to Japan of HRH the Duke of Edinburgh to Japan in 1869. His *Tales of Old Japan*, 1871, has been described by Dr Carmen Blacker as 'a classic among writings on Japan and its *ancien regime*, and a classic for folklorists too'. Mitford's writings about Japan have been collected and edited by Hugh Cortazzi in *MITFORD'S JAPAN: Memories and Recollections 1866–1906*, new edition, Japan library, 2002.
4.   *Report from the Select Committee on Diplomatic and Consular Services*, Parliamentary Papers House of Commons (PPHC), 1870 (382), vi, pp. 300–301.
5.   Hugh Cortazzi, 'The Japan Society: A Hundred-Year History', in Hugh Cortazzi and Gordon Daniels, eds., *Britain and Japan: Themes and Personalities*, (London and New York: Routledge, 1991), p. 49, and J. E. Hoare, 'Britain's Japan Consular Service', p. 104.
6.   Embassy and Consular Records, Japan (FO 262)/256, Lord Tenterden, Permanent Under Secretary, to Sir Harry Parkes, Tokyo, Consular no. 25, 4 September 1874.
7.   Aston's research was embodied in a paper he published in 1879. See W. G. Aston, 'A comparative study of the Japanese and Korean languages', *Journal of the Royal Asiatic Society*, vol. 11 (1879), 317–64.
8.   Records of the Chief Clerk's Office (FO369)/485. f262009, undated minute by W. Langley on a telegram from Tokyo, 20 June 1912.

9.   See Ruxton, *Diaries and Letters of Sir Ernest Mason Satow*, p. 269.
10. See Gordon Daniels' paper in this section.
11. For an example, see J. J. Quinn, 'The Lacquer Industry of Japan', *Transactions of the Asiatic Society of Japan (TASJ)* , (1881) vol. 9, pt. 1,1–30.
12. Carmen Blacker, 'Two Piggotts; Sir Francis Taylor Piggott (1852–1925) and Major General F. S. G. Piggott (1883–1966) in Cortazzi and Daniels, *Themes and Personalities*, p. 123–4.
13. Dennis Smith, 'Sir Charles Eliot (1862–1931) and Japan', in Cortazzi and Daniels, *Themes and Personalities*, p. 196 reproduced in this volume. See also the entry on Eliot by Sansom in the *Dictionary of National Biography*.
14. Douglas Moore Kenrick, 'A Centenary of Western Studies of Japan: The First Hundred Years of the Asiatic Society of Japan 1872–1972', *TASJ*, Third Series, vol. 14 (Dec. 1978), 394–446.

22. SIR ERNEST MASON SATOW

1.   E. M. Satow, *A Diplomat in Japan*, London: Seeley, Service & Co., 1921, p. 58.
2.   Ibid., p. 154.
3.   Quoted in Grace Fox, *Britain and Japan, 1858–1883*, Oxford: Clarendon Press, 1969, p. 423.
4.   Satow, p. 281.
5.   B. M. Allen, *The Rt Hon. Sir Ernest Satow G.C.M.G: A Memoir*, London: Kegan Paul, Trench, Trubner & Co., 1933, p. 73.
6.   Ibid, p. 79.
7.   Public Record Office PRO 30/33(11), Satow to Aston 18 January 1882.
8.   Allen, p. 87.
9.   E. M. Satow, 'Essay towards a bibliography of Siam',*Journal of the Straits Branch of the Royal Asiatic Society* 17 (1886), pp. 1–85; and 18 (1886), pp. 163–89.
10. Allen, p. 89.
11. Ibid., pp. 96-7.
12. Ibid., p. 110.
13. Ibid., p. 132.
14. Ibid., p. 134.
15. E. M. Satow, *Kuaiwa-hen, Twenty-five Exercises in the Yedo Colloquial*, Yokohama: Lane, Crawford & Co., 1873, p. iii.

23. WILLIAM GEORGE ASTON

1.   W. G. Aston, 'Japan', *Macmillan's Magazine* 26 (1872), p. 493.
2.   Ibid., p. 497.
3.   W. G. Aston, 'Takamagahara', *Transactions of the Asiatic Society of Japan* 38 (1911) 3, unnumbered page at beginning of issue.
4.   J. C. Hall, 'Eulogy upon W. G. Aston, C.M.G., D. Litt.', *Transactions of the Asiatic Society of Japan* 38 (1911), no. 5, p. v.
5.   W. G. Aston, *A Short Grammar of the Japanese Spoken Language*, 3rd edn, London: Trübner & Co., 1873, p. 83; *A Grammar of the Japanese Spoken Language*, 4th edn, Yokohama: Lane, Crawford & Co., 1888, p. 188. (Note that the word 'Short' was dropped from the title on the 4th edition).
6.   W. G. Aston, *A Short Grammar of the Japanese Spoken Language*, 1st edn, Nagasaki: F. Walsh, 1869, p. 6.
7.   *A Short Grammar*, 3rd edn, p. 3.
8.   Ibid., Preface (unpaginated).
9.   *A Grammar of the Japanese Spoken Language*, 4th edn. Preface (unpaginated).
10. W. G. Aston, *A Grammar of the Japanese Written Language with a Short Chrestomathy* (London: printed for the author at the office of *The Phoenix*, 1872), Preface (unpaginated).

11. B. H. Chamberlain, *A Handbook of Colloquial Japanese*, 4th edn, London: Crosby, Lockwood & Son, 1907, p. ii.

12. W. G. Aston, in *The Phoenix* 2 (1871–2), pp. 131–2.

13. W. G. Aston, 'Memorandum on the Loochooan and Aino languages', *Church Missionary Intelligencer and Record* 4 (1879) 8, pp. 490–1.

14. W. G. Aston, 'Hideyoshi's Invasion of Korea', *Transactions of the Asiatic Society of Japan* 6 (1878) to 11(1883).

15. British Parliamentary Papers 1883/LXXV [C.3455]: *Despatch from Her Majesty's Minister in Japan Forwarding a Report on Corea*, 'Mr Aston to Sir Harry Parkes', p. 9.

16. W. G. Aston, 'A comparative study of the Japanese and Korean languages', *Journal of the Royal Asiatic Society* 11(1879), 317–64; Bruno Lewin, 'Japanese and Korean: the problems and history of a linguistic comparison', *Journal of Japanese Studies* 2 (1976), p. 391.

17. W. G. Aston, 'An ancient Japanese classic (The *Tosa Nikki*, or Tosa Diary)', *Transactions of the Asiatic Society of Japan* 3 (1875), 2, pp. 121–30.

18. W. G. Aston, *Nihongi: Chronicles of Japan from the Earliest Times to* A.D. *697*, 2 vols, Transactions and Proceedings of the Japan Society Supplement 1, London: Kegan Paul, Trench, Trübner & Co., 1896, p. ix.

19. W. G. Aston, *A History of Japanese Literature*, London: Heinemann, 1899, p. 401.

20. Ibid., p. 386.

21. Ibid., p. 378.

22. Ibid., p. 269.

23. Ibid., p. 294.

24. Ibid., pp. 96–7.

25. W. G. Aston, *Shinto (The Way of the Gods)*, London: Longmans, Green & Co., 1905, p. 1.

26. W. G. Aston, 'Kaempfer as an Authority on Shinto', *Man* 2 (1902), 182–4.

27. *Shinto*, pp. i, 376–7.

28. Ibid., pp. 376–7.

29. *T'oung Pao* 12 (1911), p. 740.

30. George Sansom, 'Address delivered by Sir George Sansom at the Annual Ceremony [SOAS] 1956', *Journal of Asian Studies* 24 (1964–5), p. 566.

24. JOHN HARRINGTON GUBBINS

1. F. S. G. Piggott, *Broken Thread: An Autobiography*, Aldershot, 1950, p. 6.

2. Mary Fraser, *Diplomat's Wife in Japan*, Tokyo, 1899, p. 13.

3. 'Notes on a journey from Aomori to Niigata and of a visit to the Mines of Sado' in *Transactions of the Asiatic Society of Japan*, 111(1875), pp. 74–91. (Hereafter cited as *TASJ*) Also 'Review of the Introduction of Christianity into China and Japan', *TASJ*, VI (1878), 1–62, and 'Hideyoshi and the Satsuma Clan in the sixteenth century', *TASJ*, VIII (1880), 92–144.

4. K. Bourne and D. C. Watt (eds), *British Documents on Foreign Affairs*, part I, series E, 'Asia, 1860–1914', vol 3, Washington, 1989, doc. 111, Fraser to Salisbury, 26 May 1892. (Hereafter cited as *'BDOFA'*) Good accounts of Treaty revision are given in J. H. Gubbins, *Japan*, London: HMSO, 1920, pp 64–7; and A. Fraser, R. H. P. Mason and P. Mitchell, *Japan's Early Parliaments, 1890–1905*, London, 1995, chs. 5–6.

5. P. Wilkinson and Joan B. Astley, *Gubbins and SOE*, London, 1993, pp. 4–5. Also H. Cortazzi(ed.), R. H. Brunton, *Building Japan, 1869–76*, Folkestone, 1991, p. 26.

6. Sakane Yoshihisa (ed.). *Aoki Shūzō jiden*, Tokyo: Toyo bunko, 1970, pp. 117–227 is the most detailed account from the Japanese side. References to 1892–3 are found on p. 190ff.

7. Cabinet approves treaty proposals, 13 and 22 Nov. 1893, *Nihon gaikō nempyō narabini shuyō bunsho*. For Aoki's reluctance, see Sakane, *Aoki*, p. 218–19.

8. Gubbins to Foreign Office, 26 Feb. 1894 in *EDOFA*, doc. 173. Reference to Gubbins' role is found on Sakane, p. 222.

9. *BDOFA*, doc. 173.

10. *BDOFA,* doc. 173. Sakane, *Aoki,* p. 227. Gubbins' memoranda are to be found in *BDOFA,* docs 177, 180, 202, 205, 236, 238.
11. Gubbins, *Japan,* p. 67.
12. Outside Tokyo Gubbins had only served at Yokohama.
13. J. H. Gubbins, *The Making of Modern Japan,* London, 1922, p. 215.
14. Gubbins to Satow, 5 Oct. 1900 in Satow Papers (Public Record Office, Kew, PRO 30/33) 9/14.
15. Gubbins to Satow, 22 Feb. 1916 in Satow Papers 11/8.
16. Wilkinson and Asdey, *Gubbins and SOE,* p. 6.
17. *TASJ,* 1875 and 1897. In Yasui's article, *bemmo* was a refutation of certain Christian arguments.
18. J. H. Gubbins, *The Progress of Japan, 1853–71,* Oxford, 1911, p. 3.
19. Chamberlain was staying for the time being at 12 Rue de l'Athenee, Geneva.
20. Gubbins (Tudor House, Worplesdon) to Satow, 18 Dec. 1912 in Satow papers, 11/8.
21. Gubbins to Satow, 29 Dcc. 1915 in Satow Papers, 11/8.
22. Gubbins to Satow, 28 Aug. 1916 in Satow Papers, 11/8.
23. Gubbins to Satow, 12 June 1917 in Satow Papers, 11/8.
24. Wilkinson and Astley, *Gubbins and SOE,* p. 23.
25. Gubbins to Satow, 15 April 1918 in Satow Papers, 11/8.
26. J. H. Gubbins, *Japan,* London, 1920 (Foreign Office Historical Section Handbook 73, RO 42) [They were in fact joint War Office/Foreign Office/ Admiralty handbooks.]
27. 'The "Hundred Articles" and the Tokugawa government' in *Transactions of the Japan Society of London,* XVII (1918–20), pp. 128–84, delivered at the meeting on 17 Dec. 1919.
28. Gubbins to Satow, 4 and 27 Oct. 1922 in Satow Papers, 11/9.
29. Gubbins to Satow, 17 Jan. 1923 in Satow Papers, 11/9.
30. Gubbins to Satow, 29 April 1925 and 17 Feb. 1926, in Satow Papers, 11/9. His pamphlet was entitled *Socialism and the Socialist Press: an address,* 20 pages, Edinburgh: W. M. Urquhart & Sons, 1926.

25. SIR GEORGE SANSOM

1.   G. B. Sansom, *Japan: A Short Cultural History* was first published by the Cresset Press, London in 1931, and remains in print. G. B. Sansom, *A History of Japan to 1334, A History of Japan 1334–1615* and *A History of Japan, 1615–1867* were also published by the Cresset Press, in 1959, 1961 and 1964 respectively. They remain in print.
2.   For Sansom's early life see Katharine Sansom, *Sir George Sansom and Japan: A Memoir,* Tallahassee, Florida, 1972, pp. 1–3. *The Reminiscences of Sir George Sansom,* New York: Oral History Research Office, Columbia University, 1957, pp. 1–4; E. T. Williams and C. S. Nicholls (eds), *Dictionary of National Biography, 1961–1970,* Oxford 1981), pp. 922–3, and his Obituary in *The Times,* 10 March 1965.
3.   K. Sansom, *Sir George Sansom,* pp. 6–7.
4.   Sir Charles Eliot's official assessments of Sansom's qualities are reprinted in K. Sansom, *Sir George Sansom,* pp. 12–13.
5.   Letter from Sir George Sansom to Professor Marius Jansen, 1 September 1959. (Kindly supplied to the author by Professor Jansen.)
6.   G. B. Sansom, *An Historical Grammar of Japanese,* Oxford, 1928, p. vii.
7.   G. B. Sansom, *Japan: A Short Cultural History,* 1st edn, p. vii.
8.   *Times Literary Supplement,* 7 April 1932.
9.   G. B. Sansom, *Reminiscences,* p. 17.
10. Memorandum by Sansom, enclosed in Lindley to Simon, No. 574, 28 October 1932 (F 8307/39/23), FO 371/16242 cited in W. R. Louis, *British Strategy in the Far East 1919–1939,* Oxford, 1971, p. 218.
11. K. Sansom, *Sir George Sansom,* p. 32.
12. Memorandum by Sansom, 11 November 1932, enclosed in Lindley to Simon, No. 603, ii November 1932 (A 8174/53/45), cited in Louis, *British Strategy in the Far East,* p. 219.

13. K. Sansom, *Sir George Sansom*, p. 95; G. B. Sansom, *Reminiscences*, p. 36.
14. K. Sansom, *Sir George Sansom*, pp. 36, 56–68 and 77. G. B. Sansom's, *The Western World and Japan: A Study in the Interaction of European and Asiatic Cultures* was finally published by the Cresset Press, London in 1950.
15. K. Sansom, *Sir George Sansom*, p. 89.
16. Ibid., p. 92.
17. Ibid., pp. 94–7.
18. Sansom later recounted his resignation as follows: 'I had said to the Permanent Under Secretary, I really don't see why I should stay. I'm not going back to Japan. I hate your ambassador there. He's a fool', *Reminiscences*, p. 57.
19. K. Sansom, *Sir George Sansom*, p. 110.
20. Ibid., p. 114.
21. Ibid., p. 120.
22. Ibid., p. 123–4.
23. Sansom's work in wartime Washington is well summarized in Roger Buckley, *Occupation Diplomacy, Britain, the United States & Japan, 1945–1952*, Cambridge, 1982, pp. 10–13.
24. 'Sir George Sansom's views of postwar Japan', Memorandum of Conversation, 28 July 1943. Participants, G. Sansom, G.H. Blakeslee, H. Borton, Drafted by H. Borton, reprinted in Okurasho Zaiseishishitsu (ed.), *Shōwa Zaiseishi, Shūsen Kara Kōwa made*. Vol. 20 *Eibun Shiryō*, Tokyo, 1982, pp. 6–7.
25. Llewellyn Woodward, *British Foreign Policy in the Second World War*, Vol. 5, London, 1976, pp. 519–21. Sansom's role at this time is also summarized in Chihiro Hosoya, 'George Sansom, Diplomat & Historian', in I. H. Nish and C. Dunn (eds), *European Studies on Japan*, Tenterden, Kent, 1979, pp. 116–18.
26. K. Sansom, *Sir George Sansom*, p. 141.
27. Ibid., p. 154.
28. Ibid., p. 146.
29. Ibid., p. 161.
30. For the official history of the Commission, see G. H. Blakeslee, *The Far Eastern Commission: A Study in International Co-operation 1945 to 1952*, Washington, DC, 1953). For Sansom's role see Buckley, *Occupation Diplomacy*, pp. 76–9.
31. Letter from Sir George Sansom to G. C. Allen (undated). MS Add. 247/2/0 (G. C. Allen Papers, University College, London).
32. G. B. Sansom, 'Can Japan be reformed?', *Far Eastern Survey*, 2 November 2949, p. 258.
33. This preoccupation was most evident in the five volumes of the 'modernization' series published by Princeton University Press.
34. G. B. Sansom, The Western World and Japan, p. 223; see also T. C. Smith, *The Agrarian Origins of Modern Japan*, Stanford University Press, 1959.
35. G. B. Sansom, *Japan in World History*, London, 1952, p. 1.
36. Letter from Sir George Sansom to Professor Marius Jansen, 1 September 1959.
37. Marius Jansen, 'Review of G. B. Sansom, *A History of Japan to 1334*', *Journal of Asian Studies*, 18 (1958–9), pp. 501–3.
38. G. B. Sansom, *A History of Japan, 1334–1615*, p. vii.
39. John Whitney Hall, 'Review of G. B. Sansom, *A History of Japan, 1615–1867*', *Journal of Asian Studies*, 23 (1963–4), pp. 615–17.

26. BRITAIN'S JAPAN CONSULAR SERVICE, 1859–1941

* A version of this paper was given at St Anthony's College, Oxford, in February 1974. I am grateful to those who made comments, especially the late Professor D. C. M. Platt. The views expressed are my own and should not be taken as official British government policy
1. F. T. Ashton-Gwatkin, *The British Foreign Service: A discussion of the development and function of the British Foreign Service,* (Syracuse, New York: Syracuse University Press,

1951), p. 56. See also Peter Byrd, 'Regional and Functional Specialisation in the British Consular Service,' *Journal of Contemporary History*, vol. 7, nos. 1&2, p. 128; and D. C. M. Platt, *Cinderella Service: British Consuls since 1825*, (London: Longman, 1971) pp. 5, 29–36.

2.   Platt, *Cinderella Service*, pp. 125–6, 131–2.

3.   Platt, *Cinderella Service*, pp. 181–5; P D Coates, The China Consuls, (Hong Kong: Oxford University Press, 1988), pp. 7–27

4.   Foreign Office, Embassy and Consular Records China (FO 233)/3, Circular from Sir John Bonham, I Sept. 1849; *General Instructions for His Majesty's Consular Officers*, (London: Foreign Office, 1907), p. 367.

5.   Coates, *China Consuls*, Chapter 4, 'The Infant Service.'

6.   Platt, *Cinderella Service*, p. 183.

7.   Foreign Office, Japan (FO 46) 12, Malmesbury to Alcock, draft, no. 2, 1 March 1859; Coates, *China Consuls*, pp. 74–5, 502.

8.   Alexander Michie, *The Englishman in China during the Victorian Era*, (Edinburgh and London: William Blackwood and Sons, 1900), vol. 11, p. 14. See also FO 46/2, Lord John Russell to Alcock, draft. no. 44, 8 December 1859; FO 46/2, Malmesbury to Alcock, draft no. 2, 1 March 1859.

9.   Grace Fox, *Britain and Japan 1858–1883*, (Oxford: Clarendon Press, 1969), pp. 54–5; Platt, Cinderella Service, pp. 195 et seq; Foreign Office, Supplement to General Correspondence (FO 97)/269, Treasury to Foreign Office, no. 11596 2/8 of 5 August 1862.

10. FO 46/2, Malmesbury to Alcock, draft no. 51, 22 December 1859; FO 46/51, Memorandum 6 November 1863 and related papers.

11. FO 97/269, Hodgson to Lord Russell, 11 March 1861; Alcock to Russell, no. 71, 16 September 1861; Russell to Hodgson, draft, 14 January 1862, and related papers.

12. J. E. Hoare, 'Mr Enslie's Grievances', Japan Society of London *Bulletin*, no. 78, (1976), pp. 14–19

13. Foreign Office, Embassy and Consular Archives, Japan (FO 262)/ 161, Lord Clarendon to Sir Harry Parkes, no. 25, 26 February 1869; FO 262/257, Parkes to Lord Derby, no. 29 consular, draft, 28 October 1874; FO 46/254, 'Mr Enslie's Grievances'; *Japan Weekly Mail*, 25 February 1882; *London and China Express*, 13 May 1887; E. M. Satow, *A Diplomat in Japan*, (London: Seeley Service, 1921), p. 30; Sir Harry Parkes, Minutes of Evidence, *Report from the Select Committee on Diplomatic and Consular Services*, PPHC 1872 (314), VII, p. 63.

14. J. E. Hoare, Japan's *Treaty Ports and Foreign Settlements*, (Folkestone, Kent: Japan Library, 1994), pp. 56–8; Platt, *Cinderella Service*, pp. 189–90.

15. Satow, *Diplomat in Japan*, pp. 30–1.

16. Satow, *Diplomat in Japan*, pp. 17–21. Jamieson's defection led to the introduction of a bond to cover the cost of passage money: FO 17/617, E. H. Hammond to the Treasury, draft, 21 March 1865.

17. Satow, *Diplomat in Japan*, pp. 55–6.

18. Satow, *Diplomat in Japan*, pp. 57–9; *Minutes of Evidence, Report of the Committee on Oriental Studies in London*, PPHC 1909 (Cd 4561), Q. 1914.

19. Allen, *Ernest Satow*, pp. 35, 60–1; Redesdale, *Memories*, 1, 377.

20. Frank Ashton-Gwatkin, 'The meeting of John Paris and Japan', *Tsuru*, vol. 3, no. 1, p. 3; Arthur de la Mare, *Perverse and Foolish: A Jersey farmer's son in the British Diplomatic Service*, (Jersey, Channel Islands: La Haule Books, 1994), p. 71.

21. FO 262/256, Tenterden to Parkes, no. 25 consular, 4 September 1874.

22. FO 97/582, Plunkett to Salisbury, no. 25 consular, 24 July 1885.

23. Minutes of Evidence, *F!fth Report of the Royal Commission on the Civil Service*, PPHC 1914–1916, (Cd 7749) Q. 41,229; FO 262/191, Parkes to Clarendon, consular no. 50 draft, 21 July 1870; FO 262/ 227, Watkins to Granville, no 24 draft consular, 6 September 1872.

24. Foreign Office, Chief Clerk's Department (FO 369)/2152/K9097/6874/ 223, Sir John Tilley to A. Henderson, no. 322, 25 June 1930.

25. FO 83/1486, Regulations for the Joint Examination 1896.

26. *Report from the Select Committee on Diplomatic and Consular Services*, Parliamentary Papers House of Commons (PPHC), 1870 (382), vii, pp. 300–301; 5 Leathes, Minutes of Evidence, *Fifth Report of the Royal Commission on the Civil Service*, PPHC 1914–1916, (Cd 7749), Q. 38,820.
27. There is not a great deal of personal information available. Much of what is given here comes from volumes in the FO 17 series. See also *Japan Weekly Mail*, 15 December 1888; *London and China Express* 5 February 1897 for Quinn; P. F. Kornicki, 'William George Aston', in Sir Hugh Cortazzi and Gordon Daniels, editors, *Britain and Japan 1859–1991: Themes and Personalities*, (London: Routledge, 1991), pp. 64–75 reproduced in this volume.
28. The FO/17 series contain some application papers and correspondence. See also Allen, Satow, pp. 1–3 and P. F. Kornicki, 'Ernest Mason Satow', in Cortazzi and Daniels, *Britain and Japan*, pp. 76–85 reproduced in this volume; and *Japan Weekly Mail* 14 April 1888 and F. V. Dickins and S. Lane-Poole, *Life of Sir Harry Parkes*, (London: Macmillan, 1894), II, 114, footnote 1.
29. FO 262/191, Parkes to Lord Granville, draft number 69 consular, 5 November 1870.
30. *Who's who in the Far East*, 1906–7.
31. FO 97/582, Plunkett to Salisbury, no. 25 consular, 24July 1885; FO 262/ 415, Plunkett to Granville, no. 156 confid., draft, 13 September 1884 and FO 262/412, Granville to Plunkett, no. 97, 30 October 1884.
32. Obituary, Russell Robertson, *Japan Weekly Mail*, 14 April 1888; obituary, J. J. Quinn, *London and China Express*, 5 February 1897.
33. Hoare, *Japan's Treaty Ports*, pp. 18–20, 72.
34. FO 262/333, Parkes to Lord Salisbury, no. 55, draft, 15 March 1879; FO 97/582, Plunkett to Salisbury, no. 25 consular, 24 July 1885; *Japan Weekly Mail*, 5 August 1882.
35. Satow Papers (PRO 30/33)5/7, Bonar to Satow, 24 June 1896.
36. Minutes of Evidence, *Fifth Report of the Royal Commission on the Civil Service*, PPHC 1914–1916, (Cd 7749), Q. 38912; D. C. M. Platt, 'The Role of the British Consular Service in Overseas Trade, 1825–1914', *Economic History Review*, second series, Vol. XV, No. 3, (1963), p. 495. See also *Correspondence respecting the question of Diplomatic and Consular Assistance to Trade*, PPHC 1886, Commercial No. 16 Parts I and II (C. 4779 and 4779–1).
37. *Japan Gazette*, 15 September 1880.
38. *Japan Mail*, 27 September 1881.
39. J. H. Longford, 'England's Record in Japan', Japan Society of London, *Proceedings and Transactions*, Vol. VII (1905–07), p. 93; PRO 30/33/11/6, Satow to F. V. Dickins, 24 July 1893
40. PRO 30/33/15/2, Satow to Dickins, 22 August 1880.
41. FO 262/167, Parkes to Clarendon, no. 66 draft consular, 5 November 1869, enclosing Sir E Hornby to Parkes, 23 October 1869.
42. *Japan Weekly Mail*, 25 May 1878; *Tokio Times*, 5 October 1878; *London and China Express*, 13 July and 9 November 1888
43. Hoare, Japan's *Treaty Ports*, pp. 66–105; Richard T. Chang, *The Justice of the Western Consular Courts in Nineteenth Century Japan*, (Westport Conn. and London: Greenwood Press, 1984).
44. *Far East*, 17 July 1871; FO 262/655, J. Troup to H. Fraser, no. 18, 22 May 1891.
45. FO 262/209, F. Adams to Granville, draft consular nos. 49 and 52, 16 and 30 December 1871.
46. Hoare,Japan's *Treaty Ports*, pp. 31–3; Minutes of Evidence, *Fifth Report of the Royal Commission on the Civil Service*, PPHC 1914–1916 (Cd 7749), Q. 42858.
47. See the papers in FO 369/87; *General Instructions for HM Consular Officers*, (1863), enclosure no. 15; Platt, *Cinderella Service*, pp. 29–30.
48. *Japan Daily Herald* 13 September 1880.
49. E.g. FO 798/20, Dohmen to Hornby, draft no. 6, 19 June 1875.
50. See the annual *Foreign Office List; General Instructions*, 1907, pp. 53–61.

51. Minutes of Evidence, *Fifth Report of the Royal Commission on the Civil Service*, PPHC 1914–1916, (Cd 7749), Q. 42,741–4.
52. Ashton-Gwatkin, 'Meeting of John Paris and Japan', p. 3; Minutes of Evidence, *Report of the Committee on Oriental Studies in London*, PPHC 1909, (Cd 4561), XXXV, Q. 470; de la Mare, *Perverse and Foolish*, pp. 64–5; FO 369/308, Sir C MacDonald to Lord Grey, no. 4 consular, 5 January 1910; FO 369/595/42565, Sir C Greene to Consular Dept, semi-off. , 19 August 1913; *Japan Chronicle*, 19 June 1930; FO 369/2151/K2207, minutes 3 February 1930; FO 369/2323/K4122, correspondence and minutes, 1933.
53. FO 797/1, Circular to all firms, 13 September 1901; FO 369/484/15974, Treasury to the FO, 15 April 1912; FO 369/735/6584, Greene to Grey, no. 8 consular, 27 January 1914; FO 369/1003/20363, Greene to A. Balfour, consular no 79, 17 December 1917.
54. See the extensive papers in FO 369/595.
55. See, for example, FO 369/595/42565, Greene to FO, semi-off. , 19 August 1913.
56. FO 369/1167/18585, War Office to FO 1 February 1919, and minuting.
57. FO 369/2413/K7412, Sir R. Clive to Sir John Simon, no. 294, 5 June 1935; de la Mare, *Perverse and Foolish*, pp. 68–9.
58. E. g. , FO. 369/1885/K11255, Sir C Eliot to Lord Curzon, no. 308, 20 June 1921; FO 369/1978, Sir J. Tilley to Sir A. Chamberlain, no. 596, 22 November 1927.
59. Platt, *Cinderella Service*, pp. 221 Ct seq; Byrd, 'Regional and Functional Specialisation', p. 138.

APPENDIX I. THE BRITISH BOMBARDMENT OF KAGOSHIMA, 1863

Official despatches are in Public Record Office file FO 46 and as published for presentation to Parliament. I am grateful to the Admiralty Library for drawing appropriate material in their archives to my attention. I also want to record my thanks to Professor Nakasuga Tetsurō who provided valuable information from Japanese sources recorded in these notes.

1. DNB entry by John Knox Laughton.
2. Neale to Lord Russell, 26 August 1863.
3. On 6 August 1863, the day on which the British fleet left Yokohama, the *Bakufu* called an emergency meeting to consider what could be done to promote reconciliation between Satsuma and Britain. It was decided to send a number of officials (Fuchibe Tokuzō, Tateishi Tokujūrō, Yokoyama Keiichi, Shinohara Renjūrō) together with the senior representative of the Satsuma fief in Edo, Kiiri Settsu, to Satsuma. The party left Shinagawa on a *Bakufu* ship on 8 August, but the ship encountered a typhoon en route and did not reach Kagoshima bay until after the bombardment and the departure from Satsuma of the British fleet.
4. In addition Shimizu Usaburō was employed as an interpreter on board the *Euryalus*.
5. Narahara Kizaemon and Kaeda Nobuyoshi, who had been involved in the killing of Richardson at Namamugi, organized a group of some 40 samurai from the fief with a view to taking over the ships. The aristocratic-looking Machida Rokuzaemon was the senior official given the task of handing over the written reply from Satsuma while the eloquent Kōka Yoshizō was nominated as the spokesman for Satsuma. The expert swordsman Shiki Tokurō was to assassinate Kuper. In addition to the members of the party who were to board the flagship a number of samurai ready to die in a battle to overpower the fleet were going alongside the other ships in the fleet disguised as merchants selling vegetables and fruits to the crews.
6. Neale to Vice-Admiral Kuper, 14 August 1863.
7. Vice-Admiral Kuper to Neale on HMS *Euryalus* in the bay of Kagoshima, 17 August 1863. His despatch to the Admiralty dated 22 August 1863 from Yokohama on his return there was printed in *The Illustrated London News* of 7 November 1863, page 482. In this despatch Kuper reported as follows about his arrival in Kagoshima: 'Having been unable to obtain any correct information respecting the gulf or bay of

Kagoshima, and having only secured as a pilot a Japanese boatman who had been once at the place in the steamer *Fiery Cross*, it was necessary to approach with great caution. As we advanced up the gulf, however, it was found that our greatest difficulty was the extreme depth of the water, and as night overtook us when within six or seven miles of the town, we had to feel our way for nearly two hours, seeking for an anchorage; this was at last found on the western shore, near what was called the Seven Islands, but which proved to be nothing more than seven insignificant rocks close to the beech.' Kuper weighed anchor again at 7.0. a.m. on 12 August to move closer.

8.   These were the *England*, 759 tons, the *Sir George Grey*, 492 tons and the *Contest*, 350 tons.

9.   In his despatch (paragraph 12) to the Admiralty sent from Yokohama on 22 August 1863 Kuper recorded: 'At noon, during a squall accompanied by much rain, the whole of the batteries on the Kagoshima side suddenly opened fire upon the *Euryalus*, the only ship within range, but, although many shot and shell passed over and close around her, no damage was done beyond cutting away a few ropes.' Later, of course, the *Euryalus* suffered many casualties.

10. In his despatch to the Admiralty of 22 August 1863 Kuper recorded: 'I proceeded towards the batteries, opening fire upon the northernmost one with considerable effect, and passed at slow speed, along the whole line, within point blank range. Owing probably to the unfavourable state of the weather, the ships astern did not maintain their positions in as close order as I could have wished, and the *Euryalus* was consequently exposed to a very heavy and well directed fire from several of the batteries at the same time, and suffered somewhat severely'

11. In his despatch to the Admiralty of 22 August 1863 Kuper reported that the conflagration created 'continued with unabated ardour up to the time of the departure of the squadron, forty-eight hours subsequently to the first attack.'

12. In *Seapower Ashore, 200 Years of Royal Navy operations on Land*, edited by Captain Peter Hore RN, Chatham Publishing 2001.

13. Engraved portraits of Captain Joslin and Commander Wilmot were included in *The Illustrated London News* supplement dated November 14, 1863, page 501.

14. It is apparent from reports by the gunnery officer that the Armstrong guns did not function satisfactorily at Kagoshima.

15. Ernest Satow *A Diplomat in Japan*, London 1921, page 89, 'rumour said that Colonel Neale was very anxious that the Admiral should land some men and carry off a few guns as trophies of victory, but that he declined to send a single man. And men said that he [Kuper] was demoralized by the death of his flag-captain and commander.'

16. Ernest Satow *A Diplomat in Japan*. London 1921, Chapter VIII, pp 84-94.

17. Hugh Cortazzi *Dr Willis in Japan, British Medical Pioneer, 1862–1877*, London 1985. pages 34–41.

18. Admiral Kuper's despatch from Yokohama of 22 August 1863 to the Admiralty which was printed in the *Illustrated London News* of 7 November 1863 included a brief commentary from their correspondent (pages 481 and 482).

19. 'The Bombardment of Kagoshima by British Fleet, August 1863' by Commander Okuda, from the *Suikosha Kiji* of June 1908, translated by Lieutenant Neill James RN, Devonport 1937, Admiralty Library London

20. A footnote reads: 'Marshal Prince Oyama was also one of this party – translator.'

21. According to *Namamugi Ichijō* by Takeda Yasumitsu, published by Chuōkōronsha in 1975 Satsuma casualties amounted to eight dead including Saisho Seikichi and six wounded including Kawakami Tatsue. Charles Wirgman in his article of 11 December 1863 published in *The Illustrated London News* dated 20 February 1864 reported that casualties on the Satsuma side amounted to some 1500. The Satsuma authorities probably deliberately kept the published figures of casualties low in order to boost their assertion that Satsuma had won a vistory.

22. Okuda noted that on 14 August when hostilities seemed imminent Shimazu Tadayoshi, the Satsuma daimyo, 'ordered 3 submarine mines to be dropped in one

channel, but fortunately for them the British used a different channel and missed the mines.'

23. Satow *A Diplomat in Japan*, page 89.

24. John Bright (1811–89), British radical statesman and orator.

25. Grace Fox *Britain and Japan 1858–1883*, Oxford, 1969, page 117–119.

26. 'A brother flag officer, who was a member of the House and who sprang to Kuper's defence, 'in the heat of the argument, used the word "damn", and upon being called to order, created much amusement by apologizing for using language which he said "seldom fell from the lips of sailors".' This was quoted in *The Royal Navy: A History from the Earliest Times to the Death of Queen Victoria* by Sir Wm Laird Clowes, Volume VII, London, 1903, page 200.

27. *Quarterly Review*, lxv. April 1864, 499–500

28. Richard Cobden (1804–65) economist and politician described as the 'Apostle of Free Trade'.

29. The Satsuma agents who called on Neale on 9 December told some of Neale's officials that 'immediately upon the appearance of the squadron . . . the Prince of Satsuma had ordered the inhabitants to retire into the villages, and that therefore no harm had happened to the people. That if we returned to Kagoshima we should find the town nearly restored to its original state.'

30. Neale to Russell, 17 December 1863.

31. This 'written engagement' was less than had been demanded, but it was the best Neale could hope for at that time and he sensibly decided not to press the original demand. The promise to arrest those responsible for Richardson's murder was in fact no more than a ruse to buy off the British. Narahara Kizaemon, who had taken part in the attack on Richardson and had made the plans to take over the British fleet continued to play an active part in the Satsuma efforts to topple the *Bakufu* until he died fighting in 1865. Kaeda Nobuyoshi after the Meiji Resoration in 1868 became a member of the *Genrōin* and of the *Kizokuin*. The Satsuma representatives who parleyed with Neale were Iwashita Masahira (1827–1900), Shigeno Yasutsugu (1827–1910). The *Bakufu's* representatives who attended these meetings were Ukai Yaichi and Saitō Kingo. Satsuma borrowed the money needed to pay the British from the *Bakufu*.

32. Grace Fox: *Britain and Japan*, p. 102.

33. Rutherford Alcock, British Minister to Japan, was on leave in England at the time.

34. 'Master William Hennessey Parker, of the flagship, steered his vessel with great judgement, taking her at times within 400 yards of the batteries; yet Kuper continually spurred him with: "Go in closer, Parker, go in closer!" Owing to the heavy sea in which the action was fought, the decks were afloat.' This quotation comes from *The Royal Navy: A History* . . . (see note xxii) volume VII, page 200.

APPENDIX II. THE NAVAL AND MILITARY ACTION AT SHIMONOSEKI

I am grateful to the Admiralty Library for drawing my attention to various works quoted and for information about HM ships involved in the bombardment.

1. Kuper to the Secretary to the Admiralty, 15 September 1864 expanding on his brief report of 10 August.

2. 'The Americans had no suitable vessel available on the spot, but anxious to take part, they put an officer, some men, and a gun from the US corvette *Jamestown* on board a chartered steamer, the *Takiang*'. *The Royal Navy: A History from the Earliest Time to the Death of Queen Victoria* bt Sir Wm Laird Clowes, Vol VII, 1903, London.

3. Captain Hayes of HMS *Tartar* in his report to Kuper of 9 September 1864 recorded 'the valuable support' he had received 'from the able management and precision of the rifled guns of His Majesty's ship *Dupleix*, which ship invariably replied to the guns which were striking the *Tartar*, and showing an energy which reflected the highest credit on her commander.

4. The *Conqueror* which was a massive ship with a deep draught proved a liability.

5.   This despatch does not make it clear how much tough fighting took place. In the course of the afternoon of 6 September when the Naval Brigade and the Marines were engaged on shore, to quote from *The Royal Navy: A History* (see note xi): 'some gallant deeds were done and no less than three Victoria Crosses were gained'. One of these was won by Midshipman Duncan Gordon Bowes of the *Euryalus*, 'who carried a colour with the leading company, kept it with headlong gallantry in advance of all, in face of the thickest fire, his colour-sergeants having fallen, one mortally and the other dangerously wounded, and was only detained proceeding further yet by the orders of his superior officer. The colour he carried was six times pierced by musket balls.'

6.   Captain J. H. Alexander in a despatch to Admiral Kuper dated 10 September 1864 reporting on the landing by the Naval Brigade reported: 'Mr Satow of Her Majesty's Legation, Yokohama, accompanied me on all occasions, and in the thickest fire, to act as interpreter if required.'

7.   Alcock to Russell from Yokohama, 28 September 1864, received in London on 24 November.

8.   Kuper to the Secretary of the Admiralty 30 September 1864 'at Sea off the entrance to the Gulf of Yeddo [sic]'.

9.   Colin White recorded that 'The fleet anchored off many towns, but Kuper gave strict instructions that no-one was to land. However, each ship was soon surrounded by boats full of inquisitive spectators and enterprising merchants'.

10.   'The Long Arm of Seapower: The Anglo-Japanese War of 1863–64' in *Seapower Ashore, 200 Years of Royal Navy Operations on Land*, edited by Captain Peter Hore, RN, Chatham Publishing 2001.

11.   Wrecked off the China coast in 1864.

Index